C++/CLI in Action

C++/CLI in Action

NISHANT SIVAKUMAR

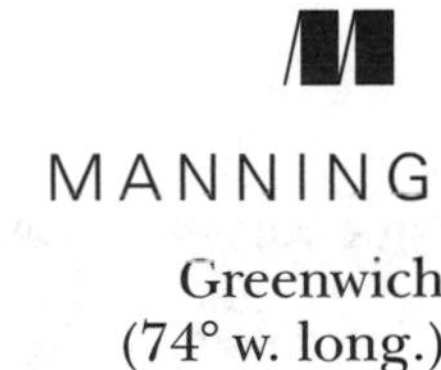

Greenwich
(74° w. long.)

For online information and ordering of this and other Manning books, please go to www.manning.com. The publisher offers discounts on this book when ordered in quantity. For more information, please contact:

Special Sales Department
Manning Publications Co.
Sound View Court 3B
Greenwich, CT 06830
Fax: (609) 877-8256
Email: orders@manning.com

Manning Publications Co.
Sound View Court 3B
Greenwich, CT 06830

Copyeditor: Tiffany Taylor
Typesetter: Denis Dalinnik
Cover designer: Leslie Haimes

ISBN 1-932394-81-8

Printed in the United States of America
1 2 3 4 5 6 7 8 9 10 – MAL – 11 10 09 08 07

To my loving wife Smitha,

who put up with my long hours of work on the book and constantly supplied me with coffee to keep me alert and awake.

Without her presence, patience, and support, this book would not have been possible.

brief contents

contents

preface

I have been using C++/CLI ever since Microsoft made the early Alpha versions of the compiler available to Beta testers and MVPs in 2003, and at some point back then, I knew I wanted to write a book about it. Having co-authored a book on its predecessor, Managed C++, a few years ago, I thought that writing a book on a subject I was very familiar with, and one that was dear to my heart in a quasi-geeky sort of way, would be an excellent thing to do. Because my life and my career managed to keep me busy, I kept postponing the book idea until Mike Stephens from Manning Publications asked if I would be interested in writing for Manning. We discussed some issues with C++ experts, including several MVPs and Microsoft VC++ team members, and we finally decided on a tentative table of contents. The next half year saw me working on the book, and the result is what you're holding in your hands (unless you're reading the e-book, in which case the previous sentence would definitely sound a tad silly).

As most authors of technical books would concur, writing each chapter—nay, each section—was an intensely stimulating process. I discovered at least one exciting new feature, technique, or idea every few days, and I would then put it into writing. As I went along, I became more convinced of the powerful capabilities of C++/CLI as a means of native-managed interop; and the fact that many developers around the world don't seem to be fully aware of what they can achieve with it spurred me on.

I have tried my best to use minimal examples that demonstrate a specific technique or set of techniques that can be applied to larger and more complex real-life development scenarios. It's my hope that I have managed to portray the power and flexibility of the C++/CLI language in the few hundred pages of this book, and that you'll derive as much information and gratification out of reading this book as I did in writing it.

acknowledgments

Rama Krishna Vavilala—My friend Rama Vavilala, who's an absolute Windows programming guru, was an immense help to me during the writing of this book. Any time I stumbled on a technical block or wanted a suggestion for resolving a specific issue, Rama had an idea or two about how to go about fixing it.

Howard Jones—Getting Howard as my development editor was one of the best things that happened to me while working on the book. He was always available, he provided useful writing tips, and helped me to follow Manning writing guidelines.

James T. Johnson—The man known as Mr. .NET in blogging circles was someone I could rely on for useful and in-depth advice about anything related to the .NET Framework during the writing of this book.

Christian Graus—My friend and colleague gave me some excellent feedback on the book, and the book's better, thanks to him.

The volunteer reviewers listed here—Rama Krishna Vavilala, Vipul Patel, James Johnson, Aleksey Nudelman, Brian Kramer, Marius Bancila, Michael Taylor, Nick Weinholt, Ayman Shoukry, Gerald Beuchelt, Berndt Hamboeck, Dave Corun, Tony Gravagno, Christian Graus, and Thomas Restrepo, who also served as the technical proofreader of the book during production. There were several review stages, and the volunteer reviewers provided lots of useful comments and suggestions, most of which helped me to improve the content of the book.

The Microsoft Visual C++ team—I have to especially thank the amazing VC++ team at Microsoft, who gave us this wonderful compiler.

Manning Publications—Beginning with publisher Marjan Bace, and all the members of the production and marketing team who worked with me on getting the book ready to go out into the world.

Mike Stephens—And finally, a big thank-you to Mike for getting me on board in the first place.

about this book

This book is targeted at intermediate or higher-level Win32/VC++ developers with basic .NET awareness who are writing new managed apps or enhancing existing VC++ apps with managed technologies like the .NET Framework, Windows Forms, WPF, or WCF. Other targets for the book include MC++ developers looking to move to the new syntax, and C# or VB.NET developers who want to write mixed-mode code and leverage the more powerful features available in C++/CLI.

The book covers the following topics:

- The new C++/CLI language syntax and semantics
- New CLI features like generics and managed templates
- Mixed-mode programming techniques
- Using .NET components from VC++ applications
- Wrapping native C++ classes and exposing them to the .NET world
- Native code—Windows Forms interop
- Native code—Avalon (WPF) interop
- Native code—Indigo (WCF) interop

This book will *not* do the following:

- *Teach you C++.* Readers are expected to be VC++ developers with intermediate or higher skills.

- *Teach you .NET.* You need some minimal awareness of the .NET Framework and its workings.
- *Dedicate chapters to specific .NET classes/libraries.* This is not a .NET book, nor is it a Base Class Library book.
- *Teach you Windows Forms, WPF, or WCF.* The book focuses on how to interop with these technologies from Visual C++.

Roadmap

The book is divided into three parts. The first part (chapters 1 through 3) introduces you to C++/CLI. The next two chapters cover mixed-mode programming, and the last part of the book (chapters 6 though 8), is devoted to how to use managed networks from native applications.

- Chapter 1 presents the new C++/CLI syntax introduced in VC++ 2005, rationalizes the need for a new syntax, explains basic syntactic concepts, and shows how you can compile and run a C++/CLI application. Concepts such as handles, CLI types, the `gcnew` operator, and boxing/unboxing are covered.
- Chapter 2 looks at CLI functionality available in C++/CLI that helps make it a first-class .NET language, including properties, delegates and events, and managed arrays. Arrays of non-CLI objects are discussed, and we look at accessing managed arrays using native pointers.
- Chapter 3 explores stack semantics and deterministic destruction, including a brief look at the garbage-collection mechanism in .NET. The chapter also covers the new function-overriding mechanisms available in C++/CLI and ends with a discussion of CLI generics and managed templates. At the end of the chapter, you should be comfortable with the C++/CLI language syntax.
- Chapter 4 is crucial, because it introduces the concept of mixed-mode programming—this book's primary subject. It bridges the previous three chapters with the next four. The chapter describes how to use CLI pointers, talks about the various interop mechanisms available and compares their performance, introduces and explains the concept of mixed types, and covers techniques to convert between native function pointers and managed delegates.
- Chapter 5 continues the coverage of mixed-mode programming and covers techniques for using native C++ libraries from managed applications. The chapter also explains how to expose a managed interface so that apps written in any CLI language—not necessarily C++—can access those native libraries. Other topics include type conversions and double thunking.

- Chapter 6 includes topics on mixing MFC with WinForms, such as hosting WinForms controls in MFC dialogs and views, and using WinForms controls to enhance the UI of an existing MFC application. The chapter ends with a look at how you can use an MFC control from a managed Windows Forms application.
- Chapter 7 briefly introduces WPF and demonstrates three different techniques to add WPF UI support to an existing native application. Because WPF is a huge topic area, this coverage is brief and introductory in nature; the chapter's main focus is interoping WPF with native code. Examples show how to host WPF controls in a native app and also how to do the reverse: host native controls in a WPF app.
- Chapter 8 briefly introduces WCF as an analogous technology to DCOM. The chapter begins with a few basic examples of writing and consuming a WCF service. The main example in the chapter is a DCOM client/server application that is migrated to a WCF platform in a step-by-step process. The chapter ends with a discussion of hosting a C++/CLI-written WCF service from within an IIS Server.
- The appendix serves as a concise introduction to .NET for those who are not familiar with it, or as a refresher for those who have used it in the past.

Source code

All source code in listings or in text is in a fixed-width font `like this` to separate it from ordinary text. Annotations accompany many of the listings, highlighting important concepts. In some cases, numbered bullets link to explanations that follow the listing.

Source code for all of the working examples in this book is available for download from www.manning.com/sivakumar or www.manning.com/C++/CLI-inAction.

Author Online

Purchase of *C++/CLI in Action* includes free access to a private web forum run by Manning Publications where you can make comments about the book, ask technical questions, and receive help from the author and from other users. To access the forum and subscribe to it, point your web browser to www.manning.com/sivakumar. This page provides information on how to get on the forum once you are registered, what kind of help is available, and the rules of conduct on the forum.

Manning's commitment to our readers is to provide a venue where a meaningful dialog between individual readers and between readers and the author can take place. It is not a commitment to any specific amount of participation on the part of the author, whose contribution to the AO remains voluntary (and unpaid). We suggest you try asking the author some challenging questions, lest his interest stray!

The Author Online forum and the archives of previous discussions will be accessible from the publisher's website as long as the book is in print.

About the author

Nishant Sivakumar is a software developer living in Atlanta who has been coding since 1990. Originally from sunny Trivandrum in India, he recently moved to Atlanta from Toronto and is just a little sad that he won't be able to play in snow anymore.

Nish has several years of experience in Visual C++ and .NET technologies and has been a Microsoft Visual C++ MVP since October 2002. Nish has also been named CodeProject MVP for 2005, 2006, and 2007. He maintains an MVP tips-and-tricks website (www.voidnish.com) where you can find a consolidated list of his articles, writings, and ideas about VC++, MFC, .NET, and C++/CLI. Nish blogs about technology and his life at blog.voidnish.com.

About the title

By combining introductions, overviews, and how-to examples, the *In Action* books are designed to help learning *and* remembering. According to research in cognitive science, the things people remember are things they discover during self-motivated exploration.

Although no one at Manning is a cognitive scientist, we are convinced that for learning to become permanent it must pass through stages of exploration, play, and, interestingly, re-telling of what is being learned. People understand and remember new things, which is to say they master them, only after actively exploring them. Humans learn *in action*. An essential part of an *In Action* guide is that it is example-driven. It encourages the reader to try things out, to play with new code, and explore new ideas.

There is another, more mundane, reason for the title of this book: our readers are busy. They use books to do a job or solve a problem. They need books that allow them to jump in and jump out easily and learn just what they want just when they want it. They need books that aid them *in action*. The books in this series are designed for such readers.

About the cover illustration

The figure on the cover of *C++/CLI in Action* is a "Member of the Divan," the Turkish Council of State or governing body. The illustration is taken from a collection of costumes of the Ottoman Empire published on January 1, 1802, by William Miller of Old Bond Street, London. The title page is missing from the collection and we have been unable to track it down to date. The book's table of contents identifies the figures in both English and French, and each illustration bears the names of two artists who worked on it, both of whom would no doubt be surprised to find their art gracing the front cover of a computer programming book...two hundred years later.

The collection was purchased by a Manning editor at an antiquarian flea market in the "Garage" on West 26th Street in Manhattan. The seller was an American based in Ankara, Turkey, and the transaction took place just as he was packing up his stand for the day. The Manning editor did not have on his person the substantial amount of cash that was required for the purchase and a credit card and check were both politely turned down. With the seller flying back to Ankara that evening the situation was getting hopeless. What was the solution? It turned out to be nothing more than an old-fashioned verbal agreement sealed with a handshake. The seller simply proposed that the money be transferred to him by wire and the editor walked out with the bank information on a piece of paper and the portfolio of images under his arm. Needless to say, we transferred the funds the next day, and we remain grateful and impressed by this unknown person's trust in one of us. It recalls something that might have happened a long time ago.

The pictures from the Ottoman collection, like the other illustrations that appear on our covers, bring to life the richness and variety of dress customs of two centuries ago. They recall the sense of isolation and distance of that period—and of every other historic period except our own hyperkinetic present.

Dress codes have changed since then and the diversity by region, so rich at the time, has faded away. It is now often hard to tell the inhabitant of one continent from another. Perhaps, trying to view it optimistically, we have traded a cultural and visual diversity for a more varied personal life. Or a more varied and interesting intellectual and technical life.

We at Manning celebrate the inventiveness, the initiative, and, yes, the fun of the computer business with book covers based on the rich diversity of regional life of two centuries ago, brought back to life by the pictures from this collection.

Part 1

The C++/CLI Language

This part of the book has three chapters that introduce the C++/CLI syntax and language semantics. Chapter 1 covers the rationale behind C++/CLI and why the old syntax had to be deprecated, followed by core concepts such as declaring and instantiating CLI types, CLI handles, and boxing and unboxing. Chapter 2 moves on to CLI-specific features such as using properties, delegates, events, and managed arrays. Chapter 3 discusses stack semantics and deterministic destruction, function overriding, CLI generics, and managed templates.

1

Introduction to C++/CLI

When C++ was wedded to CLI with a slash, it was apparent from the beginning that it wasn't going to be a celebrity marriage. The world's most powerful high level programming language—C++—was given a face-lift so that it could be used to develop on what could potentially be the world's most popular runtime environment: the CLI.

In this chapter, you'll see what C++/CLI can be used for and how C++/CLI improves the now-obsolete Managed C++ syntax. We'll also go over basic C++/CLI syntax. By the end of this chapter, you'll know how to write and compile a C++/CLI program and how to declare and use managed types. Some of the new syntactic features may take a little getting used to, but C++ as a language has never had simplicity as its primary design concern. Once you get used to it, you can harness the power and ingenuity of the language and put that to effective use.

1.1 The role of C++/CLI

C++ is a versatile programming language with a substantial number of features that makes it the most powerful and flexible coding tool for a professional developer. The Common Language Infrastructure (CLI) is an architecture that supports a dynamic language-independent programming model based on a Virtual Execution System. The most popular implementation of the CLI is Microsoft's .NET Framework for the Windows operating system. C++/CLI is a binding between the standard C++ programming language and the CLI. Figure 1.1 shows the relationship between standard C++ and the CLI.

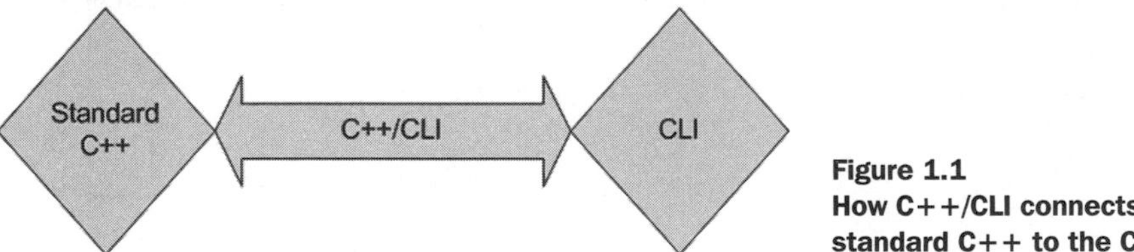

Figure 1.1 How C++/CLI connects standard C++ to the CLI

C++ has been paired with language extensions before, and the result hasn't always been pretty. Visual C++ 2005 is the first version of a Microsoft C++ compiler that has implemented the C++/CLI specification. This means three things for the C++ developer:

- C++ can be used to write applications that run on the .NET Framework. There is no need to learn a totally new language or to abandon all the C++ knowledge and experience built up through years of coding.

- C++/CLI lets developers reuse their native C++ code base, saving the agony of having to rewrite all the existing code to enable it to run on the .NET Framework.
- C++/CLI is designed to be the lowest-level language for the .NET Framework. For writing purely managed applications, it's your most powerful choice; or, as I like to say, "C++/CLI actually lets you smell the CLR (Common Language Runtime)."

Visual C++ 2005 isn't Microsoft's first attempt at providing a C++ compiler capable of targeting managed code. Both VC++ 2002 and VC++ 2003 featured a C++ compiler that supported the managed extensions to C++ (referred to as Managed C++ or MC++). As a syntactic extension, it would be an understatement to say that it was a comprehensive failure.

Now that you understand the role of C++/CLI, let's examine why it's such an invaluable inclusion among CLI languages.

The .NET Framework

It's important for you to have a basic understanding of the .NET Framework, because although this book will teach you the C++/CLI syntax before we move on to various interop mechanisms and strategies, it doesn't attempt to teach you the core details of the .NET Framework. If you've never used the .NET Framework, you should read the book's appendix ("A Concise Introduction to the .NET Framework") before you proceed further. On the other hand, if you've previously worked with the .NET Framework, you can refresh your memory by looking at these quick definitions (in no particular order) of various terms associated with the .NET Framework, which you'll encounter in this and other chapters:

- **.NET Framework:** The .NET Framework is Microsoft's implementation of the Common Language Infrastructure (CLI), which itself is an open specification that has been standardized by the ECMA (an international standards body). The .NET Framework consists of the Common Language Runtime (CLR) and the Base Class Library (BCL).
- **CLR:** The Common Language Runtime is the core of the .NET Framework and implements the fundamental aspects of the CLI such as the Virtual Execution System (VES), the Garbage Collector, and the Just in Time (JIT) compiler.
- **BCL:** The Base Class Library is an extensive set of .NET classes that is used by any .NET language (such as C#, VB.NET, C++/CLI, and so on).

- **VES**: The Virtual Execution System is the engine responsible for executing managed code, including the invocation of the Garbage Collector as well as the JIT compiler.
- **Garbage Collector**: Memory management is automatically done in the .NET Framework. The CLR includes a Garbage Collector that frees resources when they're no longer needed, so the developer doesn't need to worry about that.
- **JIT compiler**: .NET compilers (C#, VB.NET, C++/CLI, and so on) compile source code into an intermediate language called Microsoft Intermediate Language (MSIL). At runtime, the CLR uses the JIT compiler to compile this MSIL into the native code for the underlying operating system before executing it.
- **CTS**: The Common Type System (CTS) is a set of rules that specifies how the CLR can define, use, create, and manage types.
- **CLS**: The Common Language Specification (CLS) is a subset of the CTS that all languages must implement if they're to be considered CLS-compliant. CLS-compliant languages can interop with each other as long as they don't use any non-CLS-compliant features present in their specific compiler version.

I'd like to reiterate that if you're not familiar with these terms, or if you wish to understand them in more detail, please take a detour into the appendix, where most of these concepts are explained more thoroughly.

1.1.1 What C++/CLI can do for you

If you're reading this book, chances are good that you're looking to move your applications to the .NET Framework. The biggest concern C++ developers have about making the move to .NET is that they're afraid of abandoning their existing native code and having to rewrite everything to managed code. That's exactly where C++/CLI comes into the picture. You do *not* have to abandon your current native code, nor do you have to rewrite everything to managed code. That's C++/CLI's single biggest advantage—the ability to reuse existing native code.

Reuse existing native code

Visual C++ 2005 allows you to compile your entire native code base to MSIL with the flick of a single compilation switch. In practice, you may find that you have to change a small percentage of your code to successfully compile and build your applications. This is a far better option than either abandoning all your code or rewriting it entirely. Once you've successfully compiled your code for the CLR, the code can access the thousands of classes available in the .NET Base Class Library.

Access the entire .NET library

The .NET Framework comes with a colossal library containing thousands of classes that simplify your most common developmental requirements. There are classes relating to XML, cryptography, graphical user interfaces, database technologies, OS functionality, networking, text processing, and just about anything you can think of. Once you've taken your native applications and compiled them for the CLR, you can use these .NET classes directly from your code. For example, you can take a regular MFC dialog-based application and give it some encryption functionality using the .NET cryptography classes. You aren't restricted to managed libraries, because C++/CLI lets you seamlessly interop between managed and native code.

Most powerful language for interop

Although other languages like C# and VB.NET have interop features, C++/CLI offers the most powerful and convenient interop functionality of any CLI language. C++/CLI understands managed types as well as native types; consequently, you often end up using whatever library you want (whether it's a native DLL or a managed assembly) without having to worry about managed/native type conversions. Using a native library from C++/CLI is as simple as `#include`-ing the required header files, linking with the right lib files, and making your API or class calls as you would normally do. Compare that with C# or VB.NET, where you're forced to copy and paste numerous P/Invoke declarations before you can access native code. In short, for any sort of interop scenario, C++/CLI should be an automatic language choice. One popular use of interop is to access new managed frameworks such as Windows Forms from existing native applications. (Note that this technique is covered in detail in part 3 of the book.)

Leverage the latest managed frameworks

Imagine that you have a substantially large MFC application and that your company wants to give it a new look and feel. You've recently acquired an outstanding Windows Forms–based UI library from another company. Take VC++ 2005, recompile the MFC application for the CLR, and change the UI layer to use the Windows Forms library, and now you have the same application that uses the same underlying business logic with the new shiny user interface. You aren't restricted to Windows Forms or even to UI frameworks. The next version of Windows (called Windows Vista) will introduce a new UI framework called the Windows Presentation Foundation (WPF). It's a managed framework and C++/CLI will let you access it from existing native applications. When Vista is released, your applications will be able to flaunt the WPF look and feel. Note that WPF is also being made available for Windows XP, so you aren't restricted to using Vista to run WPF-based applications.

Another powerful managed framework that is coming out in Vista is the Windows Communication Foundation (WCF), which, as the name implies, is a powerful communication framework written in managed code. And yes, although you knew I was going to say it, you can access the WCF from your Visual C++ applications. Although native code reuse and powerful interop are its most popular advantages, C++/CLI is also your most powerful option to write managed applications.

Write powerful managed applications

When Brandon Bray from the Visual C++ Compiler team said that C++/CLI would be the lowest-level language outside of MSIL, he meant what he said! C++/CLI supports more MSIL features than any other CLI language; it is to MSIL what C used to be to Assembly Language in the old days. C++/CLI is currently the only CLI language that supports stack semantics and deterministic destruction, mixed types, managed templates, and STL.NET (a managed implementation of the Standard Template Library).

A natural question you may have now is why Microsoft introduced a new syntax. Why didn't it continue to use the old MC++ syntax? That's what we examine next.

1.1.2 The rationale behind the new syntax

The managed extensions to C++ introduced in VC++ 2002 were not well received by the C++ developer community. Most people appreciated the fact that they could use C++ for .NET development, but almost everybody thought the syntax was gratuitously twisted and unnatural, that the managed and unmanaged pointer usage semantics were confusing, and that C++ hadn't been given equal footing as a CLI language with other languages like C# or VB.NET. Another factor that contributed to poor Managed C++ acceptance was the fact that designer support for Windows Forms was not available in the 2002 release; although the 2003 release did introduce a designer, it wasn't as stable or functional as the designers available for C# and VB.NET, and creating pure managed applications was dreadfully unfeasible with C++.

Microsoft took the feedback from its C++ developer community seriously, and on October 6, 2003, the ECMA (an association dedicated to the standardization of Information and Communication Technology and Consumer Electronics) announced the creation of a new task group to oversee the development of a standard set of language extensions to create a binding between the ISO standard C++ programming language and the CLI. Microsoft developed and submitted full draft specifications for binding the C++ Programming Language to the Common Language Infrastructure in November 2003, and C++/CLI became an international ECMA standard in December 2005. It was expected that the ECMA would submit it to the ISO for consideration as a potential ISO standard. Visual C++ 2005 is the first publicly available compiler to support this new standard.

> **NOTE** The ECMA (the acronym originally stood for European Computer Manufacturers Association) is an association founded in 1961 that's dedicated to the standardization of Information Technology systems. The ECMA has close liaisons with other technology standards organizations and is responsible for maintaining and publishing various standards documents. Note that the old acronym isn't used anymore, and the body today goes by the name ECMA International. You can visit its website at www.ecma-international.org.

Let's take a quick look at a few of the problems that existed in the old syntax and how C++/CLI improves on these issues. If you've used the old syntax in the past, you'll definitely appreciate the enhancements in the new syntax; if you haven't, you'll still notice the stark difference in elegance between the two syntaxes.

Twisted syntax and grammar

The old Managed C++ syntax used a lot of underscored keywords that were clunky and awkward. Note that these double-underscored keywords were required to conform to ANSI standards, which dictate that all compiler-specific keywords need to be prefixed with double underscores. But as a developer, you always want your code to feel natural and elegant. As long as developers felt that the code they wrote didn't look or feel like C++, they weren't going to feel comfortable using that syntax; most C++ developers chose not to use a syntax that felt awkward.

C++/CLI introduced a new syntax that fit in with existing C++ semantics. The elegant grammar gives a natural feel for C++ developers and allows a smooth transition from native coding to managed coding.

Look at table 1.1, which compares the old and new syntaxes; you'll see what I mean.

Even without knowing the rules for either the old or the new syntax or C++/CLI, you shouldn't find it hard to decide which is the more elegant and natural of the two. Don't worry if the code doesn't make a lot of sense to you right now. Later

Table 1.1 Comparison between old and new syntaxes

<table>
<tr><th>Old syntax</th><th>C++/CLI syntax</th></tr>
<tr><td><pre>
__gc __interface I
{
};

__delegate int ClickHandler();

__gc class M : public I
{
    __event ClickHandler* OnClick;
public:
    __property int get_Num()
    {
        return 0;
    }
    __property void set_Num(int)
    {
    }
};
</pre></td><td><pre>
interface class I
{
};

delegate int ClickHandler();

ref class M : public I
{
    event ClickHandler^ OnClick;
public:
    property int Num
    {
        int get()
        {
            return 0;
        }
        void set(int value)
        {
        }
    }
};
</pre></td></tr>
</table>

in this chapter, we'll go through the fundamental syntactic concepts of the C++/CLI language. I just wanted to show you why the old syntax never became popular and how Microsoft has improved on the look and feel of the syntax in the new C++/CLI specification.

With the old syntax, every time you used a CLI feature, such as a delegate or a property, you had to prefix it with underscored keywords. For a property definition, the old syntax required separate setter and getter blocks and didn't syntactically organize them into a single block. This meant that if you carelessly separated the getter and setter methods with other code, there was no visual cue that they were part of the same property definition. With the new syntax, you put your getter and setter functions inside a property block; the relationship between them is visually maintained. To summarize my personal thoughts on this issue, with the old syntax, you feel that you're using two unrelated sublanguages (one for managed code and one for native code) with a single compiler. With the new syntax, you feel that you're using C++, albeit with a lot of new keywords: It's still a single language. Note that the VC++ team made an effort to ensure that the new keywords don't interfere with existing code bases, as you'll see later in the book.

Programmers can be compiler snobs. Many developers opined that C# and VB.NET were proper .NET languages, whereas MC++ was a second-class citizen compared to them. Let's see what has been done to the C++ language to promote it to a first-class CLI status.

Second class CLI support

Managed C++ seemed like a second-class CLI language when compared to languages like C# and VB.NET, and developers using it had to resort to contorted workarounds to implement CLI functionality. Take a trivial example such as enumerating over the contents of an `ArrayList` object. Here's what the code would look like in Managed C++:

```
IEnumerator* pEnumerator = arraylist->GetEnumerator();
while(pEnumerator->MoveNext())
{
    Console::WriteLine(pEnumerator->Current);
}
```

While languages like C# provided a `for each` construct that abstracted the entire enumeration process, C++ developers were forced to access the `IEnumerator` for the `ArrayList` object and use that directly—not a good thing, as far as Objected-Oriented abstraction rules were concerned. Now the programmer needs to know that the collection has an enumerator, that the enumerator has a `MoveNext` method and a `Current` property, and that they have to repeatedly call `MoveNext` until it returns `false`. This information should be hidden from the programmer. Requiring the internal implementation details of the collection to be directly used defeats the purpose of having collection classes, when the reason for having them is to abstract the internal details of an enumerable collection class from the programmer.

Look at the equivalent C++/CLI code:

```
for each(String^ s in arraylist)
{
    Console::WriteLine(s);
}
```

By adding constructs such as `for each`, which give developers a more natural syntax to access .NET features, the VC++ team has given us a cozy feeling that C++/CLI is now a first-class language for .NET programming. Later in this chapter, you'll see that boxing is now implicit, which means you don't have to use the gratuitous `__box` keyword required in the old syntax. If you don't know what boxing means, don't worry; it will be explained when we talk about boxing and unboxing.

Poor integration of C++ and .NET

One major complaint about Managed C++ was that C++ features such as templates and deterministic destruction weren't available. Most C++ developers felt severely handicapped by the apparent feature reductions when using MC++.

With C++/CLI, templates are supported on both managed and unmanaged types. In addition, C++/CLI is the only CLI language that supports stack semantics and deterministic destruction (although languages like C# 2.0 use indirect workarounds like the `using-block` construct to conjure up a form of deterministic destruction).

A crisp summarization would be to say that C++/CLI bridges the gap between C++ and .NET by bringing C++ features such as templates and deterministic destruction to .NET, and .NET features like properties, delegates, garbage collection, and generics to C++.

Confusing pointer usage

Managed C++ used the same `*` punctuator-based operator syntax for unmanaged pointers into the C++ heap and managed references into the CLI heap. Not only was this confusing and error-prone, but managed references were different entities with totally different behavioral patterns from unmanaged pointers. Consider the following code snippet:

```
__gc class R
{
};

class N
{
};

. . .

N* pN = new N();
R* pR = new R();
```

The two calls to `new` (shown in bold) do completely different things. The `new` call on the native class `N` results in the C++ `new` operator being called, whereas the `new` call on the managed class `R` is compiled into the MSIL `newobj` instruction. The native object is allocated on the C++ heap, but the managed object is allocated on the garbage-collected CLR heap, which has the side implication that the memory address for the object may change every time there is a garbage-collection cycle or a heap-compaction operation. The `R*` object looks like a native C++ pointer, but it doesn't behave like one, and its address can't be assumed to remain fixed. The good news is that this issue has been fixed in C++/CLI. We now have an additional `gcnew` keyword for instantiating managed objects. We also have the concept of a *handle* (as opposed to a pointer) to a managed object that uses the ^ punctuator (instead of *) as the handle operator. Later in this chapter, we'll take a more detailed look at handles and the `gcnew` operator. For now, it should suffice to note that in C++/CLI, there will be no managed/unmanaged pointer confusion.

Unverifiable code

The Managed C++ compiler could not produce verifiable code, which meant that you couldn't use it to write code that was to run under a protected environment—such as an SQL Server-stored procedure. Visual C++ 2005 supports a special compiler mode (`/clr:safe`) that produces verifiable code and disallows you from compiling any non-verifiable code by generating errors during compilation. The advantage of being able to create verifiable assemblies is that the CLR can enforce active CLR security restrictions on the running application. This gives you a wider scope to deploy your applications (for example, as SQL Server components) in secure environments like those in a banking system and in future Windows releases where code may have to be verifiable to be permitted to execute.

It should be obvious by now why Microsoft decided to bring out a new syntax. If you've never used the old syntax, you can consider yourself lucky that you can now use the powerful new C++/CLI language to write managed applications.

If you *have* used the old syntax, I strongly recommend spending some time porting the old syntax code to the new syntax as early as possible. The old syntax support (available in VC++ 2005 through the `/clr:oldSyntax` compiler switch) isn't guaranteed to be available in future VC++ versions, nor will any significant improvements be made to it. Let's now move on to our first C++/CLI program.

1.2 Hello World in C++/CLI

Before we go any further, let's write our first Hello World application in C++/CLI. In this section, we'll also look at the new compiler options that have been introduced in VC++ 2005 to support compilation for managed code. There is nothing overly-complicated about the code in Listing 1.1, but for our purposes, it does nicely to illustrate a few basic language concepts of C++/CLI.

Listing 1.1 Hello World program in C++/CLI

```
#pragma comment(lib, "Advapi32")
#include <windows.h>
#include <tchar.h>
```

```
#include <lmcons.h>
using namespace System;

int main()
{
    TCHAR buffer[UNLEN + 1];
    DWORD size = UNLEN + 1;
    GetUserName(buffer, &size);
    String^ greeting = "Hello";
    Console::WriteLine("{0} {1}",
        greeting, gcnew String(buffer));
    return 0;
}
```

❶ **Get current user**

❷ **Display greeting**

You can compile this code from the command line using the C++ compiler cl.exe as follows:

```
cl /clr First.cpp
```

Run it, and it promptly displays "Hello" followed by the current user (most likely your Windows login name) on the console. Except for the `gcnew` keyword (which we'll talk about later in this chapter), it doesn't look very different from a regular C++ program, does it? But the executable that has been created is a .NET executable that runs on the .NET Common Language Runtime. When I say *.NET executable*, I mean an MSIL program that is JIT compiled and executed by the CLR just like any executable you might create using C#, VB.NET, or another CLI language. This is a small example, but it communicates two important facts: You can use familiar C++ syntax to write .NET applications, thereby avoiding the need to learn a new language like C# or VB.NET; and you can write managed ❷ and native code ❶ within the same application.

For those of you who aren't familiar with the .NET Framework, `Console` is a .NET Framework BCL class that belongs to the `System` namespace (hence the `using namespace` declaration on top), and `WriteLine` is a static method of the `Console` class. Listing 1.1 uses native data types like `TCHAR` and `DWORD` as well as managed data types like `String`. Similarly, it uses a native Win32 API call (`GetUserName`) as well as a managed class (`System::Console`). The best part is that you do all this in a single application (within a single function, in this case). Although you may not have realized it, you've just written a mixed-mode application that mixes native and managed code. Congratulations! You can do a lot with mixed-mode coding, and you'll see far more useful applications of that technique throughout the later portions of this book.

You must have observed that I specified `/clr` as a compiler option. Let's talk a little more about that.

1.2.1 The /clr compiler option

To use the C++/CLI language features, you need to enable the `/clr` compiler switch; without it, cl.exe behaves like a native C++ compiler. The `/clr` switch creates a .NET application that's capable of consuming .NET libraries and can take advantage of CLR features such as managed types and garbage collection. You can specify suboptions to the `/clr` option to further specify the type of assembly you want created. Table 1.2 is a partial list of the `/clr` suboptions you can specify and what they do. For a more complete list, refer to the MSDN documentation for the C++ compiler command-line switches.

Now that we've discussed the command-line compiler options, let's look at how you can use the VC++ 2005 environment to create C++/CLI projects.

Table 1.2 Partial listing of `/clr` compilation modes in VC++ 2005

Compiler switch	Description
`/clr`	Creates an assembly targeting the CLR. The output file may contain both MSIL and native code (mixed-mode assemblies). This is the most commonly-used switch (which is probably why it's the default). It lets you enable CLR support to native C++ projects including, but not limited to, projects that use MFC, ATL, WTL, STL, and Win32 API. This will be the most commonly-used compilation mode throughout this book.
`/clr:pure`	Creates an MSIL-only assembly with no native code (hence *pure*). You can have native (unmanaged) types in your code as long as they can be compiled into pure MSIL. C# developers can think of this as being equivalent to using the C# compiler in unsafe mode—the output is pure MSIL but not necessarily verifiable.
`/clr:safe`	Creates an MSIL-only verifiable assembly. You can't have native types in your code, and if you try to use them, the compiler will throw an error. This compilation mode produces assemblies that are equivalent to what C# (regular mode) and VB.NET would produce.
`/clr:oldSyntax`	Enables the MC++ syntax available in VC++ 2002 and VC++ 2003. I strongly advocate that you never use this option, except where it's an absolute necessity. Even if it takes considerable time to port a large old syntax code base to the new syntax, it's still your best option in the long run. There is no guarantee that this option will be available in a future version of the VC++ compiler.

1.2.2 Using VC++ 2005 to create a /clr application

For any nontrivial program, it makes sense to use the Visual C++ development environment, although it's still good to know the compiler options available. I believe that one of the biggest reasons for the popularity of the VC++ compiler is the fact that it comes with a powerful development environment, and there's no reason we shouldn't take advantage of it. For the rest of this chapter and the next two chapters, we'll use CLR-enabled console applications as we look at the C++/CLI syntax and grammar. Those of you who want to follow along in your own console project can type in the code as it's written in the book.

NOTE In later chapters, where the examples are longer and more complex, you can use the book's companion CD, which contains full source code for the samples.

Creating a CLR console application with Visual C++ is straightforward. The steps are as follows.

1. In the New Project Wizard dialog, choose *CLR* under *Visual C++* in the *Project types* tree control on the left, and select *CLR Console Application* from the *Templates* list control on the right. You can use Figure 1.2 as a reference when doing this.
2. Enter a name for the project, and click OK.

The wizard generates quite a few files for you. The one that should interest you most is the CPP file that has the same name as the project. If you named your project Chapter01Demo, you'll see a Chapter01Demo.cpp file in your solution that contains the wizard-generated `main` method. You must have used similar wizards in the past when working on MFC, ATL, or Win32 API projects, so this should be familiar.

You'll notice something interesting about the way the generated `main` function is prototyped:

```
int main(array<System::String ^> ^args)
```

This version of `main` is compatible with the entry-point prototypes available for C# and VB.NET programs and adheres to the CLI definition of a managed entry-point function. The syntax may seem a little confusing right now (because we haven't yet begun exploring the C++/CLI syntax), but `args` is essentially a managed array of `System::String` objects that represents the command-line arguments passed to the application. Keep this important distinction in mind: Unlike

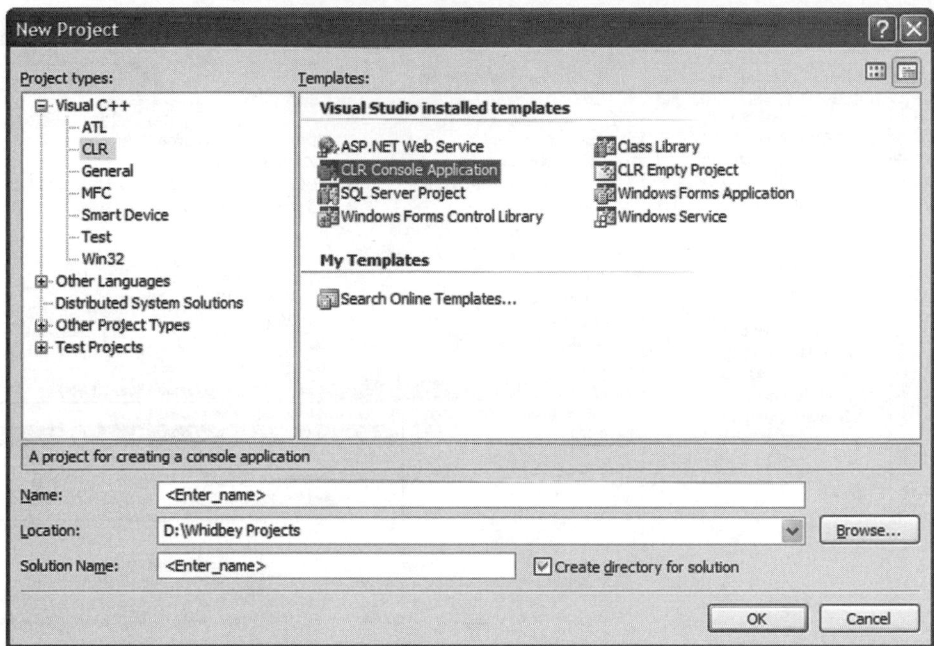

Figure 1.2 The Visual C++ 2005 New Project Wizard

the native C++ `main` prototypes, the name of the program isn't passed as the zero-indexed argument. If you run the application without any command-line arguments, the array will be empty. By default, the wizard sets the project to use the `/clr` compilation option, but you can change that by using the Project Properties dialog; you can access it by choosing Project > Properties or by using the Alt-F7 keyboard shortcut.

> **NOTE** Your keyboard shortcuts will vary depending on your VS profile. This book uses the shortcuts associated with the default VC++ profile.

Select *General* from *Configuration Properties* on the left, and you'll see an option to set the `/clr` compilation switch (you can choose from `/clr`, `/clr:pure`, `/clr:safe`, and `/clr:oldSyntax`), as shown in Figure 1.3.

Now that you've seen how to create a C++/CLI project, let's look at the type-declaration syntax for declaring CLI types (also referred to as CLR types). When you learn how to declare and use CLR types, you get a proper feel for programming on top of the CLR.

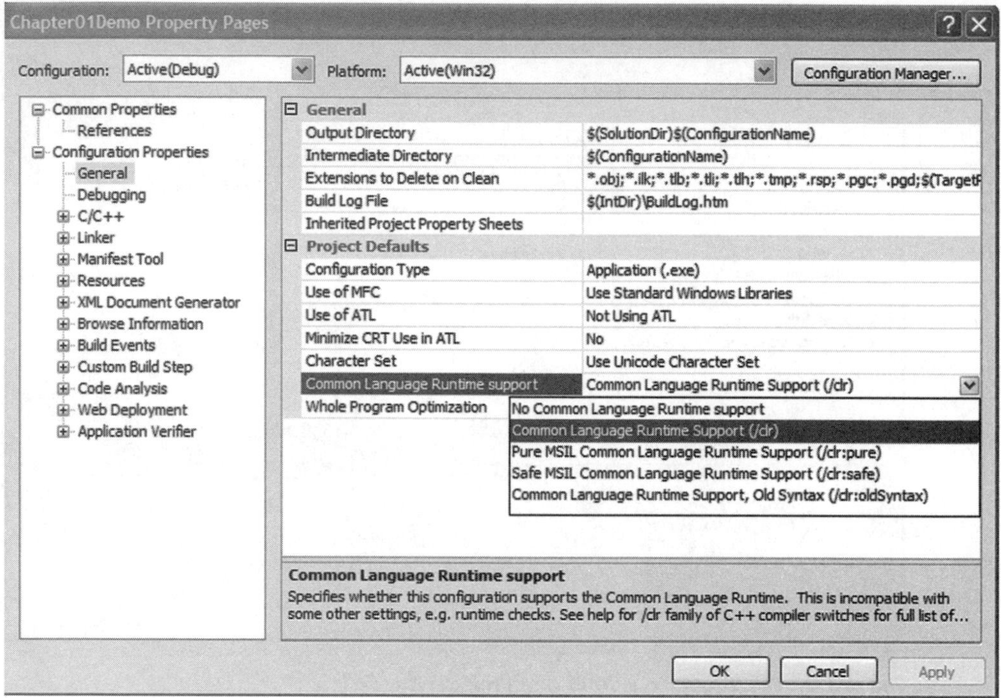

Figure 1.3 Setting the CLR compilation options using the Project Properties dialog

1.3 Declaring CLR types

In this section, we'll look at the syntax for declaring CLI (or CLR) types, modifiers that can be applied to CLI types, and how CLI types implement inheritance. C++/CLI supports both native (unmanaged) and managed types and uses a consistent syntax for declaring various types. Native types are declared and used just as they are in standard C++. Declaring a CLI type is similar to declaring a native type, except that an adjective is prefixed to the class declaration that indicates the type being declared. Table 1.3 shows examples of CLI type declarations for various types.

C# developers may be a little confused by the usage of both `class` and `struct` for both reference and value types. In C++/CLI, `struct` and `class` can be used interchangeably (just as in standard C++), and they follow standard C++ visibility rules for structs and classes. In a class, methods are `private` by default; in a struct, methods are `public` by default. In table 1.3, `RefClass1::Func` and `ValClass1::Func` are both `private`, whereas `RefClass2::Func` and `ValClass2::Func`

Table 1.3 Type declaration syntax for CLI types

CLI type	Declaration syntax

Reference types	`ref class RefClass1`
	`{`
	`    void Func(){}`
	`};`
	
	`ref struct RefClass2`
	`{`
	`    void Func(){}`
	`};`

Value types	`value class ValClass1`
	`{`
	`    void Func(){}`
	`};`
	
	`value struct ValClass2`
	`{`
	`    void Func(){}`
	`};`

Interface types	`interface class IType1`
	`{`
	`    void Func();`
	`};`
	
	`interface struct IType2`
	`{`
	`    void Func();`
	`};`

are both `public`. For the sake of clarity and consistency with C#, you may want to exclusively use `ref class` for ref types and `value struct` for value types instead of mixing `class` and `struct` for both ref and value types.

Interface methods are always `public`; declaring an interface as a struct is equivalent to declaring it as a class. This means `IType1::Func` and `IType2::Func` are both `public` in the generated MSIL. C# developers must keep the following in mind:

- A C++/CLI value class (or value struct) is the same as a C# struct.
- A C++/CLI ref class (or ref struct) is the same as a C# class.

Those of you who have worked on the old MC++ syntax should remember these three points:

- A ref class is the same as an `__gc` class.
- A value class is the same as an `__value` class.
- An interface class is the same as an `__interface`.

Spaced keywords

An interesting thing that you need to be aware of is that only three new, reserved keywords have been introduced in C++/CLI: `gcnew`, `nullptr`, and `generic`. All the other seemingly new keywords are *spaced* (or contextual) keywords. Syntactic phrases like `ref class`, `for each`, and `value class` are spaced keywords that are treated as single tokens in the compiler's lexical analyzer. The big advantage is that any existing code that uses these new keywords (like `ref` or `each`) continues to compile correctly, because it's not legal in C++ to use a space in an identifier. The following code is perfectly valid in C++/CLI:

```
int ref = 0;
int value = ref;
bool each = value == ref;
```

Of course, if your existing code uses `gcnew`, `nullptr`, or `generic` as an identifier, C++/CLI won't compile it, and you'll have to rename those identifiers.

You've seen how CLI types can be declared. Next, you'll see how type modifiers can be applied to these classes (or structs, as the case may be).

1.3.1 Class modifiers

You can specify the `abstract` and `sealed` modifiers on classes; a class can be marked both `abstract` and `sealed`. But such classes can't be derived explicitly from any base class and can only contain `static` members. Because global functions aren't CLS-compliant, you should use abstract sealed classes with `static` functions, instead of global functions, if you want your code to be CLS-compliant.

In case you're wondering when and why you would need to use these modifiers, remember that, to effectively write code targeting the .NET Framework, you should be able to implement every supported CLI paradigm. The CLI explicitly supports abstract classes, sealed classes, and classes that are both abstract and sealed. If the CLI supports it, you should be able to do so, too.

Just as with standard C++, an abstract class can only be used as a base class for other classes. It isn't required that the class contains abstract methods for it to be declared as an abstract class, which gives you extra flexibility when designing your class hierarchy. The following class is abstract because it's declared `abstract`, although it doesn't contain any abstract methods:

```
ref class R2 abstract
{
public:
    virtual void Func(){}
};
```

An interesting compiler behavior is that if you have a class with an abstract method that isn't marked `abstract`, such as the following class, the compiler issues warning C4570 (*class is not explicitly declared as abstract but has abstract functions*) instead of issuing an error:

```
ref class R1
{
public:
    virtual void Func() abstract;
};
```

In the generated IL, the class R1 is marked `abstract`, which means that if you try to instantiate the class, you'll get a compiler error (and you should). Not marking a class `abstract` when it has abstract methods is untidy, and I strongly encourage you to explicitly mark classes `abstract` if at least one of their methods is abstract. Note how I've used the `abstract` modifier on a class method in the previous example; you'll see more on this and other function modifiers in chapter 2.

Using the `sealed` modifier follows a similar syntax. A sealed class can't be used as a base class for any other class—it seals the class from further derivation:

```
ref class S sealed
{
};

ref class D : S     // This won't compile
{                   // Error C3246
};
```

Sealed classes are typically used when you don't want the characteristics of a specific class to be modified (through a derived class), because you want to ensure that all instances of that class behave in a fixed manner. Because a derived class can be used anywhere the base class can be used, if you allow your class to be inherited from, by using instances of the derived class where the base class instance is expected, users of your code can alter the expected functionality (which you want to remain unchangeable) of the class. For example, consider a banking application that has a `CreditCardInfo` class that is used to fetch information about an account holder's credit-card transactions. Because instances of this class will be occasionally transmitted across the Internet, all internal data is securely stored using a strong encryption algorithm. By allowing the class to be inherited from, there is the risk of an injudicious programmer forgetting to properly follow the data encryption implemented by the `CreditCardInfo` class; thus any instance of the derived class is inherently insecure. By marking the `CreditCardInfo` class as `sealed`, such a contingency can be easily avoided.

A performance benefit of using a sealed class is that, because the compiler knows a sealed class can't have any derived classes, it can statically resolve virtual member invocations on a sealed class instance using nonvirtual invocations. For example, assuming that the `CreditCardInfo` class overrides the `GetHashCode` method (which it inherits from `Object`), when you call `GetHashCode` at runtime, the CLR doesn't have to figure out which function to call. This is the case because it doesn't have to determine the polymorphic type of the class (because a `CreditCardInfo` object can only be a `CreditCardInfo` object, it can't be an object of a derived type—there are no derived types). It directly calls the `GetHashCode` method defined by the `CreditCardInfo` class.

Look at the following example of an abstract sealed class:

```
ref class SA abstract sealed
{
public:
        static void DoStuff(){}
private:
        static int bNumber = 0;
};
```

As mentioned earlier, abstract sealed classes can't have instance methods; attempting to include them will throw compiler error C4693. This isn't puzzling when you consider that an instance method on an abstract sealed class would be worthless, because you can never have an instance of such a class. An abstract sealed class can't be explicitly derived from a base class, although it implicitly derives from `System::Object`. For those of you who've used C#, it may be interesting to know that an abstract sealed class is the same as a C# static class.

Now that we've discussed how to declare CLI types and apply modifiers on them, let's look at how CLI types work with inheritance.

1.3.2 CLI types and inheritance

Inheritance rules are similar to those in standard C++, but there are differences, and it's important to realize what they are when using C++/CLI. The good thing is that most of the differences are obvious and natural ones dictated by the nature of the CLI. Consequently, you won't find it particularly strenuous to remember them.

Reference types (`ref class/struct`) only support `public` inheritance, and if you skip the `access` keyword, `public` inheritance is assumed:

```
ref class Base
{
};

ref class Derived : Base // implicitly public
{
};
```

If you attempt to use `private` or `protected` inheritance, you'll get compiler error C3628. The same rule applies when you implement an interface; interfaces must be implemented using `public` inheritance, and if you skip the `access` keyword, `public` is assumed:

```
interface class IBase
{
};

ref class Derived1 : private IBase {}; //error C3141
ref class Derived2 : protected IBase {}; //error C3141
ref class Derived3 : IBase {}; //public assumed
```

The rules for value types and inheritance are slightly different from those for ref types. A value type can only implement interfaces; it can't inherit from another value or ref type. That's because value types are implicitly derived from `System::ValueType`. Because CLI types don't support multiple base classes, value types can't have any other base class. In addition, value types are always sealed and can't be used as base classes. In the following code snippet, only the `Derived3` class compiles. The other two classes attempt to inherit from a ref class and a value class, neither of which is permitted:

```
ref class RefBase {};
value class ValBase {};
interface class IBase {};

value class Derived1 : RefBase {}; //error C3830
value class Derived2 : ValBase {}; //error C3830
value class Derived3 : IBase {};
```

These restrictions are placed on value types because value types are intended to be simple types without the complexities of inheritance or referential identity, which can be implemented using basic copy-by-value semantics. Also note that these restrictions are imposed by the CLI and not by the C++ compiler. The C++ compiler merely complies with the CLI rules for value types. As a developer, you need to keep these restrictions in mind when designing your types. Value types are kept simple to allow the CLR to optimize them at runtime where they're treated like simple plain old data (POD) types like an `int` or a `char`, thus making them extremely efficient compared to reference types.

Here's a simple rule you can follow when you want to decide whether a class should be a value type: Try to determine if you want it to be treated as a class or as plain data. If you want it to be treated as a class, don't make it a value type; but if you want it to behave just as an `int` or a `char` would, chances are good that your best option is to declare it as a value type. Typically, you'll want it to be treated as a class if you expect it to support virtual methods, user-defined constructors, and other aspects characteristic of a complex data type. On the other hand, if it's just a class or a struct with some data members that are themselves value types, such as an `int` or `char`, you may want to make that a value type.

One important point to be aware of is that CLI types don't support multiple inheritance. So, although a CLI type can implement any number of interfaces, it can have only one immediate parent type; if none is specified, this is implicitly assumed to be `System::Object`.

Next, we'll talk about one of the most important features that have been introduced in VC++ 2005: the concept of handles.

1.4 Handles: the CLI equivalent to pointers

Handles are a new concept introduced in C++/CLI; they replace the `__gc` pointer concept used in Managed C++. Earlier in the chapter, we discussed the pointer-usage confusion that prevailed in the old syntax. Handles solve that confusion. In my opinion, the concept of handles has contributed the most in escalating C++ as a first-class citizen of the .NET programming language world. In this section, we'll look at the syntax for using handles. We'll also cover the related topic of using tracking references.

1.4.1 Syntax for using handles

A *handle* is a reference to a managed object on the CLI heap and is represented by the ^ punctuator (pronounced *hat*).

NOTE When I say *punctuator* in this chapter, I'm talking from a compiler perspective. As far as the language syntax is concerned, you can replace the word *punctuator* with *operator* and retain the same meaning.

Handles are to the CLI heap what native pointers are to the native C++ heap; and just as you use pointers with heap-allocated native objects, you use handles with managed objects allocated on the CLI heap. Be aware that although native pointers need not always necessarily point to the native heap (you could get a native pointer pointing to the managed heap or to non-C++ allocated memory storage), managed handles have a close-knit relationship with the managed heap. The following code snippet shows how handles can be declared and used:

```
String^ str = "Hello world";
Student^ student = Class::GetStudent("Nish");
student->SelectSubject(150);
```

In the code, `str` is a handle to a `System::String` object on the CLI heap, `student` is a handle to a `Student` object, and `SelectSubject` invokes a method on the `student` handle.

The memory address that `str` refers to isn't guaranteed to remain constant. The `String` object may be moved around after a garbage-collection cycle, but `str` will continue to be a reference to the same `System::String` object (unless it's programmatically changed). This ability of a handle to change its internal memory address when the object it has a reference to is moved around on the CLI heap is called *tracking*.

Handles may look deceitfully similar to pointers, but they are totally different entities when it comes to behavior. Table 1.4 illustrates the differences between handles and pointers.

Table 1.4 Differences between handles and pointers

Handles	Pointers
Handles are denoted by the ^ punctuator.	Pointers are denoted by the * punctuator.
Handles are references to managed objects on the CLI heap.	Pointers point to memory addresses.
Handles may refer to different memory locations throughout their lifetime, depending on GC cycles and heap compactions.	Pointers are stable, and garbage-collection cycles don't affect them.
Handles track objects, so if the object is moved around, the handle still has a reference to that object.	If an object pointed to by a native pointer is programmatically moved around, the pointer isn't updated.
Handles are type-safe.	Pointers weren't designed for type-safety.

continued on next page

Table 1.4 Differences between handles and pointers *(continued)*

Handles	Pointers
The `gcnew` operator returns a handle to the instantiated CLI object.	The `new` operator returns a pointer to the instantiated native object on the native heap.
It isn't mandatory to delete handles. The Garbage Collector eventually cleans up all orphaned managed objects.	It's your responsibility to call `delete` on pointers to objects that you've allocated; if you don't do so, you'll suffer a memory leak.
Handles can't be converted to and from a `void^`.	Pointers can convert to and from a `void*`.
Handles don't allow handle arithmetic.	Pointer arithmetic is a popular mechanism to manipulate native data, especially arrays.

Despite all those differences, typically you'll find that for most purposes, you'll end up using handles much the same way you would use pointers. In fact, the `*` and `->` operators are used to dereference a handle (just as with a pointer). But it's important to be aware of the differences between handles and pointers. The VC++ team members initially called them managed pointers, GC pointers, and tracking pointers. Eventually, the team decided to call them handles to avoid confusion with pointers; in my opinion, that was a smart decision.

Now that we've covered handles, it's time to introduce the associated concept of tracking references.

1.4.2 Tracking references

Just as standard C++ supports references (using the `&` punctuator) to complement pointers, C++/CLI supports tracking references that use the `%` punctuator to complement handles. The standard C++ reference obviously can't be used with a managed object on the CLR heap, because it's not guaranteed to remain in the same memory address for any period of time. The tracking reference had to be introduced; and, as the name suggests, it tracks a managed object on the CLR heap. Even if the object is moved around by the GC, the tracking reference will still hold a reference to it. Just as a native reference can bind to an l-value, a tracking reference can bind to a managed l-value. And interestingly, by virtue of the fact that an l-value implicitly converts to a managed l-value, a tracking reference can bind to native pointers and class types, too. Let's look at a function that accepts a `String^` argument and then assigns a string to it. The first version doesn't work as expected; the calling code finds that the `String` object it passed to the function hasn't been changed:

```
void ChangeString(String^ str)
{
    str = "New string";
}
int main(array<System::String^>^ args)
{
    String^ str = "Old string";
    ChangeString(str);
    Console::WriteLine(str);
}
```

If you execute this code snippet, you'll see that `str` contains the old string after the call to `ChangeString`. Change `ChangeString` to

```
void ChangeString(String^% str)
{
    str = "New string";
}
```

You'll now see that `str` does get changed, because the function takes a tracking reference to a handle to a `String` object instead of a `String` object, as in the previous case. A generic definition would be to say that for any type `T`, `T%` is a tracking reference to type `T`. C# developers may be interested to know that MSIL-wise, this is equivalent to passing the `String` as a C# `ref` argument to `ChangeString`. Therefore, whenever you want to pass a CLI handle to a function, and you expect the handle itself to be changed within the function, you need to pass a tracking reference to the handle to the function.

In standard C++, in addition to its use in denoting a reference, the `&` symbol is also used as a unary address-of operator. To keep things uniform, in C++/CLI, the unary `%` operator returns a handle to its operand, such that the type of `%T` is `T^` (handle to type `T`). If you plan to use stack semantics (which we'll discuss in the next chapter), you'll find yourself applying the unary `%` operator quite a bit when you access the .NET Framework libraries. This is because the .NET libraries always expect a handle to an object (because C++ is the only language that supports a nonhandle reference type); so, if you have an object declared using stack semantics, you can apply the unary `%` operator on it to get a handle type that you can pass to the library function. Here's some code showing how to use the unary `%` operator:

```
Student^ s1 = gcnew Student();
Student% s2 = *s1;  // Dereference s1 and assign
                    // to the tracking reference s2
Student^ s3 = %s2;  // Apply unary % on s2 to return a Student^
```

Be aware that the `*` punctuator is used to dereference both pointers and handles, although symmetrically thinking, a ^ punctuator should been used to dereference a handle. Perhaps this was designed this way to allow us to write agnostic template/generic classes that work on both native and unmanaged types.

You now know how to declare a CLI type; you also know how to use handles to a CLI type. To put these skills to use, you must understand how CLI types are instantiated, which is what we'll discuss in the next section.

1.5 Instantiating CLI classes

In this section, you'll see how CLI classes are instantiated using the `gcnew` operator. You'll also learn how constructors, copy constructors, and assignment operators work with managed types. Although the basic concepts remain the same, the nature of the CLI imposes some behavioral differences in the way constructors and assignment operators work; when you start writing managed classes and libraries, it's important that you understand those differences. Don't worry about it, though. Once you've seen how managed objects work with constructors and assignment operators, the differences between instantiating managed and native objects will automatically become clear.

1.5.1 The gcnew operator

The `gcnew` operator is used to instantiate CLI objects. It returns a handle to the newly created object on the CLR heap. Although it's similar to the `new` operator, there are some important differences: `gcnew` has neither an array form nor a placement form, and it can't be overloaded either globally or specifically to a class. A placement form wouldn't make a lot of sense for a CLI type, when you consider that the memory is allocated by the Garbage Collector. It's for the same reason you aren't permitted to overload the `gcnew` operator. There is no array form for `gcnew` because CLI arrays use an entirely different syntax from native arrays, which we'll cover in detail in the next chapter. If the CLR can't allocate enough memory for creating the object, a `System::OutOfMemoryException` is thrown, although chances are slim that you'll ever run into that situation. (If you do get an `OutOfMemoryException`, and your system isn't running low on virtual memory, it's likely due to badly written code such as an infinite loop that keeps creating objects that are erroneously kept alive.) The following code listing shows a typical usage of the `gcnew` keyword to instantiate a managed object (in this case, the `Student` object):

```
ref class Student
{
...
```

```
};
...

Student^ student = gcnew Student();
student->SelectSubject("Math", 97);
```

The gcnew operator is compiled into the newobj MSIL instruction by the C++/CLI compiler. The newobj MSIL instruction creates a new CLI object—either a ref object on the CLR heap or a value object on the stack—although the C++/CLI compiler uses a different mechanism to handle the usage of the gcnew operator to create value type objects (which I'll describe later in this section). Because gcnew in C++ translates to newobj in the MSIL, the behavior of gcnew is pretty much dependent on, and therefore similar to, that of the newobj MSIL instruction. In fact, newobj throws System::OutOfMemoryException when it can't find enough memory to allocate the requested object. Once the object has been allocated on the CLR heap, the constructor is called on this object with zero or more arguments (depending on the constructor overload that was used). On successful completion of the call to the constructor, gcnew returns a handle to the instantiated object. It's important to note that if the constructor call doesn't successfully complete, as would be the case if an exception was raised inside the constructor, gcnew won't return a handle. This can be easily verified with the following code snippet:

```
ref class Student
{
public:
    Student()
    {
        throw gcnew Exception("hello world");
    }
};

//...

Student^ student = nullptr; //initialize the handle to nullptr

try
{
    student =  gcnew Student(); //attempt to create object
}
catch(Exception^)
{
}

if(student == nullptr) //check to see if student is still nullptr
    Console::WriteLine("reference not allocated to handle");
```

Not surprisingly, `student` is still `nullptr` when it executes the `if` block. Because the constructor didn't complete executing, the CLR concludes that the object hasn't fully initialized, and it doesn't push the handle reference on the stack (as it would if the constructor had completed successfully).

> **NOTE** C++/CLI introduces the concept of a universal null literal called `nullptr`. This lets you use the same literal (`nullptr`) to represent a null pointer and a null handle value. The `nullptr` implicitly converts to a pointer or handle type; for the pointer, it evaluates to 0, as dictated by standard C++; for the handle, it evaluates to a null reference. You can use the `nullptr` in relational, equality, and assignment expressions with both pointers and handles.

As I mentioned earlier, using `gcnew` to instantiate a value type object generates MSIL that is different from what is generated when you instantiate a ref type. For example, consider the following code, which uses `gcnew` to instantiate a value type:

```
value class Marks
{
public:
    int Math;
    int Physics;
    int Chemistry;
};

//...

    Marks^ marks = gcnew Marks();
```

For this code, the C++/CLI compiler uses the `initobj` MSIL instruction to create a `Marks` object on the stack. This object is then boxed to a `Marks^` object. We'll discuss boxing and unboxing in the next section; for now, note that unless it's imperative to the context of your code to `gcnew` a value type object, doing so is inefficient. A stack object has to be created, and this must be boxed to a reference object. Not only do you end up creating two objects (one on the managed stack, the other on the managed heap), but you also incur the cost of boxing. The more efficient way to create an object of type `Marks` (or any value type) is to declare it on the stack, as follows:

```
Marks marks;
```

You've seen how calling `gcnew` calls the constructor on the instance of the type being created. In the coming section, we'll take a more involved look at how constructors work with CLI types.

1.5.2 Constructors

If you have a ref class, and you haven't written a default constructor, the compiler generates one for you. In MSIL, the constructor is a specially-named instance method called `.ctor`. The default constructor that is generated for you calls the constructor of the immediate base class for the current class. If you haven't specified a base class, it calls the `System::Object` constructor, because every ref object implicitly derives from `System::Object`. For example, consider the following two classes, neither of which has a user-defined constructor:

```
ref class StudentBase
{
};
ref class Student: StudentBase
{
};
```

Neither `Student` nor `StudentBase` has a user-provided default constructor, but the compiler generates constructors for them. You can use a tool such as ildasm.exe (the IL Disassembler that comes with the .NET Framework) to examine the generated MSIL. If you do that, you'll observe that the generated constructor for `Student` calls the constructor for the `StudentBase` object:

```
call instance void StudentBase::.ctor()
```

The generated constructor for `StudentBase` calls the `System::Object` constructor:

```
call instance void [mscorlib]System.Object::.ctor()
```

Just as with standard C++, if you have a constructor—either a default constructor or one that takes one or more arguments—the compiler won't generate a default constructor for you. In addition to instance constructors, ref classes also support static constructors (not available in standard C++). A static constructor, if present, initializes the static members of a class. Static constructors can't have parameters, must also be `private`, and are automatically called by the CLR. In MSIL, static constructors are represented by a specially named static method called `.cctor`. One possible reason both special methods have a `.` in their names is that this avoids name clashes, because none of the CLI languages allow a `.` in a function name. If you have at least one static field in your class, the compiler generates a default static constructor for you if you don't include one on your own. When you have a simple class, such as the following, the generated MSIL will have a static constructor even though you haven't specified one:

```
ref class StudentBase
{
```

```
    static int number;
};
```

Due to the compiler-generated constructors and the implicit derivation from `System::Object`, the generated class looks more like this:

```
ref class StudentBase : System::Object
{
    static int number;
    StudentBase() : System::Object()
    {
    }
    static StudentBase()
    {
    }
};
```

A value type can't declare a default constructor because the CLR can't guarantee that any default constructors on value types will be called appropriately, although members are 0-initialized automatically by the CLR. In any case, a value type should be a simple type that exhibits value semantics, and it shouldn't need the complexity of a default constructor—or even a destructor, for that matter. Note that in addition to not allowing default constructors, value types can't have user-defined destructors, copy constructors, and copy-assignment operators.

Before you end up concluding that value types are useless, you need to think of value types as the POD equivalents in the .NET world. Use value types just as you'd use primitive types, such as `int`s and `char`s, and you should be OK. When you need simple types, without the complexities of virtual functions, constructors and operators, value types are the more efficient option, because they're allocated on the stack. Stack access will be faster than accessing an object from the garbage-collected CLR heap. If you're wondering why this is so, the stack implementation is far simpler when compared to the CLR heap. When you consider that the CLR heap also intrinsically supports a complex garbage-collection algorithm, it becomes obvious that the stack object is more efficient.

It must be a tad confusing when I mention how value types behave differently from reference types in certain situations. But as a developer, you should be able to distinguish the conceptual differences between value types and reference types, especially when you design complex class hierarchies. As we progress through this book and see more examples, you should feel more comfortable with these differences.

Because we've already talked about constructors, we'll discuss copy constructors next.

1.5.3 Copy constructors

A *copy constructor* is one that instantiates an object by creating a copy of another object. The C++ compiler generates a copy constructor for your native classes, even if you haven't explicitly done so. This isn't the case for managed classes. Consider the following bit of code, which attempts to copy-construct a ref object:

```
ref class Student
{
};

int main(array<System::String^>^ args)
{
    Student^ s1 = gcnew Student();
    Student^ s2 = gcnew Student(s1);    <-1
}
```

If you run that through the compiler (1), you'll get compiler error C3673 (*class does not have a copy-constructor*). The reason for this error is that, unlike in standard C++, the compiler won't generate a default copy constructor for your class. At least one reason is that all ref objects implicitly derive from `System::Object`, which doesn't have a copy constructor. Even if the compiler attempted to generate a copy constructor for a ref type, it would fail, because it wouldn't be able to access the base class copy constructor (it doesn't exist).

To make that clearer, think of a native C++ class `Base` with a private copy constructor, and a derived class `Derived` (that publicly inherits from `Base`). Attempting to copy-construct a `Derived` object will fail because the base class copy constructor is inaccessible. To demonstrate, let's write a class that is derived from a base class that has a private copy constructor:

```
class Base
{
public:
    Base(){}
private:
    Base(const Base&);
};

class Derived : public Base
{
};

int _tmain(int argc, _TCHAR* argv[])
{
    Derived d1;
    Derived d2(d1); // <-- won't compile
}
```

Because the base object's copy constructor is declared as `private` and therefore is inaccessible from the derived object, this code won't compile: The compiler is unable to copy-construct the derived object. What happens with a ref class is similar to this code. In addition, unlike native C++ objects, which aren't polymorphic unless you access them via a pointer, ref objects are implicitly polymorphic (because they're always accessed via reference handles to the CLR heap). This means a compiler-generated copy constructor may not always do what you expect it to do. When you consider that ref types may contain member ref types, there is the question of whether a copy constructor implements shallow copy or deep copy for those members. The VC++ team presumably decided that there were too many equations to have the compiler automatically generate copy constructors for classes that don't define them.

If you want copy-construction support for your class, you must implement it explicitly, which fortunately isn't a difficult task. Let's add a copy constructor to the `Student` class:

```
ref class Student
{
public:
    Student(){}
    Student(const Student^)
    {
    }
};
```

That wasn't all that tough, was it? Notice how you have to explicitly add a default parameterless constructor to the class. This is because it won't be generated by the compiler when the compiler sees that there is another constructor present. One limitation with this copy constructor is that the parameter has to be a `Student^`, which is OK except that you may have a `Student` object that you want to pass to the copy constructor. If you're wondering how that's possible, C++/CLI supports stack semantics, which we'll cover in detail in chapter 3. Assume that you have a `Student` object `s1` instead of a `Student^`, and you need to use that to invoke a copy constructor:

```
Student s1;
Student^ s2 = gcnew Student(s1); //error C3073
```

As you can see, that code won't compile. There are two ways to resolve the problem. One way is to use the unary `%` operator on the `s1` object to get a handle to the `Student` object:

```
Student s1;
Student^ s2 = gcnew Student(%s1);
```

Although that compiles and solves the immediate problem, it isn't a complete solution when you consider that every caller of your code needs to do the same thing if they have a `Student` object instead of a `Student^`. An alternate solution is to have two overloads for the copy constructor, as shown in listing 1.2.

Listing 1.2 Declaring two overloads for the copy constructor

```
ref class Student
{
//...
public:
    Student(){}
    Student(String^ str):m_name(str){}
    Student(const Student^)        <-- 1
    {
    }
    Student(const Student%)        <-- 2
    {
    }
};

//...

    Student s1;
    Student^ s2 = gcnew Student(s1);
```

This solves the issue of a caller requiring the right form of the object, but it brings with it another problem: code duplication. You could wrap the common code in a `private` method and have both overloads of the copy constructor call this method, but then you couldn't take advantage of initialization lists.

Eventually, it's a design choice you have to make. ❶ If you only have the copy constructor overload taking a `Student^`, then you need to use the unary `%` operator when you have a `Student` object; and ❷ if you only have the overload taking a `Student%`, then you need to dereference a `Student^` using the `*` operator before using it in copy construction. If you have both, you may end up with possible code duplication; and the only way to avoid code duplication (using a common function called by both overloads) deprives you of the ability to use initialization lists.

My recommendation is to use the overload that takes a handle (in the previous example, the one that takes a `Student^`), because this overload is visible to other CLI languages such as C# (unlike the other overload)—which is a good thing if you ever run into language interop situations. The unary `%` operator won't really slow down your code; it's just an extra character that you need to type. I also suggest that you stay away from using two overloads, unless it's a specific case of a library that will be exclusively used by C++ callers; even then, you must consider the issue of code duplication.

Now you know that if you need copy construction on your ref types, you must implement it yourself. So, it may not be surprising to see in the next section that the same holds true for copy-assignment operators.

1.5.4 Assignment operators

The copy-assignment operator is one that the compiler generates automatically for native classes in standard C++, but this isn't so for a ref class. The reasons are similar to those that dictate that a copy constructor isn't automatically generated. The following code (using the `Student` class defined earlier) won't compile:

```
Student s1("Nish");
Student s2;
s2 = s1; // error C2582: 'operator =' function
         // is unavailable in 'Student'
```

Defining an assignment operator is similar to what you do in standard C++, except that the types are managed:

```
Student% operator=(const Student% s)
{
    m_name = s.m_name;
    return *this;
}
```

Note that the copy-assignment operator can be used only by C++ callers, because it's invisible to other languages like C# and VB.NET. Also note that, for handle variables, you don't need to write a copy-assignment operator, because the handle value is copied over intrinsically.

You should try to bring many of the good C++ programming practices you followed into the CLI world, except where they aren't applicable. As an example, the assignment operator doesn't handle self-assignment. Although it doesn't matter in our specific example, consider the case in listing 1.3.

Listing 1.3 The self-assignment problem

```
ref class Grades      <-- (1) Class with nontrivial ctor/dtor
{
    //...
};

ref class Student
{
```

```
    String^ m_name;
    Grades^ m_grades;
public:
    Student(){}
    Student(String^ str):m_name(str){}
    Student% operator=(const Student% s)
    {
        m_name = s.m_name;
        if(m_grades) [#2]
            delete m_grades;      <-- Possible problem if
        m_grades = s.m_grades;    (2) self-assignment occurs
        return *this;
    }
    void SetGrades(Grades^ grades)
    {
        //...
    }
};
```

In the preceding listing, ❶ assume that `Grades` is a class with a nontrivial constructor and destructor; thus, in the `Student` class assignment operator, before the `m_grades` member is copied, ❷ the existing `Grades` object is explicitly disposed by calling `delete` on it—all very efficient. Let's assume that a self-assignment occurs:

```
while(some_condition)
{
    // studarr is an array of Student objects
    studarr[i++] = studarr[j--]; // self-assignment occurs if i == j
    if(some_other_condition)
        break;
}
```

In the preceding code snippet, if ever `i` equals `j`, you end up with a corrupted `Student` object with an invalid `m_grades` member. Just as you would do in standard C++, you should check for self-assignment:

```
Student% operator=(const Student% s)
{
    if(%s == this)     <-- Check for self-assignment
    {
        return *this;    <-- If it is so, return immediately
    }
    m_name = s.m_name;
    if(m_grades)
        delete m_grades;
    m_grades = s.m_grades;
    return *this;
}
```

We've covered some ground in this section—and if you feel that a lot of information has been presented too quickly, don't worry. Most of the things we've discussed so far will come up again throughout this book; eventually, it will all make complete sense to you. We'll now look at boxing and unboxing, which are concepts that I feel many .NET programmers don't properly understand—with not-so-good consequences.

1.6 Boxing and unboxing

Boxing is the conversion of a value of type `V` to an object of type `V^` on the CLR heap, which is a bit-wise copy of the original value object. Figure 1.4 shows a diagrammatic representation of the boxing process. *Unboxing* is the reverse process, where an `Object^` or a `V^` is cast back to the original value type `V`. Boxing is an implicit process (although it can be explicitly forced, as well), whereas unboxing is always an explicit process. If it sounds confusing, visualize a real box into which you put some object (say, a camera) so that you can send it via FedEx to your friend the next city. The same thing happens in CLR boxing. When your friend receives the package, they open the box and retrieve the camera, which is analogous to CLR unboxing.

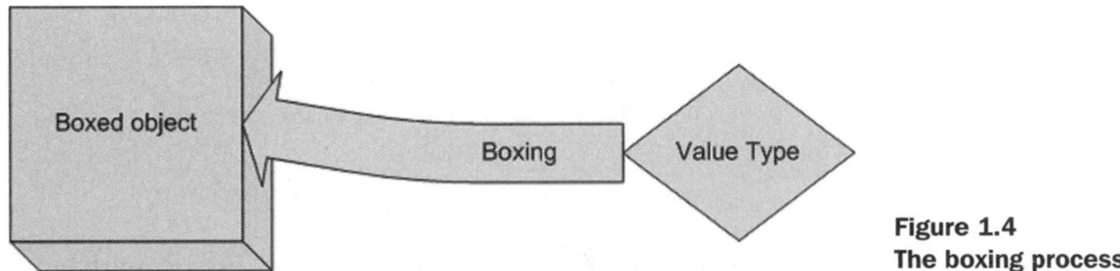

Figure 1.4
The boxing process

In this section, we'll look at how boxing is an implicit operation in the new C++/CLI syntax, how boxing ensures type safety, how boxing is implemented at the MSIL level, and how to assign a `nullptr` to a boxed value type.

1.6.1 Implicit boxing in the new syntax

Whenever you pass a simple type like an `int` or a `char` to a method that expects an `Object`, the `int` or `char` is boxed to the CLR heap, and this boxed copy is used by the method. The reason is that ref types are always references to whole objects on the CLR heap, whereas value types are typically on the stack or even on the native C++ heap. When a method expects an `Object` reference, the value type has to be copied to the CLR heap, where it must behave like a regular ref-type object. In the same way, when the underlying value type has to be retrieved, it must be unboxed back to the original value-type object. The internal boxing and unboxing mechanisms are implemented by the CLR and supported in MSIL, so all the compiler needs to do is emit the corresponding MSIL instructions.

In the old syntax, boxing was an explicit process using the `__box` keyword. Several programmers complained about the extra typing required. Because most people felt that the double-underscored keywords were repulsive, the fact that they had to use one of those keywords a gratuitous number of times in the course of everyday programming made them all the more upset. You can't blame them, as the code examples in table 1.5 show.

Table 1.5 Boxing differences between the old and new syntaxes

Explicit boxing in the old MC++ syntax	Implicit boxing in C++/CLI

int __box* AddNums(
    int __box* i, int __box* j)
{
    return __box(*i + *j);
}
 	
//...
 	
int i = 17, j = 23;
int sum = *AddNums(
    __box(i), __box(j));
Console::WriteLine(
    "The sum is {0}", __box(sum));
	int^ AddNums(int^ i, int^ j)
	{
	    return *i + *j;
	}
	
	//...
	
	int i = 17, j = 23;
	int sum = *AddNums(i, j);
	Console::WriteLine(
	    "The sum is {0}", sum);

It would be an understatement to say that the second code example is a lot more pleasing to the eye and involves much less typing. But implicit boxing has a dangerous disadvantage: It hides the boxing costs involved from the programmer, which can be a bad thing. Boxing is an expensive operation; a new object has to be created on the CLR heap, and the value type must be bitwise copied into this object. Similarly, whenever a lot of boxing is involved, chances are good that quite a bit of unboxing is also being performed. Unboxing typically involves creating the original value type on the managed stack and bitwise copying its data from the boxed object. As a developer, if you ignore the costs of repeated boxing/unboxing operations, either knowingly or unknowingly, you may run into performance issues, most often in applications where performance is a major concern.

1.6.2 *Boxing and type-safety*

When you box a value type, the boxed copy is a separate entity from the original value type. Changes in one of them won't be reflected in the other. Consider the following code snippet, where you have an `int`, a boxed object containing the `int`, and a second `int` that has been explicitly unboxed from the boxed object:

```
int i = 100;
Object^ boxed_i = i; //implicitly boxed to Object^
int j = *safe_cast<int^>(boxed_i); //explicitly unboxed
Console::WriteLine("i={0}, boxed_i={1}, j={2}", i, boxed_i, j);
i++; j--;
Console::WriteLine("i={0}, boxed_i={1}, j={2}", i, boxed_i, j);
```

The first call to `Console::WriteLine` outputs

```
i=100, boxed_i=100, j=100
```

The second call outputs

```
i=101, boxed_i=100, j=99
```

As the output clearly indicates, they're three different entities: the original value type, the boxed type, and the unboxed value type. Notice how you had to `safe_cast` the `Object^` to an `int^` before dereferencing it. This is because dereferencing is always done on the boxed value type. To get an `int`, you have to apply the dereference operator on an `int^`, and hence the cast.

NOTE The `safe_cast` operator is new to C++/CLI and replaces `__try_cast` in the old syntax. `safe_cast` is guaranteed to produce verifiable MSIL. You can use `safe_cast` wherever you would typically use `dynamic_cast`, `reinterpret_cast`, or `static_cast`. At runtime, `safe_cast` checks to see if the cast is valid; if so, it does the conversion or else throws a `System::InvalidCastException`.

When you box a value type, the boxed value remembers the original value type—which means that if you attempt to unbox to a different type, you'll get an `InvalidCastException`. This ensures type-safety when you perform boxing and unboxing operations. Consider listing 1.4, which demonstrates what happens when you attempt to unbox objects to the wrong value types.

Listing 1.4 Type-safety in boxing

```
int i = 100;
double d = 55.673;

Object^ boxed_int = i; //box int to Object^
Object^ boxed_double = d; //box double to Object^

try
{
    int x = *safe_cast<int^>(boxed_double); //compiles fine
}
catch(InvalidCastException^ e) //exception thrown at runtime
{
    Console::WriteLine(e->Message);
}

try
{
    double x = *safe_cast<double^>(boxed_int); //compiles fine
}
catch(InvalidCastException^ e) //exception thrown at runtime
{
    Console::WriteLine(e->Message);
}
```

This listing attempts to unbox a boxed `double` to an `int` and a boxed `int` to a `double`. Although the code compiles, during runtime, an `InvalidCastException` is thrown:

```
Unable to cast object of type 'System.Double' to type 'System.Int32'.
Unable to cast object of type 'System.Int32' to type 'System.Double'.
```

Note that type matching is always exact; for instance, you can't unbox an `int` into an `__int64` (even though it would be a safe conversion).

1.6.3 Implementation at the MSIL level

MSIL uses the `box` instruction to perform boxing. The following is a quote from the MSIL documentation: "The box instruction converts the raw valueType (an unboxed value type) into an instance of type Object (of type O). This is accomplished by creating a new object and copying the data from valueType into the newly allocated object."

To get a better idea of how boxing is done, let's look at how the MSIL is generated (see table 1.6).

Table 1.6 MSIL generated for a boxing operation

C++/CLI code	Generated MSIL

	`.locals init (`
	`[0] int32 i,`
	`[1] object o)`

`int i = 100;`	`IL_0000: ldc.i4.s 100` `IL_0002: stloc.0`

`Object^ o = i;`	`IL_0003: ldloc.0`
	`IL_0004: box int32`
	`IL_0009: stloc.1`

We won't decipher each MSIL instruction, but the line of code that is of interest is the instruction at location IL_0004: `box int32`. The instruction before it, `ldloc.0`, loads the contents of the local variable at the 0th position (which happens to be the `int` variable `i`) into the stack. The `box` instruction creates a new `Object`, copies the value (from the stack) into this object (using bitwise copy semantics), and pushes a handle to this `Object` on the stack. The `stloc.1` instruction pops this `Object` from the stack into the local variable at the first position (the `Object^` variable `o`). Table 1.7 shows how unboxing is done at the MSIL level.

Unboxing is the reverse process. The `Object` to be unboxed is pushed on the stack, and a cast to `int^` is performed using the `castclass` instruction. On successful completion of this call, the `Object` on the stack is of type `int^`. The `unbox int32` instruction is executed, and it converts the boxed object (on the stack) to a managed pointer to the underlying value type. This behavior is different from

Table 1.7 MSIL generated for unboxing

C++/CLI code	Generated MSIL

	`.locals init (`
	`[0] int32 x,`
	`[1] object o)`

`int x = *safe_cast<int^>(o);`	`IL_0000: ldloc.1`
	`IL_0001: castclass int32`
	`IL_0006: unbox int32`
	`IL_000b: ldind.i4`
	`IL_000c: stloc.0`

boxing where a new object is created; however, unbox doesn't create a new value type instance. Instead, it returns the address of the underlying value type on the CLR heap. The ldind.i4 instruction indirectly loads the value from the address returned on the stack by the unbox instruction. This is basically a form of dereferencing. Finally, the stloc.0 instruction stores this value in local variable 0, which happens to be the int variable x.

The basic purpose of showing you the generated IL is to give you a better idea of the costs involved in boxing/unboxing operations. When you box, you incur the cost of creating a new Object. When copying the value type into this Object, you waste CPU cycles as well as extra memory. When you unbox, you typically have to safe_cast to your value type's corresponding handle type, and the runtime has to check to see if it's a valid cast operation. Once you do that, the actual unboxing reveals the address of the value type object within the CLI object, which has to be dereferenced and the original value copied back.

Thus, both boxing and unboxing are very expensive operations. You probably won't see much of a performance decrease for simple applications, but bigger and more complex applications may be seriously affected by performance loss if you don't restrict the number of boxing/unboxing operations that are performed. Because boxing is implicit now, as a programmer you have to be that little bit extra-cautious when you convert value types to ref types, either directly or indirectly, as when you call a method that expects a ref-type argument with a value type.

1.6.4 Assigning null to a boxed value type

An interesting effect of implicit boxing is that you can't initialize a boxed value type to null by assigning a 0 to it. You have to use the nullptr constant to accomplish that:

```
int^ x1 = nullptr;
if(!x1)
    Console::WriteLine("x1 is null"); // <-- this line is executed
else
    Console::WriteLine("x1 is not null");

int^ x2 = 0;
if(!x2)
    Console::WriteLine("x2 is null");
else
    Console::WriteLine("x2 is not null");
       // ^-- this line is executed
```

In the second case, the 0 is treated as an `int`, which is boxed to an `int^`. You specifically need to use `nullptr` if you want to assign a handle to null. Note that the compiler issues warning C4965 (*implicit box of integer 0; use nullptr or explicit cast*) whenever it can.

When you have two overloads for a function that differ only by a value type argument, with one overload using the value type and the other using the boxed value type, the overload using the value type is given preference:

```
void Show(int)
{
    Console::WriteLine(__FUNCSIG__);
}
void Show(int^)
{
    Console::WriteLine(__FUNCSIG__);
}
```

Now, a call such as

```
Show(75);
```

will call the `Show(int)` overload instead of the `Show(int^)` overload. Keep in mind that, when selecting the best overload, the compiler gives lowest priority to one that requires boxing. If you had another overload that required a nonboxing cast, that overload would receive preference over the one that requires boxing. Given three overloads, one that takes an `int`, one that takes a `double`, and one that takes an `int^`, the order of precedence would be

```
[first] void Show(int)
[second] void Show(double)
[third] void Show(int^)
```

To force an overload, you can do a cast to the argument type for that overload:

```
Show(static_cast<int^>(75));
```

Now that we've covered boxing and unboxing, I suggest that you always consciously keep track of the amount of boxing that is done in your code. Because it's an implicit operation, you may miss out on intensive boxing operations; but where boxing occurs, there is bound to be unboxing, too. If you find yourself having to do a lot of unboxing, review your code to see if it overuses boxing, and try to redesign your class to reduce the amount required. Take special care inside loops, which is where most programmers end up with boxing-related performance issues.

1.7 Summary

In this chapter, we've covered some of the fundamental syntactic concepts of the C++/CLI language. As you may have inferred by now, the basic programming concepts remain the same in C++/CLI as in standard C++. However, you need to accommodate for the CLI and everything that comes with it, such as garbage collection, handles to the CLR heap, tracking references, and the implicit derivation from `System::Object`. Topics we've covered included how to declare and instantiate CLI types; how to use handles, and how they differ from pointers; and how boxing and unboxing are performed when converting from value types to reference types.

The designers of C++/CLI have gone to great lengths to ensure as close a similarity to the standard C++ language as is practically possible, but some changes had to be made due to the nature of the CLI (which is a different environment from native C++). As long as you're aware of those differences and write code accordingly, you'll do well.

Although C++/CLI's biggest strength is its ability to compile mixed-mode code, you need to be familiar with the core CLI programming concepts before you can begin writing mixed-mode applications. With that view, in the next couple of chapters we'll explore the CLI features that are supported by C++/CLI, such as properties, delegates and events, CLI arrays, CLI pointers, stack semantics, function overriding, generics, and managed templates.

2 Getting into the CLI: properties, delegates and arrays

The major aim in developing C++/CLI was to make it a first-class CLI language, and a first-class CLI language needs to provide full support for intrinsic CLI semantics and concepts like CLI properties, delegates and events, and managed arrays. The designers of the language have been careful to maintain a C++-style syntax while providing the full functionality required to implement a specific CLI concept. To implement CLI features that couldn't be semantically expressed using standard C++ syntax, compromises have been made; on occasion, syntactic constructs may look somewhat odd, at least from a C++ perspective. One notable example is the syntax for managed arrays. But by using spaced and contextual keywords, the designers of the language have avoided (or minimized) the addition of new reserved words to the C++/CLI language.

Some of the topics we'll cover in this chapter are more a part of the CLI programming methodology than an explicit part of the C++/CLI syntax; but because they play an important role in C++/CLI programming, you need a thorough understanding of these concepts. In later chapters, when we begin to deal with mixed-mode programming, many of the topics we'll discuss in this chapter will come in handy—especially the section on pinning and interior pointers. Those of you who have done a lot of template programming may be tickled by the pronounced similarity in syntax used for CLI arrays and CLI pointers. Those of you who have never used templates may find the syntax a tad daunting. Don't worry about that. As with all things C++, it takes a little while to get used to.

We'll begin this chapter with a look at CLI properties.

2.1 Properties

Properties are entities that appear to behave like fields, but are internally handled by getter and setter accessor functions. They can be scalar properties (that behave like fields) or indexed properties (that behave like array fields). Unlike the old syntax, where you had to explicitly write `get_` and `set_` functions (which was a hassle), the C++/CLI syntax for properties is more intuitive and is similar to the syntax used in C#—although I'm sure the similarity is purely coincidental.

Properties have associated types. Although the syntax for accessing properties is the same as that used for accessing fields (or arrays, in the case of indexed properties), properties don't represent storage locations. That's where the accessor functions come into play—the getter accessor is used when you read a property, and the setter accessor is used when you write to a property. Figure 2.1 shows a diagrammatic representation of how a property wraps getter and setter functions for a private data store.

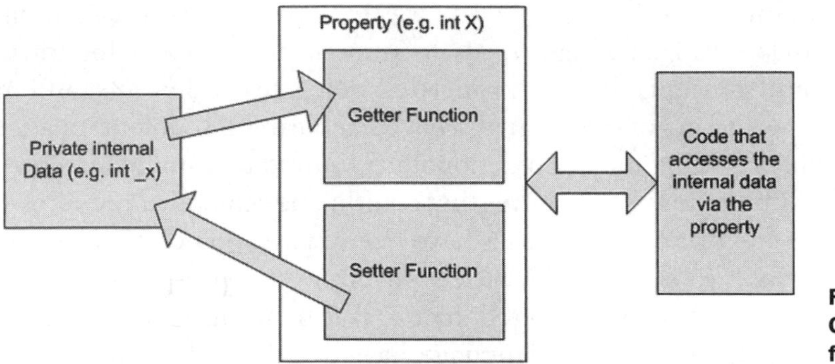

Figure 2.1 Getter and setter functions

To use an analogy, properties are like post office boxes—you can send someone a letter using their post office box number, but that's not their physical address. They either get your letter directly from the post office box, or it gets routed to their physical address. Note that properties can only be applied to `value` and `ref` types; they can't be applied to native types—at least as of VC++ 2005.

In this section, we'll discuss both scalar and indexed properties. We'll also touch on how properties work with inheritance, trivial properties, static properties, and default indexed properties. We'll start with scalar properties.

2.1.1 Scalar Properties

Scalar properties let you implement an abstraction layer for fields. You can have read-only, write-only, and read-and-write scalar properties, depending on whether you've implemented one or both `get` and `set` functions.

Let's consider a `Student` class. Assume that you need to store the age of a student in the class; for that purpose, you have a `private int` field (`_Age`). The requirement is that the age should not be accessed before it has been set; and if an attempt is made to do so, you have to throw an exception. You also need to ensure that a student is between ages 4 and 17; if an attempt is made to assign an age outside that range to a `Student` object, you throw another exception. Listing 2.1 shows how this is implemented using a property.

Listing 2.1 A class with a scalar property

```
ref class Student
{
private:
    int _Age;
     . . .
public:
```

```
    property int Age
    {
        int get()
        {
            if( _Age == 0 )
                throw gcnew InvalidOperationException(
                    "Age has not been set");
            return _Age;
        }
        void set(int x)
        {
            if( x<4 || x>17 )
                throw gcnew ArgumentOutOfRangeException(
                    "Invalid age");
            _Age = x;
        }
    }
    . . .
};
```

Property definition ❶

Get accessor method ❷

Set accessor method ❸

This code listing has a class with a single scalar property named `Age` ❶ with both `get` and `set` functions. If the property hasn't been set, and an attempt is made to read the property, an exception is thrown from the `get` method ❷. Similarly, if an attempt is made to set the property to an invalid age, an exception is thrown from the `set` method ❸. The following sample code shows how the property can be used, and when it throws an exception:

```
Student^ stud = gcnew Student();
//Console::WriteLine(stud->Age); // Throws exception from get()
//stud->Age = 3; // Throws exception from set()
stud->Age = 13; // Calls Age::set(13)
Console::WriteLine(stud->Age);  // Calls Age::get()
```

The compiler generates two instance methods named `get_Age` and `set_Age`, where `get_Age` is basically the `get` method you wrote and `set_Age` is the `set` method. Whenever you read the property, `get_Age` is called; and whenever you write to it, `set_Age` is called. In short, the property syntax is merely syntactic sugar for getter and setter methods.

Note that although MSIL doesn't insist on precisely this naming scheme for the getter and setter methods, the C++ compiler is strict about these names and as such always uses this format for property accessor methods. If you try to declare a method that is named using a `get_` or `set_` prefix that conflicts with a property name, the method throws a compiler error. The following method, if added to the `Student` class, won't compile:

```
ref class Student
{
. . .
    int get_Age()
    {
        return 42;    ❶ Error C3675
    }
```

This code ❶ throws a compiler error C3675: *'Student::get_Age': is reserved because 'Student::Age' is defined*.

You'll often find yourself writing properties that minimally wrap a private field, where the getter method returns the field and the setter method sets it, with no extra validation code. At such times, you may hope that the code will be automatically written for you. Guess what? That's exactly what trivial properties do for you.

Trivial properties

Trivial properties are properties where the compiler generates the getter and setter functions for you, as well as the backing storage. For instance, you can redesign the `Student` class as follows:

```
ref class Student
{
public:
    property int Age;
};
```

In this code snippet, `Age` is a trivial property. The compiler generates a `private` field of the same type as the property (an `int32` in MSIL) and names it `'<backing_store>Age'`. The quotes in the field name ensure that there is no chance for a name clash, because no CLI language (as of today) allows quotes in variable names. Minimal getter and setter methods are generated, where the getter returns this `private` field and the setter sets it to the passed-in value. Trivial properties are useful when you're designing classes and you have a field that you may have to refactor into a property in the future. Changing the class structure in the future may not be such a good idea, because it's a breaking change and may affect other code. For instance, if reflection is used on this class, changing a field to a property could have nasty side effects because reflection treats fields and properties differently. In addition, all callers need to be recompiled because the MSIL for accessing a property differs from that for accessing a field. As another example, a derived class may be directly accessing a protected field without knowing that it has now been wrapped by a property. Because the derived class bypasses the property validation, this may result in disallowed values being set for that field.

Although your first reaction might be to wonder whether you'll ever want to use trivial properties, you'll probably find that most of your properties are simple getter/setter abstractions for `private` fields. Using trivial properties will save you a lot of typing and will help you avoid the nasty habit of using public field members. I'm sure most of you know this, but let me remind you that public fields break encapsulation, which is one of the most basic concepts in Object Oriented Programming. Also, as C++ developers, you're understandably concerned about the performance of your code. From that perspective, it should be satisfying to know that trivial properties are typically inlined by the JIT compiler, which means the performance is the same as that for a field.

For most purposes, properties behave like methods, which isn't surprising considering that properties basically consist of one or two accessor methods. And just like methods, properties also work with inheritance.

Properties and inheritance

You can declare properties as `virtual` (which results in `virtual` getter and setter methods), although to override the property in the derived class, the derived class property needs to have the same type as the base class property. Consider a class `ButtonBase` that is used as a base class for writing custom button classes, with an inner struct `BaseData`, such that the class `ButtonBase` has a `BaseData` property. For the sake of this example, let's assume that `BaseData` is a nontrivial class with some unique, immutable data associated with it. In the setter method, instead of assigning the passed-in value to the backing store, you just copy over some data (which in this example consists of an `int`).

`ButtonBase` and `BaseData` will be used as base classes (surprise!) for other, more complex classes, so that any class that derives from `ButtonBase` will have a `BaseData`-derived `struct` associated with it. Therefore, the `Data` property is declared as `virtual`. See listing 2.2.

Listing 2.2 The base class with a `virtual` property

```
ref class ButtonBase
{
public:
    ref struct BaseData        <-- Inner struct used
    {                              to hold data
        int x;
    };
private:
    BaseData^ _bd;
public:
```

```
    ButtonBase() : _bd (gcnew BaseData())
    {
    }
    virtual property BaseData^ Data // virtual property
    {
        BaseData^ get() // implicitly virtual
        {
            return _bd;
        }
        void set(BaseData^ val) // implicitly virtual
        {
            _bd->x = val->x;
        }
    }
};
```

Let's derive a class `BitmapButton` from `ButtonBase` with an associated inner struct `DerivedData` that's derived from `BaseData`. `DerivedData` is a more complex class than `BaseData`, which in this example translates to an extra `int` member. See listing 2.3.

Listing 2.3 The derived class that overrides the `virtual` property

```
ref class BitmapButton: ButtonBase
{
public:
    ref struct DerivedData : ButtonBase::BaseData
    {
        int y;
    };
private:
    DerivedData^ _bd;
public:
    BitmapButton () : _bd(gcnew DerivedData())
    {
    }
    BitmapButton (int x, int y) : _bd(gcnew DerivedData())
    {
        _bd->x = x;
        _bd->y = y;
    }
    virtual property BaseData^ Data              ❶ Property same type as base
    {
        BaseData^ get() override // override keyword required
        {
            return _bd;
        }
        void set(BaseData^ val) override // override required
```

```
            {
                try
                {
                    _bd->x = val->x;
                    _bd->y = safe_cast<DerivedData^>(val)->y;
                }
                catch(InvalidCastException^)
                {
                    //log an error
                }
            }
        }
    };
```

Though you need a `DerivedData` property, you have to use a `BaseData` property ❶ in the derived class, because `virtual` properties require that the property type be the same in base and derived classes. When you access the `DerivedData` members in the setter method, you need to do a `safe_cast` to `DerivedData`. Notice how you need to explicitly specify the `override` keyword; you'll see more on that in chapter 3, when we cover function overriding in C++/CLI.

To test whether `virtual` properties behave as expected, you can use the following code:

```
ButtonBase ^ b = gcnew BitmapButton();        <-- Assign BitmapButton to ButtonBase variable
BitmapButton ^ d1 = gcnew BitmapButton (17,23);
b->Data = d1->Data;                           <-- Assign to base property
BitmapButton::DerivedData^ data =
    safe_cast< BitmapButton::DerivedData^>(b->Data);
Console::WriteLine(
    "b->Data : x = {0}, y = {1}", data->x, data->y);
```

Access virtual property Data

The output of the `Console::WriteLine` is (as expected)

```
b->Data : x = 17, y = 23
```

You can have different access levels for your getter and setter functions, which may be useful in circumstances where you want to give public read access to your properties, and at the same time you want to restrict write access to derived classes, without exposing the private backing store. Listing 2.4 demonstrates how you can do this using a `virtual` property with a protected set method and a public get method:

Listing 2.4 Using different access levels for get and set methods

```
ref class BaseStudent
{
private:
    String^ name;                          ❶ Backing store is still private
public:
    virtual property String^ Name          ❷ Must be virtual
    {
    protected:
        void set(String^ s)                Set accessor is protected
        {
            name = s;
        }
    public:
        String^ get()
        {
            return name;
        }
    }
};

ref class Student : BaseStudent
{
public:
    virtual property String^ Name
    {
        void set(String^ s) override       Override virtual setter
        {
            BaseStudent::Name = s;         ❸ Use protected base setter
        }
    }
};
```

The `Name` property is kept `virtual` ❷ so that derived classes can override the `set` method. Notice how the class design demonstrates a technique in which base classes can permit derived classes to have restricted write access to a specific member ❸ by allowing them to use the property setter (which is `protected`) but disallowing them direct access to the backing storage, which is `private` ❶. Note that when you specify different access modifiers for your property's accessor functions, the property itself needs to have higher visibility than its accessors. Thus, a public property can have protected accessors, but a protected property can't have a public accessor method.

So far, all the properties we have looked at are instance properties, but it's possible to have static properties that wrap static fields.

Static properties

Properties can be static, in which case the generated accessor methods are static too. Listing 2.5 shows an example of a class with a static read-only property.

Listing 2.5 Class with a static property

```
ref class Process
{
private:
    static int _LastProcessID = 0;
public:
    static property int LastProcessID
    {
        int get()
        {
            return _LastProcessID;
        }
    }
    Process(int pid)
    {
        _LastProcessID = pid;
    }
};
```

Although the example code shows a read-only static property, nothing is stopping you from giving it a set accessor method, if you require. Static properties provide the same functionality for static members of a class that instance properties provide for instance members. Use a static property when you need to expose a static member of a class to a calling class through a property. Now that we've covered scalar properties, let's discuss indexed properties.

2.1.2 Indexed properties

In this section, we'll talk about indexed properties as well as default index properties. Indexed properties are similar to scalar properties, except that you can now use one or more indexes as property arguments (hence the name).

Indexed properties enable array-like access to a member object. There is also support for a default index property that lets you access the object instance directly as an array. Continuing the classroom examples, let's write a class that stores the test results for a student and exposes those results via an indexed property called `Score`. See listing 2.6.

Listing 2.6 Class with a named indexed property

```
using namespace System::Collections; //for Hashtable

ref class TestResult
{
    Hashtable^ ht;
public:
    TestResult() : ht(gcnew Hashtable())
    {
    }
    property int Score[String^]
    {
        int get(String^ name)                    <-- Name argument is index
        {
            if(ht->ContainsKey(name))
                return safe_cast<int>(ht[name]);
            else
                return 0;
        }

        void set(String^ name, int score)          <-- Score argument is value to set
        {
            ht[name] = score;
        }
    }
};
```

Named indexed property definition

The class internally uses a `Hashtable` object to store its data. The basic difference from the earlier samples is that `Score` is an indexed property; the index is a `String^` that represents the name of a student whose score is to be set or retrieved. The following code snippet shows how this indexed property can be used:

```
TestResult^ tres = gcnew TestResult();
tres->Score["Nish"] = 975;          <-- Same as Score::set("Nish", 975)
tres->Score["Smitha"] = 955;
tres->Score["Ivor"] = 850;
tres->Score["Pat"] = 915;

while(true)
{
    Console::Write("Enter name (^C to exit) : ");
    String^ name = Console::ReadLine();
    int score = tres->Score[name];     <-- Same as Score::get(name)
    if(score)
        Console::WriteLine("{0} has a score of {1}", name, score);
    else
        Console::WriteLine("Name not found in database");
}
```

So far, you've written named, indexed properties. It's possible, however, to leave the name out, in which case they are called default indexed properties.

Default indexed properties

Default indexed properties allow array-like access on an object instance; they are indexed properties that are essentially nameless. C# developers may be interested to know that they are the same as C# indexers. Typically, you use default indexed properties on a class that contains a collection—for instance, a `Window` class that has a collection of window property objects. It's syntactically easier for the user to directly read and write properties by using an array-like syntax on the object instance. Listing 2.7 demonstrates such a class.

Listing 2.7 Class with a default indexed property

```
ref class Window
{
    Hashtable^ wndProperties;
public:
    Window() : wndProperties(gcnew Hashtable())
    {
    }
    property Object^ default[String^]          <-- ❶ Specify default indexed property
    {
        void set(String^ wndproperty, Object^ value)
        {
            wndProperties[wndproperty] = value;
        }

        Object^ get(String^ wndproperty)
        {
            return wndProperties[wndproperty];
        }
    }
};
```

Here you use the `default` keyword ❶ to specify a default indexed property. Listing 2.8 shows how the class can be used.

Listing 2.8 Using the default indexed property

```
Window^ w = gcnew Window();
w["Color"]  = Color::BurlyWood; // index applied directly on object
w["Title"] = "My Application 2.0";
w["Size"] = Size(100,80);
```

```
Console::WriteLine(w["Color"]); // index applied directly on object
Console::WriteLine(w["Title"]);
Console::WriteLine(w["Size"]);
Console::WriteLine(w["DoesNotExist"]); // returns a nullptr
```

Default indexed properties are convenient, involve less typing, and often seem to be more intuitive compared to having a named, indexed property.

Next, we'll look at two other important CLI features: delegates and events. Throughout this book, you'll see more realistic applications of these CLI features, so it's important that you understand the core concepts.

2.2 Delegates and events

Delegates are the CLI equivalent of C++ function adaptors. A delegate can wrap one or more methods that match the delegate definition, and all the encapsulated functions can be invoked by invoking the delegate using the same syntax used to invoke a function. Delegates have a close association with events. Events allow a CLI object to provide notifications, and an event is declared as a handle to a delegate type. You can hook event handlers to an object by adding callable entities to the delegate that represents a particular event. Delegates and events are heavily utilized in the Windows Forms classes, where nearly all of the UI classes use events for various notifications. Callers can hook onto these events by providing handlers that match the event's delegate signature.

To get a better idea of what events and delegates look like in the real world, think of a simple button on a form. Several events are associated with that button, such as mouse events. When you move the mouse over the button, a mouse-move event occurs; when you click the button, a left-click event occurs; and so on. CLI events are similar. In the Windows Forms classes, such user-interface events directly map to CLI events. There may be functions that are triggered when one or more of these events occur; for instance, an on-left-click function may be invoked when the left-click event is generated. A CLI delegate can wrap such a function so that when an event occurs, the delegate associated with that event is said to be *invoked*, which results in one or more functions being executed.

In the next few sections, we'll explore the usage and syntax of delegates and events in C++/CLI.

2.2.1 Delegates

Delegates are defined using the contextual keyword `delegate`, and all delegates implicitly derive from the `System::MulticastDelegate` class. A delegate declaration looks similar to a function declaration, except for the `delegate` keyword. Here's how you define a delegate that encapsulates functions that return `void` and take an `int` as argument.

```
delegate void DelegateShowInt(int);
```

Listing 2.9 demonstrates how functions are added to an instance of this delegate and how the delegate is invoked.

Listing 2.9 Setting up and using a delegate

```
ref class R
{
public:
    static void Show(int num)        <-- Static method matching delegate signature
    {
        Console::WriteLine(num);
    }
};

ref class G
{
public:
    void DoubleAndPrint(int num)     <-- Instance method matching delegate signature
    {
        Console::WriteLine(2 * num);
    }
};

. . .

DelegateShowInt^ dsi =
gcnew DelegateShowInt(&R::Show);     <-- (1) Instantiate delegate using static method
dsi += gcnew DelegateShowInt(
gcnew G(), &G::DoubleAndPrint);      <-- (2) Use += operator to add instance method
dsi(19);                             <-- (3) Invoke delegate
```

When adding static methods ❶, you use the constructor that takes the address of the static method (such as `&R::Show`); but when adding instance methods ❷, you use the constructor that takes a reference to an instance on which to invoke the function whose address you pass as the second argument. Also note how you use the `+=` operator to add a function to the delegate's invocation list (see figure 2.2).

When the delegate is invoked ❸, the encapsulated functions are called in the same order in which they were added. You can remove a function from the invocation list using the -= operator. You can add the same method more than once to a delegate's invocation list.

When you add a function to a delegate, you're basically adding it to the delegate's function-invocation list. When you remove a function from a delegate, you're removing it from the function-invocation list. Invoking a delegate essentially means that each function in the delegate's invocation list is executed one by one.

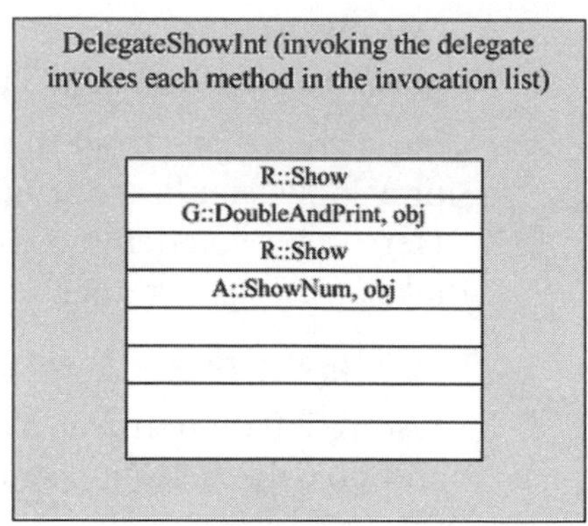

Figure 2.2 Delegate invocation list

Table 2.1 shows a sequence of operations on a delegate, along with the invocation list. You can see what happens when you add or remove a method from a delegate. The second column lists the functions in the delegate's invocation list in the order in which they will be executed when the delegate is invoked.

Be aware that when you add entries to or remove entries from the invocation list, a new invocation list is created and assigned to the delegate. This happens

Table 2.1 Invocation order for a delegate

Code	Invocation order

`G^ g = gcnew G();`
`DelegateShowInt^ dsi = nullptr;`
`dsi += gcnew`
`  DelegateShowInt(&R::Show);`
	`R::Show`

`dsi += gcnew DelegateShowInt(g,` `  &G::DoubleAndPrint);`	`R::Show` `G::DoubleAndPrint`

`dsi += gcnew DelegateShowInt(&R::Show);`	`R::Show`
	`G::DoubleAndPrint`
	`R::Show`

`dsi -= gcnew DelegateShowInt(g,` `  &G::DoubleAndPrint);`	`R::Show` `R::Show`
`dsi -= gcnew` `  DelegateShowInt(&R::Show);`	`R::Show`

because an invocation list can't be changed once it has been created. The `+=` operator translates to the `Delegate::Combine` method in the generated MSIL, whereas the `-=` operator translates to `Delegate::Remove`. Both `Combine` and `Remove` return new delegates of type `Delegate^`, so the compiler generates code to cast the returned delegate to the type of the delegate on which the operators were used.

Whenever you declare a delegate, the compiler generates a sealed class in the MSIL that is derived from `System::MulticastDelegate`. One of the member methods that's generated is the `Invoke` method, which is called every time you invoke the delegate. Obviously, `Invoke` has the same signature as the delegate definition. `Invoke` is marked with the `forwardref` and `runtime` attributes (among others), where `forwardref` indicates that the method body isn't specified in the declaration, and `runtime` indicates that the method body will be generated by the CLR. So, using the delegate invocation syntax,

```
dsi(25);
```

is equivalent to doing this:

```
dsi->Invoke(25);
```

So far, you've invoked delegates synchronously, which is a blocking operation. Next, you'll see how to asynchronously invoke a delegate, which is a nonblocking operation.

Asynchronously invoking a delegate

When you use the delegate invocation syntax (or call `Invoke` on the delegate), you invoke the delegate synchronously, which means that until every callable entity in the delegate's invocation list executes and returns, your code blocks. Consider the following code snippet, which includes a delegate `DelegateDoWork` and a function `DoWork` that matches the delegate signature:

```
delegate void DelegateDoWork();     // delegate definition

void DoWork()// method that matches delegate signature
{
    using namespace System::Threading;
    Console::WriteLine("Starting work...");
    Thread::Sleep(3000);
    Console::WriteLine("Work done!");
}
```

In this example, to simulate a complex task, you call `Sleep(3000)` inside `DoWork`; doing so pauses the executing thread for 3 seconds. Listing 2.10 sets up a delegate and invokes it.

Listing 2.10 Synchronous invocation of a delegate

```
DelegateDoWork^ ddw = gcnew DelegateDoWork(&DoWork);
Console::WriteLine("Before invoking delegate");
ddw();
Console::WriteLine("Delegate invoked. Moving on!");
```

The output is

```
Before invoking delegate
Starting work...
Work done!
Delegate invoked. Moving on!
```

The output clearly indicates that the thread stopped executing until the delegate call finished. This may not be desirable under certain circumstances, especially when you're invoking a call across an application domain (which might mean intranet or even internet communication). This is where asynchronous delegate invocation can be used.

In addition to the `Invoke` method, the compiler generates two methods called `BeginInvoke` and `EndInvoke` for the delegate class, with the `forwardref` and `runtime` attributes. These methods are used for asynchronous invocation. When you call `BeginInvoke`, the CLR queues the call to execute the delegate's callable entities on the thread pool, and control immediately returns to the calling thread, which can continue execution. Once the delegate has finished executing all of its callable entities, the callback (if any) specified in `BeginInvoke` is called. You can then handle any post-delegate code there. By calling `EndInvoke`, the return value (if any) of the delegate can be obtained. Listing 2.11 demonstrates asynchronous invocation.

Listing 2.11 Asynchronous invocation of a delegate

```
void CallBack(IAsyncResult^ ar)        <-- Callback passed to BeginInvoke
{
    using namespace System::Runtime::Remoting::Messaging;
    safe_cast<DelegateDoWork^>(                        | A little casting
        dynamic_cast<AsyncResult^>(                    | effort is required
            ar)->AsyncDelegate)->EndInvoke(ar);        |
}

. . .
```

```
Console::WriteLine("Before invoking delegate asynchronously");
ddw->BeginInvoke(gcnew AsyncCallback(&CallBack), nullptr);
Console::WriteLine("Delegate invoked asynchronously. Moving on!");
Console::ReadKey(true);
```

The output of this code is

```
Before invoking delegate asynchronously
Delegate invoked asynchronously. Moving on!
Starting work...
Work done!
```

The output shows that the `BeginInvoke` call returned immediately, whereas the delegate was invoked in parallel in a separate thread. The return value and arguments for the compiler-generated `BeginInvoke` and `EndInvoke` functions closely match the delegate definition. `BeginInvoke` always has the same arguments as the delegate in addition to a couple of extra arguments (for state management); `EndInvoke`'s return type matches that of the delegate. The callback function has to match the signature for the `AsyncCallback` delegate, and it's invoked once the asynchronous delegate execution has been completed. Figure 2.3 shows a diagrammatic representation of asynchronous delegate invocation.

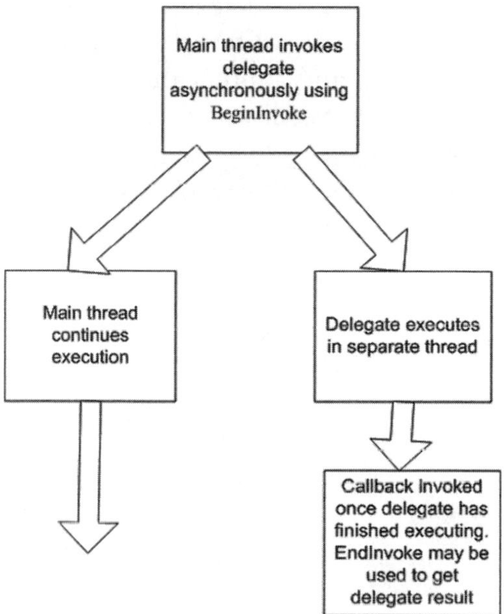

Figure 2.3
Asynchronous invocation of a delegate

A typical use of asynchronous delegate invocation occurs when the object is on a remote machine—possibly on the Internet, where the time needed to finish invoking the delegate may be nontrivial depending on the network speed. Another common use involves a time-consuming operation like a delegate that wraps methods that update a substantially sized database. It makes sense under such circumstances to use asynchronous invocation. You save yourself the trouble of managing multithreaded code and let the CLR create and manage the threads, especially because it knows how to do it well.

Let's look at events that basically use delegates in their declaration syntax.

2.2.2 Events

An event allows a class to provide notifications that a caller can hook onto by providing suitable event handlers. A CLI event is analogous to a real-life event, like a winter sale at a store. Customers who want to be notified of the winter sale can leave their phone number with store personnel and are then notified when the sale begins.

An event is declared using the `event` keyword. The type of the declaration is a handle to a delegate such that any event handlers that hook onto this event must match the delegate's signature. Let's write a simple class that generates random numbers with two events: one that notifies about the generation of an even number, and another that notifies about the generation of a number that is divisible by 9. See listing 2.12.

Listing 2.12 A random number generator class with two events

```
delegate void NumberHandler(int);        ① Delegate declarations for events

ref class NumberGenerator
{
    Random^ rand;
public:
    event NumberHandler^ OnEvenNumber;          ② Event member
    event NumberHandler^ OnDivisibleByNine;        declarations

    NumberGenerator() : rand(gcnew Random())
    {
    }
    void GenerateNumbers(int count)
    {
        for(int i=0; i<count; i++)
        {
            ProcessEvents(rand->Next());
        }
    }
    void ProcessEvents(int number)
    {
        if(number%2 == 0)
            OnEvenNumber(number);             ③ Invoke event
        if(number%9 == 0)                        handlers
            OnDivisibleByNine(number);
    }
};
```

Notice that you define a delegate type ❶ `NumberHandler`, which you can use later to declare the two event members ❷ `OnEvenNumber` and `OnDivisibleByNine`. In `ProcessEvents`, you invoke the event handlers ❸ for each of the events, depending on certain conditions that satisfy the event. Listing 2.13 shows how you set up event handlers to an instance of this class.

Listing 2.13 Hooking event handlers to the class defined in listing 2.12

```
void Number_Even(int number)
{
    Console::WriteLine(
        "Even number generated : {0}", number);
}

void Number_NineFactor(int number)
{
    Console::WriteLine(
        "A number divisible by 9 generated : {0}", number);
}

. . .

NumberGenerator^ ng = gcnew NumberGenerator();
ng->OnDivisibleByNine +=
    gcnew NumberHandler(Number_NineFactor);
ng->OnEvenNumber +=
    gcnew NumberHandler(Number_Even);
ng->GenerateNumbers(20);
```

Event handlers for events

Adding event handlers to events

If you compile and execute this code, you'll see the event handlers getting invoked, although the output will vary depending on the random numbers that are generated. In this example, you pass an `int` to both of the event handlers, but most of the .NET Framework classes use an `EventArgs`-derived object as the argument for their event handlers. If you're extending a .NET Framework class, you should do that, too, to be consistent.

The events in this example are both trivial events. The compiler generates the required accessor functions and the backing storage for storing the event handler delegate. Let's write another class with a nontrivial event. This time, let's use an `EventArgs`-derived class as the event handler parameter so you can see how that's typically implemented.

Authors of technical books are notorious for inventing some of the most contorted and seemingly pointless code samples you'll ever find. As an author who's done that in the past and who expects to keep doing that for a good while longer,

I can assure you that I do so with the best of intentions and that my fundamental objective is to demonstrate a coding concept with a simple example that is easy to assimilate.

On that note, let's write a class that searches for a word in a string and, if it finds that word, raises an `OnFindWord` event. Using nontrivial events, you'll make it so that only one handler can be associated with the `OnFindWord` event at any one time. If you attempt to add a second handler, it will be ignored (the event continues to be associated with the previous handler). Listing 2.14 shows the `EventArgs` derived class:

Listing 2.14 Deriving a class from `EventArgs`

```
ref class FindWordEventArgs : EventArgs
{
public:
    property String^ Word;             Trivial properties
    property int Index;
    FindWordEventArgs(String^ word, int index)
    {
        Word = word;                (1) Properties can't be
        Index = index;                  directly initialized
    }
};
```

Note how you have to set the properties in the constructor (1) because properties can't be directly initialized like normal fields. This is how you define the delegate for the event handler:

```
delegate void FindWordHandler(FindWordEventArgs^);
```

Instead of having a delegate that takes two arguments (one for the word and one for its index), you use an `EventArgs`-derived class, just as most of the Framework classes do. Look at listing 2.15.

Listing 2.15 The `WordFinder` class with a nontrivial event

```
ref class WordFinder
{
    String^ str;
    FindWordHandler^ _FindWordHandler;     <-- Backing store for
public:                                        event delegate
    WordFinder(String^ s) : str(s),
        _FindWordHandler(nullptr){}
    void FindWord(String^ word)
    {
```

```
        int index = 0;
        for each(String^ w in str->Split(' '))
        {
            if(word->CompareTo(w) == 0)
                OnFindWord(
                    gcnew FindWordEventArgs(w, index));
            index++;
        }
    }
    event FindWordHandler^ OnFindWord
    {
        void add(FindWordHandler^ handler)
        {
            if(_FindWordHandler == nullptr)
                _FindWordHandler = handler;
        }
        void remove(FindWordHandler^)
        {
            _FindWordHandler = nullptr;
        }
        void raise(FindWordEventArgs^ args)
        {
            if(_FindWordHandler)
                _FindWordHandler(args);
        }
    }
};
```

Invoke event handler

If event handler not set, set it

Clear event

Check for nullptr, invoke event

(1) Nontrivial event definition

For the nontrivial event, you have to declare the event accessor methods (1), `add`, `remove`, and `raise`, on your own. In this example, you take advantage of custom accessor methods by customizing the event in such a way that it can only be hooked to a single handler at a time. Note that this example serves to demonstrate the syntax for using nontrivial events; and in a real-world scenario, you'd want to directly use a delegate and expose it via a property rather than use an event that's then restricted to a single delegate. The following code shows how you can instantiate and use the `WordFinder` class:

```
void WordFoundHandler(FindWordEventArgs^ args)
{
    Console::WriteLine("Word '{0}' found at index {1}",
        args->Word, args->Index);
}

. . .

WordFinder^ wf = gcnew WordFinder(
    "C++ VB Java C# Cobol C++ Java Fortran C++ Lisp");
```

User-defined event handler

```
wf->OnFindWord += gcnew FindWordHandler(WordFoundHandler);
wf->FindWord("C++");
```

Note that you can't treat an event member as a typical data member. For instance, you can't set it to `nullptr`:

```
wf->OnFindWord = nullptr; // this throws error C3918
```

However, if you're using nontrivial events, you can add a `ResetOnFindWord` method that sets the backing storage delegate to `nullptr`, which accomplishes the same thing:

```
void ResetOnFindWord()
{
    _FindWordHandler = nullptr;
}
```

Most of the .NET Framework classes use a delegate called `EventHandler` (mscorlib.dll) for handling events. Here's how it's prototyped:

```
public delegate void EventHandler (Object^ sender, EventArgs^ e)
```

The first parameter represents the source of the event, which is the instance of the class where the event occurred, whereas the second parameter provides extra information about the event. When you design your classes, if you want to keep in sync with the .NET libraries, complete your event handler's name with *EventHandler* (for example, `NumberFoundEventHandler`), use an `EventArgs`-derived class, and name it so that it ends with the string *EventArgs*, as in `NumberFoundEventArgs`.

In the next section, we'll look at another important CLI feature: managed arrays.

2.3 CLI Arrays

CLI arrays (also referred to as *managed arrays*) are allocated on the CLR heap and are typical garbage-collected ref type objects. A CLI array has an associated rank (or dimension) that determines the number of indexes that can be associated with each array element. An array with a rank of 1 is referred to as a *single-dimensional array*, whereas an array with a rank greater than 1 is referred to as a *multidimensional array*. Although they're similar to native C++ arrays (that are allocated on the native heap), CLI arrays are entirely different entities, and you should be clear about the differences.

In the next few sections, we'll discuss various aspects of CLI arrays. From now on, whenever I mention the word *array*, be aware that I'm talking about a CLI array. If I need to talk about a native array, I'll explicitly say *native array*.

We'll discuss the usage of single-dimensional, multidimensional, and jagged arrays. We'll also cover parameter arrays, the use of arrays as function arguments and function return types, and using `System::Array` methods on user-declared arrays. We'll end the section on arrays with a discussion of advanced topics like using arrays of non-CLI objects, and how you can directly manipulate a CLI array using native pointers. Let's get started with the basic concepts of using CLI arrays.

2.3.1 Basic CLI array concepts

The syntax used to declare an array resembles that of C++ templates. Here's how you declare a single-dimensional array of `int`s:

```
array<int>^ arr;
```

Note that you declare the array as a handle type, because an array is a ref type on the CLR heap. Although the array element in this case is a value type (and hence there is no ^ punctuator), the array itself is a ref type (hence the ^). If you declare an array of a ref type, you must use the handle type on the element too:

```
array<String^>^ strarr;
```

Every CLI array automatically inherits from `System::Array`. Imagine a pseudo-template type array that looks like this:

```
namespace cli
{
    template<typename T, int rank = 1>
        ref class array : System::Array {};
}
```

The cli namespace

Note that the `cli` namespace is implicitly available when you're compiling a `/clr`-enabled project or solution. It's as if you put `using namespace cli` on top of all your source files. Several language elements, such as `array`, `pin_ptr`, and so on, are under this namespace to avoid conflicts with user-defined variables or types. If you define a symbol using the same name as one of the C++/CLI language elements under the `cli` namespace, then within a block where that symbol has visibility, you must use the fully qualified names when you use those C++/CLI language elements. See the following code:

```
char array;
cli::array<int>^ arr;
cli::array<String^>^ strarr;
```

Without the `cli::` prefix, this code would not compile.

The first template-style argument to the array declaration is the type of the array. For instance, you can specify an `int` or a `String^` as shown earlier. The second argument (which defaults to 1) specifies the rank of an array. Because the pseudo-template is derived from `System::Array`, your array is automatically a `System::Array` object. An example of using `System::Array` methods on CLI arrays will be introduced later.

The element type and rank of an array are fixed. You can't change them once an array has been declared. You also can't declare an array using stack semantics (which we'll cover later in this chapter), so arrays are always accessed using a handle variable. Because they can be accessed only via handles, arrays don't have a copy constructor or an assignment operator. Thus the array element type should not require copy construction or copy assignment.

2.3.2 *Single-dimensional arrays*

Single-dimensional arrays are CLI arrays with a rank of 1. If you don't explicitly specify a rank when declaring the array, 1 is assumed (because the default value for rank is 1 in the pseudo-template type of an array).

Consider the following code snippet, which declares, instantiates, and uses an array of `int`s. Except for the difference in the array declaration and instantiation syntax, the syntax for setting array elements and accessing their values is the same as that used for native arrays:

```
array<int>^ intarr = gcnew array<int>(3);        // Declare and create array
intarr[0] = 77;                                   // Assign values
intarr[1] = 66;                                   // to elements
intarr[2] = intarr[0] + intarr[1];
Console::WriteLine("{0} {1} {2}",                 // Access array values
    intarr[0], intarr[1], intarr[2]);
```

The syntax for using a `ref` type element is similar:

```
array<String^>^ strarr = gcnew array<String^>(10);
for(int i=0; i<10; i++)
strarr[i] = String::Concat(
    "String No. ", i.ToString());
for(int i=0; i<10; i++)
    Console::WriteLine(strarr[i]);
```

CLI arrays are fully supported at the MSIL level. When you `gcnew` a single-dimensional array type, the compiler generates the `newarr` MSIL instruction. For setting and reading array elements, the compiler generates one of the various `stelem` and `ldelem` MSIL instructions. Note that `newarr` isn't used for multidimensional arrays or for arrays that aren't zero-based.

2.3.3 Multidimensional arrays

Multidimensional arrays are those with a rank greater than 1. Note that they aren't arrays of arrays (also called *jagged arrays*) and aren't to be confused with the standard C++ notion of multidimensional arrays (those are jagged arrays). Suppose you have a list of people and cities that are to be stored in a table. Listing 2.16 shows the use of a 2-dimensional array to store this table (where each person has an associated city).

Listing 2.16 Populating a multidimensional array

```
array<String^, 2>^ employees =          <-- Rank specified as 2
    gcnew array<String^, 2>(3,2);       <-- lst dimension's length: 3, 2nd: 2

employees[0,0] = "Nish";
employees[0,1] = "Toronto";
employees[1,0] = "Chris";               Populate values
employees[1,1] = "Melbourne";
employees[2,0] = "Mike";
employees[2,1] = "LA";

Console::WriteLine("Name\t\tCity");
Console::WriteLine("--------------------");
for(int i=0; i<3; i++)
{
    for(int j=0; j<2; j++)
        Console::Write("{0}\t\t", employees[i,j]);     Read values back from array
    Console::WriteLine();
}
```

The square-brackets syntax for accessing array elements is intuitive and easy on the eyes. To further simplify the syntax, you can directly initialize the array instead of using a gcnew followed by a bunch of statements setting the various elements. The following code shows how to use direct initialization for the previous example:

```
array<String^, 2>^ employees =
{
    {"Nish","Toronto"},
    {"Chris","Melbourne"},
    {"Mike","LA"}
};
```

Figure 2.4 shows a diagrammatic representation of a 2D array. Note that it doesn't represent actual memory layout and is only a figurative representation of the array data.

Nish	Toronto
Chris	Melbourne
Mike	Los Angeles
Wally	Trivandrum
Jambo	Columbus

Figure 2.4 A 2-dimensional array

Unlike single-dimensional arrays, multidimensional arrays are created using the `newobj` MSIL instruction. The CLR Execution Engine provides CLI arrays with two instance methods named `Get` and `Set`. Not surprisingly (given their names), `Get` is used to read element values of an array while `Set` is used to write element values of an array. For multidimensional arrays, the compiler generates calls to these `Get`/`Set` methods whenever you read or write an array element. Note that multidimensional arrays are always rectangular in dimension.

2.3.4 *Jagged arrays*

Jagged arrays, which some people erroneously confuse with multidimensional arrays, are arrays of arrays and can be nonrectangular. You can think of a jagged array as an array that has an element type that is an array type. A jagged array is not a multidimensional array: It is a single-dimensional array whose element happens to be an array type. Figure 2.5 shows a jagged array. If you compare it with figure 2.4 (a 2D array), the difference is obvious—with the jagged array, each array element is a reference to another single-dimensional array. Note that a jagged array can also be an array of multidimensional arrays.

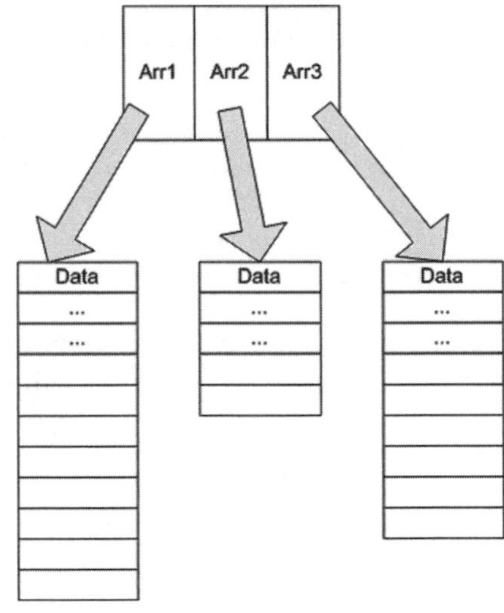

Figure 2.5 A jagged array

Here's how you can create a jagged array of `ints`:

```
array<array<int>^>^ jagarr = gcnew array<array<int>^> (5);
```

The jagged array in this snippet (`jagarr`) has a rank of 1 (single-dimensional) and a length of 5, which can be easily verified:

```
Console::WriteLine("Rank = {0}; Length = {1}",
    jagarr->Rank, jagarr->Length); // Output : Rank = 1; Length = 5
```

Each element in this jagged array is an array of `int`s; thus, they need to be created too. Notice how you use a couple of `System::Array` properties (`Rank` and `Length`) on the array. You'll see more about this in section 2.3.8.

```
for(int i=0, j=10; i<5; i++, j+=10)
{
      jagarr[i] = gcnew array<int> (j);
}
```

Each of the element arrays is of a different length (although the same dimension); hence, this jagged array is nonrectangular. Compare that with a multidimensional array that is always rectangular. (You can create a rectangular jagged array by making sure each of its element arrays is of the same length.) In our example of a jagged array, each element array is single-dimensional, but with increasing lengths in multiples of 10:

```
for(int i=0; i<5; i++)
    Console::WriteLine("Rank = {0}; Length = {1}",
    jagarr[i]->Rank,jagarr[i]->Length);
```

The output of this snippet is

```
Rank = 1; Length = 10
Rank = 1; Length = 20
Rank = 1; Length = 30
Rank = 1; Length = 40
Rank = 1; Length = 50
```

You aren't restricted to one level of jaggedness. The following is an example of a doubly jagged array (an array of arrays of arrays of `int`):

```
array<array<array<int>^>^>^ arr1 = gcnew
    array<array<array<int>^>^>(5);
```

Doesn't that syntax hurt your eyes? It definitely hurts mine! That's where a couple of `typedef`s come in handy:

```
typedef array<array<int>^> JaggedInt32Array;
typedef array<JaggedInt32Array^> DoublyJaggedInt32Array;
```

Now, you can do something like this for the doubly jagged array:

```
DoublyJaggedInt32Array^ arr2 = gcnew DoublyJaggedInt32Array(5);
```

And here's how you set up each array element:

```
for(int i=0; i<5; i++)
    arr2[i] = gcnew JaggedInt32Array(10 * (i+1));
```

That's a better proposition for the eyes! I recommend that whenever you need to have complicated jagged array declarations, you always use typedefs, such as those illustrated here, to simplify the declarations. Doing so will make your code a lot clearer and thus easier to maintain.

2.3.5 Arrays as function arguments

Arrays depict several characteristics of regular CLI types. One of them is their ability to be used as function arguments. Let's look at a function that accepts a tracking reference to a String array and initializes it using the other arguments to the function, namely an int representing the desired length for the array and a token string that's to be used to initialize the array members:

```
void InitStringArray(array<String^>^% strarr,
    String^ token, int len)
{
    strarr = gcnew array<String^>(len);
    for(int i=0; i<len; i++)
        strarr[i] = String::Concat(token, " : ", i);
}
```

Notice how the array argument is passed as a tracking reference; if you don't do this, a copy of the handle is passed to the function. The newly created array would be assigned to this copy, which would mean that the calling code's original handle would remain the same as it was originally, which isn't what you want. Remember, if you don't need the function to modify the passed-in array, you don't need to use a tracking reference. Here's how you call the InitStringArray function:

```
array<String^>^ arr;
InitStringArray(arr, "Item",7);
for(int i=0; i<7; i++)
    Console::WriteLine(arr[i]);
```

The compiler ensures type-correctness for functions that take arrays as arguments. The following code won't compile:

```
array<int>^ intarr;
InitStringArray(intarr, "Item",7); // Compiler error here
```

The function expects an array of String^ objects, whereas you've attempted to pass an array of ints to it. Arrays can also be used as function return types, as you'll see in the next section.

2.3.6 Returning arrays from functions

Returning arrays from functions is just as easy as passing them to functions. The function in listing 2.17 returns an array of `int`s that represent the Fibonacci numbers. (This may bring back pleasant memories of school, when you had to write programs in Interpreted Basic to generate the Fibonacci and other series. If those memories are nightmares, however, the author would like to absolve himself of any responsibility for the same.)

Listing 2.17 Function that returns part of the Fibonacci series

```
array<int>^ GetFibonacciArray(int count)
{
    array<int>^ arr = gcnew array<int>(count);// create array
    if(count > 0)
    {
        arr[0] = 0; // set first number
        if(count > 1)
        {
            arr[1] = 1; // set second number
            if(count > 2)
            {
                int index = 2;
                while(index < count) // generate numbers
                {
                    arr[index] = arr[index-1] + arr[index-2];
                    index++;
                }
            }
        }
    }
    return arr; // return array
}
```

Here's an example of how to use the function:

```
array<int>^ fibarr = GetFibonacciArray(10);
for(int i=0; i<fibarr->Length; i++)
  Console::Write("{0}, ",fibarr[i]);
```

Because an array is a managed object, both the function and the caller need not worry about cleaning it up after use. The Garbage Collector takes care of that. The fact that CLI arrays are type-safe managed objects is what allows them to be used as function arguments and function return types. You'll find yourself using both of these abilities frequently.

Next, we'll look at an interesting feature: parameter arrays. They are implemented using a custom IL attribute rather than with direct support at the MSIL level.

2.3.7 *Parameter arrays*

A function with a variable number of arguments has as its last argument a special array called a *parameter array*. C++/CLI supports a type-safe variable argument list mechanism using parameter arrays. There can be only one parameter array per function, and it must be the last argument. The parameter array is specified using the ellipses (...) prefix. An example of a function that takes a parameter array follows:

```
void Show(String^ name, ...array<int>^ scores)    ❶
{
    Console::Write("Scores by {0} : ", name);
    if(scores->Length == 0)
        Console::WriteLine("none");
    else
    {
        for(int i=0; i<scores->Length; i++)
            Console::Write("{0} ", scores[i]);
        Console::WriteLine();
    }
}
```

The first argument to the function is a `String^`. The second is a parameter array ❶ of type `int`. This means you can call the function with the `String^` argument (mandatory) and zero or more `int` arguments. Here's an example of how this function can be called:

```
Show("Nish"); // parameter array will be an empty array
Show("Smitha", 77, 88, 65); // parameter array will be of length 3
Show("Megan", 100); // parameter array of length 1
Show("Howard", 88, 93); // parameter array of length 2
```

Note that, in the generated IL, the function is prototyped to take a first argument of `String^` and a second argument of type `array<int>^`, but the parameter array argument is given the attribute `ParamArrayAttribute`. When you write code like this,

```
Show("Nish");
Show("Smitha", 77, 88, 65);
```

the compiler generates MSIL equivalent to this:

```
Show("Nish", gcnew array<int>(0));
Show("Smitha", gcnew array<int>{77, 88, 65});
```

Thus, parameter arrays aren't really an MSIL feature. They are implemented using a custom attribute, and CLI languages may or may not support them. Thus, they are more of a syntactic shortcut than a CLR feature!

`Console::WriteLine`, which is one of the most commonly used .NET class methods, uses a parameter array of `System::Objects` in one of its overloads. This overload lets you pass a format string as the first argument and five or more `Objects` as extra arguments, depending on your format string. If you're wondering where I came up with the number five, `WriteLine` has four overloads that take the format string followed by one, two, three, and four `Object` arguments, respectively. The parameter array overload comes into play only for calls with more that four format specifier objects. This was done for optimization reasons. (An array is always slower than passing direct objects because in the case of the array, the array elements must be extracted.) When you do something like this

```
Console::WriteLine(
    "i={0} y={1} i+y={2} i-y={3} i*y={4}",
    i, y, i+y, i-y, i*y);
```

you're actually doing the equivalent of this:

```
Console::WriteLine(
    "i={0} y={1} i+y={2} i-y={3} i*y={4}",
    gcnew array<Object^>{i, y, i+y, i-y, i*y});
```

If you examine the generated IL, the code generated is identical. All that the parameter array does is save you some keystrokes and provide a neater and more intuitive syntax.

2.3.8 *Using System::Array methods*

As I mentioned earlier in this chapter, every array implicitly inherits from the `System::Array` .NET `Library` class. This lets you use any `System::Array` method or property on arrays. Let's look at a few examples. Consider the following function, which searches for a specific string in an array and returns a `bool` that specifies whether the string was found:

```
bool DoesNameExist(array<String^>^ arr, String^ name)
{
    Array::Sort(arr);
    return Array::BinarySearch(arr, name)>-1;
}
```

You use the `Sort` and `BinarySearch static` methods of the `Array` class, both of which accept a `System::Array` argument. Although this function takes only string arrays, it's just as easy to have a function that accepts any CLI array as an argument, as in the following example:

```
void ShowArrayInfo(Array^ arr)
{
    Console::WriteLine("Length = {0}, Rank = {1}",
        arr->Length, arr->Rank);
    Console::WriteLine("Array contents : ");
    for(int i=0; i<arr->Length; i++)
        Console::WriteLine(arr->GetValue(i));
}
```

The public properties `Length` and `Rank` and the public method `GetValue` are used in this function, without knowing the type of the array element. An example of calling this function with an `int` array follows:

```
array<int>^ intarr = {1, 4, 8, 4};
ShowArrayInfo(intarr);
```

The output will be

```
Length = 4, Rank = 1
Array contents :
1
4
8
4
```

To iterate through the contents of an array, you use a `for` loop, and you loop on an index variable until it equals the `Length` property of the array. But an array is automatically a .NET collection object, because `System::Array` implements the `ICollection` and `IEnumerable` interfaces (and according to the CLI, that's what makes a class a collection class); like any collection class, an array can be iterated using the `for each` spaced keyword.

Using for each on an array

The compiler's typical behavior when it encounters `for each` loops on collection classes is to get the `IEnumerator` for the collection and loop on `MoveNext` until it returns `false`. However, for an array, this can be a seriously low-performance operation compared to looping using a regular `for` loop. Because the array's length is a known entity (through the `Length` property), and an array's index is sequential, it makes better programming sense to loop using a regular `for` loop until you hit the length of the array. The good news is that you don't have to do that, because the compiler does it for you by treating the array as a special case. When the compiler encounters a `for each` loop on an array, the MSIL it generates is equivalent to using a `for` loop with an index that's incremented until it equals the `Length` property of the array. Consider the following code snippet, which uses `for each`:

```
array<int>^ intarr = {1, 4, 8, 4};
int tot = 0;
for each(int y in intarr)
  tot += y;
```

This generates code that's nearly equivalent to the following:

```
array<int>^ intarr = {1, 4, 8, 4};
int tot = 0;
for(int i=0; i<intarr->Length; i++)
{
  int y = intarr[i];
  tot += y;
}
```

Don't worry about the fact that I said "nearly." The only difference is that the compiler-generated code works on a copy of the array handle rather than on the original array handle. As far as you're concerned, the knowledge that using a `for each` on an array won't slow down your code is what's important. If the compiler has taken precautions to ensure standard enumeration semantics, that's even better. My suggestion is to exclusively use `for each` with arrays, except where your index increment isn't sequential.

Here's something to watch out for when using `for each` loops. Look at the following code:

```
int main()
{
    array<String^>^ strarr = gcnew array<String^>(5);
    int count = 0;
    for each(String^ s in strarr)
        s = gcnew String(count++.ToString());
    for each(String^ s in strarr)
        Console::WriteLine(s);
    return 0;
}
```

If you expect it to output 0, 1, 2, 3, and 4 on separate lines, you're going to be disappointed, because it prints five blank strings. What happened?

Look at this line: `for each(String^ s in strarr)`. `s` is a local handle that is a copy of the current iterated element in `strarr`. The operative word is *copy*. When you `gcnew` the `String`, you assign it to this local handle and not to the array element. The right way to write the `for each` loop is `for each(String^% s in strarr)`.

Note that you don't have to do this for the second loop because you're only reading the array. C# people should be aware that C# won't let you specify a `foreach` (no space in the C# keyword) loop with a `ref` (ref is the C# equivalent for the C++ `^%` usage) loop variable.

2.3.9 Array covariance

A handle to an array of type D (where D is a derived class) has an automatic conversion to a handle to an array of type B (where B is a direct or indirect base class for D). This property of CLI arrays is called *array covariance*. Here's an example:

```
array<Object^>^ objarr = gcnew array<String^>(10);
```

You assign an array of type `String^` to an array handle of type `Object^`. Because `String^` is inherited from `Object^`, this is a valid conversion. Note that array covariance is limited to arrays of ref types. The following code won't compile, because `int` is a value type:

```
array<Object^>^ objarr = gcnew array<int>(10); // This won't compile
```

If you use a boxed `int` as the element type, it will compile, because a boxed `int` is a ref type and thus has a conversion to `Object^`:

```
array<Object^>^ objarr = gcnew array<int^>(10);
```

This sort of conversion is a lot more useful than the implicit conversion to `System::Array` because you can specify the common base type of array that you want to accept, instead of generically using `Array` objects in your code. To illustrate this using a simple example, think of a `School` class that has an `AddStudents` method that takes an array of `Student` objects as an argument. There might be specialized students in that school, such as math students (represented by the `MathStudent` class, which is derived from `Student`) or biology students (represented by the `BiologyStudent` class, again derived from `Student`). This is the class structure:

```
ref class Student{};
ref class MathStudent : Student{};
ref class BiologyStudent : Student{};

ref class School
{
public:
  void AddStudents(array<Student^>^ arr){}
};
```

When you add students to a `School` object, you can directly add math or biology students using arrays of the derived `Student` types:

```
School^ school = gcnew School();
array<MathStudent^>^ matharr = gcnew array<MathStudent^>(10);
array<BiologyStudent^>^ biolarr = gcnew array<BiologyStudent^>(10);
school->AddStudents(matharr);
school->AddStudents(biolarr);
```

By using a covariant array as the argument, you ensure type safety, because now, only arrays whose element type is derived from `Student` can be added to the `School` object. Had you used `System::Array` as the argument to `AddStudents`, nothing would stop a slipshod programmer from passing an array of `String` objects to the `AddStudents` method.

2.3.10 Arrays of non-CLI objects

A CLI array's element can't be a native type, but a pointer to a native type is allowed. Although it probably won't be a common scenario, there may be times when you want to store native objects in a managed array; at such times, this technique can be handy. Consider the following native class:

```
class CNative
{
public:
    CNative()
    {
        Console::WriteLine(__FUNCTION__);
    }
    ~CNative()
    {
        Console::WriteLine(__FUNCTION__);
    }
};
```

It doesn't do a lot except print the function signature in both the constructor and the destructor, which lets you keep track of the lifetime of `CNative` objects.

You can declare an array as follows:

```
array<CNative*>^ arr = gcnew array<CNative*>(2);
for(int i=0; i<arr->Length; i++)
{
    arr[i] = new CNative();
}
// now, you can use arr as required
```

Everything looks good, except that `CNative` is a native type, so its objects won't be garbage-collected. When the array `arr` goes out of scope and gets garbage-collected, its member elements don't get cleaned up. This means you have a memory leak. If you run this code, you'll see the following output:

```
CNative::CNative
CNative::CNative
```

Two CNative objects are constructed, but you don't see any destructor calls—these objects are leaked, because for native objects, you must delete what you new. If you know for sure when arr has finished being used, you can manually delete each native object in arr, although this may not be a feasible option all the time:

```
for(int i=0; i<arr->Length; i++)
{
    delete arr[i]; // delete each native object manually
}
```

A more general solution is to use such arrays of native objects as members of CLI classes, which gives you the option to clean up the native objects in the class destructor (destructors and finalizers will be covered in the next chapter). This is how you write such a class:

```
ref class R
{
private:
    array<CNative*>^ arr;
    //. . .
public:
    R()
    {
        arr = gcnew array<CNative*>(2);
        for(int i=0; i<arr->Length; i++)       Create and
        {                                       initialize array
            arr[i] = new CNative();
        }
    }
    ~R()
    {
        for(int i=0; i<arr->Length; i++)
        {                                       (1) Manually delete
            delete arr[i];                          each object
        }
    }
    //. . .
};
```

When an object of type R gets destructed, the array members (the CNative objects) get deleted too (1), thereby circumventing the memory leak. In this class, you put the deletion code in the destructor. You should use stack semantics when declaring objects of type R to take advantage of deterministic destruction when the object goes out of scope. (If this doesn't make sense now, don't worry; the next chapter discusses stack semantics, destructors, and finalizers in detail.) When R's destructor is called, each element in the array gets deleted, and you see the following output confirming that fact:

```
CNative::~CNative
CNative::~CNative
```

The most important thing you need to keep in mind when using CLI arrays of native objects is that although the array itself is a managed object that will eventually get garbage-collected, the array elements are native objects that need to be manually deleted. Let's look at how you can directly manipulate the contents of an array using native pointers.

2.3.11 Directly accessing CLI arrays using native pointers

Sometimes, it's good to have direct access to an array through a pointer. This gives you a fast access mechanism to manipulate the array, because you sidestep the CLR's array-access mechanism, which isn't as performant as direct pointer access. The example in listing 2.18 has an `array` of `int`s, where you use a native pointer to increment each `int` by 1.

Listing 2.18 Using a native pointer on a CLI array

```
void DirectArrayAccess()
{
    array<int>^ intarr = gcnew array<int>(5);
    for(int i=0; i<intarr->Length; i++)
        intarr[i] = i * 100;
    pin_ptr<int> pin = &intarr[0];                 <-- 1 Pin array on heap
    int* pintarr = pin; [#2]
    int* plast = pintarr + intarr->Length;          <-- 2 Get pointers to first, last elements

    while(pintarr < plast)
    {
        (*pintarr++)++;                             <-- 3 Increment each element and pointer
    }

    for each(int i in intarr)
        Console::WriteLine(i);
}
```

You use a pinning pointer to pin the array object ❶ in the CLR heap (to prevent it from being moved around by the Garbage Collector). You do so using the `pin_ptr` keyword, which we'll discuss in detail later in this book. For now, understand that once an object's address is assigned to a pinning pointer, the GC knows that it should not move that object around in the CLR heap. The pinning pointer takes the address of the first element (index 0) in the array, which is also the address of the array. You then assign this to a native `int*` ❷. Now you have a native `int*` pointing to the first element in the array. You also initialize a pointer `plast` to point to memory just after the last element in the array. The GC always allocates memory sequentially, so you know that the address of the last element can be calculated by adding the length of the array to the `int*` pointing to the first element of the array.

Now that you have pointers to the beginning and end of the array, you use regular pointer arithmetic to increment each element in the array ❸. You use one `++` operator to increment the pointer and another to increment its contents. The output of the code snippet shows that each array element has been incremented by 1, proving that the native pointer manipulated the CLI array, which is what you set out to do.

In general, unless you have specific reasons to write high-performant code, perhaps inside a frequently accessed code block that manipulates a substantially sized array, it's better to use CLI array semantics to access the array, because you don't run the risk of doing incorrect pointer math and corrupting memory. You also get all the benefits of CLI type-safety. Another problem with using pointers to access arrays is that you inherently have to pin the array first, and this may cause heap fragmentation problems. I'll talk more about this later in this book when I cover pinning pointers.

With that we come to the end of our coverage of CLI arrays. We have discussed basic array concepts, the usage of single-dimensional, multidimensional. and jagged arrays, using arrays as function arguments and return values, using parameter arrays in variable argument functions, array covariance, creating arrays of non-CLI objects, and manipulating arrays using native pointers. That's a lot of stuff, and you may want to grab a cup of coffee to soothe your aching brain for a while. On a few occasions, we encountered concepts we haven't covered yet, such as pinning pointers and CLI destructors, but we'll discuss those topics in later chapters.

2.4 Summary

The three topics we looked at in this chapter—properties, delegates and events, and managed arrays—are all important CLI functionalities supported by C++/CLI. They are essentially .NET features, and to interop with .NET code and be efficient as a CLI language, it was important that C++/CLI support them properly. Not only has C++/CLI supported these features immaculately, they have also been implemented with as similar a C++ style syntax as was feasible. You'll encounter them frequently when you're doing managed (or mixed-mode) coding, which makes it essential that you know how they work and how to use them.

At this point, we are almost, but not quite, ready to jump into mixed-mode programming. We still need to cover some significant C++/CLI features, such as stack semantics and deterministic destruction, function overriding, and generic programming (using CLI generics and managed templates). We'll do that in the next chapter.

3

More C++/CLI: stack semantics, function overriding, and generic programming

I'd like you to understand a few more concepts properly before we venture into interop techniques and mixed-mode programming. This chapter will round off our coverage of the basic C++/CLI syntax and concepts. The three topics I'll cover in this chapter aren't directly related to each other; however, they're fundamental to using C++/CLI, and thus it's important that we cover them early in the book.

We'll start with stack semantics and deterministic destruction, which overcomes the issue of nondeterministic finalization that's prevalent in a garbage-collected environment; we'll also take a brief look into the garbage-collection algorithm used by the CLR. Stack semantics is one of the most popular language-specific features in C++/CLI and is one feature that stands out due to the fact that no other CLI compiler supports it. We'll cover the new function-overriding features that have been added to C++/CLI and that aren't available in standard C++, and see how they enhance the flexibility of the language. Function-overriding semantics deviate from standard C++. Those of you who come from a strong native C++ background may find the new semantic behavior a little confusing initially, but as you see some examples, the confusion will slowly pass.

We'll round off the chapter with a discussion on the two distinct generic programming methods that are available in C++/CLI: CLI generics and managed templates. We'll look at how CLI generics compares with templates, where each mechanism is useful, and how you can mix them for maximum flexibility and value. By the end of this chapter, you should be set for diving into the mixed-mode programming techniques that will be covered in the rest of this book.

3.1 Stack semantics and deterministic destruction

A lot of C++ programmers were unhappy with the nondeterministic finalization approach required by the .NET garbage-collection algorithm. C++ programmers were so used to the Resource Acquisition Is Initialization (RAII) idiom, where they expected a destructor to be called when an object went out of scope or when `delete` was explicitly called on it, that a nondeterministic destructor didn't fit with their expectations or requirements. Microsoft alternatively offered the Dispose pattern, where classes had to implement an `IDisposable` interface and manually call `Dispose` on their objects when they went out of scope. The problem was that this required the programmer to manually and consistently call `Dispose` on an object whenever the object needed to be finalized. The situation became worse when the object had managed member objects that themselves would need to have `Dispose` called on them, which meant that they, too, had to implement `IDisposable`.

C++/CLI gives you separate destructor and finalizer semantics. The destructor is deterministically invoked, thereby satisfying the RAII idiom. The fact that an object can have a deterministic destructor also allowed the VC++ team to add support for stack semantics to the language, something that, as of today, isn't available in any other CLI language. Note that it's entirely possible that the designers of C++/CLI explicitly had stack semantics in mind when they decided to implement a deterministic destruction mechanism in the language semantics. In this section, we'll discuss the new destructor and finalizer semantics, take a brief look at the .NET garbage-collection process, and also talk about stack semantics and how they're internally implemented.

3.1.1 The new destructor and finalizer syntaxes

In C++/CLI, the destructor and finalizer are separate entities, and a class can choose to implement one or both of those entities. The destructor for a class is called when an object of that type is deleted manually using a call to `delete`, whereas the finalizer is called during garbage collection. A destructor is analogous to your throwing an empty soda can into the waste bin on your own; a finalizer is analogous to your dropping it on the floor, and a janitor picking it up and putting it into the waste bin during one of their cleaning cycles.

For automatic variables that use stack semantics (discussed later in this chapter), the destructor is automatically called when the object goes out of scope. Destructors provide a deterministic mechanism to clean up an object, whereas a finalizer provides a nondeterministic mechanism to clean up an object when it gets garbage-collected. For destructors, the syntax used is the same as in Standard C++:

```
~Typename()
{
}
```

Finalizers use a totally new syntax introduced in C++/CLI:

```
!Typename()
{
}
```

Listing 3.1 shows a typical class, with a constructor, destructor, and finalizer.

Listing 3.1 Class with a constructor, destructor, and finalizer

```
ref class R
{
public:
    R()
    {
        Console::WriteLine(__FUNCSIG__);
    }
    ~R()
    {
        Console::WriteLine(__FUNCSIG__);
    }
protected:
    !R()
    {
        Console::WriteLine(__FUNCSIG__);
    }
};
```

To see them in action, let's write a trivial program that creates two objects of type `R`, deletes one of them manually (thereby bringing the destructor into play), and allows the other to be garbage-collected (bringing the finalizer into play). Here's what the little program looks like:

```
int main()
{
    R^ r1 = gcnew R(); // Object r1 created
    R^ r2 = gcnew R(); // Object r2 created
    Console::WriteLine("About to delete r1");
    delete r1; // r1's destructor is invoked
    Console::WriteLine("Exiting main");
    return 0;
} // r2 gets garbage collected
```

The output of running this program is

```
R::R
R::R
About to delete r1
R::~R
Exiting main
R::!R
```

When you call `delete` on `r1`, `r1`'s destructor is invoked, just like in standard C++. For `r2`, however, you don't manually call `delete`, which means the Garbage Collector (GC) cleans it up during the next garbage-collection cycle. Because this is a small program, the GC comes into play only when the program has exited its `main` function. At that time, when the GC cleans up the objects on the CLR heap, it calls the finalizer on the `r2` object. This explains why you see `R::!R` displayed after `main` has exited in the program output. The GC doesn't call a finalizer for the `r1` object because the destructor has already been called for it.

Before we look at how the compiler generates MSIL for destructors and finalizers, you need to understand the basic concepts of .NET garbage collection.

Garbage collection

CLI `ref` objects are allocated from the CLR's managed heap. These objects are automatically freed by the .NET Garbage Collector when they're no longer required. The GC is analogous to the janitor we talked about earlier, who cleans up after you, picking up garbage and dumping it into the waste bin. As a developer, this means you only need to allocate objects. You don't have to manually free those objects; that is done for you by the CLR. This can be counterintuitive to you as a C++ developer. In C++, you're always told that you must delete objects that you allocate or else suffer the pangs of a memory leak.

You may wonder how the GC knows that an object is no longer in use and can be freed up. That's what we'll talk about in this section. I'll keep the discussion as brief and simple as I can, because I only want you to understand how objects are freed by the GC and when finalizers are called. For a more detailed study of the .NET garbage-collection algorithm, refer to books that specifically focus on the workings of the CLR.

When a .NET application is executed, the CLR reserves a large contiguous block of memory for the managed heap; and when you create `ref` objects, the CLR allocates them on this managed heap in a contiguous manner. It keeps a pointer to the next available free space. I'll refer to it as `pNextObject` in this discussion. Initially, `pNextObject` points to the beginning of the managed heap. As new objects are created, `pNextObject` is incremented to point to the beginning of the free memory block. Figure 3.1 is a block diagram that shows how `pNextObject` points to the next available free block of memory. Whenever a new object is to be created, the CLR needn't hunt for a free block of memory: It creates the object starting at the memory location pointed to by `pNextObject`. It then increments `pNextObject` by the size of the just-created object. This is why memory allocation is extremely fast and efficient in .NET, when compared to traditional C++, where the native heap allocator has to

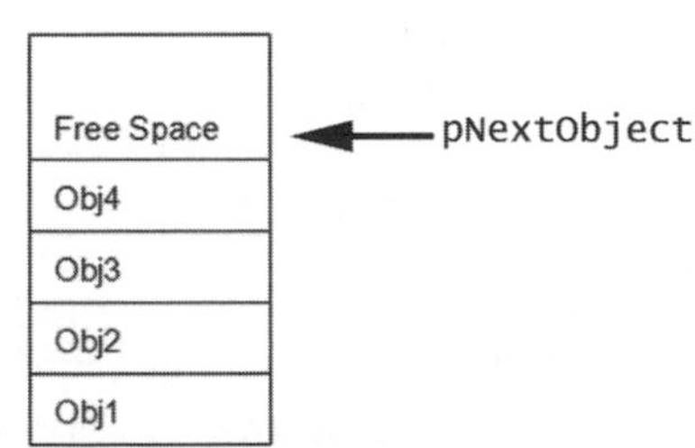

Figure 3.1 A representation of the managed heap showing the `pNextObject` pointer

search for a free memory block from a linked list of pointers to available memory blocks. If RAM was infinite, the .NET memory-allocation process would be perfect. Unfortunately, RAM is not only finite, but its finiteness can also be conspicuous when you start developing real-world applications! What happens when you run out of space? When the managed heap is full and a new object needs to be created, a garbage-collection cycle is performed. (Note that this isn't the only scenario in which a garbage-collection cycle can occur.)

Before we look at what happens during a garbage-collection cycle, you need to understand the concept of roots. A *root* is a memory location that is essentially a reference to a managed object on the heap or a `nullptr`. All global and static objects are part of a .NET application's roots. Other roots include currently active stack variables in any thread of the application, as well as CPU registers that hold references to objects on the CLR heap. When a garbage-collection cycle occurs, the GC assumes that the entire managed heap is garbage and starts building a list of reachable objects by walking through its list of roots. An object is deemed *reachable* if it can be accessed directly or indirectly through a root. For example, a root may point to an object `A` that may have a member that points to an object `B`. Although `B` can't be directly reached from that root, it can be indirectly reached via object `A`. Thus it's deemed reachable. Figure 3.2 shows a diagrammatic representation of a reachable object. Object `B` is a reachable object, whereas objects `C`

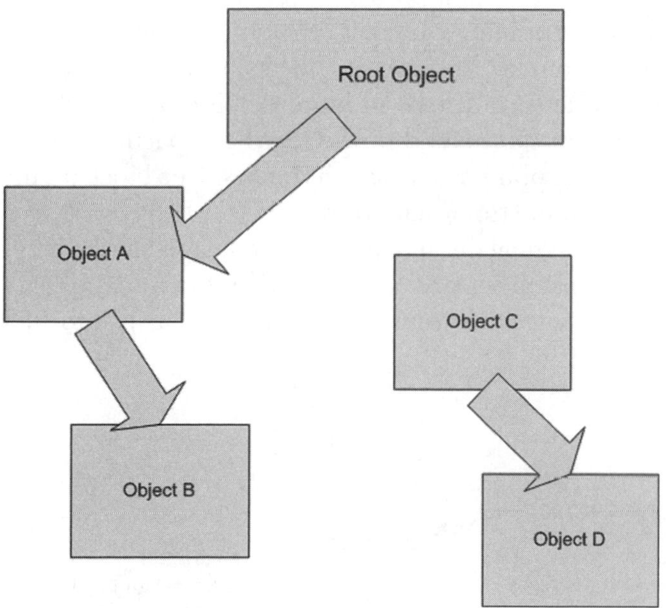

Figure 3.2 Reachable objects

and `D` are nonreachable objects because they don't have a direct or indirect connection to a root.

Once the GC has built up a list of reachable objects, every object in the managed heap that isn't in this list is considered garbage. The GC proceeds to compact the heap by moving the reachable objects down the heap, so that it ends up with one contiguous block of memory. A diagrammatic representation of this is shown in figure 3.3. Of course, this invalidates every managed pointer that refers to any of the objects that were relocated during compaction; thus, the CLR updates all those references to point to the new memory locations. This explains why interior pointers (covered in the next chapter) and managed reference handles aren't affected by garbage-collection cycles. Because they get updated by the CLR, they always refer to the original object. You can also understand why a native pointer, which knows nothing about the CLR, won't work with managed objects. A native pointer continues to point to where it was pointing to, regardless of whether the GC has relocated the object that was being pointed to. That is the case because native pointers were not designed for a garbage-collected memory system such as the one the CLR provides. As far as a native pointer is concerned, the memory address it points to is fixed and never changes. If you want it to point to some other memory location, you need to manually change the pointer to point to that new memory address.

Note that the GC won't relocate pinned objects (pinning is covered in the next chapter; for now, just be aware that a pinned object remains in a fixed memory location for the duration of pinning). It can't efficiently compact the heap when there are a substantial number of pinned objects. This leads to the heap-fragmentation problem that we'll discuss in more detail in a later chapter, when we discuss pinning pointers. At the end of the heap-compaction operation, the GC updates the `pNextObject` pointer to point to the first free block of memory, so that the next allocation is done from that address.

You may wonder whether going through the entire managed heap every time you run out of memory is all that efficient. My answer is that it most definitely would be inefficient to do so. It makes better sense to classify the heap into hierarchical

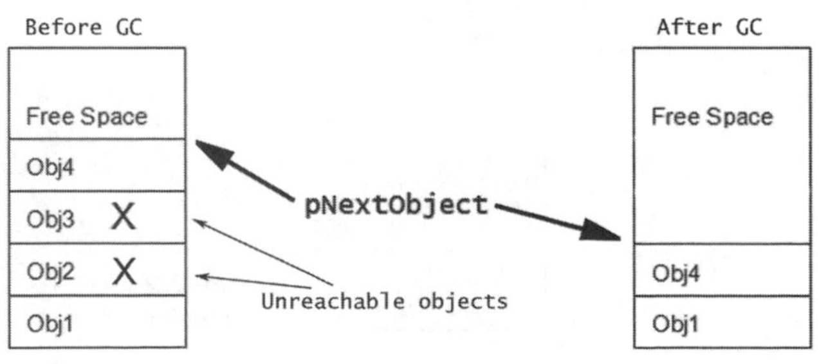

Figure 3.3
A typical garbage-collection cycle

regions so that the most frequent garbage-collection operations are performed on the lowest region, and garbage-collection cycles are less frequently done on higher regions. Apparently, the designers of the .NET garbage-collection algorithm thought so, too. In my explanation of the garbage-collection algorithm so far, I've presumed that the managed heap is considered a single entity. In reality, however, the .NET GC uses a generational algorithm. All newly-allocated objects are put into Generation-0 of the heap. A garbage-collection cycle is always performed on a generation rather than on the entire heap. When Generation-0 runs out of memory, a Gen-0 garbage-collection cycle takes place. At the end of the garbage-collection cycle, all remaining objects are promoted to Generation-1. The assumption made here is that objects surviving a garbage-collection cycle are likely to be long-living objects. They're then promoted to a higher generation so that they will be exposed to fewer garbage-collection cycles. Eventually, Generation-1 may run out of space, too. When that happens, a Gen-1 GC cycle occurs, and all remaining objects are promoted to Generation-2, the highest garbage-collection generation.

Generation-2 garbage-collection cycles are rare; when they happen, objects that are still alive remain in Generation-2, because there is no higher generation. Typically, globals and static objects in a long-running application end up in Generation-2 and stay there throughout the life of the application. Generation-1 contains medium-lifetime objects; garbage-collection cycles do occur in Gen-1, although they aren't frequent. Gen-0 contains all newly-allocated objects; garbage-collection cycles happen frequently in Gen-0. If your head is feeling a tad heavy with all that information, don't lose sleep over it; the working of the GC is entirely transparent to you, the developer. It's advantageous to have an idea of how it works, but it's not imperative to remember every implementation detail. With that happy thought, let's continue.

The large object heap

The CLR has a separate heap for allocating large objects: the *large object heap*. Objects that are around 80KB or more are allocated from the large object heap. The large object heap isn't generational; during a garbage-collection cycle, objects aren't relocated, and there is no compaction. This is because moving large objects isn't efficient and because only large objects are allocated here, the risk of fragmentation is minimal. Except for the fact that the large object heap is nongenerational and doesn't perform memory compaction, it behaves exactly like the generational-managed heap.

One last thing I'd like to cover in this section is how the GC calls finalizers on objects that are to be finalized. Whenever you create an object that has a finalizer, a pointer to this object is added to a Finalization queue maintained by the CLR. During a garbage-collection cycle, once the garbage objects (objects that don't have reachable roots) have been identified, the GC checks to see if any of these objects are in the Finalization queue. If a garbage object is in the Finalization queue, the GC removes its entry from that queue and adds it to another queue called the F-Reachable queue, where the *F* stands for *Finalization*. Like a global or a static variable, the F-Reachable queue is considered to be a root. The moment the GC moves the pointer to the object from the Finalization queue to the F-Reachable queue, the object is no longer garbage because it now has a reachable root. This process in which an object transitions from being garbage back to being reachable is called *object resurrection*. Because the object isn't garbage anymore, the GC promotes it to the next-higher generation.

Every managed application has a special runtime thread that is responsible for calling finalizers. If the F-Reachable queue is empty, this thread remains dormant; but whenever objects are added to the F-Reachable queue, this thread wakes up and removes each object from the queue after calling its finalizer, until the queue is empty. At this point, these objects have gone back to their unreachable state and will be cleaned up during the next garbage-collection cycle. As you can see, objects with finalizers aren't as efficient as those without, because at least two garbage-collection cycles are required to clean them up.

Garbage-collection cycles are expensive operations; they consume valuable CPU cycles. The roots have to be traversed, the heap must be compacted, managed pointers to relocated objects have to updated, objects must be promoted to higher generations, finalizers have to be called, and pinned objects must be left alone. Although having a garbage-collected memory manager is convenient, typically you'll find that it's less efficient than native memory management. As far as my experience goes, however, the generational garbage-collection algorithm developed by the CLR team is outstanding. If you code with a little understanding of how the GC works, you can minimize the performance hits associated with automatic memory management. You should now have a basic understanding of how the GC works and how finalizers are invoked.

IL implementation for destructors and finalizers

In our coverage of garbage collection, you saw how finalizers are invoked automatically by the GC before objects are cleaned up. It's apparent that .NET directly supports finalizers. But there was no mention of destructors. This is because the .NET Framework's memory model of automatic garbage collection isn't conducive to the concept of deterministic destructors. Given this backdrop, C++/CLI uses the Dispose pattern to implement destructor and finalizer semantics.

The C++/CLI Dispose pattern uses the following rules:

- If a class has either a finalizer (`!typename`) or a destructor (`~typename`), the compiler generates a `Dispose(bool)` method for that class. The compiler-generated code checks the `bool`, and if a `true` value is passed, it calls the destructor (`~typename`); if a `false` value is passed, it calls the finalizer (`!typename`).
- For any object that defines a destructor (`~typename`), the compiler automatically implements the `System::IDisposable` interface for that object and also generates a `Dispose()` method that satisfies that interface. This compiler-generated `Dispose` method calls `Dispose(true)` so that the destructor (`~typename`) is executed. It then calls `GC::SuppressFinalize(this)`, which removes that object from the Finalization queue, because the object need not be finalized now that its destructor has been called.
- For any object that defines a finalizer (`!typename`), the compiler automatically generates a `Finalize` method that overrides `System::Object::Finalize()`. This compiler-generated `Finalize` method calls `Dispose(false)` so that the finalizer (`!typename`) is executed.

The next example has a destructor as well as a finalizer; the compiler generates a `Dispose()` method, a `Dispose(bool)` method, and a `Finalize()` method. If you examine the generated IL, you'll see that the structure of the generated class looks like listing 3.2.

Listing 3.2 Pseudo-code showing the compiler-generated methods

```
ref class R
{
public:
    R() {...}                    <- Class constructor
    void Dispose(){...}          <- (1) Effective destructor
protected:
    void Finalize(){...}         <- (2) Finalizer override
    void Dispose(bool){...}      <- Dispose pattern helper function
private:
    void !R(){...}               <- (3) Finalizer body
    void ~R(){...}               <- (4) Destructor body
};
```

Notice how the destructor (4) and finalizer (3) methods you declare are put into the private section of the class. In the generated class, `Dispose()` (1) is the effective destructor. It eventually invokes `~R` through `Dispose(true)`. Similarly, `Finalize()` ❷ is the effective finalizer that's called by the GC; it eventually invokes `!R` through `Dispose(false)`. When you call `delete` on a CLI object that has a destructor, the compiler generates a call to `Dispose()`. Note that a corollary of this compiler behavior is that you can use `delete` in C++/CLI to dispose any object that implements `IDisposable` (including those that were written in C# or VB.NET).

You should now be comfortable with how destructors and finalizers are implemented by the compiler. With that knowledge, we'll look at the remarkable mechanism used to support stack semantics for `ref` objects in C++/CLI.

3.1.2 Stack semantics

In this section, we'll discuss how C++/CLI supports stack semantics; how it's internally implemented; and how class members are handled when using stack semantics. Essentially, stack semantics lets you declare and use a `ref` type as an automatic variable. Thus, instead of

```
R^ r = gcnew R();
delete r; // optional
```

you can do this with stack semantics:

```
R r;
```

You don't have to worry about manually calling `delete`, because when the variable goes out of scope, the destructor is called. In the handle version, if you didn't call `delete`, the object would have to wait for the next garbage-collection cycle before it gets finalized. Not only is this less efficient (as we discussed earlier), but for objects that access scarce resources like file handles, it's important to execute clean-up code as early as possible. Stack semantics solves both these problems—objects declared using stack semantics never need to be finalized (because they're always destructed). They also need not be manually deleted, because the compiler generates the destructor call for you when they go out of scope.

> **Types that can't use stack semantics**
>
> Three reference types can't use stack semantics: delegates, arrays, and `System::String` objects. These types are specially treated by the CLR, and the compiler can't generate destructors for them. It's a pity, really, because having to use handle variables for arrays and strings (which are probably the two most commonly used types) breaks code uniformity (if you're using stack semantics for everything else); but it's a CLR-imposed restriction and not the compiler's fault.

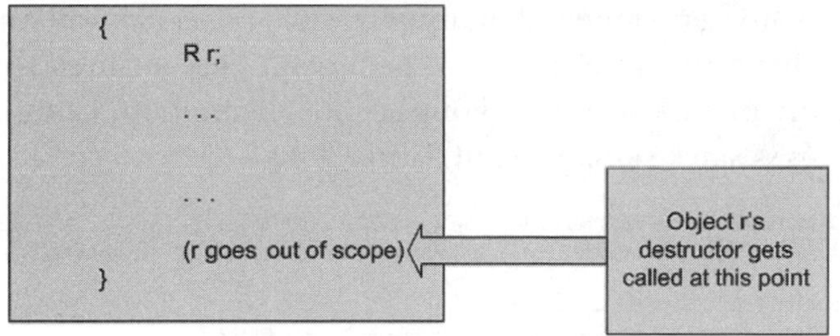

Figure 3.4
Stack object's destructor gets called at the end of its scope

Figure 3.4 shows how a stack object's destructor gets called when it goes out of scope, typically at the end of the method or block where it has been declared.

Let's write a function that opens two text files and writes the contents of both of those files to a new text file. In other words, it concatenates two text files to a third file. You'll use the `StreamWriter` and `StreamReader` classes in the `System::IO` namespace. In the first version of the function, you manually clean up the writer and reader objects; see listing 3.3.

Listing 3.3 File-concatenation code without stack semantics

```
void ConcatFilestoFile(String^ infile1,
                       String^ infile2, String^ outfile)
{
    String^ str;
    StreamReader^ sr1;
    StreamReader^ sr2;
    StreamWriter^ sw;
    try
    {
        sr1 = gcnew StreamReader(infile1);
        sr2 = gcnew StreamReader(infile2);
        sw = gcnew StreamWriter(outfile);
        while(str = sr1->ReadLine())
            sw->WriteLine(str);
        while(str = sr2->ReadLine())
            sw->WriteLine(str);
    }
    finally
    {
        delete sr1;
        delete sr2;
        delete sw;
    }
}
```

Not only do you have to remember to manually call `delete` on all three file objects, but you also have to use a `try-finally` block. This ensures that if an exception is thrown, any previously created objects are cleaned up. Compare that with the version that uses stack semantics, in listing 3.4.

Listing 3.4 File-concatenation code using stack semantics

```
void ConcatFilestoFile(String^ infile1,
                       String^ infile2, String^ outfile)
{
    String^ str;
    StreamReader sr1(infile1);
    StreamReader sr2(infile2);
    StreamWriter sw(outfile);
    while(str = sr1.ReadLine())
        sw.WriteLine(str);
    while(str = sr2.ReadLine())
        sw.WriteLine(str);
}
```

Not only is this version shorter and easier to read, but you don't need to use a `try-finally` block (because the compiler does that for you, as you'll soon see). Notice that you don't call `delete`. Instead, you let the objects get destructed when they go out of scope, which (as illustrated in listing 3.4) is when the function exits. That should help you appreciate how stack semantics brings a remarkable level of convenience to managed coding.

Implementing stack semantics

Consider that you have a function that uses a `StreamReader` object to read one line from a file. The compiler generates the necessary `try-finally` blocks and the calls to `Dispose` in the generated MSIL (see table 3.1).

If you think about it, the compiler is writing code for you that you'd normally have to write on your own. This code may feel wrong because it looks as if there will be double calls to `delete` when an exception is thrown. However, the MSIL uses `fault` handlers (and not `finally` handlers) to do this. If an exception is thrown, the code in the `catch` (`fault`) block executes, and then control leaves the block—meaning the second `delete` never executes in such a scenario. A `fault` handler is similar to a `finally` handler, except that the `fault` block is executed only if its associated `try` block throws an exception. (Because there's no `fault`-equivalent keyword in C++, I used `catch` to show the pseudo-code.)

Table 3.1 Compiler-generated code that simulates stack semantics: single object

<table>
<tr><th>C++/CLI code</th><th>Code (pseudo) generated by the compiler</th></tr>
<tr><td><pre>void ReadOneLine()
{
    StreamReader sr("c:\\fil1");
    sr.ReadLine();
}</pre></td><td><pre>void ReadOneLine ()
{
    StreamReader^ sr =
        gcnew StreamReader("c:\\fil1");
    try
    {
        sr->ReadLine();
    }
    catch(Exception^)
    {
        delete sr; // sr->Dispose
    }
    delete sr; // sr->Dispose
}</pre></td></tr>
</table>

Let's add to the complexity of the function by using an additional `StreamReader` object (see table 3.2).

The code the compiler generates is perfect; each object is deleted when it would normally have gone out of scope, and proper `try-catch` blocks ensure that only those objects are destroyed that need to be. (Again, remember that the `catch` blocks above are `fault` blocks in the MSIL; I used `catch` as a pseudo-equivalent in C++.) In short, the compiler has not only saved you time, but it has also generated optimized code that would have been difficult to emulate had you tried to code it on your own. The moment I added an additional disposable object, the code complexity increased substantially. Try to imagine how complex it would be with functions that have half a dozen or more disposable objects, with some of them possibly used in conditional blocks; I dare say even the most experienced developers would find it tedious and difficult to get it all right, not to mention how long it would take.

If your class needs to have member objects that are themselves disposable, you can declare them using stack semantics. The compiler will generate the required creation and disposal code for you.

Handling member objects

Think of a custom file reader class (let's call it `MyFileReader`) that uses a custom file stream object (let's call it `CustomFileStream`) to read from a special device. Assume that both these classes use scarce resources and need to be disposed of deterministically. All you need to do is to declare a `CustomFileStream` member

Table 3.2 File-concatenation code without stack semantics: multiple objects

C++/CLI code	Code (pseudo) generated by the compiler

<pre>void ReadOneLine()
{
  StreamReader sr("c:\\fil1");
  StreamReader srnew("c:\\fil2");
  sr.ReadLine();
  srnew.ReadLine();
}</pre>
	<pre>void ReadOneLine()
	{
	  StreamReader^ sr =
	    gcnew StreamReader("c:\\fil1");
	  try
	  {
	    StreamReader^ srnew =
	      gcnew StreamReader("c:\\fil2");
	    try
	    {
	      sr->ReadLine();
	      srnew->ReadLine();
	    }
	    catch(Exception^)
	    {
	      delete srnew; // Dispose
	    }
	    delete srnew; // Dispose
	  }
	  catch(Exception^)
	  {
	    delete sr; // Dispose
	  }
	  delete sr; // Dispose
	}</pre>

using automatic variable (stack) semantics; the compiler takes care of creating and destroying the object for you:

```
ref class MyFileReader
{
public:
  CustomFileStream m_stream; // this is all you need to do
  MyFileReader(){}
  ~MyFileReader(){}
  . . .
};
```

The compiler generates code to instantiate the `CustomFileStream` member in the constructor. Here's what it looks like in MSIL (pseudo C++ code):

```
MyFileReader()
{
  m_stream = gcnew CustomFileStream();
}
```

It also generates the required clean-up code in the `Dispose(bool)` method. Here's what that'll look like in the generated MSIL (pseudo C++ code):

```
void Dispose(bool bDispose)
{
  if(bDispose) // Destructor
  {
    try
    {
      this->~MyFileReader();
    }
    finally
    {
      delete m_stream;
    }
  }
  //...
}
```

With stack semantics on `ref` types, you get to have all the advantages of an automatic garbage-collected memory management system, as well as enjoy the benefits of the RAII paradigm. Using the RAII model, stack objects follow scoping rules and destructors get called when an object goes out of scope. Note that the compiler doesn't allow you to declare a method for a `ref` class that has the same signature as one of the compiler-generated `Dispose` overloads. You also can't call `Dispose` directly on a `ref` object handle. Instead, you have to either use `delete` or change your code to use stack semantics.

3.1.3 Guidelines for using destructors and stack semantics

Here are some general strategies that you can exercise to get the best out of using stack semantics. Like all suggestions, they depend on your situation and therefore should be used only after you consider your specific coding scenario!

Whenever possible, prefer a destructor to a finalizer. A finalizer is more expensive than a destructor, because the GC always promotes finalizable objects to a higher generation. If they have a pending finalizer, even short-lived objects will be promoted to Gen-1. You also have little control over when the finalizer gets called, unlike with a destructor, which gets invoked deterministically. This can be vital in cases where you have a resource that needs to be deallocated. For instance, imagine a network file stream class that writes some data to a network stream. Now, assume that the clean-up code that flushes the stream and closes the network connection socket is in a finalizer. The network connection has to be kept open until the finalizer gets executed sometime in the unpredictable future. Other applications that may need a network connection are forced to wait if all available connections are in use. Or, even worse, if the connection drops, there is a possibility of data loss, because you haven't flushed the contents of the stream yet. A destructor avoids all such issues.

If your disposable class has a handle member that needs to be disposed, manually delete that member in the destructor. Consider a disposable class that has a member object that doesn't have a default constructor; that member can't be used as an automatic variable. Therefore, you're forced to use a handle to that object as the member. If you don't manually `delete` that member in the destructor, that member will be nondeterministically finalized during a future garbage-collection cycle, and you don't get the performance advantage or the predictability of using stack semantics. The following code snippet demonstrates how you can do that. The class `AutoFile` has a destructor where it manually deletes its `Resource` member, which had to be used as a handle because it didn't have a default constructor:

```
ref class AutoFile
{
  Resource^ m_Res;
public:
  AutoFile()
  {
    m_Res = gcnew Resource(1000); // no default constructor
  }
  ~AutoFile()
  {
    delete m_Res; // manually clean up here
  }
};
```

For classes that have both a destructor and a finalizer, call `!T()` *from* `~T()`. Once a destructor gets executed, because a call is made to `GC::SuppressFinalize`, the object is removed from the Finalization queue and its finalizer is never called. If there is some cleanup code in the finalizer that isn't present in the destructor, this may result in unpredictable behavior. By calling the finalizer from the destructor, you ensure that it's definitely called. You may think you can work around this by putting the clean-up code in the finalizer into the destructor as well, but doing so results in code duplication. This makes changes and updates difficult because they have to be done twice, and in my opinion is best avoided.

3.2 Function overriding

Standard C++ has simple function overriding rules. If a derived class method matches a base class method's name and signature, it implicitly overrides the base class method. For non-`virtual` functions, the rules are the same in C++/CLI. But for `virtual` functions in ref classes, C++/CLI implements a different set of rules not available in standard C++, such as explicit overriding, renamed overriding, and multiple overriding. In this section, you'll see how these new overriding features are implemented; we'll also look at how to declare and use sealed and abstract functions.

3.2.1 Explicit overriding

Virtual functions in derived classes need to explicitly state whether they're overriding the base class method or not. The compiler issues error C4485 if you attempt an implicit override. Two keywords can be applied to a derived class `virtual` function:

- `override` means the function overrides the base class function.
- `new` means this is an entirely new function that hides the base class function.

Consider listing 3.5, which has a base class `Robot` and a derived class `HouseRobot`.

Listing 3.5 Explicit overriding example

```
#define SHOW Console::WriteLine(__FUNCTION__)

ref class Robot
{
public:
    virtual void Greet(){SHOW;}
    virtual void Walk(){SHOW;}
};

ref class HouseRobot : public Robot
{
public:
    virtual void Greet() override {SHOW;}      <-- 1 Override base class method
    virtual void Walk()new {SHOW;}             <-- 2 Hide base class method
};

int main()
{
    Robot^ rob = gcnew HouseRobot();
    rob->Greet();                              <-- 3 Invoke HouseRobot::Greet
    rob->Walk();                               <-- 4 Invoke Robot::Walk
    return 0;
}
```

This code listing has a base class `Robot` with two `virtual` methods, `Greet` and `Walk`, that are also implemented in the derived class, `HouseRobot`. In the derived class, for method Greet ❶, you specify the override modifier, which indicates that this method overrides the base class method of the same name and signature. For method Walk ❷, you specify the new modifier, which means this method doesn't override the base class method; rather, it hides the base class method and treats it as an independent virtual method. Later, when you create a HouseRobot object and assign it to a Robot handle, the call to Greet ❸ will invoke the derived class method because it's an override for the base class method of the same name. However, the call to Walk ❹ invokes the base class method, because the method in the derived class is treated as an independent function (although it has the same name and signature).

In short, all you need to remember is that for virtual methods of ref types, you have to specify override or new if a derived class method has the same name and signature as the base class method. When you specify override, you get behavior that's equivalent to that in Standard C++, whereas when you specify new, the method in the derived class is treated as an independent method that doesn't override the base class method.

3.2.2 Renamed overriding

Renamed (or named) overriding allows you to specify the base class virtual method that is being overridden, even when the base class method name doesn't match the derived class method name. This gives you the flexibility of using appropriate names for derived class methods and at the same time overriding methods in the base class with a different name. Listing 3.6 takes the previous example and modifies it to demonstrate renamed overriding.

Listing 3.6 Renamed overriding example

```
ref class Robot
{
public:
    virtual void Greet(){SHOW;}
    virtual void Walk(){SHOW;}
};

ref class HouseRobot : public Robot
{
public:
    virtual void SayHello() = Robot::Greet {SHOW;}
    virtual void Walk() new {SHOW;}
    virtual void Run() = Robot::Walk {SHOW;}
};
```

❶ SayHello overrides Greet method
❷ Walk: new method in derived class
❸ Run overrides Walk

```
int main()
{
    Robot^ rob = gcnew HouseRobot();
    rob->Greet();                        ◁┘ ❹ Invoke HouseRobot::SayHello
    rob->Walk();    ◁┐ Invoke
    return 0;        ❺ HouseRobot::Run
}
```

The derived class, `HouseRobot`, has methods named `SayHello` ❶, which overrides the `Greet` method in the base class; `Walk` ❷, which is a new method that doesn't override the base class method of the same name; and `Run` ❸, which overrides the `Walk` method in the base class. When you invoke `Greet` ❹ on a `Robot` handle that is a reference to a `HouseRobot` object, `SayHello` from the derived class gets invoked. Similarly, when you invoke `Walk` ❺, `Run` from the derived class gets invoked. It's interesting (and possibly confusing to a first-timer) that the `Walk` method is present in both the base and derived classes, but the override for the base class `Walk` method is the derived class `Run` method. The ability to rename a method override in a derived class gives you a higher level of flexibility when designing complex class hierarchies. Renamed overriding can be extended so that a derived class function can override multiple methods, and that's what we'll look at next.

3.2.3 *Multiple overriding*

Although ref types can't have multiple base classes, they can implement one or more interfaces in addition to having a base class. Sometimes, you may want to have a function in a derived class that overrides both a base class method and an interface method. That's where multiple overriding comes into play. Let's continue with the robot class example and add an interface, `IHumanoid`, into the class hierarchy; see listing 3.7.

Listing 3.7 Multiple overriding example

```
ref class Robot
{
public:
    virtual void Greet(){SHOW;}
};

interface class IHumanoid
{
    virtual void Talk();
};
```

```
ref class HouseRobot : public Robot, public IHumanoid
{
public:
    virtual void SayHello() =
        Robot::Greet, IHumanoid::Talk {SHOW;}
};

int main()
{
    Robot^ rob = gcnew HouseRobot();
    IHumanoid^ hum = safe_cast<IHumanoid^>(rob);
    rob->Greet();
    hum->Talk();
    return 0;
}
```

1 SayHello overrides Greet, implements Talk

2 Invoke HouseRobot::SayHello

3 Invoke HouseRobot::SayHello

The class `HouseRobot` is derived from `Robot`. In addition, it implements the interface `IHumanoid`. `HouseRobot` has a single method `SayHello` ❶, which overrides both `Robot::Greet` and `IHumanoid::Talk` using renamed overriding. Thus, multiple overriding is essentially a kind of renamed overriding, except that more than a single method is overridden. Later, when `Greet` is called on a `Robot` handle holding a `HouseRobot` object ❷, `HouseRobot`'s `SayHello` is invoked. Similarly, when `Talk` is called on an `IHumanoid` handle holding the same `HouseRobot` object ❸, it's again `HouseRobot`'s `SayHello` that is invoked.

3.2.4 Sealed and abstract functions

A `virtual` function marked with the `sealed` modifier can't be overridden in a derived class. Consider the `Robot` class hierarchy example. Assume that a function named `ShutDown` is declared in the base `Robot` class; this function contains fundamental code to switch off a robot. It's important that derived classes don't override this method, because if they're allowed to do that, and a derived class implements this function improperly, it could pose a security risk where a malfunctioning robot couldn't be switched off. That's where it's desirable to mark the `ShutDown` function as sealed, as shown in listing 3.8.

Listing 3.8 Sealed function example

```
ref class Robot
{
public:
    virtual void Greet(){SHOW;}
    virtual void Shutdown() sealed {SHOW;}
};
```

1 Robot::ShutDown: marked sealed

```
ref class HouseRobot : public Robot
{
public:
    virtual void Greet() override {SHOW;}
    virtual void Shutdown() override {SHOW;}    ◁ ❷ Compiler throws error C3764
};
```

Because Robot::Shutdown ❶ is marked as sealed, it can't be overridden in a derived class. Any attempt to do so results in a compiler error ❷. Note that the following code will compile:

```
ref class HouseRobot : public Robot
{
public:
    virtual void Greet() override {SHOW;}
    virtual void Shutdown() new {SHOW;}
};
```

It compiles because here HouseRobot::ShutDown doesn't override the sealed function in the base class; instead, it creates an entirely new function, albeit with the same name. Another modifier that can be applied to a function is abstract. An abstract function is equivalent to a pure virtual function, but using the abstract modifier allows for syntactic uniformity. The following code snippet demonstrates both syntactic forms:

```
ref class Robot abstract
{
public:
    virtual void Greet(){SHOW;}
    virtual void Work1() abstract;    ◁ Workl: abstract method
    virtual void Work2() = 0;    ◁ Work2: also abstract method
};
```

This code snippet uses both syntactic styles for declaring abstract methods. The compiler generates identical MSIL for both styles. Therefore, it's up to you to decide what style to use. I suggest that you use the abstract modifier because it ensures syntactic uniformity with the rest of the function modifier syntaxes. Also note how I marked the class Robot as an abstract class. If I hadn't done this, the compiler would issue warning C4570 (*a class with abstract methods is not explicitly declared to be abstract*). Even if you ignore the warning, the class will be marked as abstract in the generated MSIL. I recommend that you explicitly mark a class as abstract if it contains at least one abstract method.

You may or may not encounter situations where you can apply all those features, but they're directly supported by the CLR, and the C++/CLI compiler supports them too. The good thing is that if you ever need to implement some such functionality or class design, you know that C++/CLI will let you do so.

3.3 Generics and managed templates

Generics (it's treated as a singular word) is a CLI feature introduced in .NET 2.0 that allows you to use parameterized types. If you haven't used templates before, you may not know what a parameterized type is. Put simply, a parameterized type is defined using one or more type parameters that are unknown until the type is first declared or defined. Once you see some sample code later in this and following sections, things will become more apparent. An analogy is to think of device-specific remote controls, such as one for the TV, one for the DVD player, one for your AC, and so on. A generic remote control can work with any of these devices, if you specify which device you want to use it with (this is analogous to the type parameter).

Although similar to C++ templates (which also use parameterized types), generics is directly supported by the CLR. There are some important differences in their behavior, compared to templates. In addition to generics, C++/CLI also supports managed templates, which basically extend the C++ template mechanism to managed types and functions. In this section, we'll discuss both generics and managed templates, and also evaluate their differences. Note that although both C# and VB.NET support generics, C++/CLI is the only language (currently) to support managed templates.

3.3.1 Why have parameterized types?

I'll use the proverbial stack class to explain why you need parameterized types. If you've used templates in the past, you may want to skip to the next section, where I describe the syntax for using CLI generics. Consider the following simple stack class:

```
ref class Stack
{
array<Object^>^ m_StackItems;
public:
    Stack(){...}
    void Push(Object^){...}
    Object^ Pop(){...}
};
```

The class internally uses an `Object` array to store the items, and the `Push` method accepts an `Object^`, whereas the `Pop` method returns an `Object^`. I chose `Object^`

as the type of the stack item so that you can store any CLI type using this class. Assume that for a specific application, you need to create three different stacks: one to store strings, one to store objects of a specific managed type, and one to store numbers. This is what the code looks like:

```
Stack^ stringstack = gcnew Stack();
stringstack->Push("Nish");
String^ s = safe_cast<String^>(numstack->Pop());    ❶ Object^ cast to String^

Stack^ customstack = gcnew Stack();
customstack->Push(gcnew SomeType());
SomeType^ z = safe_cast<SomeType^>(customstack->Pop());    ❷ Object^ cast to SomeType^

Stack^ numstack = gcnew Stack();
numstack->Push(100);    ❸ Int boxed to Object^
int x = *safe_cast<int^>(numstack->Pop());    ❹ Object^ unboxed to int
```

For the string stack and the custom stack, the `Pop` operations ❶ and ❷ require explicit casts to the expected type of the item—`String^` in the case of the string stack, and `SomeType^` in the case of the custom stack. Not only is this pointlessly tiring to write, but the cast requirement means that the CLR must do runtime type-checking on the objects that are being cast, which affects the performance of the code. When you use the stack to store numbers, you'll immediately notice the inefficiency introduced when using the `Push` and `Pop` operations. When you `Push` a number ❸, the `int` has to be boxed to an `Object`; when you `Pop` it back ❹, the `Object` has to be unboxed back to an `int`. Earlier, you saw that both boxing and unboxing are expensive operations that consume precious CPU cycles, thereby affecting code performance. Thus far, this class hasn't been impressive in terms of performance. But that's not all; the class isn't type-safe either. For example, the following code compiles fine:

```
numstack->Push("Smitha");
int y = *safe_cast<int^>(numstack->Pop());
```

You've incorrectly pushed a string to the number stack and then unboxed it back to an `int`. The compiler compiles it fine; as far as it's concerned, the stack stores and retrieves `Object` items. During runtime, the previous code results in a runtime exception. In summary, not only is the stack class inefficient in terms of performance, but it's also deficient in enforcing type safety. If parameterized types were not an option, the only way to get around these drawbacks would be to write three separate stack classes: one for an `int`, one for a `String`, and one for the custom type. For example, you'd have an `IntStack` class for the number stack and a `StringStack` class for the string stack:

```
ref class IntStack
{
array<int>^ m_StackItems;
public:
    IntStack(){...}
    void Push(int){...}
    int Pop(){...}
};

ref class StringStack
{
array<String^>^ m_StackItems;
public:
    StringStack(){}
    void Push(String^){}
    String^ Pop(){return nullptr;}
};
```

Not only would this result in an abominable level of code duplication, but for every new stack type you need, you'd have to write a new class. Clearly, this is the wrong way to approach the problem. That's where parameterized types come into the picture; they solve the performance issues related to superfluous casting, and they also ensure strict type safety. In the next section, you'll see how CLI generics can be used to write a generic stack class that overcomes the drawbacks in the one you wrote in this section.

3.3.2 Generics syntax for classes and functions

If you've used templates before, you'll notice the remarkable similarity in syntax. Be aware that this was intentionally done, to give C++ programmers a natural feel for the generics syntax.

Here's how the generic stack class looks in code, using CLI generics:

```
generic<typename T> ref class Stack     <-1 Class declared as generic
{
    array<T>^ m_StackItems;     <-2 Array's element is parameterized type
public:
    Stack(){...}
    void Push(T){...}     <-3 Push now accepts parameterized type
    T Pop(){...}     <-4 Pop returns parameterized type
};
```

The most interesting thing about this code snippet is the declaration of the class ❶. You use the `generic` keyword to specify that this is a generic class (the syntax is the same as that for a C++ template class, except that the keyword `template` is replaced with the keyword `generic`). You also specify a parameterized type named `T`, using the `typename` keyword. Note that you aren't limited to one parameterized type; you can have as many as you require. The rest of the class uses this parameterized type, instead of the type-unsafe `Object^` used in the previous version of the class. If you look at the array declaration ❷, you'll see that the type of the array is the parameterized type `T`. This type is known only when the generic class is first declared. Similarly, the `Push` method ❸ accepts a `T` object, and the `Pop` method ❹ returns a `T` object. To see this generic class in action, let's use it to declare the `number`, `string`, and custom stacks used in the previous example:

```
Stack<String^>^ stringstack = gcnew Stack<String^>();
stringstack->Push("Howard");
String^ s = stringstack->Pop();

Stack<SomeType^>^ customstack = gcnew Stack<SomeType^>();
customstack->Push(gcnew SomeType());
SomeType^ z = customstack->Pop();

Stack<int>^ numstack = gcnew Stack<int>();
numstack->Push(100);
int x = numstack->Pop();
```

❶ **String ^ as parameterized type**

❷ **Custom as parameterized type**

❸ **Int as parameterized type**

When you declare objects of a generic type, you need to specify the type of the expected parameterized types; in the example, there is only one such parameterized type. You declare a string stack ❶ by specifying `String^` as the parameterized type. The `Push` method now accepts a `String^`, and the `Pop` method returns a `String^`. Thus, there is no casting involved; it's as if you had a stack class where the type of the stack was a `String^`. Similarly, for the custom stack ❷, you specify `SomeType^` as the parameterized type, and thus `Push` accepts a `SomeType^` object while `Pop` returns one. For the number stack ❸, the parameterized type is an `int`. Both `Push` and `Pop` accept and return an `int`, respectively, which means no boxing or unboxing is involved. Figure 3.5 shows a diagrammatic representation of a stack implementation using generics.

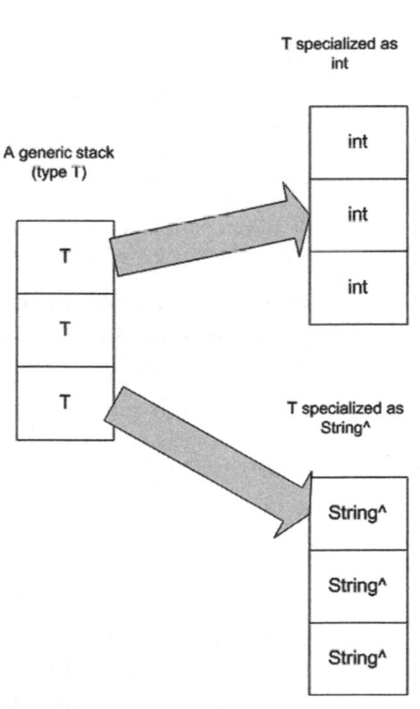

Figure 3.5 A generic stack implementation

Clearly, the generic version of the stack class has improved on performance by avoiding a requirement for casting, boxing, and unboxing of types. That's not all; generic classes also enforce type safety. Consider the following piece of code, which tries to push a string into the number stack and a number into the string stack:

```
stringstack->Push(100);
numstack->Push("Smitha");
```

Both lines of code fail to compile. The parameterized type for the string stack has been specified to be a `String^`, and thus the compiler won't allow you to pass an `int` to the `Push` method. Similarly, for the number stack, `Push` expects an `int`, and thus it won't accept a string. You aren't restricted to generic classes. You can have a nongeneric class with one or more generic functions, and you can also have a global generic function. Here's how you declare a nongeneric class with a generic method:

```
ref class R
{
public:
    void Func(){}
    generic<typename T> void GenericFunc(){}
};
```

The method named `Func` is a normal method, whereas the method named `GenericFunc` is a generic method. The class itself is nongeneric. Here's how you invoke the generic method:

```
R^ r = gcnew R();
r->Func();
r->GenericFunc<float>();      // (1) Type parameter must be specified
r->GenericFunc<char>();
```

When you invoke the generic method (1), you have to specify the generic type parameter. In the previous snippet, the first time you call the function, you specify a `float`; the second time, you specify a `char`. An example of a global generic function that takes two generic parameters follows:

```
generic<typename T1, typename T2>
    void DoSomething(T1 t1, T2 t2)
{...}
```

As you can see, the syntax for global generic functions is the same as that for a generic method of a nongeneric class. You may not find yourself using nongeneric classes with generic methods that often, but if you ever have to, it's good to know that it's possible. Similarly, global generic functions, which aren't portable with other languages like C# or VB.NET, are also something that you won't use frequently; but again, they can be used where required. For example, let's write a generic global method that moves the contents of one generic stack to another:

```
generic<typename STACKTYPE> void MoveStack(
    Stack<STACKTYPE>^ source, Stack<STACKTYPE>^ dest)
{
    STACKTYPE item;
    while(item = source->Pop())
        dest->Push(item);
}
```

Notice how you use the generic-type parameter for the function (`STACKTYPE`) as the generic-type parameter for the two generic `Stack` arguments—`source` and `dest`. The function `MoveStack` now takes two arguments, both of type `Stack<STACKTYPE>`. The compiler strictly enforces this so that if you attempt to pass in a generic stack whose generic type is a different type from `STACKTYPE`, it won't compile. Using this function looks something like this:

```
Stack<String^>^ stringstacknew = gcnew Stack<String^>();
MoveStack<String^>(stringstack, stringstacknew);
```

Although you could make this function a `static` member of the `Stack` class, I chose to use a global function, because the function doesn't use the generic type parameters for the class directly. If it was a static method of the class, you'd have to pass in a meaningless type parameter for the class, which is ignored by the `MoveStack` method. To explain this more clearly, if you wrote it as a static method of the `Stack` class, you'd have to call it this way:

```
Stack<sometype>::MoveStack<String^>(stringstack, stringstacknew);
```

You'd have to pass in a type (any type, it doesn't matter) to the `Stack` class. Because it would be a pointless thing to do, I chose to implement this as a global function.

In short, generic classes and functions improve on performance by allowing you to generically work on a parameterized type (or types) and also to enforce type safety at the compilation level. By default, the compiler assumes that the generic-type parameter is a `System::Object`, which means you can invoke any `System::Object` method or property on the parameterized type argument. Frequently, you'll want to do more than that, which is where the constraint mechanism comes into play.

3.3.3 Constraint mechanism

The constraint mechanism allows you to specify one or more constraints for each generic-type parameter. When an instance of that generic type is created, the generic types that are specified are bound by these constraints. If a generic type that you specify doesn't satisfy the constraints on that generic-type argument, the compiler throws an error. If that sounds a little fuzzy, the following example should make it clear.

Consider a generic DogShow class that lets dogs perform tricks, where the exact type of the dog is specified as a generic-type parameter. All trick dogs are expected to know some common tricks, and these are abstracted in an interface called ITrickDog that is defined as follows:

```
interface class ITrickDog
{
    void Bark();
    void Sit();
    void WagTail();
    void RollOver();
};
```

Now, you're going to write your DogShow class using a generic-type parameter that imposes the constraint that the type of the parameter has to be ITrickDog. See listing 3.9.

Listing 3.9 Generic DogShow class with a constraint

```
generic<typename TDOG> where TDOG:ITrickDog          ❶ Constraint specified using where clause
    ref class DogShow
{
    TDOG m_dog;          ❷ Generic type parameter used as private member
public:
    DogShow()
    {
        m_dog = Activator::CreateInstance<TDOG>();          ❸ Generic type instantiated
    }
    ~DogShow()
    {
        delete m_dog;
    }
    void DoTricks(int count)
    {
        for(int i=0; i<count; i++)
        {
            m_dog->Bark();
            m_dog->Sit();          ❹ ITrickDog methods invoked
            m_dog->WagTail();
            m_dog->RollOver();
        }
    }
};
```

The most interesting part of this code listing is the class declaration ❶, where you use the `where` clause to specify a constraint on the `TDOG` generic-type parameter. This tells the compiler that `TDOG` will be of type `ITrickDog`. During the instantiation of a `DogShow` object, the compiler won't let you pass in a generic parameter that isn't an `ITrickDog` type. The class has a private member `m_dog` ❷ that is of type `TDOG`, the generic-type parameter. In the constructor ❸, you'll notice something a little unusual—the fact that you use `Activator::CreateInstance<T>` to create the object. You have to do that because the C++/CLI compiler won't let you `gcnew` a generic-type parameter. This is so because there is no way the compiler can be sure the generic-type parameter will have a suitable constructor available, because that information isn't known during compilation time. Note that a special constraint called the constructor constraint is available, which is satisfied if the generic-type parameter has a public parameterless constructor. Using that constraint lets you use `gcnew` on a generic-type parameter. Here's how you use the constructor constraint on the previous class:

```
generic<typename TDOG> where TDOG:ITrickDog,gcnew()
    ref class DogShow
```

Notice the use of `gcnew()` in the constraint list following the `where` keyword. You can directly use `gcnew` on the parameter type instead of resorting to `Activator::CreateInstance<T>` to create the object. (*Note that you can't use the* `gcnew` *constraint for nondefault constructors*). Now the `DogShow` constructor can be rewritten as follows:

```
m_dog = gcnew TDOG();
```

Getting back to listing 3.9, in the `DoTricks` method ❹, you'll see that you invoke `ITrickDog` methods on the `m_dog` member variable. The compiler lets you do this because it knows that `m_dog` will be an `ITrickDog` object because of the constraint. If you attempt to instantiate a `DogShow` object using a non-`ITrickDog` generic-type parameter, you get the following compiler error:

```
DogShow<Object^>^ ds = gcnew DogShow<Object^>();
. . .
error C3214: 'System::Object ^' :
    invalid type argument for generic parameter 'TDOG' of
    generic 'DogShow', does not meet constraint 'ITrickDog ^'
```

The proper way to do this is to use a class that implements the `ITrickDog` interface as the generic-type parameter, similar to the following code:

```
ref class MyDog : ITrickDog
{
public:
```

```
        virtual void Bark(){...}
        virtual void Sit(){...}
        virtual void WagTail(){...}
        virtual void RollOver(){...}
    };
    . . .
    DogShow<MyDog^>^ ds = gcnew DogShow<MyDog^>();
    ds->DoTricks(2);
```

Because `MyDog` implements `ITrickDog`, it satisfies the constraints imposed on the `TDOG` generic-type parameter. To put it briefly, by default, the generic-type parameter is as limited as a `ref` type can be and is treated as a `System::Object`. Every constraint you add increases the number of methods or properties that can be applied on the type parameter while at the same time constraining the number of types that can be used as the generic type. In this way, constraints are a powerful means to improve the flexibility of generic types, but you'll run into issues with the generic constraint mechanism when dealing with simple types.

3.3.4 Issues with the constraint mechanism and simple types

When you want to use generics with simple types (like `int` or `float`), the problem is that it's not possible to specify a constraint for them that will allow elementary operations like + and – on the generic-type parameters. Consider the following generic class:

```
generic<typename T> ref class Score
{
    T m_t;
public:
    Score(T t) : m_t(t){}
    void Add(T t)
    {
        m_t += t;      <-- (1) Line won't compile
    }
    . . .
};
```

The addition attempt (1) won't compile because the compiler can't know for sure that the generic-type parameter supports the `+=` operator. There is no way for you to tell the compiler using a constraint that the types are expected to support the `+=` operator.

How do you work around this problem? If .NET supported an interface called `IAddable`, you could use that as the constraint, but .NET doesn't support any such interface. Let's write such an interface:

```
generic<typename T> interface class IAddable
{
    void Add(T);
};
```

It's a generic interface with just a single function named `Add` that has the generic-type parameter as an argument. You can now modify the `Score` class as follows:

```
generic<typename T> where T:IAddable<T> ref class Score
{
    T m_t;
public:
    Score(T t) : m_t(t){}
    void Add(T t)
    {
        m_t->Add(t);
    }
};
```

Notice how you specify an `IAddable<T>` constraint for the generic-type parameter. You also change the call to the `+=` operator in the `Add` method to a call to `IAddable::Add` method. Of course, to use this class you have to use types that implement `IAddable`. For example, assuming you need to use an `int` as the generic-type parameter, you have to wrap this `int` in a `MyInt` `struct` (or `class`) that implements `IAddable`:

```
ref struct MyInt : IAddable<MyInt^>
{
    int m_int;
    virtual void Add(MyInt^ x)
    {
        m_int += x->m_int;
    }
};
```

Now you can use the generic class as follows:

```
MyInt^ myint1 = gcnew MyInt();
myint1->m_int = 99;
MyInt^ myint2 = gcnew MyInt();
myint2->m_int = 88;
Score<MyInt^>^ sc1 = gcnew Score<MyInt^>(myint1);
sc1->Add(myint2);
```

That solution works, but it has its own set of disadvantages. For one, you can't directly use simple types with the generic class because for each simple type, you have to wrap the simple type in a class that implements `IAddable`. In this example, you wrap the `int` type, but you also have to write wrappers for `int`, `float`, `double`, `char`, and any other simple type you intend to use as type parameters.

And that's not all; `IAddable` just specifies the addition interface. You also need to write other interfaces like `ISubtractable`, `IDivisble`, and so on, and then have each of your wrapper classes implement all of these interfaces if you need to support operations other than addition. To go through that much work just to get a generic class working with simple types may not be worth the time and effort.

Let's see how you can improve on this solution. To solve the issue of having to write and implement separate interfaces for each numerical operation on a simple type is easy: You write an interface that encompasses all the commonly done numerical operations. Here's what the interface looks like:

```
generic<typename T> interface class INumericalOperations
{
    T Add( T t1, T t2 );
    T Subtract( T t1, T t2 );
    T Multiply( T t1, T t2 );
    T Divide( T t1, T t2 );
. . .
};
```

I've only shown the most common operations in this code snippet, but you may want to add other operations that are applicable to your scenario. Anyway, you have only one interface to worry about now, so that has solved one problem.

Let's approach the other issue now: the fact that you need to write wrapper classes for every simple type you need to use. To solve that, you can use a variation of the adapter pattern. You have an adapter class that is unimaginatively called `NumericalAdapter`, which has several private classes where each class implements the `INumericalOperations` interface for a specific simple type (like `int` or `float`). There's also a generic `GetNumericalAdapter` method that returns the corresponding `INumericalOperations` object for a specific type. Listing 3.10 shows the partial class listing. (It shows only two of the adapters, one for `int` and one for `float`; the rest of the adapters have to be similarly implemented.)

Listing 3.10 An implementation of the adapter pattern

```
ref class NumericalAdapter
{
private:
    ref class IntNumericalAdapter :
        INumericalOperations<int>
    {
    public:
        virtual int Add( int t1, int t2 )
        { return t1+t2; }
        virtual int Subtract( int t1, int t2 )
```

❶ Type adapter to handle int

```
        { return t1-t2; }
        virtual int Multiply( int t1, int t2 )
        { return t1*t2; }
        virtual int Divide( int t1, int t2 )
        { return t1/t2; }
    };
    ref class FloatNumericalAdapter :
        INumericalOperations<float>
    {
    public:
        virtual float Add( float t1, float t2 )
        { return t1+t2; }
        virtual float Subtract( float t1, float t2 )
        { return t1-t2; }
        virtual float Multiply( float t1, float t2 )
        { return t1*t2; }
        virtual float Divide( float t1, float t2 )
        { return t1/t2; }
    };

    . . . // similar adapters for other types

public:
    generic<typename T> static INumericalOperations<T>^
        GetNumericalAdapter()
    {
        Type^ typ = T::typeid;
        if( typ == int::typeid)
        {
            return dynamic_cast<INumericalOperations<T>^>(
                gcnew IntNumericalAdapter());
        }
        if( typ == float::typeid)
        {
            return dynamic_cast<INumericalOperations<T>^>(
                gcnew FloatNumericalAdapter());
        }

        . . . // check for and return other adapters

        throw gcnew Exception("Unsupported type");
    }
};
```

❶ **Type adapter to handle int**

❷ **Type adapter to handle float**

❸ **Get compile-time type**

❹ **Instantiate and return int adapter**

❺ **Instantiate and return float adapter**

The adapter classes that represent each type (like `int` or `float`) are implemented as private inner classes of the `NumericalAdapter` class. I've only shown the adapters for `int` ❶ and `float` ❷ in the code. Depending on your scenario, you'll want to implement adapters for every simple type that may be required somewhere. In

GetNumericalAdapter, you use the typeid keyword ❸ that returns the compile time type of the type that's passed to it (and it does support generic type parameters, too). Once you have the type of the generic-type parameter, you compare that with the various types you support (the code only shows comparisons for int and float); once a matching type is found ❹ and ❺, you instantiate and return an adapter object for that specific type. Now you can rewrite the Score class as follows:

```
generic<typename T> ref class Score
{
    T m_t;
public:
    Score(T t) : m_t(t){}
    void Add(T t)
    {
      m_t = NumericalAdapter::GetNumericalAdapter<T>()->Add(m_t, t);
    }
};
```

In the Add method, you use the NumericalAdapter class to get an adapter for the specific generic type and call Add on the returned adapter. You can do something similar for any other numerical operation like Subtract or Divide, too. Using the class is also straightforward now, and you can use simple types directly instead of having to implement and use unnecessary wrapper classes:

```
Score<int>^ sc1 = gcnew Score<int>(85);
sc1->Add(90);
```

That's a lot better, isn't it? The caller doesn't need to know about the complexities of the adapter pattern you implemented, and that's what you set out to do. Later in this chapter, when we cover managed templates, you'll see how such a scenario can be more easily handled using managed templates (although they aren't portable to other languages like C# and VB.NET).

3.3.5 Comparison with templates

In this section, you'll see how generics, although syntactically and conceptually similar to C++ templates, differ from templates in various ways. Understanding the differences between generics and templates will help you comprehend some of the limitations encountered when using generics.

The biggest difference between templates and generics is in how they're instantiated. Generics are instantiated at runtime by the CLR, whereas templates are instantiated at compile time by the C++ compiler. A generic type is compiled into MSIL and exists as a part of the generated assembly. Templates, on the other hand, don't exist after the compilation phase, and specialized classes are generated for every template specialization encountered by the compiler. Consider the following code snippet:

```
template<typename T> class X{...};     Template definition
. . .
X<int> x1;        Template
X<char> x2;       specializations
```

In the generated source code, the compiler generates two separate classes, both of which are the same as the template class `X`, but with one major difference: The template-type parameter is replaced by an `int` in one class and by a `char` in the other. Meanwhile, the template class `X` doesn't get compiled into the generated executable (or library); it vanishes. If there are no instantiations of a template class, it's equivalent to that class not being there. Now, consider the following code snippet, which shows equivalent generics-based code:

```
generic<typename T> ref class X{...};
. . .
X<int> x1;
X<char> x2;
```

In the generated MSIL, there is only one class, but it's marked as a generic class. This is possible because generics is an intrinsic CLI feature and is supported at the MSIL level. Earlier in this chapter, you saw how CLI generics supports a constraints feature that lets you apply constraints to the generic-type parameter. With templates, you don't need to explicitly specify a constraint for a template-type parameter; instead, the compiler follows a lazy constraint-enforcement pattern. When I say *lazy*, I mean the compiler validates the methods invoked on an instance of a template type only when it encounters any such instances invoking that method. The following example should clarify this. Notice how you make a call to a function `CopyData` on a variable that is of the template-parameter type (that could be any type). This wouldn't be possible with generics unless you added constraints to the generic parameter type that would allow such a call:

```
template<typename T> class X
{
    T m_t;
public:
    void Func()
    {
        m_t.CopyData();        (1) Compiler permits call to CopyData
    }
};

...
```

```
void F()
{
    X<CData> x1;       ❷ Compiler doesn't validate parameter
    x1.Func();         ❸ Check performed at this point
}
```

When the compiler sees that the template method `Func` ❶ issues a call to a function named `CopyData`, it compiles it without any issues (*in reality, no code is generated until the code calling that method is strictly necessary in the resulting binary*). Later, ❷ the template class is instantiated using a type parameter of `CData`; again, the compiler doesn't check to see if `CData` has a method named `CopyData`. But when the instantiated template `x1` invokes a call to the `Func` method ❸, and within the `Func` method a call is made to `CopyData`, the compiler validates the call and compiles the code only if such a call can legally be made. If `CData` doesn't have a callable entity named `CopyData`, the compiler throws an error. This mechanism, where a constraint check on the template calls is left until the last possible moment, is why it's called a lazy constraint pattern. Templates don't have the problem with simple types that generics have, where you saw how to work around the problem of using operators like `+=` on a generic-parameter type. With a template, you can do something like the following:

```
template<typename T> T Add(T t1, T t2)
{
    return t1 + t2;
}
```

Because the compiler validates template instantiations only when they occur, the previous code easily compiles. Of course, if you attempt to instantiate a template using a type parameter that doesn't support the `+` operator, the compiler throws an error. Templates can do this because they're implemented at compilation time and the compiler is able to perform the validation at that time. With generics, the CLR instantiates them at runtime; at that time, if a mismatching type parameter is encountered, the runtime would throw an exception and halt execution, which wouldn't be a good thing. Thus, with generics, it's imperative that constraints are specified so the compiler knows for sure that the code will work fine when the CLR eventually instantiates a generic-type instance.

The differences between templates and generics don't stop there. Templates allow nontype parameters, which isn't supported by generics. For example, you can do this with templates:

```
template<typename T, int x = 0> class A{...};
```

In this code snippet, the parameter `x` is an `int` and not a type. You'll see more on this in the next section, when we discuss managed templates. For now, be aware that you can't use nontype parameters with a generic class or function.

Another feature supported by templates is user-defined specialization. Again, this isn't available with CLI generics. This feature allows you to define specialized classes or functions that handle specific types. The following code snippet shows such an example:

```
template<typename T> class A{...};
template<> class A<int>{...};
```

The first line is the primary template definition, and the second line is a user-defined specialization for `int`. This is used whenever `int` is specified as the template-type parameter. Generics doesn't support this feature. We'll discuss this a bit more when we cover managed templates in the next section.

One last difference I want to talk about is the support for *mix-in classes*. A simple definition for a mix-in class is a template class that is derived from a type parameter. You'll see an example of such a class in the next section, but the following code snippet shows what a mix-in declaration looks like:

```
template<typename T> class A : public T {};
```

In this snippet, the template class `A`, when instantiated, is a child of the specified type parameter. You can't do that with generic classes. At this point, you may wonder why we even have generics when templates seem a lot more powerful and functional. The answer is that templates are a C++ compiler feature and don't work across CLI languages because none of the other languages support it. Generics is an intrinsic CLI feature, and your generic classes and libraries can be consumed by any CLI language that supports generics. In the next section, you'll see how to mix generics and templates so that you can use templates and at the same time expose a generic interface for other CLI languages. Another advantage of using generics over templates is that your generic classes are compiled into MSIL assemblies as generic types (because MSIL supports generic types) and can thus be accessed across assemblies. Templates exist only within the assembly where they're used; to use a template, you need access to the source code definition for that template. Table 3.3 lists these differences.

They both have their uses and their proponents. My personal feeling is that, as C++ developers programming for the .NET framework, it's great that you can utilize both these methods. Whenever I want my classes to be accessible to other CLI languages, I use generics or a mixture of templates and generics, with the

Table 3.3 A quick comparison of generics and templates

Generics	Templates
Instantiated at runtime by the CLR	Instantiated during compilation by the C++ compiler
Uses the type constraint mechanism to resolve calls on type parameters	Use lazy constraint evaluation on types at the point of instantiation and/or invocation of calls on the parameters
Doesn't support nontype parameters	Support both type and nontype parameters
Doesn't support user-defined specialization	Support user-defined specialization for classes and functions
Can't derive from generic parameter types	Can derive from template parameter types
Is a cross-language feature	Are a C++ only feature
Supports cross-assembly access	Can be used only via source code access and are visible only within the assembly where they're used

public generic interface wrapping the internal template implementation. But if I'm writing a C++-only application or library, I may prefer templates for the additional flexibility and power they offer. Eventually, it's all about using the right tool for the job. After seeing how templates offer a lot of functionality that's not available in generics, it must be a huge relief to know that C++/CLI supports templates for managed types. You can call them managed templates, which is what we'll discuss in the next section.

3.3.6 Managed templates

In addition to CLI generics, C++/CLI supports templates for CLI types such as ref classes, value classes, and CLI interface classes. These managed templates follow the same rules and syntax as native templates. Unlike generics, managed templates are resolved at compile time and reside exclusively in the generated assembly, which means you can't access them from outside the assembly. Declaring a managed template is exactly the same as declaring a native template. If you rewrote your stack class using a template, it would look like this:

```
template<typename T> ref class TStack
{
    array<T>^ m_StackItems;
public:
    TStack(){}
    void Push(T){}
    T Pop(){...}
};
```

The only thing that differentiates the template declaration from a native template declaration is that the class is a ref type and contains managed members. Interestingly, the only difference from the generic version of the class you wrote earlier is the keyword `template`, which has replaced the keyword `generic`. As you saw in the previous section, templates support several features not available in generics, such as user-defined specialization.

Template specialization

Managed templates support user-defined specializations. For example, in the stack class, assume that you need to treat `System::String` stacks differently from stacks of other types. To do that, you write a specialization for `System::String` as shown in the following code:

```
template<typename T> ref class TStack
{
    array<T>^ m_StackItems;
public:
    TStack(){}
    void Push(T){}
    T Pop(){...}
};

template<> ref class TStack<String^>
{
    array<String^>^ m_StackItems;
public:
    TStack(){}
    void Push(String^){}
    String^ Pop(){...}
};
. . .
TStack<char>^ charstk;
TStack<String^>^ strstk;
```

Primary template class (annotates the first class)
Specialization for String ^ (annotates the second class)
Use primary template (annotates `TStack<char>^ charstk;`)
Use specialization for String ^ (annotates `TStack<String^>^ strstk;`)

The declaration of the specialization is similar to the primary template except that there is no `typename` clause and, instead, the class directly uses `String^` as the element type of the stack. This is useful where you need the template class to behave differently for certain types. The flexibility provided by user-defined specializations allows you to choose different implementations for different template-type arguments. For example, for the previous string stack, you may want to set a maximum length on the strings that can be pushed onto the stack. This is where the specialization comes into play. As another example, if you have a template class that's used as part of a math library, you can have different algorithms for integers and floating-point numbers. Another template feature not available in generics is the use of nontype parameters.

Nontype parameters

Nontype parameters give you increased flexibility when using templates. Let's take the stack class and add an `int` parameter to it that specifies the initial size of the internal array that stores the stack elements:

```
template<typename T, int size = 10> ref class TStack
{
    array<T>^ m_StackItems;
public:
    TStack() : m_StackItems(gcnew array<T>(size)){}
    void Push(T){}
    T Pop(){...}
};
```

You have a parameter named `size`, which is an `int` (nontype) parameter with a default value of 10. Setting the default value allows you to use the class without having to explicitly specify the initial size of the array. Here's how you can use the class now:

```
TStack<char>^ charstk1;
TStack<char, 25>^ charstk2;
```

For the first instantiation, the parameter `size` is taken as 10 (the default value you specified in the template declaration), whereas for the second instantiation, the parameter `size` is 25 (which you explicitly specify).

Support for mix-ins

A template class can be inherited from a type parameter; this supports a programming model called *mix-ins*. A full discussion of mix-in-based programming is beyond the scope of this book, but for those of you who haven't encountered the model before, here's a simple template-based mix-in class that gives a sequence number to every object that's instantiated:

```
int g_sequence = 0;

template<typename T> ref class Sequence : public T
{
    int m_sequenceid;
public:
    Sequence()
    {
        m_sequenceid = g_sequence++;
    }
    property int SequenceID
    {
        int get()
        {
```

```
            return m_sequenceid;
        }
    }
};
```

This class uses a global variable (`g_sequence`) as a sequence counter, and a sequence identifier is associated with every instance of this mix-in class. A read-only property named `SequenceID` is also defined that returns the sequence identifier of an instance. Using this class looks something like the following code snippet:

```
Sequence<RefType> obj1;
Sequence<Object> obj2;
Sequence<Exception> obj3;
. . .
Console::WriteLine(obj1.SequenceID); //0
Console::WriteLine(obj2.SequenceID); //1
Console::WriteLine(obj3.SequenceID); //2
```

You declare three objects, all of them of different types, using the mix-in template; later you print out the sequence identifiers. The big advantage is that you can take a number of unrelated classes and add a common set of functionalities to all of them through the mix-in. Of course, this is a simple example. In the real world, mix-ins are often used for far more useful and complex situations. Having seen how templates can derive from template-type parameters, it may interest you to know that templates can derive from a generic type, too.

Mixing templates and generics

Templates are much more flexible than generics. But templates can't be used outside their containing assembly, which makes it impossible to expose templates from a library. However, there is a way to work around this problem. Templates can inherit from generic types. Taking advantage of this, you can implement and expose a set of generic interfaces from a library, where the library has templates that implement these generic interfaces. You can then provide an adapter class that instantiates specific templates and returns them through the publicly exposed interface. Let's do that with the stack class. The first thing you need to do is to define the generic interface:

```
generic<typename T> public interface class IStack
{
public:
    void Push(T);
    T Pop();
};
```

The `IStack` generic interface is the public interface for the library. Once you implement the generic interface, the next step is to write the templates that implement these interfaces:

```
template<typename T> ref class TStack : IStack<T>
{
    array<T>^ elements;
public:
    virtual void Push(T t)
    {...}
    virtual T Pop()
    {...}
};
```

Note that, although I've only shown the primary template, an actual implementation often involves user-defined template specializations. Now you need to write an adapter class that returns a generic interface back to the caller from whom you must hide the template details. You use the same technique you used earlier to implement a generic class that supports numerical operations on its type parameters:

```
public ref class Factory
{
public:
    generic<typename T> static IStack<T>^ GetGStack()
    {
        if(T::typeid == int::typeid)
        {
            return (IStack<T>^) gcnew TStack<int>();
        }
        if(T::typeid == String::typeid)
        {
            return (IStack<T>^) gcnew TStack<String^>();
        }
        . . .
        throw gcnew Exception("Unknown type");
    }
};
```

Based on the requested type of the generic parameter, you return specialized template objects that are optimal for the required type. The code snippet shows only two cases, for `int` and `String`, but an actual adapter (or factory) class would have multiple cases. The caller now uses this `Factory` class to request the generic object they want and uses it as if it was a generic type. The caller need not support templates, which means your library can now be used from other languages like C# and VB.NET that don't support templates. Here's some C# code that shows how to use the factory class:

```
static void Main(string[] args)
{
    IStack<string> strstack = Factory.GetGStack<string>();
    strstack.Push("apples");
    strstack.Push("oranges");
}
```

This technique of using specialized templates for internal implementation and then exposing them through generic interfaces outside the assembly has been extensively used in the design of the STL.NET library that's currently being developed by Microsoft.

3.4 Summary

We've come to the end of our coverage of basic C++/CLI concepts. In this and the two previous chapters, we've discussed the new syntactic and conceptual features that have been introduced with C++/CLI so that it can be used to target the .NET Framework. In this chapter, you learned some of the more advanced CLI concepts supported by C++/CLI, such as stack semantics, function overriding, CLI generics, and managed templates. At this point, you should be able to write managed applications and take full advantage of the .NET Framework class library. Armed with this knowledge, you can move into the next level, which is to mix managed and native code to write applications that leverage both native and managed libraries. In the next chapter, we'll introduce mixed-mode programming and explore such concepts as CLI pointers, mixed types, interop mechanisms, and converting between delegates and function pointers.

Part 2

Mixing managed and native code

Part 2 consists of two chapters that introduce the concept of mixed-mode programming and how native code can be consumed from managed applications. This part bridges the first part of the book with the third part. Chapter 4 covers CLI pointers, interop mechanisms, mixed types, and converting function pointers to delegates. Chapter 5 explores type conversions, double thunking, writing a CLI wrapper for a native API, wrapping an MFC extension DLL, writing a custom CCW, and how a single mixed-mode DLL can be consumed by both managed and native callers.

4 Introduction to mixed-mode programming

In the previous three chapters of this book, we've gone through the syntax and semantics of the C++/CLI language. It's now time to step it up a gear and move into the world of *mixed-mode programming*.

When I say mixed-mode programming, I mean mixing managed and native code in the same assembly. You can't do that with any other CLI language, because except for C++/CLI, every other CLI compiler only understands managed code. Because C++ is intrinsically an unmanaged programming language, mixing managed and native code is absolutely within its capabilities. Of course, things don't work the same way in managed code as they do in native code. The types are different; memory allocation is manual in one and automatic in the other; the API is different; and so on. When you mix the two, you need to be able to accommodate the use of managed and native types together, to convert between types, and to smoothly interop between the managed and native code.

I'm going to show you the basic techniques that you can apply in your mixed-mode programming projects. By the end of this chapter, you'll be pretty comfortable with mixed-mode programming concepts. We'll begin with a look at the concept of CLI pointers and discuss both pinning pointers and interior pointers. We'll also discuss how they can be used to perform typical pointer operations. CLI pointers are frequently required when you're doing mixed-mode programming, especially when you're utilizing native APIs that accept pointer arguments. Thus it's important to understand how they work and how they can be used to interop between native and managed code.

We'll also briefly look at the various interop mechanisms available for mixing managed and native code, such as COM Callable Wrappers (CCW), P/Invoke, and C++ interop. Although we'll be exclusively using C++ interop in this book, it's important to be aware of the other mechanisms available and their pros and cons when compared with C++ interop.

We'll also examine how mixed types can be implemented using C++/CLI; in the course of the discussion, you'll learn how to develop a managed smart pointer class that will handle automatic resource deallocation for a native resource when used in a managed class. Mixed types will be a prominent feature in your mixed-mode programming adventures; thus, a good understanding of how to use them will be extremely beneficial to you.

We'll round off the chapter with a discussion of how to convert between CLI delegates and unmanaged function pointers using two new methods added in .NET 2.0 to the `Marshal` class. This knowledge will be useful to you when wrapping native API that uses unmanaged function pointers as callbacks.

4.1 Using interior and pinning pointers

You can't use native pointers with CLI objects on the managed heap. That is like trying to write Hindi text using the English alphabet—they're two different languages with entirely different alphabets. Native pointers are essentially variables that hold memory address locations. They point to a memory location rather than to a specific object. When we say a pointer points to an object, we essentially mean that a specific object is at that particular memory location.

This approach won't work with CLI objects because managed objects in the CLR heap don't remain at the same location for the entire period of their lifetime. Figure 4.1 shows a diagrammatic view of this problem. The Garbage Collector (GC) moves objects around during garbage-collection and heap-compaction cycles. A native pointer that points to a CLI object becomes garbage once the object has been relocated. By then, it's pointing to random memory. If an attempt is made to write to that memory, and that memory is now used by some other object, you end up corrupting the heap and possibly crashing your application.

C++/CLI provides two kinds of pointers that work around this problem. The first kind is called an *interior pointer*, which is updated by the runtime to reflect the new location of the object that's pointed to every time the object is relocated. The physical address pointed to by the interior pointer never remains the same, but it always points to the same object. The other kind is called a *pinning pointer*, which prevents the GC from relocating the object; in other words, it pins the object to a specific physical location in the CLR heap. With some restrictions, conversions are possible between interior, pinning, and native pointers.

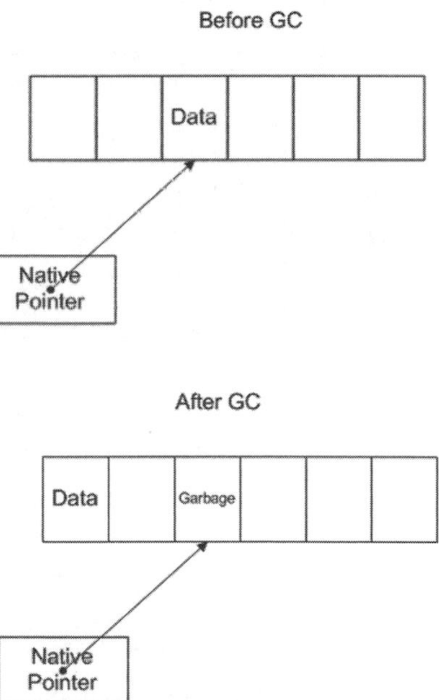

Figure 4.1 Problem using a native pointer with a managed object

Pointers by nature aren't safe, because they allow you to directly manipulate memory. For that reason, using pointers affects the type-safety and verifiability of your code. I strongly urge you to refrain from using CLI pointers in pure-managed applications (those compiled with `/clr:safe` or `/clr:pure`) and to use them strictly to make interop calls more convenient.

4.1.1 Interior pointers

An *interior pointer* is a pointer to a managed object or a member of a managed object that is updated automatically to accommodate for garbage-collection cycles that may result in the pointed-to object being relocated on the CLR heap. You may wonder how that's different from a managed handle or a tracking reference; the difference is that the interior pointer exhibits pointer semantics, and you can perform pointer operations such as pointer arithmetic on it. Although this isn't an exact analogy, think of it like a cell phone. People can call you on your cell phone (which is analogous to an interior pointer) wherever you are, because your number goes with you—the mobile network is constantly updated so that your location is always known. They wouldn't be able to do that with a landline (which is analogous to a native pointer), because a landline's physical location is fixed.

Interior pointer declarations use the same template-like syntax that is used for CLI arrays, as shown here:

```
interior_ptr< type > var = [address];
```

Listing 4.1 shows how an interior pointer gets updated when the object it points to is relocated.

Listing 4.1 Code that shows how an interior pointer is updated by the CLR

```
ref struct CData
{
   int age;
};

int main()
{
   for(int i=0; i<100000; i++)     <-1
      gcnew CData();

   CData^ d = gcnew CData();
   d->age = 100;

   interior_ptr<int> pint = &d->age;     <-2

printf("%p %d\r\n",pint,*pint);

   for(int i=0; i<100000; i++)     <-3
      gcnew CData();

   printf("%p %d\r\n",pint,*pint);     <-4
return 0;
}
```

In the sample code, you create 100,000 orphan `CData` objects ❶ so that you can fill up a good portion of the CLR heap. You then create a `CData` object that's stored in a variable and ❷ an interior pointer to the `int` member `age` of this `CData` object. You then print out the pointer address as well as the `int` value that is pointed to. Now, ❸ you create another 100,000 orphan `CData` objects; somewhere along the line, a garbage-collection cycle occurs (the orphan objects created earlier ❶ get collected because they aren't referenced anywhere). Note that you don't use a `GC::Collect` call because that's not guaranteed to force a garbage-collection cycle. As you've already seen in the discussion of the garbage-collection algorithm in the previous chapter, the GC frees up space by removing the orphan objects so that it can do further allocations. At the end of the code (by which time a garbage collection has occurred), you again ❹ print out the pointer address and the value of `age`. This is the output I got on my machine (note that the addresses will vary from machine to machine, so your output values won't be the same):

```
012CB4C8 100
012A13D0 100
```

As you can see, the address pointed to by the interior pointer has changed. Had this been a native pointer, it would have continued to point to the old address, which may now belong to some other data variable or may contain random data. Thus, using a native pointer to point to a managed object is a disastrous thing to attempt. The compiler won't let you do that: You can't assign the address of a CLI object to a native pointer, and you also can't convert from an interior pointer to a native pointer.

Passing by reference

Assume that you need to write a function that accepts an integer (by reference) and changes that integer using some predefined rule. Here's what such a function looks like when you use an interior pointer as the pass-by-reference argument:

```
void ChangeNumber(interior_ptr<int> num, int constant)
{
    *num += constant * *num;
}
```

And here's how you call the function:

```
CData^ d = gcnew CData();
d->age = 7;
interior_ptr<int> pint = &d->age;
ChangeNumber(pint, 3);
Console::WriteLine(d->age); // outputs 28
```

Because you pass an interior pointer, the original variable (the `age` member of the `CData` object) gets changed. Of course, for this specific scenario, you may as well have used a tracking reference as the first argument of the `ChangeNumber` function; but one advantage of using an interior pointer is that you can also pass a native pointer to the function, because a native pointer implicitly converts to an interior pointer (although the reverse isn't allowed). The following code work:

```
int number = 8;
ChangeNumber(&number, 3);          // 1 Pass native pointer to function
Console::WriteLine(number); // outputs 32
```

It's imperative that you remember this. You can pass a native pointer to function that expects an interior pointer as you do here ❶, because there is an implicit conversion from the interior pointer to the native pointer. But you can't pass an interior pointer to a native pointer; if you try that, you'll get a compiler error. Because native pointers convert to interior pointers, you should be aware that an interior pointer need not necessarily always point to the CLR heap: If it contains a converted native pointer, it's then pointing to the native C++ heap. Next, you'll see how interior pointers can be used in pointer arithmetic (something that can't be done with a tracking reference).

Pointer arithmetic

Interior pointers (like native pointers) support pointer arithmetic; thus, you may want to optimize a performance-sensitive piece of code by using direct pointer arithmetic on some data. Here's an example of a function that uses pointer arithmetic on an interior pointer to quickly sum the contents of an array of `int`s:

```
int SumArray(array<int>^% intarr)
{
    int sum = 0;
    interior_ptr<int> p = &intarr[0];          // 1 Get interior pointer to array
    while(p != &intarr[0]+ intarr->Length)     // 2 Iterate through array
        sum += *p++;
    return sum;
}
```

In this code, `p` is an interior pointer to the array ❶ (the address of the first element of the array is also the address of the array). You don't need to worry about the GC relocating the array in the CLR heap. You iterate through the array by using the `++` operator on the interior pointer ❷, and you add each element to the variable `sum` as you do so. This way, you avoid the overhead of going through the `System::Array` interface to access each array element.

It's not just arrays that can be manipulated using an interior pointer. Here's another example of using an interior pointer to manipulate the contents of a `System::String` object:

```
String^ str = "Nish wrote this book for Manning Publishing";
interior_ptr<Char> ptxt = const_cast< interior_ptr<Char> >(
    PtrToStringChars(str));            ❶
interior_ptr<Char> ptxtorig = ptxt;    ❷
while((*ptxt++)++);                    ❸
Console::WriteLine(str);               ❹
while((*ptxtorig++)--);                ❺
Console::WriteLine(str);               ❻
```

You use the `PtrToStringChars` helper function ❶ to get an interior pointer to the underlying string buffer of a `System::String` object. The `PtrToStringChars` function is a helper function declared in `<vcclr.h>` that returns a `const` interior pointer to the first character of a `System::String`. Because it returns a `const` interior pointer, you have to use `const_cast` to convert it to a non-`const` pointer. You go through the string using a `while`-loop ❸ that increments the pointer as well as each character until a `nullptr` is encountered, because the underlying buffer of a `String` object is always `nullptr`-terminated. Next, when you use `Console::WriteLine` on the `String` object ❹, you can see that the string has changed to

```
Ojti!xspuf!uijt!cppl!gps!Nboojoh!Qvcmjtijoh
```

You've achieved encryption! (Just kidding.) Because you saved the original pointer in `ptxtorig` ❷, you can use it to convert the string back to its original form using another `while` loop. The second `while` loop ❺ increments the pointer but decrements each character until it reaches the end of the string (determined by the `nullptr`). Now, ❻ when you do a `Console::WriteLine`, you get the original string:

```
Nish wrote this book for Manning Publishing
```

Whenever you use an interior pointer, it's represented as a managed pointer in the generated MSIL. To distinguish it from a reference (which is also represented as a managed pointer in IL), a `modopt` of type `IsExplicitlyDereferenced` is emitted by the compiler. A `modopt` is an optional modifier that can be applied to a type's signature. Another interesting point in connection with interior pointers is that the `this` pointer of an instance of a value type is a non-`const` interior pointer to the type. Look at the value class shown here, which obtains an interior pointer to the class by assigning it to the `this` pointer:

```
value class V
{
```

```
    void Func()
    {
        interior_ptr<V> pV1 = this;
        //V* pV2 = this; <-- this won't compile
    }
};
```

As is obvious, in a value class, if you need to get a pointer to `this`, you should use an interior pointer, because the compiler won't allow you to use a native pointer. If you specifically need a native pointer to a value object that's on the managed heap, you have to pin the object using a pinning pointer and then assign it to the native pointer. We haven't discussed pinning pointers yet, but that's what we'll talk about in the next section.

A dangerous side-effect of using interior pointers to manipulate String objects

The CLR performs something called *string interning* on managed strings, so that multiple variables or literal occurrences of the same textual string always refer to a single instance of the `System::String` object. This is possible because `System::String` is immutable—the moment you change one of those variables, you change the reference, which now refers to a new `String` object (quite possibly another interned string). All this is fine as long as the strings are immutable. But when you use an interior or pinning pointer to directly access and change the underlying character array, you break the immutability of `String` objects. Here's some code that demonstrates what can go wrong:

```
String^ s1 = "Nishant Sivakumar";
String^ s2 = "Nishant Sivakumar";

interior_ptr<Char> p1 = const_cast<interior_ptr<Char> >(
    PtrToStringChars(s1)); // Get a pointer to s1
while(*p1) // Change s1 through pointer p1
    (*p1++) = 'X';

Console::WriteLine("s1 = {0}\r\ns2 = {1}",s1,s2);
```

The output of is as follows:

```
s1 = XXXXXXXXXXXXXXXXX
s2 = XXXXXXXXXXXXXXXXX
```

You only changed one string, but both strings are changed. If you don't understand what's happening, this can be incredibly puzzling. You have two `String` handle variables, `s1` and `s2`, both containing the same string literal. You get an interior pointer `p1` to the string `s1` and change each character in `s1` to *X* (basically blanking out the string with the character *X*). Common logic would say that you have changed the string `s1`, and that's that. But because of string interning, `s1` and `s2` were both handles to the same `String` object on the CLR heap. When you change the underlying buffer of the string `s1` through the interior pointer, you change the interned string. This means any string handle to that `String` object now points to an entirely different string (the *X*-string in this case). The output of the `Console::WriteLine` should now make sense to you.

In this case, figuring out the problem was easy, because both string handles were in the same block of code, but the CLR performs string interning across application domains. This means changing an interned string can result in extremely hard-to-debug errors in totally disconnected parts of your application. My recommendation is to try to avoid directly changing a string through a pointer, except when you're sure you won't cause havoc in other parts of the code. Note that it's safe to read a string through a pointer; it's only dangerous when you change it, because you break the "strings are immutable" rule of the CLR. Alternatively, you can use the `String::IsInterned` function to determine if a specific string is interned, and change it only if it isn't an interned string.

4.1.2 Pinning pointers

As we discussed in the previous section, the GC moves CLI objects around the CLR heap during garbage-collection cycles and during heap-compaction operations. Native pointers don't work with CLI objects, for reasons previously mentioned. This is why we have interior pointers, which are self-adjusting pointers that update themselves to always refer to the same object, irrespective of where the object is located in the CLR heap. Although this is convenient when you need pointer access to CLI objects, it only works from managed code. If you need to pass a pointer to a CLI object to a native function (which runs outside the CLR), you can't pass an interior pointer, because the native function doesn't know what an interior pointer is, and an interior pointer can't convert to a native pointer. That's where pinning pointers come into play.

A pinning pointer pins a CLI object on the CLR heap; as long as the pinning pointer is *alive* (meaning it hasn't gone out of scope), the object remains pinned. The GC knows about pinned objects and won't relocate pinned objects. To continue the phone analogy, imagine a pinned pointer as being similar to your being forced to remain stationary (analogous to being pinned). Although you have a cell phone, your location is fixed; it's almost as if you had a fixed landline.

Because pinned objects don't move around, it's legal to convert a pinned pointer to a native pointer that can be passed to the native caller that's running outside the control of the CLR. The word *pinning* or *pinned* is a good choice; try to visualize an object that's pinned to a memory address, just like you pin a sticky note to your cubicle's side-board.

The syntax used for a pinning pointer is similar to that used for an interior pointer:

```
pin_ptr< type > var = [address];
```

The duration of pinning is the lifetime of the pinning pointer. As long as the pinning pointer is in scope and pointing to an object, that object remains pinned. If the pinning pointer is set to `nullptr`, then the object isn't pinned any longer; or if the pinning pointer is set to another object, the new object becomes pinned and the previous object isn't pinned any more.

Listing 4.2 demonstrates the difference between interior and pinning pointers. To simulate a real-world scenario within a short code snippet, I uses `for` loops to create a large number of objects to bring the GC into play.

Listing 4.2 Code that compares an interior pointer with a pinning pointer

```
for(int i=0; i<100000; i++)              Fill portion
   gcnew CData();                        of CLR heap

CData^ d1 = gcnew CData();
for(int i=0; i<1000; i++)                (1)
   gcnew CData();
CData^ d2 = gcnew CData();

interior_ptr<int> intptr = &d1->age;     <-(2)
pin_ptr<int> pinptr = &d2->age;          <-(3)

printf("intptr=%p pinptr=%p\r\n",        <- Display pointer
   intptr,pinptr);                          addresses before GC

for(int i=0; i<100000; i++)              (4)
   gcnew CData();

printf("intptr=%p pinptr=%p\r\n",        <- Display pointer
   intptr,pinptr);                          addresses after GC
```

In the code, you create two `CData` objects with a gap in between them (1) and associate one of them with an interior pointer to the `age` member of the first object (2).

The other is associated with a pinning pointer to the `age` member of the second object ❸. By creating a large number of orphan objects, you force a garbage-collection cycle ❹ (again, note that calling `GC::Collect` may not always force a garbage-collection cycle; you need to fill up a generation before a garbage-collection cycle will occur). The output I got was

```
intptr=012CB4C8 pinptr=012CE3B4
intptr=012A13D0 pinptr=012CE3B4
```

Your pointer addresses will be different, but after the garbage-collection cycle, you'll find that the address held by the pinned pointer (`pinptr`) has not changed, although the interior pointer (`intptr`) has changed. This is because the CLR and the GC see that the object is pinned and leave it alone (meaning it doesn't get relocated on the CLR heap). This is why you can pass a pinned pointer to native code (because you know that it won't be moved around).

Passing to native code

The fact that a pinning pointer always points to the same object (because the object is in a pinned state) allows the compiler to provide an implicit conversion from a pinning pointer to a native pointer. Thus, you can pass a pinning pointer to any native function that expects a native pointer, provided the pointers are of the same type. Obviously, you can't pass a pinning pointer to a `float` to a function expecting a native pointer to a `char`. Look at the following native function that accepts a `wchar_t*` and returns the number of vowels in the string pointed to by the `wchar_t*`:

```
#pragma unmanaged
int NativeCountVowels(wchar_t* pString)
{
   int count = 0;
   const wchar_t* vowarr = L"aeiouAEIOU";
   while(*pString)
      if(wcschr(vowarr,*pString++))
         count++;
   return count;
}
#pragma managed
```

Here's how you pass a pointer to a CLI object, after first pinning it, to the native function just defined:

```
String^ s = "Most people don't know that the CLR is written in C++";
pin_ptr<Char> p = const_cast< interior_ptr<Char> >(
   PtrToStringChars(s));
Console::WriteLine(NativeCountVowels(p));
```

> **#pragma managed/unmanaged**
>
> These are `#pragma` compiler directives that give you function-level control for compiling functions as managed or unmanaged. If you specify that a function is to be compiled as unmanaged, native code is generated, and the code is executed outside the CLR. If you specify a function as managed (which is the default), MSIL is generated, and the code executes within the CLR. Note that if you have an unmanaged function that you've marked as unmanaged, you should remember to re-enable managed compilation at the end of the function

`PtrToStringChars` returns a `const` interior pointer, which you cast to a non-`const` interior pointer; this is implicitly converted to a pinning pointer. You pass this pinning pointer, which implicitly converts to a native pointer, to the `NativeCountVowels` function. The ability to pass a pinning pointer to a function that expects a native pointer is extremely handy in mixed-mode programming, because it gives you an easy mechanism to pass pointers to objects on the CLR heap to native functions. Figure 4.2 illustrates the various pointer conversions that are available.

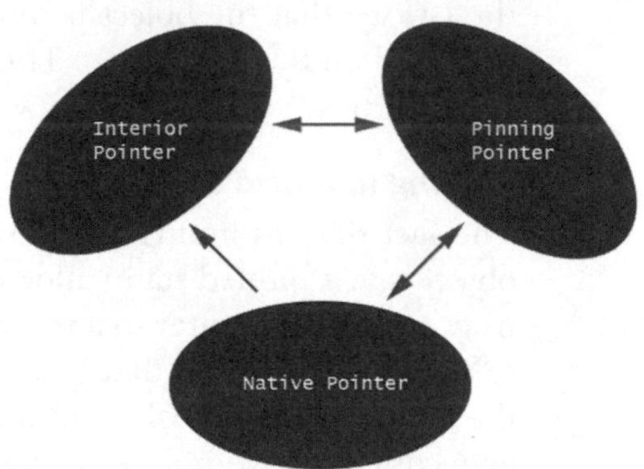

Figure 4.2 Pointer conversions between native, interior, and pinning pointers

As you can see in the figure, the only pointer conversion that is illegal is that from an interior pointer to a native pointer; every other conversion is allowed and implicitly done. You have seen how pinning pointers make it convenient for you to pass pointers to CLI objects to unmanaged code. I now have to warn you that pinning pointers should be used only when they're necessary, because tactless usage of pinning pointers results in what is called the *heap fragmentation problem*.

The heap fragmentation problem

Objects are always allocated sequentially in the CLR heap. Whenever a garbage collection occurs, orphan objects are removed, and the heap is compacted so it won't remain in a fragmented condition. (We covered this in the previous chapter when we discussed the multigenerational garbage-collection algorithm used by the CLR.) Let's assume that memory is allocated from a simple heap that looks like figures 4.3 through 4.6. Of course, this is a simplistic representation of the CLR's GC-based memory model, which involves a more complex algorithm. But the basic principle behind the heap fragmentation issue remains the same, and thus this simpler model will suffice for the present discussion. Figure 4.3 depicts the status of the heap before a garbage-collection cycle occurs.

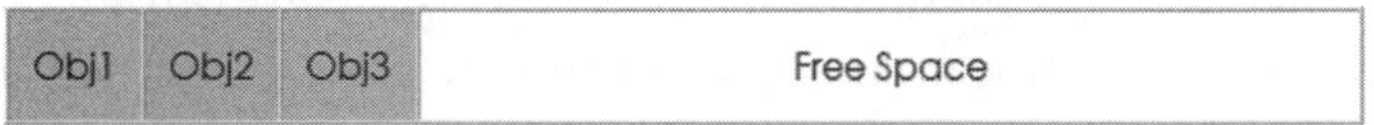

Figure 4.3 Before a garbage-collection cycle

There are presently three objects in the heap. Assume that `Obj2` (with the gray shaded background) is an orphan object, which means it will be cleaned up during the next garbage-collection cycle. Figure 4.4 shows what the heap looks like after the garbage-collection cycle.

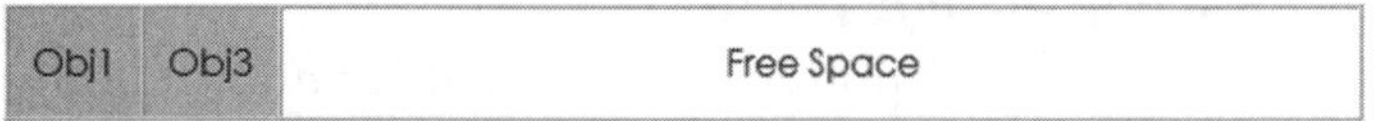

Figure 4.4 After a garbage-collection cycle (assuming no pinned objects)

The orphan object has been removed and a heap compaction has been performed, so `Obj1` and `Obj3` are now next to each other. The idea is to maximize the free space available in the heap and to put that free space in a single contiguous block of memory. Figure 4.5 shows what the heap would look like if there was a pinned object during the garbage-collection cycle.

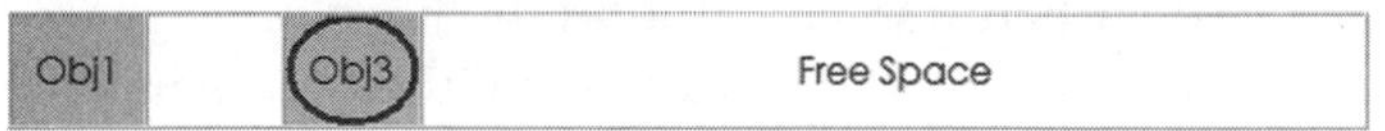

Figure 4.5 After a garbage-collection cycle (one pinned object)

Assume that `Obj3` is a pinned object (the circle represents the pinning). Because the GC won't move pinned objects, `Obj3` remains where it was. This results in fragmentation because the space between `Obj1` and `Obj2` cannot be added to the large continuous free block of memory. In this particular case, it's just a small gap that would have contained only a single object, and thus isn't a major issue. Now, assume that several pinned objects exist on the CLR heap when the garbage-collection cycle occurs. Figure 4.6 shows what happens in such a situation.

Figure 4.6 After a garbage-collection cycle (several pinned objects)

None of those pinned objects can be relocated. This means the compaction process can't be effectively implemented. When there are several such pinned objects, the heap is severely fragmented, resulting in slower and less-efficient memory allocation for new objects. This is the case because the GC has to try that much harder to find a block that's large enough to fit the requested object. Sometimes, although the total free space is bigger than the requested memory, the fact that there is no single continuous block of memory large enough to hold that object results in an unnecessary garbage-collection cycle or a memory exception. Obviously, this isn't an efficient scenario, and it's why you have to be extremely cautious when you use pinning pointers.

Recommendations for using pinning pointers

Now that you've seen where pinning pointers can be handy and where they can be a little dodgy, I'm going to give you some general tips on effectively using pinning pointers.

Unless you absolutely have to, don't use a pinning pointer! Whenever you think you need to use a pinning pointer, see if an interior pointer or a tracking reference may be a better option. If an interior pointer is acceptable as an alternative, chances are good that this is an improper place for using a pinning pointer.

If you need to pin multiple objects, try to allocate those objects together so that they're in an adjacent area in the CLR heap. That way, when you pin them, those pinned objects will be in a contiguous area of the heap. This reduces fragmentation compared to their being spread around the heap.

When making a call into native code, check to see if the CLR marshalling layer (or the target native code) does any pinning for you. If it does, you don't need to pin your object before passing it, because you'd be writing unnecessary (though harmless) code by adding an extra pinning pointer to the pinned object (which doesn't do anything to the pinned state of the object).

Newly-allocated objects are put into Generation-0 of the CLR heap. You know that garbage-collection cycles happen most frequently in the Generation-0 heap. Consequently, you should try to avoid pinning recently allocated objects; chances are that a garbage-collection cycle will occur while the object is still pinned.

Reduce the lifetime of a pinning pointer. The longer it stays in scope, the longer the object it points to remains pinned and the greater the chances of heap fragmentation. For instance, if you need a pinning pointer inside an `if` block, declare it inside the `if` block so the pinning ends when the `if` block exits.

Whenever you pass a pinning pointer to a native pointer, you have to ensure that the native pointer is used only if the pinning pointer is still alive. If the pinning pointer goes out of scope, the object becomes unpinned. Now it can be moved around by the GC. Once that happens, the native pointer is pointing to some random location on the CLR heap. I've heard the term *GC hole* used to refer to such a scenario, and it can be a tough debugging problem. Although it may sound like an unlikely contingency, think of what may happen if a native function that accepts a native pointer stores this pointer for later use. The caller code may have passed a pinning pointer to this function. Once the function has returned, the pinning will quickly stop, because the original pinning pointer won't be alive much longer. However, the saved pointer may be used later by some other function in the native code, which may result in some disastrous conditions (because the location the pointer points to may contain some other object now or even be free space). The best you can do is to know what the native code is going to do with a pointer before you pass a pinning pointer to it. That way, if you see that there is the risk of a GC hole, you avoid calling that function and try to find an alternate solution.

Note that these are general guidelines and not hard rules to be blindly followed at all times. It's good to have some basic strategies and to understand the exact consequences of what happens when you inappropriately use pinning pointers. Eventually, you have to evaluate your coding scenario and use your judgment to decide on the best course.

4.2 Working with interop mechanisms

The term *interop* (short for *interoperability*) is used to represent any situation where managed and unmanaged code have to interact with each other; it includes calling managed code from unmanaged code, as well as the reverse. C++/CLI provides the same mechanisms for interop that are available in other languages like C#, such as CCW and P/Invoke. In addition, C++/CLI also provides a mechanism called *C++ interop*, which allows you to use a mixed-mode executable or DLL to handle interop scenarios. For most purposes, C++ interop is a lot more convenient, flexible and performant than the other interop mechanisms. Throughout the rest of this book, we'll use C++ interop for the mixed-mode programming ventures.

In this section, we'll look at all three of the mechanisms available in VC++ 2005 to interop between managed and unmanaged code, and compare them in terms of ease of use and performance. When we discuss CCW and P/Invoke, you'll see why you may prefer C++ interop over them whenever that is an option. Of course, you should also be aware that both CCW and P/Invoke are powerful mechanisms that are handy for specific situations where C++ interop may not be the best option.

To simplify the discussion, I have sectioned it into the two potential interop situations: accessing a managed library from native code and accessing a native library from managed code. For most real-life applications that require some sort of interop, you'll encounter at least one of these situations, and quite possibly both.

4.2.1 Accessing a managed library from native code

You'll encounter scenarios where you need to access a managed library from native code, typically when you have an existing unmanaged application and, for whatever reasons, you need to interop with a new managed library as part of enhancing or revising your application. This is analogous to trying to play a DVD on an old VCR. You need to convert the DVD data (analogous to the managed library) to a format that can be played by the VCR (analogous to your native code).

In this section, you'll see how to do this using two different techniques: The first one will use a CCW, and the second one will use C++ interop. You'll use a simple managed library that lets you order a movie from a fictitious video store. Listing 4.3 shows the interface and skeletal class implementation for such a library.

Listing 4.3 The managed library implementation for the video store

```
namespace ManLib
{
    public interface class IVideoStore
    {
        bool IsMovieAvailable(String^);
        int GetMovieID(String^);
        int GetStockCount(int);
        bool OrderMovie(int, int);
        array<String^>^ GetMovieCast(int);

    };

    public ref class VideoStore : IVideoStore
    {
    public:
        virtual bool IsMovieAvailable(String^ strMovieName)
        . . .
        virtual int GetMovieID(String^ strMovieName)
```

```
        . . .
        virtual int GetStockCount(int movieID)
        . . .
        virtual bool OrderMovie(int movieID, int count)
        . . .
        virtual array<String^>^ GetMovieCast(int movieID)
        . . .
    };
}
```

The method names are self-explanatory, so I won't attempt to describe what each method does. Next, you're going to write two different applications. One uses a CCW and the other uses C++ interop, but both applications are functionally identical. They both check if a movie is available; after checking to see if the store has it, you'll order six copies of it. The applications also display a list of the cast of characters once the order is completed. All this is done through the managed library you just defined. Let's start with the CCW caller application.

Using a CCW to access a CLI library

CCW is a mechanism available in .NET that allows a COM client (such as a native C++ or VB 6 application) to access managed objects via proxy COM objects which wrap the managed objects. Figure 4.7 shows a diagrammatic representation of how the CCW connects a CLI library with a native caller.

The CCW is responsible for all managed/unmanaged marshalling. The managed object is virtually invisible to the COM client, which sees only the CCW. Using the DVD-VCR analogy, a CCW is like an external device that reads a DVD and passes converted data to a dummy video cassette disk that can be played on a VCR.

The CCW is reference-counted (like a normal COM object) and manages the lifetime of the wrapped managed object. When its reference count reaches zero, the managed object becomes a candidate for garbage collection. A deeper explanation of CCW or COM isn't within the scope or subject matter of this book, and unless you have some basic COM awareness, the code in this section may look a little strange. You should, however, still go through it, so that when you see the C++ interop version of the same app, you'll appreciate how much simpler and more convenient C++ interop is. In general, unless you've previously done a bit of COM programming, CCW isn't something I recommend as a suitable interop mechanism. With that in mind, let's get started on the CCW caller application.

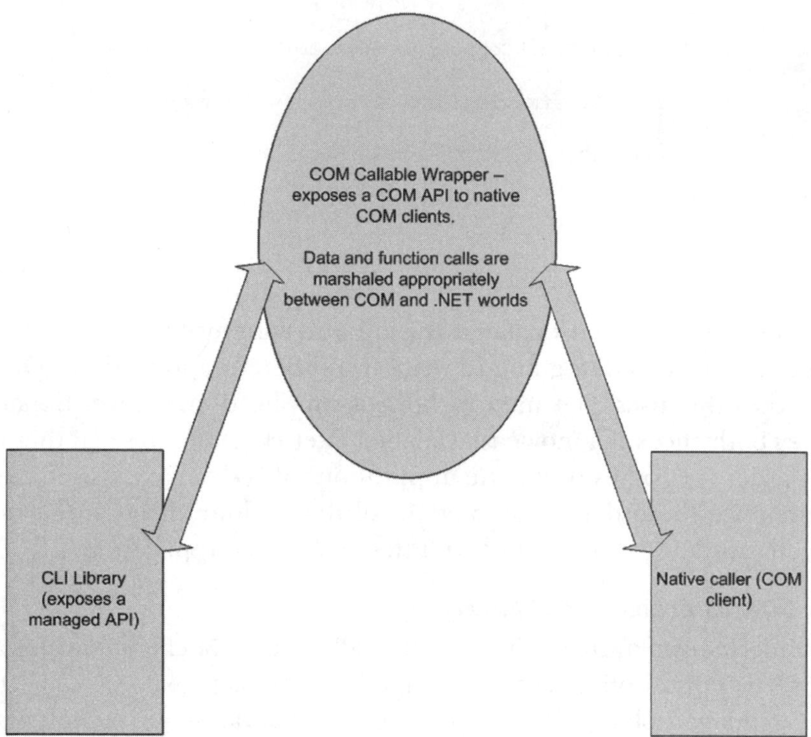

Figure 4.7 Native caller using a CCW to call into a CLI library

The managed assembly has to be registered for use by COM clients. For this, you use Regasm.exe, the Assembly Registration Tool provided with the .NET Framework. You can run the following command to register the assembly for COM access:

```
RegAsm.exe  ManLib.dll /tlb:ManLib.tlb
```

You use the `/tlb` option to output a type library file that will contain the accessible COM types within that library. You do that so you can import type information into the application by using `#import` on this tlb file. Note that only public members of public types are exposed via COM, and any other members or types will be invisible to the CCW. You can also control COM visibility of an assembly or a type at various levels of granularity using custom attributes such as `ComVisible`.

Before I show you the code for the application, look at the output you'll get when you run the final CCW application, shown in figure 4.8. You'll then know exactly what is being done as you examine the code.

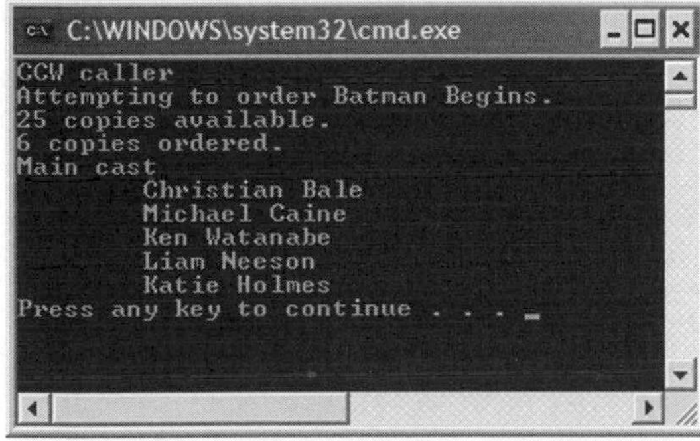

Figure 4.8
Output from the CCW caller application

Remember that the CCW caller is a native application and knows nothing of .NET or of managed types. Listing 4.4 shows the CCW caller application code.

Listing 4.4 Accessing the managed library via a CCW

```
#import "..\debug\ManLib.tlb" raw_interfaces_only      <-- Reference tlb using #import

using namespace ManLib;

void BuyMovie()
{
    cout << "CCW caller" << endl;
    ManLib::IVideoStorePtr pVidStore(__uuidof(VideoStore));      <-- Instantiates VideoStore object

    unsigned char ret = 0;
    CComBSTR strMovie = "Batman Begins";

    cout << "Attempting to order Batman Begins." << endl;
    if(SUCCEEDED(pVidStore->IsMovieAvailable(      <-- Check availability
        strMovie, &ret)) && ret)
    {
        long movieid = 0;
        if(SUCCEEDED(pVidStore->GetMovieID(strMovie, &movieid)))      <-- Retrieves movie ID
        {
            long count = 0;
            if(SUCCEEDED(pVidStore->GetStockCount(      <-- Returns number of copies
                movieid, &count)) && count > 5)
            {
                cout << count << " copies available." << endl;
                if(SUCCEEDED(pVidStore->OrderMovie(      <-- Order movie
                    movieid, 6, &ret)) && ret)
                {
                    cout << "6 copies ordered." << endl;
                    SAFEARRAY* pSA= NULL;
                    if(SUCCEEDED(pVidStore->GetMovieCast(      <-- Get cast list
                        movieid, &pSA)))
```

```
                    {
                        long lbound = 0, ubound = 0;

                        SafeArrayGetLBound (pSA, 1, &lbound);
                        SafeArrayGetUBound (pSA, 1, &ubound);

                        BSTR* s = NULL;
                        SafeArrayAccessData(pSA, (void**) &s);
                        cout << "Main cast" << endl;
                        for(long i=lbound; i<=ubound; i++)
                        {
                            wcout << "\t" << s[i] << endl;
                        }
                        SafeArrayUnaccessData(pSA);
                        SafeArrayDestroy (pSA);
                    }
                }
            }
        }
    }
}
```

Enumerates returned SAFEARRAY

The most noticeable thing about this code listing is that it's essentially COM-based in nature. There is no .NET presence syntactically in that code, and that code is only aware that it's accessing a COM object and its methods. The fact that the COM object is a CCW for an underlying managed object is imperceptible to the caller application. When you use `#import`, the compiler creates the required smart pointers to access the COM object, which saves you the trouble of manually having to call COM functions such as `AddRef`, `Release`, `QueryInterface`, and so on.

The .NET interface is now accessed via the CCW interface, which means the prototypes for the managed functions have been replaced with COM versions. As is typical in COM, all functions return an `HRESULT`. The return type in the managed code is converted to an `out` parameter of the function. For example, this is what the `IsMovieAvailable` function looks like in managed code:

```
bool IsMovieAvailable(String^);
```

And here's the COM version used in the CCW caller:

```
HRESULT IsMovieAvailable (/*[in]*/ BSTR,
    /*[out,retval]*/ unsigned char *);
```

The `String^` argument in managed code becomes a `BSTR` argument in COM code, and the `bool` return type, which is now an `out` parameter of the function, becomes an `unsigned char*`. Similarly, every other managed function has been given a COM version which uses COM types.

In the case of the `GetMovieCast` function, the COM version can be a little formidable for people without COM experience: It uses a `SAFEARRAY`, which isn't the simplest of the COM types. The original managed function, which looked like this

```
array<String^>^ GetMovieCast(int);
```

has been converted to the following COM version:

```
HRESULT GetMovieCast (/*[in]*/ long, /*[out,retval]*/ SAFEARRAY**);
```

Although the CLR marshalling layer takes care of type conversions between the managed and the COM world, the caller is responsible for freeing native resources once they're no longer required. You'll notice how you use `SafeArrayDestroy` to free the `SAFEARRAY` once you finish iterating through its contents. You can simplify the `SAFEARRAY` usage considerably by using the ATL `CComSafeArray` wrapper class, but I wanted to use straight COM to exemplify the differences between the CCW approach and the C++/CLI approach that will be discussed in the next section.

As I said, unless you're reasonably comfortable with COM and prepared to be responsible for native resource deallocation (or be familiar with using ATL wrapper classes), CCW can be intimidating. Of course, if your native application is COM-based and already makes extensive use of COM, CCW is the most natural choice and will merge smoothly with the rest of your native code. If not, then I strongly recommend that you don't use CCW; instead, you should use C++ interop. Moving on to the C++ interop version of the app you wrote previously, you'll appreciate how convenient it can be compared to CCW.

Preserving method signature for CCW

In the example, the return type of the managed method is converted to an `out` parameter in the COM method, and the return type is changed to an `HRESULT`. This can be inconvenient at times, because you need to check the `HRESULT` for success. You also need to pass a pointer to the original return type as a final argument. If you have control over the managed library and have the option of modifying the original managed code, you can use the `MethodImplAttribute` attribute with `MethodImplOptions::PreserveSig` on those methods where you want the signature to be preserved. For example, if you applied it to the `IsMovieAvailable` method, you'd get the following COM method: `unsigned char IsMovieAvailable([in] BSTR)`, which is a little closer to the original managed method. You can also directly use the return type instead of having to pass a pointer to a variable.

Using C++ interop to access a CLI library

The C++ interop caller app is functionally identical to the CCW caller app. However, although the CCW caller was a native C++ application, the C++ interop caller has to be compiled with the /clr compilation switch—if not the whole application, then at least those source files that will access the managed library. You also need to add a reference to the managed library in the project settings. Figure 4.9 shows a diagrammatic view of a mixed-mode application accessing a CLI library via C++ interop. Using the DVD-VCR analogy, C++ interop is analogous to directly adding support for playing a DVD to your old VCR by adding a DVD player to the device (analogous to enabling /clr compilation).

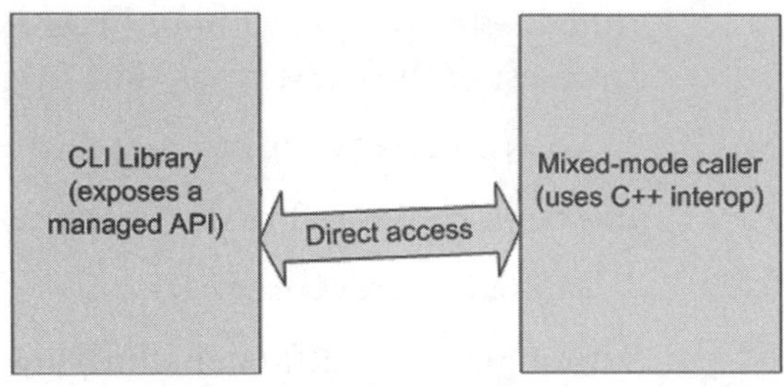

Figure 4.9 Accessing a CLI library using C++ interop

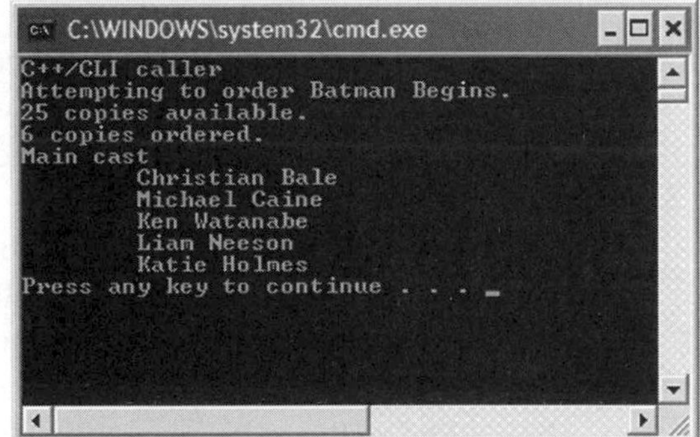

Figure 4.10 Output from the C++ interop caller application

As you did with the CCW, look at the output you'll get when you run the final C++ interop application; see figure 4.10.

Listing 4.5 shows the code for the C++ interop version of the application. Not only is it shorter than the CCW version, but it directly uses CLI types to access the managed library.

Listing 4.5 Accessing the managed library via C++ interop

```
void BuyMovie()
{
    cout << "C++/CLI caller" << endl;
    VideoStore^ vidstore = gcnew VideoStore();        <-- Instantiate VideoStore object
    cout << "Attempting to order Batman Begins." << endl;
    System::String^ strMovie = "Batman Begins";
    if(vidstore->IsMovieAvailable(strMovie))
    {                                                   Invoke VideoStore methods
        int movieid = vidstore->GetMovieID(strMovie);
        int count = 0;
```

```
            if((count = vidstore->GetStockCount(movieid)) > 5)
            {
                cout << count << " copies available." << endl;
                if(vidstore->OrderMovie(movieid, 6))
                {
                    cout << "6 copies ordered." << endl;
                    cout << "Main cast" << endl;
                    for each(System::String^ s in
                        vidstore->GetMovieCast(movieid))    <-- 1 Enumerate String array
                    {
                        System::Console::WriteLine("\t{0}", s);
                    }
                }
            }
        }
    }
```

Enumerate String array (1)

Invoke VideoStore methods

As you can see, this is conventional C++/CLI code, except that it's part of a primarily unmanaged application that has had `/clr` enabled. In other words, you're seeing a mixed-mode application, albeit a simple one. You directly use CLI types like `String^` and CLI arrays, and thus there is no need to convert managed types to native types. In a real-life scenario, unless the original native application is COM-based, the mere fact that you didn't have to go through the exacting chore of enumerating a `SAFEARRAY` and can instead have the luxury of using `for each` (1) on the returned `String^` array should itself be reason enough to choose C++ interop over CCW in such a situation. Although I am firmly in favor of C++ interop over CCW, it is imprudent to take an uncompromising approach to all interop scenarios. There are situations where CCW is best and other situations (the majority, in my opinion) where C++ interop is more suitable. In the next section, we'll compare the two mechanisms to see where each is the better choice.

Comparison of the two techniques

You've seen two different techniques to access a managed library from a native application. One uses the CCW mechanism supported by the .NET Framework, and the other uses C++ interop supported by the C++/CLI compiler. The CCW caller is typically a native application (although you can do CCW from a mixed-mode app too), whereas the C++ interop caller has to enable `/clr` and is always a mixed-mode application. If you aren't prepared to use a mixed-mode caller application, CCW is your better choice, because C++ interop requires mixed-mode compilation.

If you aren't familiar with COM, or if your caller app isn't primarily COM-based, using CCW has the obvious disadvantage that you'll be forced to do quite a bit of COM programming. In most cases, you'll be responsible for freeing COM resources such as `SAFEARRAY`s and `BSTR`s. And unless you can apply the `MethodImplAttribute` with the `PreserveSig` option on your managed methods (which requires that you have source code access to the managed library), you'll also have to handle `out` parameters for your return types because the COM methods will return `HRESULT`s. If you use C++ interop, you'll directly use C++/CLI to access the managed library using .NET types.

Another issue with using CCW is that CCW lets you instantiate only those objects that have a default constructor. If an object has only nondefault constructors, you can't use that object through CCW. You can write another factory class that will instantiate and return an object of the type you want, but doing so adds unnecessary work and is possible only in scenarios where you can change the managed library. There are no such issues with C++ interop.

The last issue is that of performance. Although the performance improvement will vary depending on the scenario where interop is applied, typically C++ interop is much more performant than CCW. With CCW, the managed/unmanaged transitions are handled by the CCW marshalling layer. With C++ interop, you have more direct control over what you do, because you can choose to use managed types by default and convert to native types only where required.

Summarizing these points, my recommendation is to use CCW only when you have to, such as when the native app is COM-based and you don't want to bring in `/clr` compilation. For all other scenarios, C++ interop is your fastest and most convenient option. In later chapters, you'll see how you can take advantage of C++ interop when you mix managed technologies such as Windows Forms, Avalon, and so on, with native technologies like MFC. Now that you've seen how to access managed libraries from native code, let's look at the reverse process in the next section—accessing native libraries from managed code.

4.2.2 Accessing a native library from managed code

In this section, we'll look at the reverse scenario of what we covered in the previous section: accessing a native library from managed code. For example, you may want to use a native library that you have been using for years from your new managed applications, because you can't find a managed equivalent for it that's efficient enough for your purposes. Think of the DVD-VCR analogy, and swap the situation; you have a video tape, and you want to play it on your DVD player. You can approach this in two ways—one is to use the P/Invoke mechanism, and the other is to use C++ interop. We'll cover both mechanisms in this section, and we'll use the following library as the example native code:

```
class __declspec(dllexport) CStudentDB
{
public:
    CStudentDB(int id);
    int GetScore();
};

extern "C"  __declspec(dllexport) int GetStudentID(
    LPCTSTR strName);
extern "C" __declspec(dllexport) void GetStudentAddress(
    int id, LPTSTR szAddress);
```

❶ **Exported class**

❷ **Exported functions**

This code is part of a native DLL. There are two exported functions ❷, as well as an exported class ❶. You're going to write two sample programs, one using P/Invoke and the other using C++ interop, both of which will access this native DLL. Let's start with the P/Invoke sample.

Using P/Invoke to access a native DLL

P/Invoke (short for Platform Invoke) is a mechanism that allows you to call unmanaged functions declared in native DLLs from managed code by declaring those functions using the `DllImport` attribute. This is analogous to using a device that converts the video cassette data to a video stream that can be directly passed to the DVD player. The .NET P/Invoke layer does the type marshalling across the managed/unmanaged boundary. When you make a P/Invoke function call, the P/Invoke layer loads the containing DLL into the process memory (if it's not already loaded), gets the address of the unmanaged function to call, converts the managed types to native types as required, calls the function, converts the native types back to managed types as required, and returns control to the calling managed code. Figure 4.11 shows how a managed application accesses a native C-based API through P/Invoke.

All this is done transparently. As a user, it's convenient to call an unmanaged function as if it was a managed call, but you pay a price for all that convenience—performance. The managed/unmanaged transitions and data conversions slow down your application, although depending on your scenario, that may not be a big issue. Listing 4.6 shows the P/Invoke version of the program that calls into the native DLL you declared earlier.

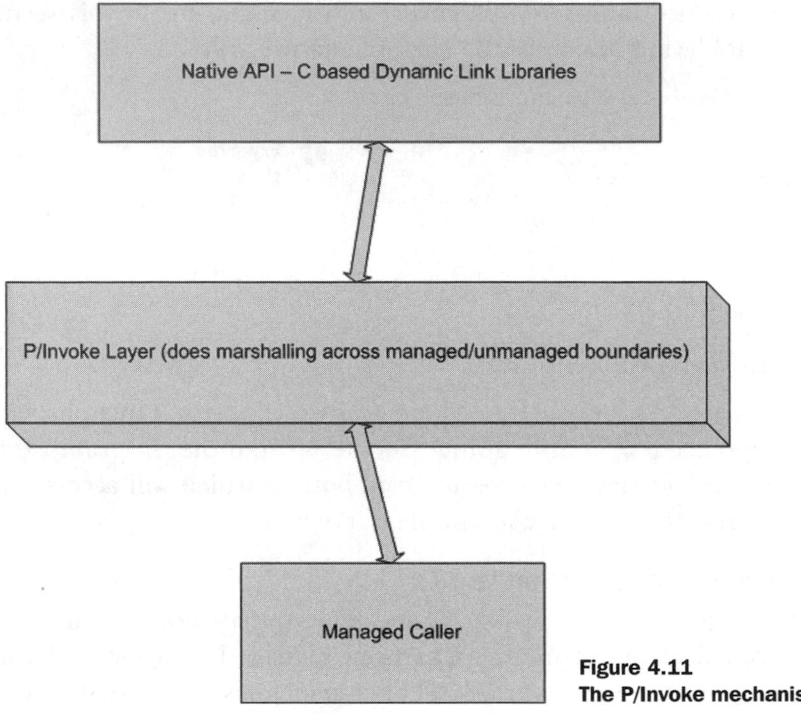

Figure 4.11 The P/Invoke mechanism

Listing 4.6 Using P/Invoke to call functions in a native DLL

```
[DllImport("Natlib.dll",CharSet=CharSet::Unicode)]
extern "C" int GetStudentID(String^ strName);
[DllImport("Natlib.dll",CharSet=CharSet::Unicode)]
extern "C" void GetStudentAddress(int id,
    StringBuilder^ szAddress);

int main(array<System::String ^> ^args)
{
    int studid = GetStudentID("Howard Jones");
    StringBuilder^ addr = gcnew StringBuilder(100);
    GetStudentAddress(studid, addr);
    Console::WriteLine("Student ID : {0}", studid);
    Console::WriteLine("Address : {0}", addr->ToString());
    return 0;
}
```

❶ **P/Invoke declaration for GetStudentID**

❷ **P/Invoke declaration for GetStudentAddress**

Directly call methods

In the code, you declare each unmanaged function that you need to call. For the `GetStudentID` function ❶, notice how the `LPCTSTR` parameter in the DLL function has been changed to a `String^` parameter in the P/Invoked function. When the call is made, the P/Invoke layer converts the `String^` to an `LPCTSTR` before making the call. Similarly, for the `GetStudentAddress` function ❷, you use a `String-Builder^`, where the native function used an `LPTSTR`. You need to use managed types that closely match the corresponding unmanaged types, or else the calls will either fail with erroneous results or you may get a crash. For example, passing an `int` where a `char*` is expected results in unpredictable behavior depending on what the native function expects that `char*` to be. `DllImport` can take several arguments; for example, in the declaration of `GetStudentAddress` ❷, you specify that the `CharSet` is `Unicode`. Because the focus of this book is on using C++ interop, I don't want to discuss the various `DllImport` options in detail, but if you ever end up using P/Invoke, you should look them up in the MSDN library.

Notice that you don't make a call into the exported class, because you can only call exported functions using P/Invoke. If you want to use the exported class and you have access to the DLL source code, you have to export a function that would wrap the calls to the class for you. For instance, you'd have to export a function from the DLL such as the following, where the function declares an instance of the class, makes a call into a class method, and returns the value returned by the class method:

```
extern "C" __declspec(dllexport)_API int GetStudentScore(int id)
{
    CStudentDB sdb(id);
    return sdb.GetScore();
}
```

Obviously, if you have a DLL that exports several classes, and you don't have the option of writing wrapper functions for them, P/Invoke isn't applicable in calling those functions. The advantage of using P/Invoke is that you can directly use managed types and let the P/Invoke layer do your data marshalling for you. The disadvantages are poorer performance and having to re-declare every function you intend to call. That's why C++ interop is so much more convenient and, for most purposes, a far more performant option. With that in mind, let's move on to the C++ interop version of the previous program.

Using C++ interop to access a native DLL

To access the native library from C++ interop, all you need to do is to `#include` the required header files and link with the required lib files. This is like adding video cassette support to a DVD player—like one of those 2-in-1 players available from your nearest Wal-Mart. Figure 4.12 shows a diagrammatic view of how a

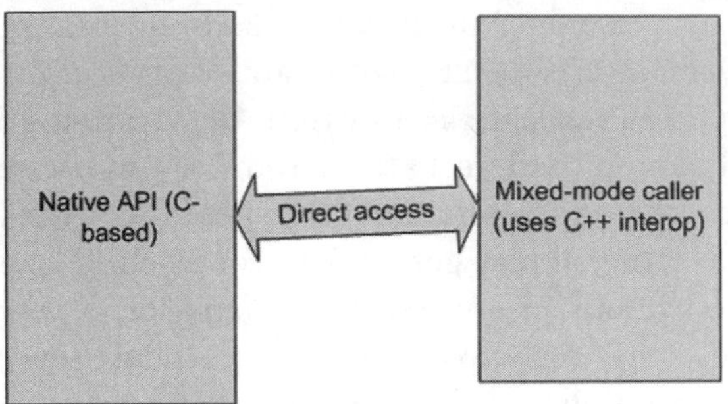

Figure 4.12 Accessing a native library using C++ interop

mixed-mode caller can directly access a native API via C++ interop; notice how there's no need for a middleman.

Once you do that, you can use the class directly, as shown in the listing 4.7.

Listing 4.7 Using C++ interop to call functions in a native DLL

```
#include "../NatLib.h" [#1]
#pragma comment(lib,"../Natlib")

using namespace System;

int main(array<System::String ^> ^args)
{
    int studid = GetStudentID(_T("Howard Jones"));
    TCHAR addr[100];
    GetStudentAddress(studid, addr);
    Console::WriteLine("Student ID : {0}", studid);
    std::wcout << L"Address : " << addr << std::endl;
    CStudentDB sdb(studid);
    Console::WriteLine("Score : {0}", sdb.GetScore());
    return 0;
}
```

Include required header and lib files

Directly call exported native functions

Instantiate exported class, and invoke methods (1)

As is typical in mixed-mode applications, you use both native objects such as `cout` as well as managed objects such as `Console`. In addition, you can easily instantiate and use the exported class (1), which you couldn't do with P/Invoke without the help of an exported helper function that would do it for you. C++ interop is more convenient to use than P/Invoke because you don't have to declare the P/Invoke functions and can directly use the native types that are expected by the native DLL. Very often, you can avoid doing managed/unmanaged type conversions except where required. But P/Invoke does have its uses too; ideally, both mechanisms should be used where they're most suitable.

Comparison of the two techniques

Now that you have seen both techniques, let's summarize the pros and cons of each. P/Invoke is directly supported by the .NET Framework, and other languages like C# and VB.NET use it exclusively to call into unmanaged API. P/Invoke is extremely advantageous for other languages like C# and VB because it lets you access the unmanaged functions using managed types. Because C# and VB only understand managed types, this is a boon for them. With C++, this isn't as advantageous considering that C++/CLI supports both managed and unmanaged types. But if your scenario requires you to compile your C++/CLI code using `/clr:pure` (generate only MSIL—no native code), then P/Invoke is your only option. C++ interop isn't compatible with `/clr:pure` because it requires a mixed-mode assembly.

If that isn't a constraint, then C++ interop is far more convenient to use than P/Invoke. With C++ interop, you don't have to declare every API function and native structure using the `DllImport` attribute. You just include the header and lib files, and directly use the API as you would have done in an unmanaged application. You can access exported classes in a DLL, something that can't be directly done using P/Invoke. Another advantage is that you can minimize the managed/unmanaged type conversions that are required. For example, suppose your app needs a result that can be obtained from calling three native functions and then doing some processing on them. With C++ interop, you can make those API calls and perform native processing on their results to obtain the final result, which can at that point be converted to a managed type. With P/Invoke, even the subresults would use managed types, thus increasing the number of type conversions required.

In general, C++ interop is more performant than P/Invoke because of fewer type-marshalling requirements. Although you can tune up P/Invoke calls by using appropriate managed types in the declarations that reduce the type conversions required during P/Invoke, you eventually end up doing type marshalling on your own. With C++ interop, you have more control over the managed/unmanaged type conversions that need to be done. And you can speed up calls into native code by putting them in `#pragma unmanaged` blocks in your source code.

In this book, we'll be using C++ interop exclusively, because although P/Invoke may have its advantages, it's primarily intended for languages like C# and VB.NET. With C++/CLI, when you have the flexibility of using a powerful mechanism like C++ interop, you don't have to use P/Invoke. Whether you're calling into managed code from native code, calling native code from managed code, or mixing managed and native calls in a single block of code, we'll use C++ interop exclusively over other mechanisms like CCW and P/Invoke.

4.3 Using mixed types

A *mixed type* is one that requires object members to be allocated on both the CLI heap and in unmanaged memory, where these object members may be directly declared in the class or inherited from a parent. A more simplistic definition is to say that a mixed type is either a native type with a managed type member, or a managed type with a native type member. In this section, we'll examine both scenarios. An analogy is to think of a clock that shows time using hour, minute, and second hands as well as using a digital display—the time is represented both in analog and digital formats.

The VC++ 2005 compiler doesn't directly support mixed types! You may be thinking, if it doesn't, then why are you discussing mixed types in this chapter? I said "doesn't directly support"—the operative word is *directly*. There are library-provided workarounds to implement mixed types, and you can even write a smart pointer class to augment the possibilities.

The ability to support mixed types is important for C++/CLI as a language. The language is primarily being promoted as the number-one choice for doing any kind of managed/unmanaged interop programming. The moment you start doing that, the first thing you need, perhaps without your even realizing it, is support for mixed types. It's not surprising, when you think about it. Say you have an extensive MFC application with hundreds of MFC-derived classes. If you attempt to add a managed library to this application, you'll soon want to add managed type members to your MFC-derived classes (those would then be mixed types). The reverse situation for a managed application is equally possible, where your managed classes need native members when you try to add some native library to the application. In later chapters, when you see real-life applications of mixed-mode programming, just about every class you write will be a mixed-mode class.

4.3.1 Native types with managed members

In this section, we'll discuss how you can declare managed types in a native class. Obviously, you can't directly declare a managed type member in a native type. If you attempt to do so, you'll be greeted with a compiler error. The following code won't compile:

```
ref class Managed{};
class Native
{
    Managed^ m;        <-- (1) Throw compiler error C3265
};
```

This code snippet throws compiler error C3265 ❶ because you attempt to declare a managed object as a native class member. To declare the managed member in the native type, you have to use the `gcroot` template class (which is declared in `<gcroot.h>`), which wraps the `GCHandle` structure (which is under the `System::Runtime::InteropServices` namespace). Here's how `gcroot` is used:

```
gcroot<MANTYPE^> pMan;
. . .
pMan = gcnew MANTYPE();      <-- (1) Wrap managed type MANTYPE
pMan->ManagedMethod();       <-- (2) Directly invoke methods of MANTYPE
```

Note how you can directly use `gcnew` to instantiate the `gcroot` variable ❶. This is possible because the `gcroot` template has an assignment `operator` that accepts a type `T`, which in this code snippet will be a `MANTYPE^`. There's also a conversion constructor for `gcroot` that takes a type `T`, which comes into play if you directly construct a `gcroot` object using `gcnew`. Similarly, you can also make `MANTYPE` method calls on the variable ❷. This is possible because `gcroot` has an `operator->` that returns a `T` (which is `MANTYPE^` in the example). In general, once you have a `gcroot<T>` variable, you can use it just as if it was a `T` variable, which is what `gcroot` is there for. Let's look at an example.

Imagine that you have a native `Grid` class that represents a grid control, which is internally bound to an XML data store. Next, assume that you have a managed `XmlDB` class, which is used to read and write data between the grid control and the XML data store. You're going to see how the native `Grid` class can have the `XmlDB` managed class as a member. The `XmlDB` class opens the Xml file in its constructor and closes the file in its destructor—thus, it's imperative that the destructor is called as soon as the grid control is closed. Here's the skeletal code listing of the managed `XmlDB` class:

```
ref class XmlDB
{
public:
    XmlDB(String^ XmlFile)
    {//Open XML data store
    }
    ~XmlDB()
    {//Close XML data store
    }
```

```
    void Read(int x, int y, String^ node)
    {//Read node data into (x,y)
    }
    void Write(int x, int y, String^ node)
    {//Write data in (x,y) into node
    }
};
```

I've kept the class simple, with both `Read` and `Write` methods, and nontrivial constructor and destructor. Listing 4.8 shows the skeletal native `Grid` class that uses `gcroot` to declare and use a member variable of type `XmlDB`.

Listing 4.8 Using `gcroot` to declare a managed member object

```
class Grid
{
    gcroot<XmlDB^> _xmldb;          <- Managed member declared using gcroot
public:
    Grid(char* XmlFile)
    {
        _xmldb = gcnew XmlDB(gcnew String(XmlFile));     <- Managed object instantiated
    }
    ~Grid()
    {
        delete _xmldb;          <- Managed object deleted in destructor
    }
    const char* GetXmlStore()
    {//Return Xml file path
    }
    void PopulateGrid()
    {//Populate grid using the Xml file
        . . .
        for(int i=0; i<rows; i++)
            for(int j=0; j<cols; j++)
                _xmldb->Read(i, j, node[i,j]);
    }
    void OnGridUpdated()
    {//Write updated cells back to the Xml file
        . . .
        for(int i=0; i<rows; i++)
            for(int j=0; j<cols; j++)
                _xmldb->Write(i, j, node[i,j]);
    }
    . . . //rest of the class goes here
};
```

(Calls made into managed object: `PopulateGrid` through the rest of the class)

You basically use the `gcroot<XmlDB^>` variable as if it was an `XmlDB^` variable. The only thing you have to watch out for is remembering to `delete` the managed object explicitly in the native destructor. The XmlDB object closes the file connection in its destructor, so it's important that you call delete as soon as the object isn't needed any longer (or else the file connection will remain open until the next garbage-collection cycle). This is such a common scenario that another template called auto_gcroot (declared in <msclr\auto_gcroot.h>) has been provided, which is almost the same as gcroot, except that it behaves like a smart pointer and has automatic resource management support. If you use auto_gcroot, you don't need to manually delete the managed object, because it's automatically done for you. If you re-wrote the class above using auto_gcroot, it would look like listing 4.9.

Listing 4.9 Using an auto_gcroot member

```
class Grid
{
    msclr::auto_gcroot<XmlDB^> _xmldb;
public:
    Grid(char* XmlFile)
    {
        _xmldb = gcnew XmlDB(gcnew String(XmlFile));
    }
    const char* GetXmlStore()
    {//Return Xml file path
    }
    void PopulateGrid()
    {//Populate grid using the Xml file
     . . .
    }
    void OnGridUpdated()
    {//Write updated cells back to the Xml file
     . . .
    }
};
```

❶ Use auto_gcroot instead of gcroot

There are no changes except that you use auto_gcroot instead of gcroot ❶, and you don't have to call delete on the managed object, which is why you don't have a destructor. Of course, if the Grid class needs some resource cleanup, it will have a destructor, but it won't have to call delete on the auto_gcroot object. Now that you have seen how to have native types with managed members using gcroot and auto_gcroot, let's move ahead and see how to do the reverse—have managed types with native members.

4.3.2 Managed types with native members

As of VC++ 2005, the compiler won't permit you to put a whole native object member into a managed class. The following code won't compile:

```
class Native{};

ref class Managed
{
    Native m_n;          // (1) Compiler error C4368
};
```

The attempt to declare a native member ❶ throws compiler error C4368: *cannot define 'm_n' as a member of managed 'Managed' : mixed types are not supported*. But it's permissible to have a pointer to a native object. The code in listing 4.10 will compile.

Listing 4.10 Managed class with native pointer member

```
ref class Managed
{
    Native* m_n;             // Declare pointer to native object
public:
    Managed()
    {
        m_n = new Native();      // Use new to create native object
    }
    ~Managed()
    {
        delete m_n;          // (1) Manually delete native object
    }
};
```

The primary concern in this example is that you should `delete` the native object ❶ in the managed destructor. If you don't do so, there will be a memory leak, because native heap objects don't have the garbage collection and finalization support available in the CLR. In the previous section, you saw how the `auto_gcroot` template class acts as a smart pointer that automatically frees the managed resource when it goes out of scope. It would have been nice if such a class was provided for native objects too, but there isn't one provided in the library. Well, nothing stops you from rolling out your own smart pointer class that manages the native resource. Listing 4.11 shows a skeletal listing of what such a class can look like.

Listing 4.11 CAutoNativePtr skeletal listing

```
template<typename T> ref class CAutoNativePtr
{
private:
    T* _ptr;        <-- T* holds native resource
public:
    CAutoNativePtr() : _ptr(nullptr)
    . . .
    CAutoNativePtr(T* t) : _ptr(t)
    . . .
    CAutoNativePtr(CAutoNativePtr<T>% an) : _ptr(an.Detach())
    . . .
    template<typename TDERIVED>
        CAutoNativePtr(CAutoNativePtr<TDERIVED>% an)
            : _ptr(an.Detach())
    . . .                                          Constructor overloads
    !CAutoNativePtr()
    . . .
    ~CAutoNativePtr()                              Destructor and finalizer
    . . .
    CAutoNativePtr<T>% operator=(T* t)
    . . .
    CAutoNativePtr<T>% operator=(CAutoNativePtr<T>% an)
    . . .
    template<typename TDERIVED>
        CAutoNativePtr<T>% operator=(CAutoNativePtr<TDERIVED>% an)
                                                   Assignment operator overloads
    . . .
    static T* operator->(CAutoNativePtr<T>% an)    <-- Pointer to member operator overload
    . . .
    static operator T*(CAutoNativePtr<T>% an)      <-- Cast operator to T*
    . . .
    T* Detach()                                    <-- Methods to associate
    . . .
    void Attach(T* t)                              <-- and de-associate T*
    . . .
    void Destroy()                                 <-- Delete underlying T*
    . . .
};
```

Now let's implement the various pieces of this class one by one. Doing so will also give you an example of how to implement a smart pointer class using managed code. Let's begin with the constructor overloads; see listing 4.12.

Listing 4.12 `CAutoNativePtr` constructor overloads

```
CAutoNativePtr() : _ptr(nullptr)        ❶ Default ctor
{
}
CAutoNativePtr(T* t) : _ptr(t)          Construct object from existing T*
{
}
CAutoNativePtr(CAutoNativePtr<T>% an)
    : _ptr(an.Detach())                 ❷ Copy ctor
{
}
template<typename TDERIVED>
    CAutoNativePtr(CAutoNativePtr<TDERIVED>% an)
        : _ptr(an.Detach())             ❸ Copy ctor specialization for derived object
{
}
```

The default constructor ❶ sets `_ptr` to a `nullptr`, whereas the constructor that takes an existing `T*` associates that `T*` with the class by assigning it to `_ptr`. Once a `T*` is associated with the class, the class is responsible for freeing that `T*` when it's no longer needed (which is when it goes out of scope). For the copy constructor ❷, you first detach the `T*` from the source object; otherwise, there will be two smart pointers associated with the same `T*`, which will result in double-deletion because both objects will attempt to delete the `T*` when it goes out of scope. By detaching the `T*` from the source object, you ensure that only one smart pointer is associated with the `T*`. You also need to have a specialization of the copy constructor ❸ to handle objects associated with a `TDERIVED*` where `TEDERIVED` is a type derived directly or indirectly from `T`.

Now, let's implement the destructor and the finalizer. You'll implement both so that even if somehow the user declares the smart pointer using handle semantics (instead of stack semantics) and then forgets to call `delete`, the `finalizer` will still free up the native resource:

```
!CAutoNativePtr()
{
    delete _ptr;
}
~CAutoNativePtr()
{
    this->!CAutoNativePtr();
}
```

Notice how you delete the native object in the finalizer and invoke the finalizer in the destructor. You do that to avoid code duplication. Let's implement the assignment operators now; you have three overloads for that, as shown in listing 4.13.

Listing 4.13 CAutoNativePtr assignment operators

```
CAutoNativePtr<T>% operator=(T* t)              ❶ Assignment from T*
{
    Attach(t);
    return *this;
}

CAutoNativePtr<T>% operator=(CAutoNativePtr<T>% an)   ❷ Assignment from another CAutoNativePtr
{
    if(this != %an) //check for self assignment
        Attach(an.Detach());
    return *this;
}

template<typename TDERIVED>
    CAutoNativePtr<T>% operator=(
        CAutoNativePtr<TDERIVED>% an)           ❸ Assignment from derived type CAutoNativePtr
{
    Attach(an.Detach());
    return *this;
}
```

The first overload ❶ takes a `T*` and is internally implemented using a call to `Attach`. You haven't seen `Attach` yet, but when you implement it, if the class is currently associated with a `T*`, it must be deleted before you take ownership of the new `T*`. The second overload ❷ is a copy assignment operator. You check for self assignment and then use `Attach` on the `T*` that is obtained by calling `Detach` on the source object. The reason you call `Detach` is the same reason as for the copy constructor: You don't want two objects holding onto the same `T*`, because that would result in double deletion. The last overload ❸ is a specialization of the copy assignment operator that handles a `CAutoNativePtr` that owns a `T`-derived object.

Let's implement the pointer-to-member and the `T*`-cast operators, both of which return a `T*`:

```
static T* operator->(CAutoNativePtr<T>% an)
{
    return an._ptr;
}
```

```
static operator T*(CAutoNativePtr<T>% an)
{
    return an._ptr;
}
```

Both operators are implemented simply and return the `T*` owned by the object. The cast to `T*` allows `CAutoNativePtr` objects to be used anywhere a `T*` is expected. The `->` operator lets a user directly access `T` methods using the `CAutoNativePtr` object (essentially, this is what makes it a smart pointer). You still have to write the `Attach`, `Detach`, and `Destroy` methods; once you do that, you'll see an example of how to use the smart pointer class. Listing 4.14 shows the last of the methods.

Listing 4.14 The `Detach`, `Attach`, and `Destroy` methods

```
T* Detach()
{
    T* t = _ptr;
    _ptr = nullptr;
    return t;
}

void Attach(T* t)
{
    if(t)
    {
        if(_ptr != t)
        {
            delete _ptr;
            _ptr = t;
        }
    }
    else
    {
#ifdef _DEBUG
        throw gcnew Exception(
            "Attempting to Attach(...) a nullptr!");
#endif
    }
}

void Destroy()
{
    delete _ptr;
    _ptr = nullptr;
}
```

❶ Detach method releases T*

❷ Attach method takes over ownership of T*

❸ Delete underlying T* object

The `Detach` method ❶ releases ownership of the `T*` by setting its internal `T*` variable to a `nullptr` and returning the original `T*`. Once `Detach` is called, the smart pointer is no longer responsible for the native object, and the caller is responsible for freeing the resource when it's no longer needed. The `Attach` method ❷ takes over ownership of a `T*`; before it does that, it deletes the currently owned `T*`, if any. It also takes some safety precautions, such as checking to see that the calling code isn't erroneously trying to re-attach an already attached `T*`, in which case `Attach` does nothing; and checking to see if the caller is attempting to attach a `nullptr`, in which case it throws an exception (only in debug mode). The `Destroy` method ❸ deletes the underlying native object and sets the smart pointer's internal `T*` variable to a `nullptr`.

That's it; you've finished writing the smart pointer class. All you need to do now is write some code to see it in action: see listing 4.15.

Listing 4.15 Using the `CAutoNativePtr` class

```
class Native
{
public:
    void F(){}
};

class Derived : public Native{};

void SomeFunc(Native){}                  Functions that take
void SomeOtherFunc(Native*){}            Native object and Native*

ref class Ref
{                                               Declare smart
    CAutoNativePtr<Native> m_native;       <--  pointer object
public:
    Ref()
    {}
                                              Constructor
    Ref(Native* pN) : m_native(pN)       <--  that takes T*
    {}
                                                          Copy constructor
    Ref(CAutoNativePtr<Native> pN) : m_native(pN)    <--  comes into play
    {}

    void Change(Native* pNew)
    {
        m_native = pNew;       <--  Assign from T*
    }

    void Change(CAutoNativePtr<Native> pNew)
    {
        m_native = pNew;       <--  Assign from another
    }                               smart pointer
```

```
        void DoStuff()                          Logical NOT
        {                                       applied via T* cast
            if(!m_native)                  <-
            {
            }
            else
            {                                   ❶ -> operator
                m_native->F();               <-   at work
                SomeFunc(*m_native);                  ❷ T* cast
                SomeOtherFunc(m_native);                at work
            }
        }

        bool DoComparisons(CAutoNativePtr<Native> a1,
            CAutoNativePtr<Native> a2, CAutoNativePtr<Native> a3)
        {
            return (a1 == a2) && (a1 != a3);   <- Operators == and !=
        }                                         applied via T* cast

        void Close()
        {
            m_native.Destroy();            <- Free native
        }                                     resource
    };

    int main()
    {
        CAutoNativePtr<Derived> d1(new Derived);
        CAutoNativePtr<Derived> d2(new Derived);

        CAutoNativePtr<Native> n1(d1);          <- Call specialized ctor
                                                   for derived types
        n1 = d2;                <- Specialized
                                   assignment operator
        return 0;                  for derived types
    }
```

The class not only takes responsibility for freeing the native resource when it's no longer required, but it also provides a convenient interface to the caller. By using the `->` operator ❶, the calling code can directly access the `T*` methods. Because of the `T*` cast, passing the smart pointer to a function that expects a `T` object or a `T*` is also possible ❷. In general, the smart pointer object can be used and handled just as if it was a `T*` object, which is what you set out to do when you wrote the class. I hope that the step-by-step implementation of the earlier class gave you a good idea of how managed classes are written and how various operators are handled.

One last topic that we'll cover in this chapter is how to bridge the gap between native function pointers and CLI delegates.

4.4 Function pointers and delegates: bridging the gap

Function pointers are often used to implement a callback mechanism in native code. A *callback function* is one that's not explicitly invoked but is automatically invoked by another function when a certain event or state is triggered. Callback functions are similar to the CLI delegate/event mechanism, where the delegate associated with the event is invoked when that event is triggered. If you haven't used callbacks before, think of them as being similar to calling up a restaurant, placing an order, and asking them to call you back on your phone once the order is ready so you can pick it up.

When you start mixing native and managed code, you'll soon encounter a situation where you need to call a native function that expects a pointer to a callback function from managed code. At that point, you'll probably find it convenient if you can pass a delegate to that function rather than a function pointer. Delegates are an intrinsic part of the CLI, so using them is more natural from managed code, compared to passing a pointer to a function. (Note that this is one scenario where the P/Invoke mechanism may be useful, because it performs behind-the-scenes conversions between function pointers and delegates.) The reverse situation is also possible, where you have native code that is using an object that takes event handlers. You may find it convenient if you can pass a pointer to a native function as the event handler method.

In .NET 2.0, the framework has two new functions called `GetFunctionPointerForDelegate` and `GetDelegateForFunctionPointer` in the `Marshal` class. These functions convert between a function pointer and a delegate (see figure 4.13).

4.4.1 Using GetFunctionPointerForDelegate

Let's start by writing a managed class that enumerates the visible windows on your desktop; internally, you'll use the `EnumWindows` API function to do the window enumeration. The `EnumWindows` API is declared as follows:

```
BOOL EnumWindows(WNDENUMPROC lpEnumFunc,LPARAM lParam);
```

The first parameter to the function is a function pointer, `typedef`-ed as `WNDENUMPROC`, which is defined as follows:

```
typedef BOOL (CALLBACK* WNDENUMPROC)(HWND, LPARAM);
```

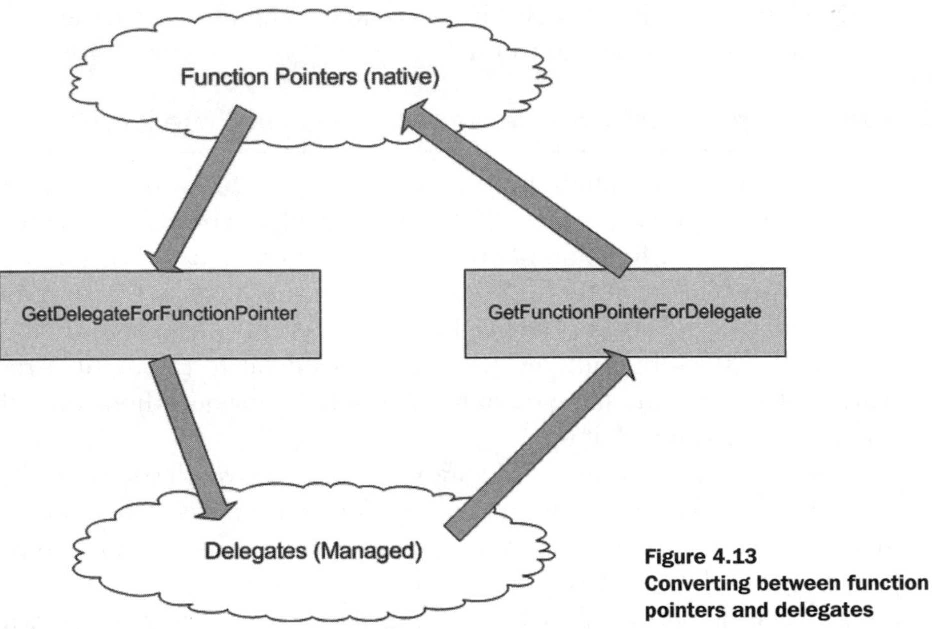

Figure 4.13 Converting between function pointers and delegates

For every window that is found, the API will call the function pointed to by `lpEnumFunc`. In the managed class, you'll declare a delegate that will serve as the managed version of this function pointer, and use that delegate to expose an event. You'll then use `Marshal::GetFunctionPointerForDelegate` to convert that delegate to a function pointer that can then be passed to the `EnumWindows` API function. Listing 4.16 shows the managed window enumeration class.

Listing 4.16 Class to enumerate windows

```
delegate bool EnumWindowsDelegateProc(
    IntPtr hwnd,IntPtr lParam);        <-- Delegate used in lieu of function pointer

ref class WindowEnumerator
{
private:
    EnumWindowsDelegateProc^ _WindowFound;        <-- Private delegate member
public:
    WindowEnumerator(EnumWindowsDelegateProc^ handler)
    {
        _WindowFound = handler;
    }
    void Init()
    {
        pin_ptr<EnumWindowsDelegateProc^> tmp =  &_WindowFound;   <-- 1 Pin delegate before passing to native code
```

```
        EnumWindows((WNDENUMPROC)
            Marshal::GetFunctionPointerForDelegate(
            _WindowFound).ToPointer(), 0);
    }
};
```

❷ Call API with converted function pointer

Note that you don't strictly need to pin the delegate ❶; you only need to ensure that the GC doesn't collect it. This is because the GC doesn't keep track of unmanaged pointers; but pinning solves that issue for you and doesn't cause any noticeable overhead in this scenario. When the call to `EnumWindows` is executed ❷, the callback that is passed to it is a native pointer to the delegate, which means this delegate is invoked for every window.

To use this class, all you need is a method that matches the `EnumWindowsDelegateProc` delegate signature. You're going to write such a method (as a static method of a class); it will display the title text of each visible window that's enumerated.

4.4.2 Using GetDelegateForFunctionPointer

You have only seen `GetFunctionPointerForDelegate` in action so far. To see the reverse function `GetDelegateForFunctionPointer`, you'll use a pointer to the native `printf` function to display each enumerated window. That way, in using a single example, you can see both conversions. Listing 4.17 shows the code for the class.

Listing 4.17 Code that performs delegate/function pointer conversions

```
ref class MyClass
{
    delegate int DispProc(String^, String^);
    static DispProc^ pDispProc = nullptr;
public:
    static MyClass()
    {
        HMODULE hLib = LoadLibrary(_T("msvcrt.dll"));
        if(hLib)
        {
            typedef int (*FUNC_PTR)(const char *, ...);
            FUNC_PTR pfn = reinterpret_cast<FUNC_PTR>(
                GetProcAddress(hLib, "printf"));
            if(pfn)
            {
                pDispProc = (DispProc^)
                    Marshal::GetDelegateForFunctionPointer(
                    (IntPtr)pfn,DispProc::typeid);
            }
            FreeLibrary(hLib);
```

❶ Delegate to display each window

❷ Convert printf function to a delegate

```
        }
    }
    static bool HandleFoundWindow(IntPtr hwnd,IntPtr lParam)
    {
        TCHAR buff[512];
        GetWindowText((HWND)hwnd.ToPointer(), buff, 511);
        if(IsWindowVisible((HWND)hwnd.ToPointer()) && _tcslen(buff))
            pDispProc("%s\r\n\r\n",gcnew String(buff));
        return TRUE;
    }
};
```

Use pDispProc to indirectly invoke printf ❸

A delegate ❶ is used to display each enumerated window. The most interesting portion in this code snippet is the static constructor ❷, where you obtain a function pointer to the `printf` function (from msvcrt.dll), convert it to a delegate, and then save it in the `pDispProc` delegate variable. In the `HandleFoundWindow` method, when you invoke the `pDispProc` delegate ❸, `printf` gets executed, because the delegate is merely a proxy to the unmanaged function pointer (that points to `printf`). In the previous class, you passed a delegate to a method expecting a function pointer, and the delegate was invoked through that function pointer. However, in this class, you pass a function pointer to a delegate, and the function pointer is invoked through the delegate. Here's a code snippet that shows how these two classes can be put to use:

```
WindowEnumerator we(gcnew EnumWindowsDelegateProc(
    MyClass::HandleFoundWindow));
we.Init();
```

As you can see, the calling code has no idea that the class internally converts the delegate to a function pointer. This ability to convert between function pointers and delegates is particularly useful when you're wrapping a native library so as to expose it to the .NET world. Languages such as C# and VB.NET only understand delegates, whereas a lot of native libraries use function pointers to provide callbacks. By using these `Marshal` class methods, you can expose delegates to languages like C# and VB.NET and internally continue to use function pointers. In the same way, when you're attempting to use a managed class that has events from native code, you can take advantage of the ability to convert a function pointer to a delegate to directly pass pointers to native methods as the event handler functions.

A trick to use assembly code from managed code

You can't have inline assembly language code in managed blocks, which rules out using them in pure MSIL modules. Even in mixed-mode modules, you'd need to restrict them to unmanaged blocks of code. Here's a trick that uses `GetDelegateForFunctionPointer` and allows you to directly execute assembly code. You can declare an unsigned `char` array containing the assembly code for a function, convert that to a delegate using `GetDelegateForFunctionPointer`, and then execute that delegate. Here' s some sample code:

```
delegate Int32 DoubleNum(Int32 x);

unsigned char pNative[] =
{
    0x55, // push ebp
    0x8B, 0xEC, // mov ebp,esp
    0x8B, 0x45, 0x08, // mov eax,dword ptr [arg]
    0x03, 0x45, 0x08, // add eax,dword ptr [arg]
    0x5D, // pop ebp
    0xC3 // ret
};

DoubleNum^ pDoubleNum = (DoubleNum^)
    Marshal::GetDelegateForFunctionPointer(
        (IntPtr)pNative, DoubleNum::typeid);

Console::WriteLine(pDoubleNum(19));
```

You should do this only if you're familiar with assembly and are sure of what you're doing. It's more of a feel-good trick rather than something you'd want to put to use in production code.

4.5 Summary

In this chapter, we've discussed some seemingly disconnected topics, but they're all important concepts in mixed-mode programming. It was vital that you understand the workings of pinning and interior pointers and also have an idea of when and when not to use them.

We also covered various interop mechanisms, and although you saw that every mechanism has its own set of advantages and best-use situations, we won't be using either CCW or P/Invoke in the rest of this book. For the sort of mixed-mode programming we'll be covering, C++ interop is the fastest and most convenient option. We'll use that exclusively for our interop needs.

We discussed mixed types and how to use the `gcroot/auto_gcroot` library's provided classes. We also implemented a similar smart pointer class for automatically managing a native resource in a managed class. We'll be using mixed types considerably in the rest of this book, and the techniques you learned in this chapter will be repeatedly put into practice.

The last topic we discussed, which was how to convert between function pointers and delegates, is something that you'll see again when writing native wrappers for managed code or managed wrappers for native code.

In the next chapter, we'll use the information gained in this and the previous chapters to demonstrate how you can access and utilize native libraries from managed applications.

5 Interoping with native libraries from managed applications

When you have extensively large native applications and libraries, it doesn't make much sense to attempt to rewrite the entire code base in .NET. If you have a car with a tape-deck music system, and you want to have MP3 support, you don't change the entire music system in the car. Instead, you buy a new MP3-player, connect it to your existing car music system, and reuse the existing infrastructure—which in this case includes the speakers and the amplifiers. Similarly, the most cost-effective option (in terms of work) is to directly interop with those native libraries from your new managed applications. With that approach, you write your new applications using the .NET Framework but continue to access and utilize the legacy unmanaged libraries that you used in the past, because they may not have managed versions ready yet, and a port to .NET is extremely difficult and impractical. In this chapter, we'll look at some example scenarios where managed/unmanaged interop is required and see how to approach such scenarios using C++/CLI. To maintain simplicity and easy comprehension, I've used minimal examples, but the same techniques can be applied to bigger real-life interop developmental efforts.

Type conversions are one of the most important aspects of mixed-mode programming, because whenever your code crosses the managed/unmanaged boundary, type conversions come into play. It's a little like having two private secretaries: one who speaks only French, and the other who speaks only English. Although you can give them independent work, sometimes they have to interact directly with each other. You need to do French/English translations for that, which would obviously be a time-consuming process. It's the same with type conversions, and thus it's important to minimize the amount of processor time spent doing type conversions. It's essential that you're comfortable with doing them and that you know the best ways to achieve them, depending on the situation.

The core example in the chapter is a CLI wrapper that you'll write for the native desktop API. The techniques used can be generically applied to a wide level of mixed-mode scenarios.

You'll also see other shorter examples, such as wrapping classes in an MFC extension DLL via a mixed-mode regular DLL and writing a custom RCW to consume a COM object. Additionally, we'll discuss a useful technique to write a single mixed-mode DLL that will export a conditionally compiled C++ class that can be consumed by both managed and native clients.

For conversions not discussed here, the techniques and .NET classes used for the conversions are pretty much the same. Once you get the hang of it, you can apply these same mechanisms to do any sort of managed/unmanaged type conversion.

5.1 Converting between managed and native types

There are several commonly required conversions between managed and unmanaged types: specifically, those dealing with strings and arrays. Managed code only understands managed types, and native code only understands native types. Thus, whether you're calling into managed code from native code or calling into native code from managed code, you need conversions in both directions. Before the interop call, you need to convert from the calling type to the target type; after the call, you need to convert back to the calling type.

Next, we'll look at various string conversions, techniques for marshalling arrays, and implementing a fixed-size array.

5.1.1 Marshalling native strings

If you can convert from `System::String` to an unmanaged type X, you can indirectly convert a `System::String` to any unmanaged type Y, where a conversion exists from X to Y. For example, if you can convert to a `char*` or a `wchar_t*`, you can automatically convert to any MFC or COM string type, because conversions to those types exist from and to a `char*` or a `wchar_t*`. We aren't going to discuss conversions to every single unmanaged type out there, but you'll see all the common ones. Let's start with conversions from and to `char*` and `wchar_t*`.

Converting from and to Ansi and Unicode strings

Converting from a `char*` to a `String^` isn't hard; the `String` class has a constructor that takes a `char*`. However, to convert a `String^` back to a `char*`, you have to use the `StringToHGlobalAnsi` method of the `Marshal` class (declared under the `System::Runtime::InteropServices` namespace), which allocates unmanaged memory and copies the contents of the `String^` into that memory. After using the `char*`, you have to manually free the allocated memory using the `FreeHGlobal` method or else suffer a memory leak. Listing 5.1 shows both conversions: from `char*` to `String^` and then back to `char*`.

Listing 5.1 Converting from `char*` to `String` and back

```
char strAnsi[] = "This is an Ansi string";
String^ str = gcnew String(strAnsi);          <-- String constructor takes char*
IntPtr p = Marshal::StringToHGlobalAnsi(str);  <-- Allocate native memory; copy String into it
char* pAnsi = static_cast<char*>(p.ToPointer());  <-- Cast IntPtr to char*
printf("%s\r\n",pAnsi);
Marshal::FreeHGlobal(p);   <-- Free native memory after using char*
```

Converting to a wchar_t* is similar; you just use the String^ constructor that takes a wchar_t* parameter. To convert back, you use StringToHGlobalUni, which is similar to StringToHGlobalAnsi, except that it creates a Unicode string. As before, you have to manually free the native memory after usage using FreeHGlobal. Listing 5.2 shows these functions in action.

Listing 5.2 Converting from wchar_t* to String and back

```
wchar_t strUni[] = L"This is an Unicode string";
String^ str =                              String constructor
    gcnew String(strUni);                  takes wchar_t*
IntPtr p =                                         Allocate native memory;
    Marshal::StringToHGlobalUni(str);              copy String to it
wchar_t* pUni =
    static_cast<wchar_t*>(p.ToPointer());          Cast IntPtr to wchar_t*
wprintf(L"%s\r\n",pUni);
Marshal::FreeHGlobal(p);    <-- Free unneeded native memory
```

Converting from and to COM strings

BSTRs are used primarily in COM. On Windows platforms, they're defined as wide character strings that are NULL terminated, but BSTRs can contain embedded NULLs too, because the memory allocated for a BSTR is preceded by a length field. Although you can convert a String to a wchar_t* and then easily convert that to a BSTR, the Marshal class provides a direct method to convert to a BSTR. You can then use that method instead of going for a two-level conversion. Converting a BSTR to a String is easy; you use the String constructor that takes a Unicode string, just as you did in the previous section. Note that you assume that the BSTR doesn't contain embedded NULLs (which it can). If you aren't sure of that, you should use the String constructor overload that allows you to specify the number of characters in the string and the start position within the character array. For the reverse conversion, you can use the StringToBSTR method of the Marshal class, which allocates a BSTR and copies the contents of the String into it. Once you're done with it, you need to call FreeBSTR to free the allocated BSTR. Listing 5.3 demonstrates this.

Listing 5.3 Converting between a BSTR and a String

```
BSTR bstr = SysAllocString(L"This is a BSTR");   <-- Allocate source BSTR
String^ str = gcnew String(bstr);   <-- Convert to String using constructor
IntPtr p = Marshal::StringToBSTR(str);
BSTR bstrnew = static_cast<BSTR>(p.ToPointer());      Convert to BSTR;
wprintf(L"%s\r\n",bstrnew);                           use as required
```

```
Marshal::FreeBSTR(p);         <— Free BSTR
SysFreeString(bstr);          <— Free original BSTR
```

Converting from and to MFC and STL strings

Conversions with an MFC `CString` are probably the most convenient among string conversions. You can use the `String` constructor with a `CString` because `CString` has an implicit cast to `LPCTSTR` that the `String` constructor can use. Converting back to a `CString` is also easy, because one of the `CString` constructors takes a `String^` parameter. Listing 5.4 shows these conversions in action:

Listing 5.4 Converting between a `CString` and a `String`

```
CString mfcstr = _T("This is a CString");
String^ str = gcnew String(mfcstr);      <— String constructor, takes LPCTSTR
CString mfcnew(str);                     <— CString constructor,
_tprintf(_T("%s\r\n"), mfcnew);             takes String ^
```

For an STL `string`, there's no direct conversion. You indirectly use the `char*` conversions by calling the `c_str` method on the `string`, which returns a `const char*`. To convert back to the STL `string`, you convert to `char*` and use that `char*` to construct a new `string` object. Listing 5.5 demonstrates these conversions:

Listing 5.5 Converting between an STL `string` and a `String`

```
using namespace std;
string stl = "This is an STL string";            (1) Construct
String^ str = gcnew String(stl.c_str());      <—     String ^
IntPtr p = Marshal::StringToHGlobalAnsi(str);            (2) Construct
string stlnew(static_cast<char*>(p.ToPointer()));            STL string
Marshal::FreeHGlobal(p);                  <—
printf("%s\r\n",stlnew.c_str());        (3) Free char*
```

A `String^` is constructed (1) using the `const char*` returned by `string::c_str`. For the reverse conversion, you construct the STL `string` using the `char*` obtained from using `StringToHGlobalAnsi` on the `String^` (2). You then free the `char*` (3), because it's no longer needed, and continue to use the STL `string`.

Although we haven't looked at every unmanaged string type, any other type can be indirectly created by converting from one of the string types we have covered in this section. Depending on your programming context, you should choose the most convenient conversion available. For instance, COM programmers may want to convert to a BSTR, whereas MFC programmers may prefer a CString. The good thing about the CString is that because of the implicit cast to LPCTSTR, it can be used anywhere a const char* or wchar_t* is expected.

5.1.2 Marshalling arrays

Another frequently-encountered requirement when doing mixed-mode coding is converting between managed and native arrays. When converting from a managed array to a native array, two approaches can be adopted.

Approach 1

If the required native array is for read-only purposes, then you don't need to create a new native array; rather, you can pin the managed array and pass a pointer to the first element. You learned how to do this in chapter 2, when we discussed managed arrays.

Here's a code snippet that illustrates how to pin the managed array and pass it to a function that expects a native array:

```
array<int>^ intarr = gcnew array<int>(10);
pin_ptr<int> pin = &intarr[0];          <-- Pin managed array
FuncIntPtr(pin);                        <-- (1) Call function with pinned pointer
```

The pinned pointer is passed directly to a function expecting a native array (1).

Approach 2

If a new native array needs to be created, you can use an overload of the Marshal::Copy method to do that. In the previous code snippet, you didn't create a new native array. If you wanted to, however, this is how you'd do it using the Marshal::Copy method:

```
int arr[10];
Marshal::Copy(intarr,0,static_cast<IntPtr>(arr),10);
```

In this snippet, the managed array is copied into a native array that you pass to the function. Note that the function won't allocate memory for the native array; that's up to the caller. The Marshal::Copy method is internally implemented using a fast memory copy and has specific overloads to handle various types of arrays.

The Marshal::Copy method also has overloads to copy a native array to a managed array, and therefore it can be used to convert in both directions. The following code snippet demonstrates this.

```
int natarr[10];
array<int>^ newarr = gcnew array<int>(10);
Marshal::Copy(static_cast<IntPtr>(natarr), newarr, 0, 10);
```

Here the contents of the native array are copied into the managed array. Array copying between managed and native arrays makes sense only for compatible types. For example, a managed array of `Char` should be copied only into a native `wchar_t` array. If you have a managed array of a managed type, it doesn't make sense to attempt to copy that to a native array, because a native array can't have a managed type as the element. But if you have a native array of a native pointer type, you can copy that into a managed array of type `IntPtr` using an overload of the `Marshal::Copy` method. Some code that illustrates this is shown here:

```
Native* natptrarr[100];
array<IntPtr>^ manarray = gcnew array<IntPtr>(100);
Marshal::Copy(static_cast<IntPtr>(natptrarr),
    manarray,0,100);
```

In this code snippet, you take advantage of the fact that an `IntPtr` can be used to hold a pointer to a native type. If you want to extract the original `Native*` out of the array, you can do the following cast:

```
Native* pNative = (Native*)manarray[0].ToPointer();
```

Managed arrays are always reference types, and thus you can't have a managed array of static size that you can use as a member of a data structure. It's possible, however, to simulate a static-size managed array.

5.1.3 Simulating a native static array with managed code

C# 2.0 has a fixed array feature that lets you specify the number of elements, so that the resulting data structure will have a size equal to the size of the total number of elements. This is useful when talking to legacy code that uses fixed-size arrays. Although there is no direct syntactic support to do the same in C++/CLI, you can simulate the C# 2.0 fixed-array behavior by implementing a class that emulates the MSIL generated by the C# compiler for a fixed-size array. The first time I saw such an implementation, it was a template class written by Shaun Miller and Brandon Bray, both from the Visual C++ team. My version is similar to theirs, except that I follow the C# 2.0 generated MSIL more closely than they did. If you use my version, shown in listing 5.6, the generated MSIL will be as close to the C# 2.0 version as possible.

Listing 5.6 Template class that emulates a C# 2.0 fixed array

```
template<typename T, int size>
[StructLayout(LayoutKind::Sequential,
    Size = sizeof(T) * size),UnsafeValueType]
public value class FixedSizeArray
```

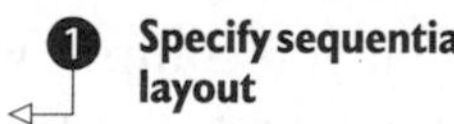

```
{
    T FixedElementField;        <-- Bogus element used as address resolver (2)
public:
    T% operator[](int index)    (3) Overloaded [] operator
    {
        return *(&FixedElementField + index);
    }
    operator interior_ptr<T>()  (4) Implicit cast to interior_ptr
    {
        return &FixedElementField;
    }
};
```

You use the StructLayout attribute ❶ to specify a sequential layout. You also use the UnsafeValueType attribute (from the System::Runtime::CompilerServices namespace), so the CLR will add buffer overflow checks. In addition, you have a bogus element that serves as an address resolver to the structure ❷. The [] operator is overloaded to return the T element at an index ❸, and an implicit cast to interior_ptr is added for pointer access support ❹. The MSIL generated for this class is close to that generated for a C# 2.0 fixed array, except for the operators you overloaded for convenience. Using this class is straightforward, and the in-memory size of the class will always be equal to the sum of the sizes of each element in the class. Here's some sample code that demonstrates how the class can be used:

```
FixedSizeArray<int, 10> arr;
arr[4] = 100;
arr[8] = 99;
Console::WriteLine("Array size : {0}",sizeof arr); // Outputs 40
interior_ptr<int> p = arr;
for(int i=0; i<10; i++)
    Console::WriteLine("Element {0} : {1}",i,*p++);
```

In this code snippet, you directly access array elements using the [] operator as well as use a pointer to iterate through the elements. In a future version of the compiler, it's probable that direct syntactic support for fixed arrays will be added. You don't have to wait until then, though, because the flexibility of the C++/CLI language allows you to write utility classes to work around such limitations.

5.2 Double thunking in mixed-mode function calls

When you compile with /clr and you have a native class in your code (one that's neither a ref class nor a value class), two entry points are generated for its methods:

a managed entry point and a native entry point. This allows both managed and native callers to call these methods, and the native entry point acts as a thunk to the managed entry point. The word *thunk* (or *thunking*) refers to the jump from the managed code to the native code (or the reverse). Those of you who moved from Win16 to Win32 programming a long while ago may remember the thunking that was required to jump from a 16-bit block of code into a 32-bit function. Thunking here is used in a similar context except that the jump is between managed and unmanaged code.

Virtual functions are always called through the native entry point, and this results in a performance issue. When a managed caller calls a virtual function in a `/clr` compiled native class, two managed/unmanaged transitions are required: the first managed-to-native transition to invoke the native entry point, and the second native-to-managed transition to invoke the managed entry point. This is referred to as *double thunking*. Figure 5.1 shows a diagrammatic representation of double thunking.

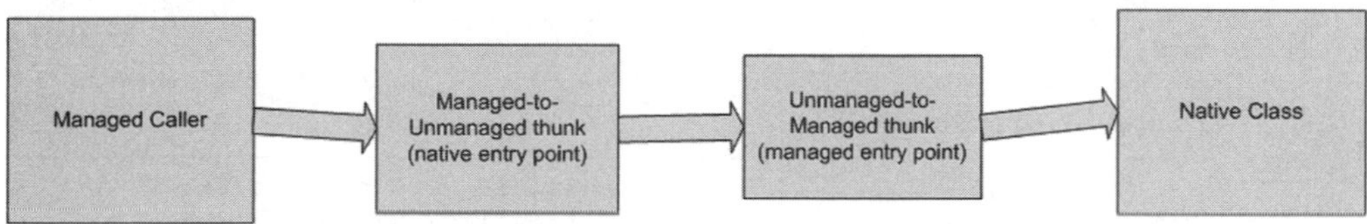

Figure 5.1 Double thunking

Let's write some code to see the effect of double thunking:

```
class N
{
public:
    N()
    {
        Console::WriteLine(__FUNCSIG__);
    }
    N(const N&)
    {
        Console::WriteLine(__FUNCSIG__);
    }
    ~N()
    {
        Console::WriteLine(__FUNCSIG__);
    }
};

class X
```

```
{
public:
    virtual void UseNVirt(N)
    {
        Console::WriteLine(__FUNCSIG__);
    }
}
```

You have a class `N` with a constructor, a copy constructor, and a destructor, and you use the `__FUNCSIG__` macro to display the function name when the functions are invoked. This allows you to trace the execution flow of the program. Now, let's write some code that invokes the `UseNVirt` virtual method of the class `X`. So that you can see the corresponding output for each relevant fragment and get a clear picture of the program flow, table 5.1 shows the code and the corresponding console output.

Table 5.1 Execution flow with double thunking

Source code	Console output

`N n;`
`X* x = new X();`
`Console::WriteLine();`
	`__thiscall N::N(void)`

`x->UseNVirt(n);`
`Console::WriteLine();`
	`__thiscall N::N(const class N &)`
	`__thiscall N::N(const class N &)`
	`__thiscall N::~N(void)`
	`void __thiscall X::UseNVirt(class N)`
	`__thiscall N::~N(void)`

`delete x;`	`__thiscall N::~N(void)`

As you can see, when you make the call to `UseNVirt`, the copy constructor for class `N` is invoked twice. This happens because two copy constructions are required: the first to call the native stub method, and the second to call the actual managed method. Thus, two thunks are involved. The first managed-to-native thunk is to call the native method, and the second native-to-managed thunk is to call the managed method. The combination of the double-thunking and the extra copy construction involved results in poorer code performance.

The resolution to this double-thunking problem is to instruct the compiler not to generate the native entry point. This is done by specifying the `__clrcall` calling convention. Specifying `__clrcall` on a method tells the compiler that the method will be called only from managed code; thus, only a managed entry point needs to be generated. Of course, this means you can't call the method from a

#pragma unmanaged block of code. Therefore, you should use this calling convention only when you're sure that the caller will always be managed. Let's add a method to the class X that uses the __clrcall calling convention and use that function in the test code. Here's the modified code for the class X:

```
class X
{
public:
    virtual void UseNVirt(N)
    {
        Console::WriteLine(__FUNCSIG__);
    }
    virtual void __clrcall UseNVirtClrCall(N)
    {
        Console::WriteLine(__FUNCSIG__);
    }
};
```

The only difference in the newly added method is that you specify it to use the __clrcall calling convention. Let's write some code that invokes this method; as before, table 5.2 shows the corresponding console output.

Table 5.2 Execution flow without double thunking

Source code	Console output

`N n;`
`X* x = new X();`
`Console::WriteLine();`
	`__thiscall N::N(void)`

`x->UseNVirtClrCall(n);`
`Console::WriteLine();`
	`__thiscall N::N(const class N &)`
	`void __clrcall X::UseNVirtClrCall(class N)`
	`__thiscall N::~N(void)`

`delete x;`	`__thiscall N::~N(void)`

This time, there's only one call to the class N copy constructor. No double thunking occurs, because there's only one entry point: the managed one. My recommendation is to liberally use __clrcall except when you know for certain that the method can be invoked by a native caller. Note that VC++ 2005 does some optimizations on its own and implicitly adds __clrcall to any method with a managed type in its signature (including the return type).

At this stage, I believe we have covered sufficient ground to move on to a discussion on how a native library can be wrapped using C++/CLI, and a managed interface exposed to the .NET world.

5.3 Wrapping a native API and exposing a CLI interface

A lot of native APIs, including most of the Windows programming API, is written in C, and as a result, the public interface consists of a large number of C-style functions. Although the .NET Framework provides interop mechanisms to invoke C-based libraries, it's far more convenient for managed callers if a managed API is exposed to them. Going back to our earlier analogy of the French and English secretaries, a CLI wrapper is equivalent to giving each of them translation booklets (in their respective languages) that contain translated versions of commonly required sentences, thus allowing them to communicate with each other without too much trouble.

In this section, you'll write a managed .NET wrapper for a set of native API functions that deals with the creation and management of virtual desktops. A .NET wrapper essentially means a managed library that exposes a purely managed interface to .NET callers while internally making the proxy calls into the native library that it's wrapping. Figure 5.2 shows the basic design that will be used to wrap the native API and expose a managed interface to managed callers.

Obviously, before you begin writing a wrapper, you have to ask yourself if you need to do that. If you're making a few scattered calls into the native API from your managed code, you may as well use the P/Invoke or C++ interop mechanism we discussed in the previous chapter. Of course, to use C++ interop, your managed application needs to be using C++. Even then, the `/clr:safe` and `/clr:pure` modes will be incompatible. Assuming that you want to expose an API to other languages like C# and VB.NET, P/Invoke is your only option. But as the occurrence of calling the unmanaged API increases, P/Invoke will not only be inconvenient (for reasons you saw earlier), but also far less performant. That's where a .NET wrapper makes sense. The wrapper you're going to write in this section will wrap a bunch of C-based Win32 API functions. Later this chapter, you'll see how

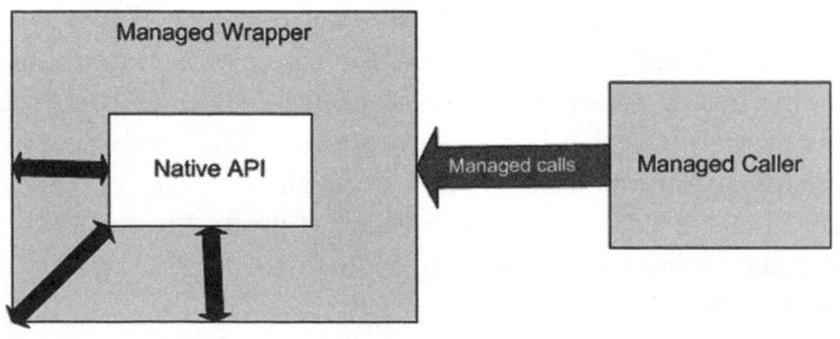

Figure 5.2 Wrapping the native API using a managed wrapper

to write wrappers for C++ classes; more specifically, you'll write a wrapper for an MFC extension library. Before you write your wrapper, let's quickly go through the API so you get an idea of the native API functions that need to be wrapped.

5.3.1 Overview of the native API

Beginning with Windows 2000, the OS directly supports multiple desktops, where a *desktop* is a logical display that can contain any number of windows and menus. Each desktop is associated with a *window station*; a window station can contain multiple desktops, all of which share the clipboard. We won't discuss how window stations and desktops work in detail; we'll limit our discussion to the creation and management of desktops on the default window station. Our aim in this section is to develop a good understanding of how a native API can be wrapped, not to write a comprehensive library for managing virtual desktops and window stations. For the example wrapper, we'll ignore the possibility of having multiple window stations and assume that you'll always be working with the default windows station that's created every time Windows boots up. Table 5.3 is a partial list of the Desktop API functions. I've listed only those functions you'll use in your wrapper.

Table 5.3 Desktop API: List of functions used

API function	Description

`CreateDesktop`	Creates a new desktop, and assigns it to the calling thread. The desktop will be associated with the active window station. If the desktop already exists, a handle is returned to this existing desktop. The `lpszDesktop` parameter is used to specify a unique case-insensitive name that will be used to identify the desktop.
	`HDESK CreateDesktop(`
	`  LPCTSTR lpszDesktop,`
	`  LPCTSTR lpszDevice,`
	`  LPDEVMODE pDevmode,`
	`  DWORD dwFlags,`
	`  ACCESS_MASK dwDesiredAccess,`
	`  LPSECURITY_ATTRIBUTES lpsa`
	`);`

`OpenDesktop`	Opens an existing desktop. Although you'll wrap it in the next section, you can use the `CreateDesktop` function to open an existing desktop. The only situation where this function is necessarily used over `CreateDesktop` is when you need to specify the `fInherit` parameter as `FALSE`, which means new processes won't inherit this desktop handle.

continued on next page

Table 5.3 Desktop API: List of functions used *(continued)*

API function	Description

	`HDESK OpenDesktop(`
	`  LPTSTR lpszDesktop,`
	`  DWORD dwFlags,`
	`  BOOL fInherit,`
	`  ACCESS_MASK dwDesiredAccess`
	`);`

`CloseDesktop`	Closes a handle to a desktop. Note that this doesn't delete the desktop. A desktop is deleted only when all processes running on it have terminated.
	`BOOL CloseDesktop(`
	`  HDESK hDesktop`
	`);`

`SwitchDesktop`	Activates and shows a specified desktop.
	`BOOL SwitchDesktop(`
	`  HDESK hDesktop`
	`);`

`GetUserObjectInformation`	Retrieves information about a specific desktop object. Although you won't directly wrap this function, you'll use it to retrieve the name of a desktop object.
	`BOOL GetUserObjectInformation(`
	`  HANDLE hObj,`
	`  int nIndex,`
	`  PVOID pvInfo,`
	`  DWORD nLength,`
	`  LPDWORD lpnLengthNeeded`
	`);`

`GetThreadDesktop`	Gets a handle to the desktop object associated with a specific thread.
	`HDESK GetThreadDesktop(`
	`  DWORD dwThreadId`
	`);`

`SetThreadDesktop`	Assigns a specific desktop to the calling thread.
	`BOOL SetThreadDesktop(`
	`  HDESK hDesktop`
	`);`

`EnumDesktopWindows`	Enumerates all top-level windows in a specific desktop. This function invokes a callback for each window that's enumerated and works similarly to the `EnumWindows` API function.
	`BOOL EnumDesktopWindows(`
	`  HDESK hDesktop,`

continued on next page

Table 5.3 Desktop API: List of functions used *(continued)*

API function	Description

	`WNDENUMPROC lpfn,`
	`LPARAM lParam`
	`);`

`EnumDesktops`	Enumerates all desktops in the current window station.
	`BOOL EnumDesktops(`
	`HWINSTA hwinsta,`
	`DESKTOPENUMPROC lpEnumFunc,`
	`LPARAM lParam`
	`);`

Note that an `HDESK` is a handle to a desktop object, just like an `HWND` is a handle to a window. As you can see from the table, nearly all the desktop API functions either take or return an `HDESK`. When you write your .NET wrapper, you'll abstract away this `HDESK` object from the managed interface because there's no need to have the managed callers directly access and manipulate the `HDESK`.

5.3.2 Writing the CLI wrapper

The primary idea of writing the wrapper is that pure-managed clients (including those written in C# or VB) can access the library and invoke calls using managed types. When writing the wrapper, I didn't put a lot of effort into maintaining a .NET-style interface. Instead, I wrote what can be termed a *thin managed wrapper* around the underlying native API. Although there's a school of thought that encourages people to write every managed API with a strong .NET flavor, my recommendation is to use the best approach for a specific scenario. In this example, I didn't want to unnecessarily complicate the code by using .NET coding elements such as exceptions, when simple boolean return types will do the job just as well, and perhaps more efficiently. However, if the wrapper will be primarily used from languages such as C# or VB.NET, then I recommend that you follow the standard .NET design guidelines.

I'll first show you the skeletal framework of what your class will look like. Then, I'll explain how the class can be used from a C# client. Once you do that, you'll see how each method or property is internally implemented and how the managed/unmanaged marshalling is implemented. Let's begin with the skeleton class, shown in listing 5.7.

Listing 5.7 Skeletal wrapper class (just the definitions)

```
namespace DesktopLibrary
{
    [UnmanagedFunctionPointer(CallingConvention::Winapi,
        CharSet = CharSet::Auto)]
    public delegate bool EnumDesktopDelegate(
        String^ strDesktop, IntPtr param);
    public delegate void EnumDesktopWindowsDelegate(
        String^ strTitle);
    BOOL CALLBACK GlobalEnumWindowsProc(
        HWND hwnd,LPARAM lParam);
    public ref class Desktop
    {
    private:
        HDESK _hDesktop;
        Desktop(HDESK hDesktop);
        static EnumDesktopDelegate^ _EnumDesktopDelegate = nullptr;
    public:
        Desktop();
        ~Desktop();
        !Desktop();
        bool Create(String^ strDesktop);
        bool Open(String^ strDesktop);
        bool Close();
        bool Activate();
        bool EnumWindowTitles();
        void RaiseWindowFound(String^ strTitle);
#pragma push_macro("CreateProcess")
#undef CreateProcess
        Process^ CreateProcess(String^ strProcessPath);
#pragma pop_macro("CreateProcess")
        property String^ Name
        {
            String^ get();
        };
        event EnumDesktopWindowsDelegate^ OnWindowFound;
        static property Desktop^ ThreadDesktop
        {
            Desktop^ get();
            void set(Desktop^);
        };
        static bool SwitchTo(Desktop^);
        static event EnumDesktopDelegate^ OnDesktopFound
        {
            void add(EnumDesktopDelegate^);
            void remove(EnumDesktopDelegate^);
        };
#pragma push_macro("EnumDesktops")
#undef EnumDesktops
```

Annotations:
1. Delegate declarations for events
2. HDESK member
3. Constructor is kept private
4. Public wrapper methods
5. Helper method
6. Return name of desktop
7. Current thread's associated desktop
8. Static method to switch desktops

Nontrivial event for desktop enumeration

9. List desktops in current window station

```
        static bool EnumDesktops(IntPtr param);     ⑨
#pragma pop_macro("EnumDesktops")
    };
}
```

A couple of delegate declarations ❶ are used to declare the events associated with enumerating windows in a desktop and enumerating desktops in the current window station. You also have a global callback that's used as part of the class's internal implementation. The important `HDESK` member ❷ is a private variable and is hidden from the calling managed client. Because you don't want to expose the `HDESK` to the clients, the constructor ❸ that takes an `HDESK` is kept private and is only used within the class. You also have a number of public methods ❹ such as `Create`, `Open`, `Close`, and so on, that act as the wrapper methods invoked by calling managed clients. Typically, each of these wrapper methods wraps a specific native method. For example, `Create` wraps the `CreateDesktop` API function, and `Close` wraps the `CloseDesktop` API function.

You also have some extra helper functions like `CreateProcess` ❺, which creates a process in a specific desktop. There's no specific desktop API function that `CreateProcess` is wrapping; it's merely a convenient function that you've added to enhance the usability of the managed interface. Similarly, you have a property called `Name` ❻, which returns the name of a desktop. Again, you implement this as a property to improve the usability level of the public managed interface by internally wrapping one specific usage of the `GetUserObjectInformation` API function, which can be used to obtain information other than just the name of the desktop. You aren't exposing the full functionality of the `GetUserObjectInformation` function, because you're only interested in the desktop's name. This is something you'll do a lot when wrapping native API: partially exposing a native method's functionality levels and hiding those functionalities that aren't needed by the managed caller.

Similar to the `Name` property, the static `ThreadDesktop` property ❼ can be used to get and set the desktop associated with the calling thread. This single property internally wraps two API functions: `GetThreadDesktop` and `SetThreadDesktop`. You also have a static `SwitchTo` method ❽ that activates a specific desktop. It's functionally identical to the `Activate` method, except that this is a static method, and internally it invokes a call to `Activate`. Again, this is a matter of convenience; you give the user multiple options to do something, which improves the flexibility of the class.

In the native API, the functions that enumerate desktops and desktop windows both invoke callback functions for every window or desktop that's enumerated. In the managed version, you provide the managed clients with events they can hook onto; the event handlers do the same role in managed code that the callbacks do in native code. You implement the two events differently. For the `OnDesktopFound` event, you use a delegate that's a managed version of the native callback, and internally you use `GetFunctionPointerForDelegate` to convert the delegate into a function pointer. For the `OnWindowFound` event, you use a delegate that's simpler than the native callback; and internally, a global callback is used, which transfers the call to the event handler. You implement the two events differently so that you get an idea of both techniques: The former technique uses a thin delegate wrapper over the native callback, and the latter uses a more abstract delegate wrapper over the native callback. What we've discussed so far will become far more lucid later when you see the implementation for each function and property of the wrapper class.

One interesting thing you'll have noticed is that for both `CreateProcess` ❺ and `EnumDesktops` ❾, you use a bunch of `#pragma` preprocessor macros as well as a `#undef` macro. You have to do this because both `CreateDesktop` and `EnumDesktops` are Win32 API functions with both Ansi and Unicode versions. For example, with `CreateDesktop`, `CreateDesktopA` is the Ansi version, whereas `CreateDesktopW` is the Unicode version. The Win32 header files declare a macro named `CreateProcess` that will evaluate to `CreateProcessA` in Ansi compilation mode and `CreateProcessW` in Unicode compilation mode. Every time the preprocessor sees the macro `CreateProcess`, it converts it to either the Unicode or the Ansi versions. The preprocessor can't determine if you're calling the Win32 API or declaring a new function; it replaces every macro it finds with the right Ansi or Unicode version. In your code, when the preprocessor sees your managed functions named `CreateProcess` and `EnumDesktops`, depending on whether Ansi or Unicode compilation is enabled, it replaces the names with the *A* or *W* versions. Because you don't want your public managed functions to be renamed with *A* or *W* prefixes, you need to temporarily undefine the macro, make your declaration, and then redeclare the macro. The following code snippet shows what you typically do in such situations:

```
#pragma push_macro("EnumDesktops")          <-- Save macro value to preprocessor stack
#undef EnumDesktops                         <-- Undefine macro
    static bool EnumDesktops(IntPtr param);
#pragma pop_macro("EnumDesktops")           <-- Restore macro value from stack
```

Note that you have to do this in both header and CPP files; in fact, you have to do this for every instance where you use functions that have names that clash with a Win32 API name. In general, I strongly suggest that you avoid using names that clash with Win32 API functions. In the example, I chose to use two such names to show you how to use these macros, but in real-life situations you should avoid this as far as possible, because it's a bother to have to go through the *macro-save, macro-remove, macro-restore* routine every time.

Using the wrapper class from C#

Before we discuss the implementation of each method and property, let's see how a C# client can use the wrapper class. Listing 5.8 is a C# console app that uses the wrapper library to create a new desktop, runs Notepad in the new desktop, and then returns to the primary desktop. It also enumerates all active desktops before it terminates.

Listing 5.8 C# client that calls your managed wrapper

```
class Program
{
    static bool FoundDesktop(string s, IntPtr param)
    {
        Console.WriteLine(s);
        return true;
    }

    static void FoundWindow(string s)
    {
        Console.WriteLine(s);
    }

    static void Main(string[] args)
    {
        Desktop dorig = Desktop.ThreadDesktop;
        Desktop dnew = new Desktop();
        dnew.Create("nish");
        Desktop.ThreadDesktop = dnew;
        dnew.Activate();
        dnew.CreateProcess("c:\\windows\\notepad.exe");
        MessageBox.Show("pause","hey");
        dorig.Activate();
        Desktop.ThreadDesktop = dorig;

        dnew.OnWindowFound +=
            new EnumDesktopWindowsDelegate(FoundWindow);
        dnew.EnumWindowTitles();

        dnew.Close();

        Desktop.OnDesktopFound +=
```

Event handlers for EnumWindowTitles, EnumDesktops

Save current desktop

Create and show new desktop; run Notepad

Restore original desktop

Enumerate windows on created desktop

```
                new EnumDesktopDelegate(FoundDesktop);
            Desktop.EnumDesktops(IntPtr.Zero);
        }
    }
```

Enumerate all desktops in system

When you run this app, it creates a new desktop, launches Notepad, and pops up a message box. If you dismiss the message box without closing Notepad, the desktop remains alive, so that the next time you activate this desktop (by running the app again) you'll see the previous instance of Notepad as well as the new one that's just been launched. Try leaving the desktop alive, and run the app a few times, so that you'll get a few instances of Notepad running; doing so will give you some output when you enumerate the windows in that desktop. To make sure the desktop is killed, close all running instances of Notepad, and then dismiss the message box.

Implementation of the wrapper class

In this section, we'll go through every method and property in the wrapper class and discuss how they were implemented and why they were implemented in that particular way, where appropriate. We'll start with the two constructors: the public parameter less constructor and the private constructor that takes an `HDESK` parameter:

```
Desktop::Desktop() : _hDesktop(nullptr)
{
}

Desktop::Desktop(HDESK hDesktop) : _hDesktop(hDesktop)
{
}
```

There's not much code. The default constructor assigns the `_hDesktop` member to a `nullptr`, whereas the private overload that takes an `HDESK` parameter uses it to initialize the `_hDesktop` member. You also have a destructor and a finalizer, both of which invoke the `Close` method, in case the client doesn't manually do so (and calling `Close` on an already-closed `Desktop` object is harmless):

```
Desktop::~Desktop()
{
    Close();
}

Desktop::!Desktop()
{
    Close();
}
```

Next, here's the `Create` method that wraps the `CreateDesktop` API function:

```
bool Desktop::Create(String^ strDesktop)
{
    if(_hDesktop && !Close())
        return false;
    pin_ptr<const wchar_t> pStr = PtrToStringChars(strDesktop);
    _hDesktop = CreateDesktop(CW2CT(pStr),
        nullptr, nullptr,0,GENERIC_ALL,nullptr);
    return !(_hDesktop==nullptr);
}
```

❶ Check for and close open HDESKOP

❷ Pin String ^ to get wchar_t*

❸ Invoke native API function

In the `Create` method, you first check to see ❶ if the `Desktop` object already represents an open desktop; if so, you call `Close` on the handle (where `Close` is a wrapper function for the `CloseDesktop` API call). Next, you need to convert the `String` to a `const TCHAR*`, which is what the `CreateDesktop` function expects as the first parameter. You do that ❷ by using `PtrToStringChars` to get an interior pointer to the `String`'s buffer and then pinning that buffer. You pin the buffer so that you can pass the pointer to the native function call ❸. Observe how you change the `HDESKTOP` return type of the `CreateDesktop` call to a simpler `bool` return type for the managed code. When wrapping native API, this is something you'll probably find yourself doing often, because in most cases, there is no need to expose the actual native return type to managed code. It's far more convenient to substitute the return type with a managed type, such as `bool`.

The following code shows the `Open` method, which is implemented similarly to the `Create` method you just saw. The only difference here is that you call the `OpenDesktop` API function instead of the `CreateDesktop` function:

```
bool Desktop::Open(String^ strDesktop)
{
    if(_hDesktop && !Close())
        return false;
    pin_ptr<const wchar_t> pStr = PtrToStringChars(strDesktop);
    _hDesktop = OpenDesktop(CW2CT(pStr), 0, TRUE, GENERIC_ALL);
    return !(_hDesktop==nullptr);
}
```

By the way, for both `Open` and `Create` methods, because you only require a const `TCHAR*` to pass onto the native function, you don't have to create a new `TCHAR` buffer using one of the `Marshal` class methods discussed earlier in this chapter. Instead, you pass a pinned pointer to the internal buffer, thereby saving the overhead of having to create a new `TCHAR` buffer and then copy the contents of the `String` into it. Next, let's look at the relatively simple `Close` method that wraps the `CloseDesktop` API function:

```
bool Desktop::Close()
{
    return CloseDesktop(_hDesktop)!=FALSE;
}
```

An interesting point in this code is how you convert the native `BOOL` return type (which is merely a `typedef` for `int`) to the managed code-compatible `bool` return type. You do the same thing for the `ActivateDesktop` call too, as shown here:

```
bool Desktop::Activate()
{
    return SwitchDesktop(_hDesktop)!=FALSE;
}
```

Next, we'll look at the `CreateProcess` method. As noted previously, the desktop API doesn't provide any function to create a process on a specific desktop. Obviously, however, any managed client that will be using your wrapper library will want to run apps on desktops that are created. So, you provide them with a `CreateProcess` method that internally uses the `CreateProcess` Win32 API function (not connected in any way with the desktop API) to spawn an application on a particular desktop. Listing 5.9 shows this method.

Listing 5.9 The `CreateProcess` member function

```
#pragma push_macro("CreateProcess")
#undef CreateProcess
Process^ Desktop::CreateProcess(String^ strProcessPath)
{
#pragma pop_macro("CreateProcess")
    pin_ptr<const wchar_t> pStr = PtrToStringChars(strProcessPath);
    PROCESS_INFORMATION ProcessInfo;
    STARTUPINFO StartupInfo;
    ZeroMemory(&StartupInfo, sizeof(StartupInfo));
    StartupInfo.cb = sizeof StartupInfo ;
    LPTSTR lpName = new TCHAR[Name->Length + 1];
    pin_ptr<const wchar_t> pName = PtrToStringChars(Name);
    _tcscpy_s(lpName,Name->Length + 1,CW2CT(pName));        (1) Set desktop name
    StartupInfo.lpDesktop = lpName;                              in StartupInfo
    Process^ ret = nullptr;
    if(::CreateProcess(CW2CT(pStr), NULL,
        NULL,NULL,FALSE,0,NULL,                         Get Process object for
        NULL,&StartupInfo,&ProcessInfo))              newly-started application
    {
        ret = Process::GetProcessById(ProcessInfo.dwProcessId);
        CloseHandle(ProcessInfo.hThread);
        CloseHandle(ProcessInfo.hProcess);                 Create process in
    }                                                      specific desktop
    delete lpName;
```

```
        return ret;
    }
```

Essentially, you set the `lpDesktop` parameter of the `StartupInfo` variable ❶ to the name of the desktop you retrieve using the `Name` property. When you call `CreateProcess`, the newly-spawned application is associated with the desktop you specified. You then return a managed `Process` object to the calling client so the caller can manipulate the process as required. Thus, although managed wrappers hide a lot of native functionality from managed clients, they can also add to the managed interface utility methods, such as this one, that don't directly map to a corresponding native API function.

Let's look at the various property accessor functions. Listing 5.10 shows the `Name` property, which is a get-only property.

Listing 5.10 The `Name` property

```
String^ Desktop::Name::get()
{
    if(!_hDesktop)
        return nullptr;
    DWORD dwReqLen = 0;
    GetUserObjectInformation(_hDesktop,
        UOI_NAME, nullptr, 0, &dwReqLen);
    int factor = sizeof(TCHAR) / sizeof(char);
    LPTSTR szBuff = new TCHAR[dwReqLen/factor + 1];
    GetUserObjectInformation(_hDesktop,
        UOI_NAME, szBuff, dwReqLen, &dwReqLen);
    String^ tmp = gcnew String(szBuff);
    delete szBuff;
    return tmp;
}
```

Call native API and retrieve desktop name

Convert unmanaged buffer into String^

There is no `GetDesktopName` API function in the desktop API, but there is a `GetUserObjectInformation` function that retrieves information about a desktop or window station, including the name of the desktop. You don't want to wrap the entire `GetUserObjectInformation` function, so you essentially hide that function, use part of the information it returns, and expose that as a read-only `Name` property to the managed clients. Again, this is an abstraction that's done to improve the usability of the managed interface. Let's look at the `ThreadDesktop` property, which has both `get` and `set` accessors:

```
Desktop^ Desktop::ThreadDesktop::get()
{
    HDESK hCur = GetThreadDesktop(GetCurrentThreadId());
    if(hCur)
        return gcnew Desktop(hCur);
    else
        return nullptr;
}

void Desktop::ThreadDesktop::set(Desktop^ desktop)
{
    SetThreadDesktop(desktop->_hDesktop);
}
```

The `set` accessor calls the `SetThreadDesktop` API function and is basically a full wrapper for the API function. But the `GetThreadDesktop` API function can be used to retrieve the desktop associated with any specific thread, whereas you only need to get the desktop associated with the calling thread. You abstract away the `thread-id` parameter by hard-coding a call to `GetCurrentThreadId` in the call to `GetThreadDesktop`. This is a case where the managed wrapper wraps a specialized case of the unmanaged API, where you have hard-coded one of the parameters to the API call.

Earlier, you saw how the `Activate` method was implemented. `Activate` is an instance method, and to provide a means for the calling client to directly activate a desktop without having to resort to using an instance of a `Desktop` object, I've provided a static method called `SwitchTo`, which delegates the call to the `Desktop` object's `Activate` method:

```
bool Desktop::SwitchTo(Desktop^ desktop)
{
    return desktop->Activate();
}
```

This is more of a convenience function and is provided only to give the caller an extra option. I wanted to show you an example of having a static method and an instance method that are functionally much the same.

You only have enumeration methods left now, along with their respective event handlers. I've implemented the two events differently so you get to see two different techniques for wrapping native functions with callbacks. For the `EnumDesktops` function, you use a nontrivial event. The delegate directly matches the native callback function prototype, which means you can use the `GetFunctionPointerForDelegate` method to convert the delegate to a function pointer that can be passed to the native API function.

You may wonder why you go to all the trouble of implementing a nontrivial event just to restrict it to a single-event handler. The reason is that it's better than any of the alternatives. If you implemented a property to expose the delegate, nothing stops a caller from hooking multiple methods to that property. Then again, you could modify the `EnumDesktops` method to take a delegate argument (that would serve as the callback), but that would be too unnatural a technique for a managed interface (even for one as thin as the one you're writing). Although it may not be the most commonly-used technique, I eventually settled for a single-event-handler implementation of a nontrivial event. Of course, it's still not foolproof, and an obstinate user can hook multiple methods to the event by directly hooking a multicast delegate to the event, but that is an unlikely scenario. Listing 5.11 shows the nontrivial event declarations as well as the `EnumDesktops` method.

Listing 5.11 Code to enumerate desktops

```
void Desktop::OnDesktopFound::add(EnumDesktopDelegate^ d)
{
    _EnumDesktopDelegate = d;
}

void Desktop::OnDesktopFound::remove(EnumDesktopDelegate^ d)
{
    _EnumDesktopDelegate = nullptr;
}

#pragma push_macro("EnumDesktops")
#undef EnumDesktops
bool Desktop::EnumDesktops(IntPtr param)
{
#pragma pop_macro("EnumDesktops")
    HWINSTA hwinsta = GetProcessWindowStation();
    if(hwinsta && _EnumDesktopDelegate)
    {
        pin_ptr<EnumDesktopDelegate^> pDelegate = &_EnumDesktopDelegate;
        EnumDesktops(hwinsta,
            (DESKTOPENUMPROC)Marshal::GetFunctionPointerForDelegate(
                _EnumDesktopDelegate).ToPointer(),
            (LPARAM)param.ToPointer());
    }
    return false;
}
```

Annotations: **Ensures only one event handler is associated** (add); **Removing sets internal delegate to nullptr** (remove); **Pin delegate first**; **Get function pointer; call native API function** ❶

You saw this technique in the last chapter when we discussed how to convert between delegates and function pointers. You're now seeing a real-life application for that technique. When you make the call to the `EnumDesktops` function ❶, the default behavior of the marshalling layer (when the managed client is C#) is to marshal `String^` objects to Ansi strings. This is OK when you're building an Ansi version of the library. It will fail, however, in an Unicode version, because a Unicode string is expected, whereas the marshalling layer continues to use an Ansi string. To avoid this, you explicitly use the `UnmanagedFunctionPointer` attribute on the delegate declaration and specify the `CharSet` parameter to be `CharSet::Auto`, which specifies that the `String^` is to be converted to the appropriate string (either Unicode or Ansi) by the marshalling layer. Here's the delegate declaration once more, so you needn't turn back a few pages to look at it:

```
[UnmanagedFunctionPointer(CallingConvention::Winapi,
    CharSet = CharSet::Auto)]
public delegate bool EnumDesktopDelegate(
    String^ strDesktop, IntPtr param);
```

You specify the `UnmanagedFunctionPointer` attribute, which controls the marshalling behavior of a delegate, and you specify `CharSet::Auto` as the character set to use. In my opinion, it's a little peculiar that the C# compiler uses Ansi string marshalling as the default, especially when you consider that in .NET, all strings are in Unicode.

Thus, for this event, you use a nontrivial event so you can pin the delegate. Note that pinning isn't mandatory here: You just need to keep the delegate alive, not necessarily fixed at a specific location. You use pinning as an easy way to ensure that the object isn't collected by the GC (although that can alternatively be achieved by allocating a `GCHandle` to the delegate). You must also use a custom attribute on the delegate declaration to ensure that the string is converted properly, but calling the native API is easy. You convert the delegate to a function pointer using the `GetFunctionPointerForDelegate` method. Now, let's see how you implement the `EnumWindowTitles` method and its associated event using a different technique.

The callback prototype accepted by `EnumWindowTitles` is defined to take an `HWND` as well as a user-defined parameter. Instead of exposing this in equivalent delegate form to the managed world, you'll abstract away the `HWND` and the user-defined parameter. You'll provide the managed client with a delegate that takes a `String^` parameter, which will represent the title text of the enumerated window. You achieve this by declaring a global callback function that's internally used by the native API. This global callback function will invoke the managed event handler for every enumerated window. Here you're basically taking a native function with native arguments (like `HWND`) and wrapping it using a managed function with managed argument types (such as `String^`). Reusing our French and English secretaries analogy, this is like taking a French sentence that refers to a major city in France and exposing a translated English version that replaces the major French city with a British one, such as London. You're not only translating the French words to English, but you're also transliterating some of the objects used in the sentence to those that are contextually more suited to an English speaker.

Listing 5.12 shows the global callback, the `EnumWindowTitles` method, as well as the `RaiseWindowFound` helper method that you use to invoke the event.

Listing 5.12 Code to enumerate desktop windows

```
bool Desktop::EnumWindowTitles()
{
    if(!_hDesktop)
        return false;
    pin_ptr<Desktop^> ptr = &(Desktop^)this;                    ❶ Pin current instance of object
    return EnumDesktopWindows(_hDesktop,                        ❷ Pass pinned object as callback parameter
        GlobalEnumWindowsProc, (LPARAM) ptr)==TRUE;
}

void Desktop::RaiseWindowFound(String^ strTitle)                ❸ Helper function used to invoke event
{
    OnWindowFound(strTitle);
}

BOOL CALLBACK DesktopLibrary::GlobalEnumWindowsProc(
    HWND hwnd,LPARAM lParam)
{
    int len = GetWindowTextLength(hwnd);
    LPTSTR pBuff = new TCHAR[len + 1];
    GetWindowText(hwnd, pBuff, len + 1);
    interior_ptr<Desktop^> ptr = (interior_ptr<Desktop^>)(void*)lParam;   ❹ Convert LPARAM to interior pointer
    if(_tcslen(pBuff) > 0)
        (*ptr)->RaiseWindowFound(gcnew String(pBuff));          ❺ Invoke event through Desktop pointer
    delete[] pBuff;
    return TRUE;
}
```

This technique passes a pointer to the `Desktop` object to the unmanaged callback and then has the unmanaged callback use this pointer to invoke the managed event handler. In `EnumWindowTitles`, you pin the current `Desktop` instance ❶ and then pass that as the user-defined parameter to the `EnumDesktopWindows` API function ❷. The `RaiseWindowFound` method ❸ is a helper function to invoke the event handler because you can't directly invoke a trivial event from outside the class. In the global callback function, you convert the `LPARAM` back to an interior pointer to the passed-in `Desktop` object ❹. You then call the `RaiseWindowFound` method through this pointer ❺. Thus, control is transferred to the managed event handler indirectly via the unmanaged callback.

Compared with the previous technique, there are some advantages here. You don't have to declare a nontrivial event; you don't have to use any custom attributes on the delegate declaration; and you can choose a user-friendly delegate that returns the title text for each window (whereas the original unmanaged callback was relatively more complicated). Thus, you provide an abstracted and simpler interface for the calling client. But internally, you have to use a global callback. You have to pass a `Desktop` pointer to this callback and then have the callback transfer control back to the managed event handler.

Both techniques have advantages and disadvantages. The former technique is simpler to implement, but it exposes the internal callback details to the managed client. The latter technique is more complicated to implement, but the managed interface is more user-friendly. In general, unless the native callback uses unmanaged types that don't have direct managed equivalents (such as a native handle like an `HWND` or an `HDESKTOP`), it's better to use the former technique of converting the delegate into a function pointer using `GetFunctionPointerForDelegate`, because the code is now simpler. Thus, it's easier to maintain. For other situations, the more complicated mechanism of using a global callback that transfers control to the managed event handler is the better solution because you get to hide unnecessary native API details from the managed interface.

You've probably noticed how you've put into practice several of the techniques you learned in the previous four chapters. That's how it will be throughout the rest of this book. In this section, the managed wrapper you wrote was for a native API consisting of C-style global function calls.

5.4 Exposing an MFC extension DLL to .NET

Explaining an MFC extension DLL isn't within the scope of this book. If you don't know what it is, you should read about it in your copy of the MSDN library. You may be thinking that you could use the same technique you used in the previous section to wrap the extension DLL. Well, that won't work out, because an MFC extension DLL can only be used by an MFC regular DLL or by an MFC application. If you attempt to directly wrap it, as you wrapped the desktop API in the previous section, the calling application will need to be an MFC application, which severely restricts the wrapper. You can't use it from C# and VB.NET clients, nor can you use it from purely managed C++/CLI applications. The solution you're going to apply is simple: You'll write a regular MFC DLL with `/clr` compilation turned on that will contain the managed wrapper class. Calling clients will use this regular MFC DLL and use the wrapper that proxies the calls into the original extension DLL. Figure 5.3 shows a diagrammatic representation of this design.

Let's look at the example extension DLL that we'll use to demonstrate this technique.

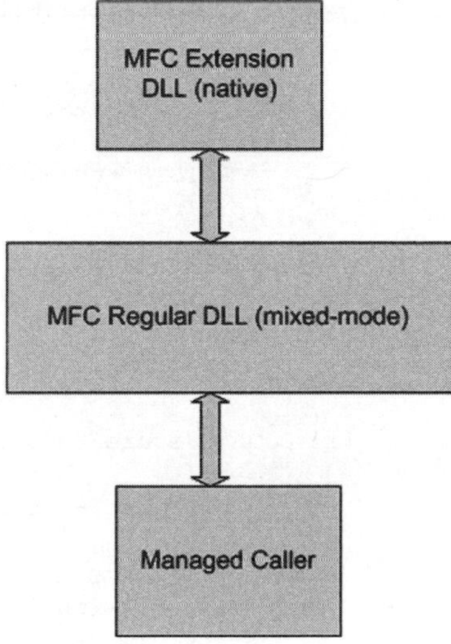

Figure 5.3
Wrapping an extension DLL

5.4.1 Overview of the MFC extension DLL

Our example MFC extension DLL exports a single class called `CSecureStdioFile`, which is derived from the MFC class `CStdioFile`. The class adds elementary encryption support by overriding the `ReadString` and `WriteString` functions to use simple XOR-based encryption. Note that this sort of encryption is easy to break, and I use it merely to demonstrate the techniques involved in wrapping an MFC extension DLL. Here's the declaration for the exported class:

```
class AFX_EXT_CLASS CSecureStdioFile : public CStdioFile
{
public:
    virtual void WriteString(LPCTSTR lpsz);
    virtual LPTSTR ReadString(LPTSTR lpsz, UINT nMax);
    virtual BOOL ReadString(CString& rString);
};
```

You have overrides for both overloads of the `ReadString` method as well as for the `WriteString` method. The idea is that a caller can use this class where they previously used the `CStdioFile` class, without having to change any code. Listing 5.13 shows the implementations of these methods.

Listing 5.13 The secure overrides

```
void CSecureStdioFile::WriteString(LPCTSTR lpsz)
{
    CString str = lpsz;
    for(int i=0; i<str.GetLength(); i++)
    {
        str.SetAt(i, 0xFF ^ str[i]);
    }
```

Each character is XOR encrypted

```
    CStdioFile::WriteString(str);
}

LPTSTR CSecureStdioFile::ReadString(LPTSTR lpsz, UINT nMax)
{
    LPTSTR ret = CStdioFile::ReadString(lpsz, nMax);
    if(ret)
    {
        for(LPTSTR p = lpsz; *p; p++)
            *p ^= 0xFF;
    }
    return ret;
}
BOOL CSecureStdioFile::ReadString(CString& rString)
{
    BOOL ret = CStdioFile::ReadString(rString);
    if(ret)
    {
        for(int i=0; i<rString.GetLength(); i++)
        {
            rString.SetAt(i, 0xFF ^ rString[i]);
        }
    }
    return ret;
}
```

Each character is XOR encrypted

LPTSTR is directly XOR decrypted

CString is directly XOR decrypted

A calling app can use `CSecureStdioFile` just as if it was using `CStdioFile`, except that the resulting file that's created will be pretty much indecipherable (because each character will be XOR-ed with 0xFF).

5.4.2 Writing the managed regular MFC DLL wrapper

The role of the MFC regular DLL is to proxy the calls from a managed caller into the extension DLL. The MFC regular DLL project has the `/clr` compilation mode enabled. You'll use the `CAutoNativePtr` template class that you wrote in the previous chapter to manage the native `CSecureStdioFile` object, which will be a member of the managed wrapper class. Listing 5.14 shows the declaration of the wrapper class.

Listing 5.14 Declaration of `CSecureStdioFileManaged`: the wrapper class

```
#include "../MfcExtensionLib/SecureStdioFile.h"
#include "AutoNative.h"
#include <vcclr.h>
#include <AtlBase.h>
using namespace System;
```

```
public ref class CSecureStdioFileManaged
{
private:
    CAutoNativePtr<CSecureStdioFile> m_pFile;        ❶ Declare native member using CAutoNativePtr
public:
    CSecureStdioFileManaged();
    enum class OpenFlags
    {
        ModeCreate = CFile::modeCreate,             ❷ Managed enum that partially wraps CStdioFile flags
        ModeRead = CFile::modeRead,
        ModeWrite = CFile::modeWrite
    };
    bool Open(String^ strFileName, OpenFlags flags);
    void Close();                                   ❸ Managed wrapper methods
    String^ ReadString();
    void WriteString(String^ str);
};
```

By using the `CAutoNativePtr` template class ❶, you don't need to worry about deallocating the native object. Notice how you have a managed `enum` ❷ that contains a partial set of the various `CFile` modes used by `CStdioFile`. Other `CFile` modes are available, but these are the only ones you'll be exposing via the managed interface. You also have managed wrapper methods ❸ for each of the `CStdioFile` methods that you'll expose to the managed clients. Let's look at the implementations of the various wrapper methods. Here's the constructor:

```
CSecureStdioFileManaged::CSecureStdioFileManaged()
    : m_pFile(new CSecureStdioFile())
{
}
```

The constructor is simple and exists merely to initialize the native `CStdioFile` object represented by the `m_pFile` `CAutoNativePtr` member. This `m_pFile` member is used by the wrapper methods to proxy the call into the native class. The following code shows the wrappers for the `Open` and `Close` methods:

```
bool CSecureStdioFileManaged::Open(
    String^ strFileName, OpenFlags flags)
{
    pin_ptr<const wchar_t> ptr = PtrToStringChars(strFileName);   ❶ Pin String^ and pass to native method
    return m_pFile->Open(W2CT(ptr),(UINT)flags)!=FALSE;          ❷ Convert BOOL to bool for return type
}

void CSecureStdioFileManaged::Close()
{
    m_pFile->Close();
}
```

Because the native `Open` method expects a `const TCHAR*`, you use `PtrToStringChars` ❶ to return an interior pointer to the passed-in `String^`, you pin that pointer, and then pass that as the path to the file to open. For the flags, you cast the managed `enum` to an `UINT`. The return type from the native `Open` method is a `BOOL`, which you convert to a `bool` by doing an inequality comparison with `FALSE` ❷. The `Close` wrapper is even simpler, because there are no types to convert between managed and unmanaged; you merely call the `native Close` method. The same technique is used for the `ReadString` and `WriteString` wrappers:

```
String^ CSecureStdioFileManaged::ReadString()
{
    CString str;
    if(m_pFile->ReadString(str))
        return gcnew String(str);
    else
        return nullptr;
}

void CSecureStdioFileManaged::WriteString(String^ str)
{
    m_pFile->WriteString(CString(str));
}
```

Both methods call the corresponding native method using the `m_pFile` member. Notice how you use the return type in `ReadString` to indicate whether you've reached the end of the file. The native method returns `FALSE`, if there is nothing more to read. In the wrapper method, you indicate that by returning a `nullptr`. When a valid string is read in, you return that as a `String^` by converting the `CString` to a `String^`. For the `WriteString` wrapper, you call the native `WriteString` method by converting the `String^` to a `CString`. Notice how you repeatedly use, in various fashions, the managed/unmanaged type conversion techniques covered in earlier chapters. In my opinion, if you're comfortable with managed/unmanaged type conversions, half the trouble in doing mixed-mode programming is behind you.

Now that you've written the managed wrapper, any managed client, such as a C# client or a C++/CLI safe-mode application, can directly use this DLL and consume the managed class. Listing 5.15 shows how the wrapper class is used from a managed console application.

Listing 5.15 Using the secure string class

```
int main(array<System::String ^> ^args)
{
    CSecureStdioFileManaged f;
    String^ path = Path::Combine( Path::GetDirectoryName(
        Environment::CommandLine->Replace("\"",""),
        "\\ManTestFile.txt" );
    f.Open(path, CSecureStdioFileManaged::OpenFlags::ModeCreate
        |CSecureStdioFileManaged::OpenFlags::ModeWrite);
    f.WriteString("Hello, this is a test");
    f.Close();

    f.Open(path, CSecureStdioFileManaged::OpenFlags::ModeRead);
    Console::WriteLine(f.ReadString());
    f.Close();
    return 0;
}
```

In this example, you create a file, write a string to it, close it, re-open the file, read and display the string, and close the file again. The output of the program isn't particularly exciting: It displays the string you wrote to the file. However, if you open the created file (ManTestFile.txt) using a text editor such as Notepad, you'll see some random illegible characters (the effect of XOR-ing). The calls to `Open`, `Close`, `WriteString`, and `ReadString` are made on the managed object exposed by the managed regular DLL, which in turn proxies the calls into the native extension DLL. For the application to execute, both DLLs need to be present (either in the current directory or in the search path).

You have a purely managed EXE calling into a mixed-mode DLL that in turn calls into a native DLL. Although the example in this section is a simple class, the same technique can be used to write managed wrappers for any MFC extension DLL. The size and complexity of the wrapper functions may vary, but the core idea will remain the same. By now, you'll probably have recognized a common pattern that you use when wrapping native libraries. Both in the previous section, where you wrapped a C-based desktop API, and in this section, where you wrapped an MFC-based class, the most important job is doing the type conversions and deciding what portions of the native API are to be exposed to the managed world. Again, I'd like to stress that you must be comfortable with converting types between the native and the CLI world, and you should also know when to use what sort of conversion. As you see more examples and application scenarios in the rest of this chapter and in the book, you'll get more comfortable with doing that and making the right type of marshalling choices.

5.5 Accessing a COM object via a custom RCW

Languages like C# and VB.NET access COM servers by using tlbimp.exe (type library importer) to generate a runtime callable wrapper (RCW) assembly, and then directly use the classes in this RCW. C++/CLI allows you to use the same technique; but this technique, although easy to use, has a couple of disadvantages:

- You add a dependency on the RCW assembly.
- The RCW classes and methods are direct conversions of the COM functions. Sometimes, the resulting class structure may not adhere to a typical CLI interface.

C++/CLI gives you another mechanism to access the COM server, where you write a custom wrapper class that exposes a managed interface to calling clients. This solves both the disadvantages that I just mentioned. There is no dependency on an RCW assembly, because the custom RCW can be a part of the main application. Because you have direct manual control over the wrapper (as opposed to having tlbimp.exe generate it for you), you can use a more CLI-style public interface. Be aware that a custom RCW involves more work than a tlbimp-generated RCW. As an analogy, think of a remote control with a favorite-channel list, which makes it easy for an old person, say your granny, to directly go to a channel of her choice by pressing a single button, rather than having to type in or scan through a humongous list of channels. The favorite-channel list wraps the underlying channel selection and exposes a simpler interface that's more familiar to the end user, your granny. Similarly, the custom RCW hides most of the underlying COM interface and instead exposes a more .NET-like interface for calling clients.

In this section, you'll write a custom RCW for a simple COM server and then access the COM server through this wrapper. Figure 5.4 shows the basic design of the custom RCW and how managed and mixed-mode callers can access the COM library.

5.5.1 The COM object to interop with

As your example COM server, you'll write a simple ATL-based COM DLL that can be used to create a shell shortcut link as well as to parse an existing shell shortcut link. The following listing shows what the COM interface looks like:

```
interface ILink : IDispatch
{
    [id(1), helpstring("method CreateLink")] HRESULT CreateLink(
        [in] BSTR FullPath, [in] BSTR LinkPath,
```

```
        [in] BSTR Description, [in] BSTR WorkingDir);
    [id(2), helpstring("method ResolveLink")] HRESULT ResolveLink(
        [in] BSTR LinkPath, [out] BSTR* FullPath,
        [out] BSTR* Description, [out] BSTR* WorkingDir);
};
```

The two method names are self-explanatory. `FullPath` represents the target of the shortcut link; `Description` represents the comment associated with a shortcut link (you see this comment when you hover your mouse over a shortcut in Explorer); and `WorkingDir` is the startup directory for the shortcut. These three variables are [in] arguments for `CreateLink` and are [out] arguments for `ResolveLink`, whereas the `LinkPath` argument is an [in] argument in both functions and specifies the path to the shortcut file. The implementations for these two functions are shown in listing 5.16 and use the shell's `IShellLink` and `IPersistFile` interfaces to create and resolve the shortcut links. A deeper explanation of using these two shell interfaces doesn't fit within the scope of the book. If you don't understand the COM code, don't worry too much. Our primary intention is to focus on writing the RCW rather than on understanding how the COM object is implemented.

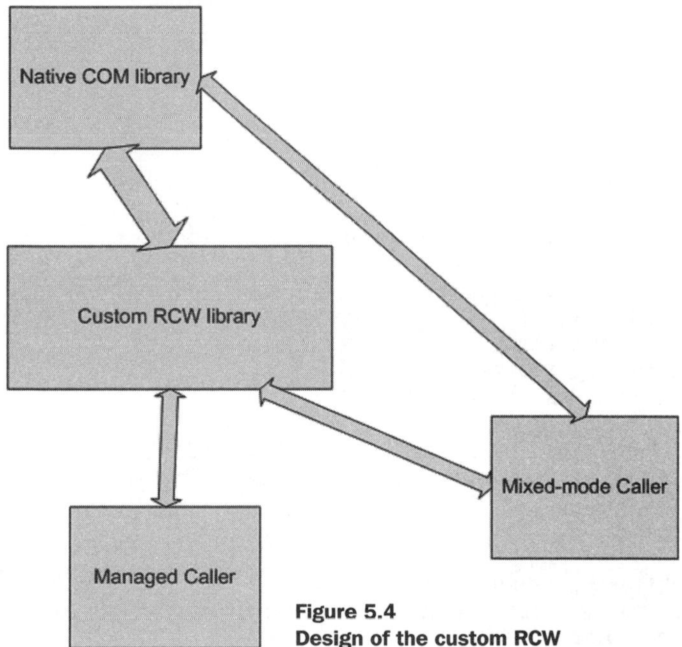

Figure 5.4
Design of the custom RCW

Listing 5.16 The `CreateLink` and `ResolveLink` methods

```
STDMETHODIMP CLink::CreateLink(
    BSTR FullPath, BSTR LinkPath,
        BSTR Description, BSTR WorkingDir)
{
    IShellLink* psl = NULL;
    HRESULT  hr = CoCreateInstance(CLSID_ShellLink, NULL,
        CLSCTX_INPROC_SERVER, IID_IShellLink, (LPVOID*) &psl);    <-- Create IShellLink object
    if (SUCCEEDED(hr))
    {
        IPersistFile* ppf = NULL;

        psl->SetPath(FullPath);
        psl->SetWorkingDirectory(WorkingDir);      Set parameters
        psl->SetDescription(Description);

        hr = psl->QueryInterface(IID_IPersistFile,(LPVOID*)&ppf);    <-- Get IPersistFile of IShellLink object

        if (SUCCEEDED(hr))
        {
            hr = ppf->Save(LinkPath, TRUE);    <-- Create and save shortcut
            ppf->Release();
        }
        psl->Release();
    }
    return hr;
}

STDMETHODIMP CLink::ResolveLink(
    BSTR LinkPath, BSTR* FullPath,
        BSTR* Description, BSTR* WorkingDir)
{
    IShellLink* psl = NULL;
    WIN32_FIND_DATA wfd={0};
    TCHAR szFullPath[MAX_PATH];
    TCHAR szDescription[INFOTIPSIZE];
    TCHAR szWorkingDir[MAX_PATH];

    HRESULT hr = CoCreateInstance(CLSID_ShellLink, NULL,
        CLSCTX_INPROC_SERVER, IID_IShellLink, (LPVOID *) &psl);    <-- Create IShellLink object

    if (SUCCEEDED(hr))
    {
        IPersistFile* ppf = NULL;
        hr = psl->QueryInterface(IID_IPersistFile, (LPVOID *)&ppf);    <-- Get IPersistFile of IShellLink object
        if (SUCCEEDED(hr))
        {
            hr = ppf->Load(LinkPath, STGM_READ);    <-- Load and initialize shortcut file
            if (SUCCEEDED(hr))
            {
```

```
                hr = psl->Resolve(GetDesktopWindow(), 0);
                if (SUCCEEDED(hr))
                {
                    hr = psl->GetPath(szFullPath,MAX_PATH,
                        &wfd,SLGP_UNCPRIORITY);
                    if (SUCCEEDED(hr))
                        hr = psl->GetDescription(
                          szDescription,INFOTIPSIZE);
                    if (SUCCEEDED(hr))
                        hr = psl->GetWorkingDirectory(
                          szWorkingDir,MAX_PATH);

                    if (SUCCEEDED(hr))                          Retrieve
                    {                                           parameters
                        *FullPath = SysAllocString(
                          CT2W(szFullPath));
                        *Description = SysAllocString(
                          CT2W(szDescription));
                        *WorkingDir = SysAllocString(
                          CT2W(szWorkingDir));
                    }
                }
            }
            ppf->Release();
        }
        psl->Release();
    }
    return hr;
}
```

I won't explain the functions because this section is about writing a custom wrapper over a COM object, any COM object, and thus the implementation of the COM methods doesn't matter. We'll now look at the custom RCW you're going to write, which will expose this COM object to managed code.

5.5.2 Writing the custom RCW

You'll need to declare a COM object as a member of the managed wrapper class, and although you could technically use the `CAutoNativePtr` template class to do that, doing so would involve two layers of smart pointers—the `CAutoNativePtr` class and the COM smart pointer class. A simpler and better way is to use the `msclr::com::ptr` class, which is a managed COM wrapper class declared in `<msclr\com\ptr.h>`. Listing 5.17 shows the custom RCW class in its entirety.

Listing 5.17 The custom RCW class

```
#include <msclr\com\ptr.h>

#import "../ShellLink/Debug/ShellLink.tlb"

using namespace System;
using namespace System::Runtime::InteropServices;
using namespace ShellLinkLib;

ref class ShellLink
{
private:
    msclr::com::ptr<ILink> lnkptr;                    <-- 1 Declare COM object using com::ptr
public:
    ShellLink()
    {
        lnkptr.CreateInstance(__uuidof(Link));        <-- 2 Create COM object in constructor
    }

    property String^ FullPath;                        | 3 Properties representing
    property String^ Description;                     |   parameters
    property String^ WorkingDir;                      |

    bool CreateLink(String^ LinkPath)
    {
        IntPtr lp = Marshal::StringToBSTR(LinkPath);      | Allocate
        IntPtr fp = Marshal::StringToBSTR(FullPath);      | BSTRs from
        IntPtr dc = Marshal::StringToBSTR(Description);   | String objects
        IntPtr wd = Marshal::StringToBSTR(WorkingDir);    |

        HRESULT hr = lnkptr->CreateLink(              <-- Invoke CreateLink
            static_cast<BSTR>(fp.ToPointer()),            method on COM object
            static_cast<BSTR>(lp.ToPointer()),
            static_cast<BSTR>(dc.ToPointer()),
            static_cast<BSTR>(wd.ToPointer()));

        Marshal::FreeBSTR(wd);                        |
        Marshal::FreeBSTR(dc);                        | Free BSTRs
        Marshal::FreeBSTR(fp);                        | after use
        Marshal::FreeBSTR(lp);                        |
        return SUCCEEDED(hr);
    }

    bool ResolveLink(String^ LinkPath)
    {
        BSTR pFullPath = NULL;
        BSTR pDescription = NULL;
        BSTR pWorkingDir = NULL;

        IntPtr lp = Marshal::StringToBSTR(LinkPath);
```

```
            HRESULT hr = lnkptr->ResolveLink(                      Invoke ResolveLink
                static_cast<BSTR>(lp.ToPointer()),                 method on COM
                &pFullPath, &pDescription, &pWorkingDir);          object

        if(SUCCEEDED(hr))
        {

        FullPath = Marshal::PtrToStringBSTR((IntPtr)pFullPath);
        Description = Marshal::PtrToStringBSTR((IntPtr)pDescription);
        WorkingDir = Marshal::PtrToStringBSTR((IntPtr)pWorkingDir);

        SysFreeString(pFullPath);                                  Set property
        SysFreeString(pDescription);     Free BSTRs allocated      String objects
        SysFreeString(pWorkingDir);      by COM method

        }

        Marshal::FreeBSTR(lp);
        return SUCCEEDED(hr);
    }
};
```

The wrapper class uses the same technique to expose the COM object that you used in the previous section when you wrapped the MFC class in the extension DLL. Note how you use the `msclr::com::ptr` class ❶ to allow the `ref` class to have a COM smart pointer member. You create the COM object in the constructor ❷ and don't explicitly call `Release`, because the managed COM smart pointer does that for you. The wrapper methods, `CreateLink` and `ResolveLink`, aren't very different from the wrapper methods you saw earlier. The native types (which in this case happen to be COM types) are exposed as managed types, and the native-managed type conversions are performed by the wrapper methods. For both wrapper methods, you change the number of arguments from four (as in the COM methods) to one. You delegate the functionality of the other parameters to the three properties ❸—`FullPath`, `Description` and `WorkingDir`—thereby achieving a more CLI-style interface than would be possible using tlbimp.exe and direct RCW. Note that you can convert the `HRESULT` returned (in case of an error) to a .NET exception using the `Marshal::GetExceptionForHR` method.

Essentially, you've written a customized wrapper (hence the name custom RCW), as opposed to the RCW generated by tlbimp.exe, where you don't have the option to manually customize the managed interface.

5.5.3 Using the custom RCW

Accessing the COM object via the custom RCW is straightforward—and the COM details are hidden from the managed callers. The following code demonstrates how the wrapper can be used:

```
ShellLink lnk1;
lnk1.FullPath = "d:\\mp3";
lnk1.Description = "Hmmmmmmmmm - nice";
lnk1.WorkingDir = "d:\\";
lnk1.CreateLink(
    "C:\\Documents and Settings\\Nish\\Desktop\\StartD.lnk");

ShellLink lnk2;
lnk2.ResolveLink(
    "C:\\Documents and Settings\\Nish\\Desktop\\StartD.lnk");
Console::WriteLine(lnk2.FullPath);
Console::WriteLine(lnk2.Description);
Console::WriteLine(lnk2.WorkingDir);
```

This code creates a shortcut to d:\mp3 on the desktop and then reads back the information from the shortcut and displays it on the console. Had you used tlbimp.exe, you wouldn't have the convenience of using properties; you also wouldn't have a return type to check for success. Note that although I haven't done so in this code, both wrapper methods return a `bool` that indicates whether the COM methods were successful. And the best part is that there is no dependency on an interop DLL (the RCW wrapper generated by tlbimp.exe).

In this chapter, you've now seen three different types of wrappers: one that wraps the desktop API, another that wraps an MFC extension DLL, and now this custom wrapper for a COM server. The core techniques used in all three wrappers remain the same: A mixed class proxies the calls into the native library, whether that's a C-based DLL, an MFC extension library, or a COM server. In each case, the wrapper class and the original native class are two separate entities. It would be interesting if you didn't have to have separate classes for managed and native callers, wouldn't it? In the next section, you'll see a technique that allows you to use a single mixed-mode DLL, which exposes a C++ interface that both managed and native clients can use.

5.6 Writing a single mixed-mode DLL for both managed and native clients

The technique that will be demonstrated in this section is one that was introduced by Paul DiLascia for his April 2005 column in *MSDN Magazine*, although he used

VC++ 2003 and the old managed extensions syntax. You'll use a modified version of his technique that will work with VC++ 2005. The basic idea is to export a mixed class (a native class with a `gcroot`–ed managed member) from a mixed-mode DLL and to provide a header file for the export that conditionally hides the managed methods when compiled without the `/clr` compilation mode. The size of the class, as viewed from a native client and a managed client, will be kept the same (you'll see how to do that later in the section). The native clients will see a native class and invoke native methods on instances of that class, without needing to know anything about the internal managed implementation. The managed clients will see a non-CLI mixed class with both managed and native methods and can choose to use either the managed interface directly or the native methods, depending on the scenario. You can think of it as similar to driving one of those new car models with a shiftronic automatic transmission: You can drive it like an automatic car, as well as go into manual mode when you want to. Similarly, with your mixed-mode DLL, you can choose to invoke the library natively or via managed code; the choice is up to you. Figure 5.5 shows a diagrammatic representation of how the mixed-mode DLL is designed.

Note that, strictly speaking, this section may not fully fit under the subject stated in the chapter's title—calling native code from managed applications—because here, you have a native application calling into a mixed-mode DLL that exports a native C++ interface. But the technique can be useful under certain

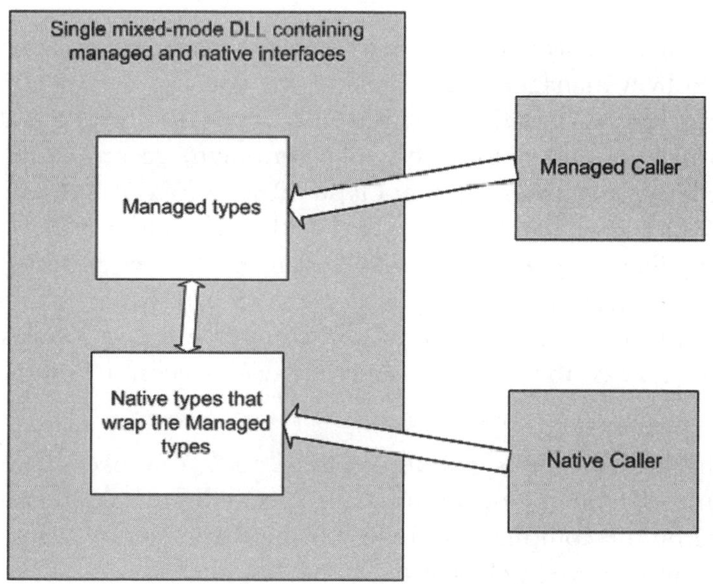

Figure 5.5 Mixed-mode DLL containing managed and native interfaces

circumstances. Both managed and native clients can utilize the same mixed-mode DLL, where the managed clients see the managed interface too (whereas the native clients don't), which is achieved through conditional compilation. Personally, I feel that this technique can be advantageous when your calling code may be either managed or native but you want to provide a caller-independent interface. I'll use up one of my author-privilege cards to put this section into this chapter, even though pedantically speaking, it may not wholly match the chapter topic. You'll start by writing a native class that will wrap the `System::Object` .NET class.

5.6.1 Wrapping the System::Object class

Every managed class has `System::Object` as a direct or indirect base class, and by wrapping `System::Object` in a native class, you can use this wrapper class as a base class for any class that will wrap a managed class. It may sound a little confusing, but when you see an example later, it will become clear. This is what a bare-bones wrapper class for the `System::Object` class looks like:

```
class CNativeObject
{
protected:
#ifdef _MANAGED
    gcroot<Object^> m_ObjHandle;
#else
    intptr_t m_ObjHandle;
#endif
};
```

As I mentioned earlier, the size of the class, as seen by a native caller, must be the same as that seen by a managed caller. This is why you use a `#ifdef` to check whether the macro `_MANAGED` is defined. If it's defined, you know that the `/clr` compilation mode is enabled, and you specify a member of type `gcroot <Object^>`. If `/clr` isn't enabled, you specify a member of type `intptr_t`. You can do this safely because the size of a `gcroot` handle is the same as the size of an `intptr_t` object. Under 32-bit compiling, `intptr_t` is a `typedef` for an `int` (4 bytes), whereas under 64-bit compiling, `intptr_t` is a `typedef` for `__int64` (8 bytes). This matches the size of a `gcroot`, which is 4 bytes under 32-bit compilation and 8 bytes under 64-bit compilation. It's easy to verify this using the `sizeof` operator, as shown here:

```
Console::WriteLine(sizeof gcroot<Object^> == sizeof intptr_t);
```

The output of this line of code is guaranteed to be `True`. You take advantage of this guarantee in the technique of conditionally specifying managed and native types, depending on the compilation mode. Listing 5.18 shows a more refined wrapper for the `System::Object` class using this technique.

Listing 5.18 The CNativeObject class declaration

```
#ifdef _MANAGED
#include <vcclr.h>
using namespace System;
using namespace System::Runtime::InteropServices;
#endif

#include <string>


class COMMONLIB_API CNativeObject
{
protected:
#ifdef _MANAGED
    gcroot<Object^> m_ObjHandle;
#else
    intptr_t m_ObjHandle;
#endif
public:
#ifdef _MANAGED
    //Managed methods
    gcroot<Object^> operator ->();
#endif
public:
    //Native methods
    CNativeObject(void);
    std::string ToString();
    virtual void CreateManagedObject();
};
```

❶ Class's one and only data member

❷ Conditionally compiled managed members

❸ Always compiled native members

As you can see, there is only one data member for the class ❶; this data member will be a `gcroot<Object^>` when `/clr` is enabled and an `intptr_t` otherwise. You also have an overload for the `->` operator ❷ that's conditionally compiled for managed code, and a bunch of native methods ❸, such as `ToString`, which wraps `System::Object::ToString`, and `CreateManagedObject`, which creates the managed `System::Object` reference. The basic idea is that a native caller sees only the native code, whereas a managed caller sees a mixed-mode class.

Because both `ToString` and `CreateManagedObject` use managed code, you don't inline them. Instead, you put them in the CPP file along with the constructor. Listing 5.19 shows how these functions are defined.

Listing 5.19 CNativeObject implementation

```
CNativeObject::CNativeObject(void)
{
    m_ObjHandle = nullptr;      <-- Set m_ObjHandle to nullptr
}

gcroot<Object^> CNativeObject::operator ->()
{
    return m_ObjHandle;     <-- (1) -> operator returns underlying m_ObjHandle
}

string CNativeObject::ToString()
{
    IntPtr ptr = Marshal::StringToHGlobalAnsi(
        (*this)->ToString());
    string str = reinterpret_cast<char*>(
        static_cast<void*>(ptr));
    Marshal::FreeHGlobal(ptr);
    return str;
}                               (2) Convert returned String^ to an std::string

void CNativeObject::CreateManagedObject()
{                                                  (3) Explicit function to
    m_ObjHandle = gcnew Object();         <--      instantiate managed object
}
```

The `->` operator overload ❶ is there for managed callers who can directly access the underlying managed object and apply methods or properties on it. Of course, they may have directly used the wrapped managed object, but in that case, the managed object may not necessarily be in an assembly that's referenced by default. This way, they can also use a native method as and when required. The `ToString` wrapper ❷ merely converts the `String^` returned by the managed object to an `std::string` so that native callers can use it. The `CreateManaged-Object` method ❸ is used to explicitly create and instantiate the managed object. It's a `virtual` method, and thus a `CNativeObject*` that refers to a derived class object that wraps a managed type will always be guaranteed to call the appropriate method. Notice that you only wrap `System::Object` selectively, because for this example, you don't need every member in the `System::Object` class. Next, let's see how to derive a class from `CNativeObject` that will wrap a specific managed type. For the example, I have chosen the `MD5CryptoServiceProvider`, which can be used to compute MD5 hashes.

5.6.2 Writing derived class wrappers

In this section, you'll derive a class from `CNativeObject` that will wrap the `MD5CryptoServiceProvider` selectively. You'll wrap only the `ComputeHash` method, to keep the example short and simple, but if you so require, you should be able to use similar techniques to wrap the entire functionality of the managed class. You don't need to add a `MD5CryptoServiceProvider` member to this class. Instead, you'll use the `gcroot<Object^>` member of the `CNativeObject` class to hold the `MD5CryptoServiceProvider` object. This is possible because every managed object indirectly derives from `System::Object`. Listing 5.20 shows the class declaration.

Listing 5.20 Writing a `CNativeObject` derived class

```
#include "NativeObject.h"

#ifdef _MANAGED
using namespace System::Security::Cryptography;
#endif

class COMMONLIB_API CNativeMD5CryptoServiceProvider
    : public CNativeObject
{
public:
#ifdef _MANAGED
    //Managed methods
    gcroot<MD5CryptoServiceProvider^> operator ->();      <-- 1 Overload operator -> to return wrapped type
#endif
public:
    virtual void CreateManagedObject();                   <-- 2 Override explicit creation method
    bool ComputeHash(const unsigned char* input,          <-- 3 Expose method exposed from managed type
        unsigned char* output, int* plen);
};
```

Notice how you overload operator `->` in the class ❶, except that this time it returns a `gcroot<MD5CryptoServiceProvider^>`, which allows managed clients to directly use the `MD5CryptoServiceProvider` object. You also need to override `CreateManagedObject` ❷ so that the right managed object is instantiated (in this case, an `MD5CryptoServiceProvider` object). You also have a single method, `ComputeHash` ❸, which internally uses an overload of the managed `ComputeHash` method. As I mentioned earlier, this example exposes only one overload of the hashing function, so I can keep the example simple and still demonstrate the core techniques that are being used. You can easily wrap every method available in the managed type using pretty much the same techniques shown. Listing 5.21 gives the method implementations.

Listing 5.21 The managed wrapper methods

```
void CNativeMD5CryptoServiceProvider::CreateManagedObject()
{
    m_ObjHandle = gcnew MD5CryptoServiceProvider();    <-- 1 Create MD5CryptoServiceProvider instance
}

bool CNativeMD5CryptoServiceProvider::ComputeHash(
    const unsigned char* input, unsigned char* output, int* plen)
{
    bool ret = true;
    int inlen = (int)strlen((const char*)input);
    array<unsigned char>^ buffer = gcnew array<unsigned char>(inlen);
    for(int i=0; i<inlen; i++)
        buffer[i] = input[i];
    array<unsigned char>^ hash = (*this)->ComputeHash(buffer);   <-- 2 Invoke managed ComputeHash
    int hashlen = hash->Length;
    if(hashlen > *plen)
    {
        *plen = hashlen;
        return false;
    }
    *plen = hashlen;
    for(int i=0; i<hashlen; i++)
        output[i] = hash[i];
    return ret;
}

gcroot<MD5CryptoServiceProvider^>
    CNativeMD5CryptoServiceProvider::operator ->()
{
    return (MD5CryptoServiceProvider^)(Object^)m_ObjHandle;   <-- 3 Cast gcroot to MD5CryptoServiceProvider
}
```

In `CreateManagedObject` ❶, you instantiate the `MD5CryptoServiceProvider` object and store it in the `m_ObjHandle` variable, which is a `gcroot<Object^>` and can thus store any managed object. In the `->` operator overload ❸, you return an `MD5CryptoServiceProvider^`, which allows you to directly access the managed object when you need it. You see this in the `ComputeHash` wrapper method, where the `this` pointer is dereferenced ❷, and then by using the `->` operator, you extract the underlying managed object and invoke the managed `ComputeHash` on it.

Both `CNativeObject` and `CNativeMD5CryptoServiceProvider` are put into a mixed-mode DLL and exported as C++ classes. For any managed class, whether it's a .NET Framework class, a custom class that you wrote, or one from a third-party library, you only need to derive a class from `CNativeObject` as you did here and write wrapper methods for those functions that you need access to.

The native caller

The native caller is a pure native C++ application that uses the exported native C++ classes from the DLL without being aware that it's calling into a mixed-mode DLL. Listing 5.22 shows a simple native client that computes and displays the MD5 hash for a string.

Listing 5.22 Native calling code

```
int _tmain(int argc, _TCHAR* argv[])
{
    CNativeObject n;
    n.CreateManagedObject();
    string s = n.ToString();
    cout << s << endl;

    CNativeMD5CryptoServiceProvider md5;
    md5.CreateManagedObject();
    cout << md5.ToString() << endl;

    unsigned char output[512];
    int len = 511;
    if(md5.ComputeHash((const unsigned char*)
        "Hello world. This is a test.", output, &len))
    {
        cout << hex << uppercase;
        for(int i=0; i<len; i++)
            cout << (int) output[i] << " ";
    }
    cout << endl;
    return 0;
}
```

This code is pretty simple, and there's not much to explain. The two calls to `ToString` invoke the managed `ToString` methods on the respective objects. This is obvious from the output of the program:

```
System.Object
System.Security.Cryptography.MD5CryptoServiceProvider
EF BD F0 71 15 AB 2F 7D FF 50 C9 1F 83 27 44 3E
```

You can see from the managed types that are displayed that the .NET methods were in action. The best part is that the calling code is a pure native application.

The managed caller

Although I'm going to show you a purely managed client, it may as well be a mixed-mode application. As I mentioned earlier, the managed client can directly use the managed object; but in certain cases (such as when you have abstracted some functionality and written a simpler interface to some API), it may be easier to use a common interface (the mixed-mode DLL) from both managed and native clients. The managed client can use the object directly as a native object and invoke the native helper methods, if any; and whenever it requires the underlying managed object, that's easily available, too. Listing 5.23 shows the managed client app.

Listing 5.23 The managed caller

```
CNativeMD5CryptoServiceProvider md5;
md5.CreateManagedObject();                    // ❶ Use native interface
String^ str = "Text to be hashed";
array<unsigned char>^ buffer =
    gcnew array<unsigned char> (str->Length);
int index = 0;
for each(wchar_t c in str)
    buffer[index++] = (unsigned char)c;
array<unsigned char>^ hash = md5->ComputeHash(buffer);   // ❷ Use managed interface
for each(unsigned char c in hash)
    Console::Write("{0:X2} ",c);
Console::WriteLine();
```

In this example, you create the managed object using the native interface ❶, but because the caller is managed, the managed interface is available too, which allows you to directly invoke the managed methods using the `->` operator ❷. Obviously, this isn't as useful as being able to use the DLL from the native caller, because the managed caller doesn't need to use the wrapper. However, it still gives you an extra level of flexibility, in that the managed caller can flip between using the native interface and the managed interface, depending on which is most convenient. For instance, if it needs to handle native types, it may call the native method, thereby avoiding type conversions, whereas it can use the managed interface when it's dealing with managed types.

In conclusion, I'd like to recommend that you use this technique only if you need to and/or if you have client applications that can't use the `/clr` compilation model. For all other purposes, you'll be much better off (in terms of convenience and lower chances for bugs) if you use the much-more-straightforward mixed-mode approach.

5.7 Summary

At this point in the book, we've covered enough ground that you can effortlessly access native code from a managed-caller application. We covered three different types of native wrappers in this chapter. The first one was the wrapper you wrote for the native Desktop API. You then wrote a mixed-mode regular DLL that wrapped an extension DLL. Finally, you wrote a custom RCW to wrap a COM object. For all three examples, you used the knowledge acquired in the earlier syntax chapters, and particularly the information from the previous chapter on mixed-mode techniques. For any sort of mixed-mode scenario, where you need to consume an unmanaged library from a managed application, you can apply one or more of the techniques covered in this chapter. The core concepts remain the same. It's just that, for a large real-world application, you'll end up writing that many more wrappers.

The last section in the chapter was a little different from the rest, in that we talked about a technique that allows a mixed-mode DLL to export a C++ class that exposes a purely native interface to native callers, and a mixed-mode interface to managed callers. Although not a commonly-required scenario, when you need to access managed code from a native caller without having to resort to CCW techniques (perhaps to avoid COM calls), this technique can be extremely valuable to know.

In the rest of this book, each chapter will discuss how to interop your native code with specific managed frameworks, such as Windows Forms or Avalon. But even there, you'll find that most of the techniques are basic variations on those that have been covered in this and earlier chapters. That's the good thing about mixed-mode programming: Although it may seem daunting in the beginning, the more you work on it, the easier and smoother it gets. Eventually, you'll be as comfortable doing mixed-mode coding as you are with anything else.

Part 3

Using managed frameworks from native applications

This part's three chapters show you how to consume popular managed frameworks from native applications; each chapter focuses on one such managed framework. Chapter 6 discusses Windows Forms and MFC interop, and covers topics such as hosting Windows Forms controls in MFC dialogs and views, using Windows Forms controls to give MFC apps an Office 2003–style UI, and using an MFC control from a Windows Forms application. Chapter 7 briefly introduces WPF and explains three approaches to consuming WPF from C++/CLI applications. The chapter also covers how to host a WPF control in a native application using two different techniques and finishes with a discussion of hosting a native control in a WPF application. Chapter 8 introduces WCF and shows how a typical DCOM-based client-server application can be migrated to WCF. The chapter rounds off with a discussion on hosting WCF services from an IIS server.

6 Interoping Windows Forms with MFC

The interop examples you saw in the previous chapter were mostly scenarios where a managed application was utilizing a native library. Beginning with this chapter, we're going to look at specific managed frameworks that can be used from native applications using C++/CLI interop mechanisms. We'll focus on interop mechanisms for mixing the Windows Forms UI library with applications that are written using MFC classes.

MFC has been one of the most popular class frameworks for Visual C++ development, and a vast majority of VC++ UI applications are written in MFC. Windows Forms is a powerful UI framework available in the .NET Base Class Library that has been gaining in popularity over the last couple of years. It's extremely useful at times to be able to use Windows Forms in an application that's currently using MFC, perhaps to use a new modern-day UI control that was written using Windows Forms. With VC++ 2005 and C++/CLI, doing that isn't hard, and MFC has been boosted with some Windows Forms interop classes that ease the process for you. The MFC library has been more or less frozen (as far as enhancements go) and hasn't changed much in the last two Visual C++ releases, whereas Windows Forms is a constantly enhanced framework. Any new UI enhancements and improvements will most likely be in the Windows Forms API, and being able to interop between the two frameworks means that existing MFC applications can leverage this new functionality. You can think of using Windows Forms in MFC applications as analogous to using French phrases in English sentences. It's not an exact analogy, but the core idea of enhancing the English literature using a foreign language is similar to what Windows Forms does for MFC.

It's not possible to discuss every possible MFC/Windows Forms interop scenario in a chapter, or even in a dozen chapters. But the majority of interop requirements can be isolated into a few specific scenarios. Once you know how to handle those scenarios, mixing Windows Forms and MFC is a straightforward task. That's what we're going to do in this chapter; we'll look at some of the more commonly-required tasks when interoping MFC and Windows Forms. Because teaching Windows Forms is beyond the scope of this chapter, it's assumed that you're already familiar with the fundamentals of using the Windows Forms framework.

Techniques we'll cover in this chapter include hosting a Windows Forms control in an MFC dialog, and hosting a Windows Forms control as an MFC view. That covers two of the most popular UI window options available in MFC: views and dialogs. We'll discuss how to use some of the new menu and toolbar classes available in Windows Forms (WinForms) 2.0 to give an existing MFC application a more modern UI without changing its core functionality—only the UI is changed. You'll also see an example of directly using a WinForms control as an MFC dialog, which can be handy in certain scenarios. We'll wind up the chapter with an example of hosting an MFC control directly in a Windows Forms application. Although there is no direct library support to do that, we use some basic interop techniques to host a CWnd-derived MFC control inside a WinForms window (or form). We'll begin the chapter with a simple WinForms example so that I can quickly talk about how a WinForms form relates to a native window. If you're familiar with how WinForms is implemented, you can skip this section.

6.1 A simple Windows Forms application

Windows Forms is the user interface framework provided by the .NET Base Class Library. Although it's essentially a wrapper around the Win32 API, unlike MFC, which is a thin wrapper over the API, Windows Forms is at a far higher level; it's also an extremely feature-rich class library that lets you develop rich UIs without needing to poke into the native API. It's such a vast topic that it's impossible to provide even a brief introduction in this chapter. You need to learn more about WinForms from other sources, because my coverage will be minimal—just enough to help you make sense of the interop scenarios that we'll cover in the rest of the chapter.

Visual Studio 2005 provides a powerful development environment for writing WinForms applications. For the example, you won't use the capabilities of VS 2005; instead, you'll write the WinForms application by hand. You'll start with a simple program that brings up a window on screen (or a WinForms form, as it's called in .NET). Continuing with the analogy of French phrases in English, consider this application similar to writing your first essay in French—not too detailed, but just enough to expound basic French language concepts.

Here are the steps you need to follow to get this first program up and running:

1. Create an empty CLR project using VS 2005.
2. Change the `SUBSYSTEM` linker setting to `/SUBSYSTEM:WINDOWS`.
3. Set the entry-point function as `main`.
4. Add references to System.dll and System.Windows.Forms.dll.
5. Add a CPP file to the project (call it simple.cpp) that will contain the following code:

```
using namespace System;
using namespace System::Windows::Forms;

[STAThreadAttribute]
```

```
int main(array<System::String ^> ^args)
{
    Application::EnableVisualStyles();
    Application::Run(gcnew Form());      // 1 Initiate message loop and show form
    return 0;
}
```

Compile and run the program, and you'll see a nice window on your screen. The line of code that is of interest is the call to the static `Run` method of the `Application` class ❶. It initiates the application message loop and shows the `Form` object that you pass to it. You use the default `Form` object, so the window that's created doesn't have a title, but it has a title bar. It has maximize and minimize buttons, and it can be moved around on the screen, as well as sized. Thus, a `Form` object basically wraps a Win32 window, just like the `CWnd` MFC class, except that the wrapping is done at a level high enough to virtually hide the internal Win32 window implementation details.

The internal `HWND` that represents the Win32 window can be accessed via the `Handle` property of a `Form`. Let's see how you can use that `HWND` directly in a Win32 API call. You'll need to `#include <windows.h>` as well as `<tchar.h>`, and then make the following changes to the `main` function:

```
[STAThreadAttribute]
int main(array<System::String ^> ^args)
{
    Application::EnableVisualStyles();
    Form^ form = gcnew Form();
    SetWindowText((HWND)form->Handle.ToPointer(),
        _T("Hello World"));
    Application::Run(form);
    return 0;
}
```

Note that when you use Windows Forms, normally there is no need to access the `HWND` directly, especially for a triviality such as changing the title text of the window. You do so here to see how it can be done, so you understand how a WinForms `Handle` relates to a native `HWND`. This will be handy when you're mixing native UI frameworks with Windows Forms, where an API would expect an `HWND` parameter.

Note that the `Handle` property is inherited from the `Control` class (which is an indirect base class of the `Form` class). The `Control` class is used as a base class by WinForms classes that represent a UI and includes child controls such as buttons, edit boxes, combo boxes, and so on. The core idea that you need to keep in mind is that WinForms is fundamentally a Win32 API wrapper, and every WinForms `Form` or `Control` is essentially a native `HWND`-based Win32 window.

6.2 Hosting a Windows Forms control in an MFC dialog

In this section, you'll see how to put a WinForms control into an MFC dialog using the `CWinFormsControl` MFC class added in VC++ 2005. Although both MFC and WinForms wrap the same underlying Win32 windows, they use two totally different UI architectural models. Thus, you can't just drag and drop a Forms control into an MFC dialog as you would normally do with a standard dialog control. That's where the `CWinFormsControl` class comes into play. `CWinFormsControl` is a templated `CWnd`-derived class that provides functionality to host a WinForms control directly in an MFC application. Doing this is similar to having a trusted old Toyota Corolla (analogous to the MFC application) and adding fancy new BMW-brand headlights (the WinForms control) to it. Figure 6.1 shows a diagrammatic representation of hosting a WinForms control in an MFC dialog.

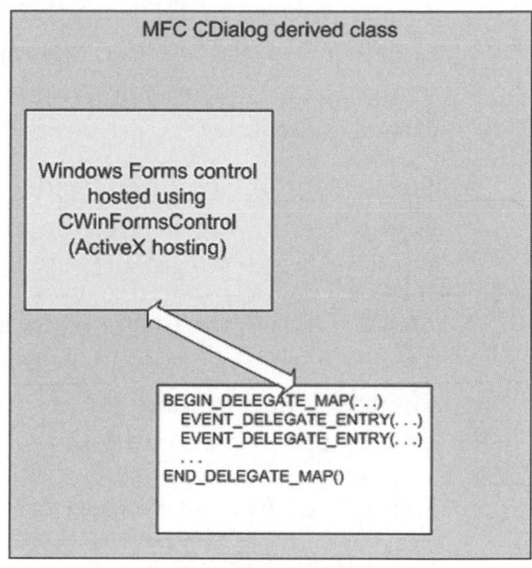

Figure 6.1 Hosting a WinForms control in a dialog

For the example application, you'll put a `MaskedTextBox` control on a dialog box. The techniques you use here can be repeated for any other WinForms control, including custom components, such as the one you wrote earlier. The `MaskedTextBox` is an extended `TextBox` control derived from `TextBoxBase` (the same base class from which `TextBox` also inherits), which provides functionality to filter the input text through a `Mask` property. At the end of this section, you'll have an application that looks like Figure 6.2. The following summarizes

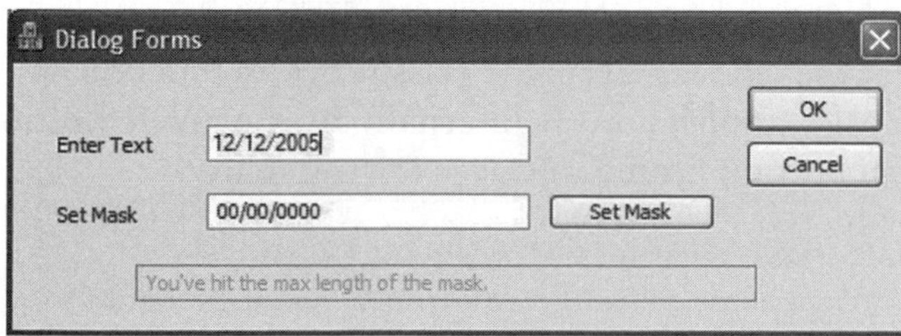

Figure 6.2 Using the `MaskedTextBox` in an MFC dialog

the steps you'll complete in the following sections to get the application up and running:

Step 1 Create the MFC project.

Create a new dialog-based MFC application using the wizard, name the project as `DialogForms`, and enable `/clr` compilation, which you'll need to use the WinForms control.

Step 2 Add the required header files.

Add the following header file `#include` to your stdafx.h: `<afxwinforms.h>` (you need it for `CWinFormsControl`).

Step 3 Modify the dialog resource.

Modify your dialog resource so it has the controls shown in figure 6.2, with one change. Where you see the `MaskedTextBox` control in the figure, put a static control. You should end up with the controls listed in table 6.1.

Table 6.1 Controls that are added to the dialog resource

Control	Description
`IDC_MASKED_EDIT`	A placeholder for the `MaskedTextBox` control.
`IDC_EDITMASK`	Map to a `CEdit` DDX variable named `m_Mask`.
`IDC_BUTTONMASK`	Add an `ON_BN_CLICKED` entry, and map that to the `OnBnSetMask` method.
`IDC_EDIT_STATUS`	Map to a `CEdit` DDX variable named `m_StatusEdit`, and make it read-only.
`IDC_STATIC`	Set the caption to **Set Mask**.
`IDC_STATIC`	Set the caption to **Enter Text**.

Step 4 Add a `CWinFormsControl` member variable.

Add a `CWinFormsControl<MaskedTextBox>` variable to the dialog header file:

```
CWinFormsControl<System::Windows::Forms::MaskedTextBox> m_MaskedEdit;
```

As I mentioned earlier, the `CWinFormsControl` class provides functionality to host a .NET control in an MFC application. It internally uses ActiveX hosting techniques and provides an uncomplicated interface for you to use.

Step 5 Associate the member variable with a dialog control id.

In the dialog class's `DoDataExchange`, add a call to `DDX_ManagedControl`:

```
void CDialogFormsDlg::DoDataExchange(CDataExchange* pDX)
{
    CDialog::DoDataExchange(pDX);
    DDX_ManagedControl(pDX, IDC_MASKED_EDIT, m_MaskedEdit);
. . .
}
```

The call to `DDX_ManagedControl` creates the `MaskedTextBox` control and associates it with the resource-id `IDC_MASKED_EDIT`. Internally, `DDX_ManagedControl` is implemented using `CWinFormsControl`'s `CreateManagedControl` method. `CreateManagedControl` has several overloads, and `DDX_ManagedControl` uses the one that accepts a placeholder resource ID that represents a static control. The static control is destroyed, and the managed control is created using the dimensions of the original static control and with the same resource-id.

Step 6 Add an event handler declaration.
Add the event handler declaration in the header file of the dialog class:

```
void OnMaskInputRejected(System::Object^,
    System::Windows::Forms::MaskInputRejectedEventArgs^);
```

Note that this method is a member of the MFC `CDialog`-derived class. This means the managed event handler is a member of the native MFC class. The next step will show you how that is made possible.

Step 7 Add the delegate map to the dialog class.
Set up the delegate map in a public section of your dialog class declaration:

```
BEGIN_DELEGATE_MAP( CDialogFormsDlg )
    EVENT_DELEGATE_ENTRY( OnMaskInputRejected, System::Object^,
        System::Windows::Forms::MaskInputRejectedEventArgs^ )
END_DELEGATE_MAP()
```

The delegate map allows you to use an MFC class function as a delegate by calling `MAKE_DELEGATE` on it. Internally, a delegate proxy is created that proxies the managed delegate invocation to the native MFC method that represents the event handler. Part of the magic is done by a template class called `delegate_proxy_factory` that's declared in the <msclr\event.h> header file. This class has a `gcroot` member for a template parameter-dependent `delegate_proxy_type` that gets defined as part of the expansion of the `BEGIN_DELEGATE_MAP` and `END_DELEGATE_MAP` macros. This `delegate_proxy_type` has a pointer to the containing native class. The `EVENT_DELEGATE_ENTRY` macro expands into a member function within the `delegate_proxy_type` class and internally invokes the corresponding native method using the pointer to the native class. In short, the managed events are proxied into the native methods.

Step 8 Add code to the `OnBnSetMask` method.

You'll now add code to the `OnBnSetMask` function (which is the button-click handler for the set-mask button):

```
void CDialogFormsDlg::OnBnSetMask()
{
   CString strMask;
   m_Mask.GetWindowText(strMask);
   m_MaskedEdit->Clear();
   m_MaskedEdit->Mask = gcnew System::String(strMask);
}
```

You retrieve the text from the edit control representing the mask and set it to the `Mask` property of the `MaskedTextBox` control via the `CWinFormsControl<MaskedTextBox>` member variable.

Step 9 Initialize the WinForms control.

Initialize the `MaskedTextBox` control in `OnInitDialog`:

```
BOOL CDialogFormsDlg::OnInitDialog()
{
    CDialog::OnInitDialog();

    // . . .

    m_MaskedEdit->PromptChar = L' ';
    m_Mask.SetWindowText(L"00/00/0000");
    OnBnSetMask();
    m_MaskedEdit->MaskInputRejected +=
        MAKE_DELEGATE(
        System::Windows::Forms::MaskInputRejectedEventHandler,
        OnMaskInputRejected) ;
    return TRUE;
}
```

You set the `PromptChar` property to a space (the default is an underscore); this will be the character shown in the `MaskedTextBox` control when no input is available. You then add an event handler to the `MaskInputRejected` event using the `MAKE_DELEGATE` macro. The macro takes two arguments: The first specifies the delegate type of the event, and the second specifies the native method that will be used as the event handler. The delegate is constructed using the `m_delegate_map_proxy` member (of type `delegate_proxy_factory`) that was inserted earlier using the delegate map, and the corresponding managed method of the `delegate_proxy_type` class is set as the event handler. Eventually, when this delegate is invoked, the corresponding native method (of the same name) will be invoked, as discussed earlier.

Step 10 Add the `OnMaskInputRejected` event-handler function.

Now, you just need to add the `OnMaskInputRejected` event handler function to the dialog class:

```
void CDialogFormsDlg::OnMaskInputRejected(System::Object^,
    System::Windows::Forms::MaskInputRejectedEventArgs^ args)
{
  if(m_MaskedEdit->MaskFull)
  {
    m_StatusEdit.SetWindowText(
        L"You've hit the max length of the mask.");
  }
  else if(args->Position == m_MaskedEdit->Mask->Length)
  {
    m_StatusEdit.SetWindowText(L"You are at the end of the mask.");
  }
  else
  {
    m_StatusEdit.SetWindowText(L"Bad entry. Check your input!");
  }
}
```

The `MaskInputRejected` event is raised when the user attempts to input something that doesn't match the `Mask`. This code checks for various conditions that may have resulted in the input being rejected; you show an appropriate message in the status message edit box.

That's it: You can compile and run the application. Test various masks to see the `MaskedTextBox` control in action. It took a little more effort to use the WinForms control in the MFC dialog that it would have taken to use it directly in a WinForms application. But if you have an existing MFC application, this is a far more convenient and faster method than rewriting the entire application using WinForms. Also remember that the same steps that you carried out here can be used to host any WinForms control in an MFC dialog.

Although MFC dialogs are promising candidates for hosting WinForms controls, sometimes you may want to directly use a WinForms control as an MFC view window. That's what we'll talk about in the next section.

Let's now go through the various steps in more detail.

6.3 Hosting a Windows Forms control as an MFC view

Hosting a WinForms control as a `CView` can be trickier compared to hosting it on a dialog, but there are workarounds to all the issues that crop up. In this section, you'll write an SDI MFC application that will host the `DataGridView` WinForms control introduced in the .NET Framework 2.0 version. For the analogy-happy folks out there, you can think of this as trying to put a Pontiac G6 body on a Toyota Corolla—doable, but with a few hiccups that need to be resolved.

You'll use the `CWinFormsView` MFC class, which provides functionality to host a WinForms control as an MFC view. Figure 6.3 shows a diagrammatic representation of how you use the `CWinFormsView` class.

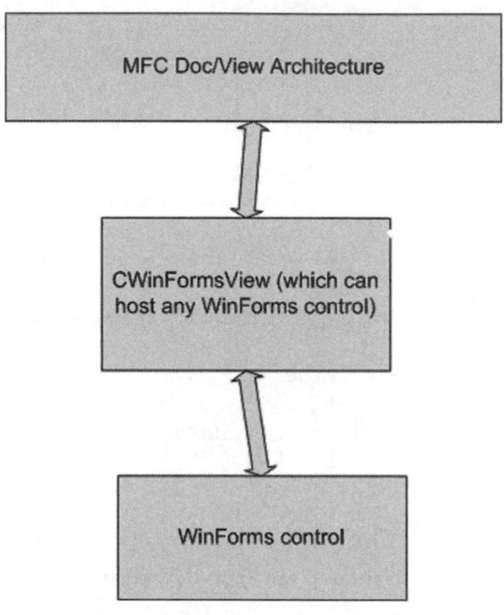

Figure 6.3 Using a WinForms control as an MFC view

When you use the `CWinFormsView` class, the WinForms control is created as a child of the original `CView` (or `CView`-derived) window and resized to fit within the view; thus, the `HWND` for the `CView` and the `HWND` for the embedded WinForms control won't be the same. The `DataGridView` control is an advanced class with extensive data integration capabilities. In the example, you'll use it to display XML data, and also to allow the user to make changes and save those changes back to the XML file. Not only do you need to put the WinForms control inside the view, but you also need to appropriately handle file open/save functionality so that the default MFC functionality is overridden with the custom handlers. Figure 6.4 shows what the final application will look like.

Here are the steps you'll follow to get the application up and running:

Step 1 Create the application project.

Create a new SDI MFC application, and enable `/clr` compilation. Add references to the `System.Data` and `System.Xml` assemblies, because you'll need them for using specific features of the `DataGridView` control. Name the project `MfcDataGridView`.

Step 2 Add the required header files.

Add the following `#include` to the stdafx.h file. You need it for the `CWinFormsView` class:

```
#include <afxwinforms.h>
```

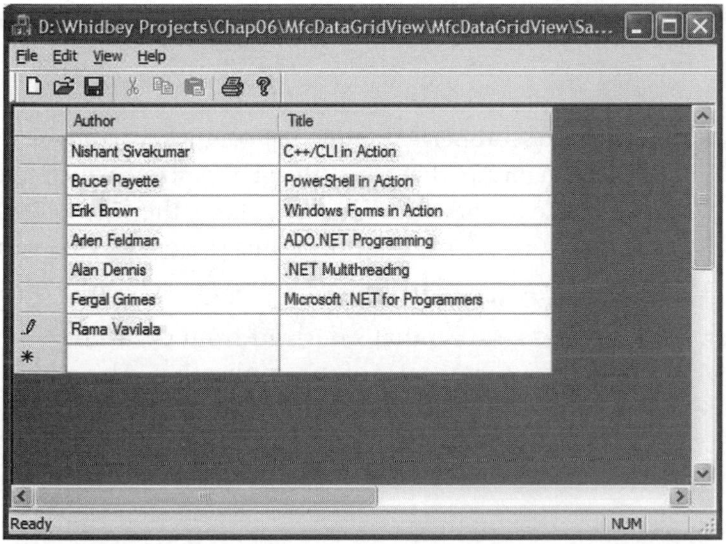

Figure 6.4 Example that demonstrates hosting the `DataGridView` control as an MFC view

Step 3 Create the container control.

There's a problem in the ActiveX-based hosting used by the MFC-WinForms classes that prevents a `DataGridView` control from binding to its data source when it's directly used as the view window using the `CWinFormsView` class. To work around this problem, you need to put the `DataGridView` control as a child of a `UserControl`-derived class and then host this `UserControl`-derived class as the view window. To do so, add the following `UserControl`-derived class to the project, which serves as a container (or holder) for the `DataGridView` control:

```
using namespace System;
using namespace System::Windows::Forms;

ref class HolderControl : UserControl
{
    DataGridView^ m_dgView;
public:
    HolderControl()
    {
        m_dgView = gcnew DataGridView();
        m_dgView->Dock = DockStyle::Fill;
        Controls->Add(m_dgView);
    }
    property DataGridView^ TheDataGridView
    {
        DataGridView^ get()
        {
```

❶ Fill entire control

```
                return m_dgView;
            }
        }
    };
```

Notice how you set the Dock property of the DataGridView control to DockStyle::Fill ❶. This way, you ensure that when the view is sized, which means the UserControl is sized too (done by the CWinFormsView class), the DataGridView control automatically fills the entire UserControl and thus the entire view window.

Step 4 Create the CWinFormsView-derived class.
Next, add a new class (CDataGridView) that's derived from CWinFormsView, which you'll use as the base class for the main view of the application. Also add a CString member variable (m_XmlFile) that will hold the full path to the XML file:

```
class CDataGridView : public CWinFormsView
{
. . .
protected:
    CString m_XmlFile;
. . .
};
```

Step 5 Call the appropriate CWinFormsView constructor.
You now need to modify the CDataGridView constructor so that it calls the appropriate version of the CWinFormsView constructor. Change the CDataGridView constructor to the following:

```
CDataGridView::CDataGridView() :
    CWinFormsView(HolderControl::typeid)
    ,m_XmlFile(_T(""))
{
}
```

You pass the type of the HolderControl class to the CWinFormsView constructor. The CWinFormsView class will now be responsible for creating and maintaining the HolderControl class as a child control.

Step 6 Change the main view to derive from CDataGridView.
Change the main view class so that it derives from CDataGridView instead of from CView (the default). Replace all instances of CView with CDataGridView in both the CPP and the H files of the CMfcDataGridViewView class.

Just to reassess where you are, at this point, you have written enough code to host the DataGridView. You now need to write code to allow the application to open and save XML data. That's what you'll accomplish in the remaining steps.

Step 7 Add a `GetControl` helper function.

Add a helper function that will return a `DataGridView^`, which will be a reference to the underlying WinForms control. The `CWinFormsView` version of `GetControl` is called, which returns a reference to the underlying `HolderControl^`, and you retrieve the `DataGridView` control using the `TheDataGridView` property that you defined earlier (in step 3):

```
DataGridView^ CDataGridView::GetControl(void)
{
    return safe_cast<HolderControl^>(
        __super::GetControl())->TheDataGridView;
}
```

Later, whenever you need to directly access the underlying `DataGridView` control, you can conveniently use this `GetControl` method.

Step 8 Add helper functions for open/save/new handlers.

In later steps, you're going to add functionality to the `CDataGridView` class so that it handles opening and saving XML files directly. One of the aims in doing this is to avoid having to modify the `CDocument`-derived class in the project. The fewer files you need to modify, the better, especially if you're applying these techniques on an application that's far larger than the simple SDI demo. Let's first write a couple of helper functions to indicate to the Document-View system that the XML data has been modified (or not); these helper functions can then be used by the open/save/new handlers:

```
int CDataGridView::ShowPromptForSaveDialog(void)
{
    return AfxMessageBox(_T("Save changes to ")
        + m_XmlFile + _T("?"),
        MB_YESNOCANCEL|MB_ICONQUESTION);
}

bool CDataGridView::DoModifiedCheck(void)
{
    if(GetDocument()->IsModified())
    {
        int ret = ShowPromptForSaveDialog();
        if(ret == IDCANCEL)
            return false;
        if(ret == IDYES)
            OnFileSave();
    }
    return true;
}
```

The `ShowPromptForSaveDialog` method mimics (although not identically) the message box shown by MFC when you attempt to close a document (either via closing the app or via opening another document), and the document has been modified and not been saved. The `DoModifiedCheck` method checks if the document's modified flag is set and, if so, uses the `ShowPromptForSaveDialog` method to prompt the user, emulating regular MFC behavior in response to the user's choice.

Step 9 Add the delegate map and the event handlers.

In the previous step, you wrote helper functions that check the document's modified flag to determine if a save is pending. In this step, you write code that sets the document's modified flag whenever the data grid has been modified. To do so, add event handlers to the `UserAddedRow`, `UserDeletedRow`, and `CellValueChanged` events of the `DataGridView` control. Just as in the example in the previous section, you declare a delegate map to map the MFC methods to managed delegates:

```
BEGIN_DELEGATE_MAP(CDataGridView)
    EVENT_DELEGATE_ENTRY(OnUserAddedRow,
        Object^, DataGridViewRowEventArgs^)
    EVENT_DELEGATE_ENTRY(OnUserDeletedRow,
        Object^, DataGridViewRowEventArgs^)
    EVENT_DELEGATE_ENTRY(OnCellValueChanged,
        Object^, DataGridViewCellEventArgs ^)
END_DELEGATE_MAP()
```

The events are hooked up in the `OnInitialUpdate` method of the `CDataGridView` class, as shown here:

```
void CDataGridView::OnInitialUpdate()
{
    CWinFormsView::OnInitialUpdate();

    GetControl()->UserAddedRow += MAKE_DELEGATE(
        DataGridViewRowEventHandler,OnUserAddedRow);
    GetControl()->UserDeletedRow += MAKE_DELEGATE(
        DataGridViewRowEventHandler,OnUserDeletedRow);
    GetControl()->CellValueChanged += MAKE_DELEGATE(
        DataGridViewCellEventHandler,OnCellValueChanged);
}
```

The event-handler implementations are simple—all they do is set the document's modified flag:

```
void CDataGridView::OnUserAddedRow(Object^,
    DataGridViewRowEventArgs^)
{
    GetDocument()->SetModifiedFlag(TRUE);
}
```

```
void CDataGridView::OnUserDeletedRow(Object^,
    DataGridViewRowEventArgs^)
{
    GetDocument()->SetModifiedFlag(TRUE);
}

void CDataGridView::OnCellValueChanged(Object^,
    DataGridViewCellEventArgs ^)
{
    GetDocument()->SetModifiedFlag(TRUE);
}
```

You're now at a point where you can implement the code for opening/saving XML documents.

Step 10 Add file-open and -save methods that bind the XML to the `DataGridView` control.

Add an `OnFileOpen` method as shown here. It binds the opened XML file to the `DataGridView` control:

```
void CDataGridView::OnFileOpen()
{
    if(DoModifiedCheck())
    {
        CFileDialog fd(TRUE);

        TCHAR dirbuff[MAX_PATH + 1];
        if(GetModuleFileName(NULL, dirbuff, MAX_PATH + 1) &&
            PathRemoveFileSpec(dirbuff))
        {
            fd.m_pOFN->lpstrInitialDir = dirbuff;
        }

        fd.m_pOFN->lpstrFilter = _T("XML Files (*.xml)\0*.xml\0");
        if(fd.DoModal() == IDOK)
        {
            using namespace System;
            using namespace System::Data;
            DataSet^ ds = gcnew DataSet();
            ds->ReadXml(gcnew String(                              // 1 Read XML into dataset
                m_XmlFile = fd.GetPathName()));
            GetControl()->DataSource = ds;                         // 2 Bind to dataset
            GetControl()->DataMember = ds->Tables[0]->TableName;   // Specify table to use
            AfxGetMainWnd()->SetWindowText(
                m_XmlFile + _T(" - ") + AfxGetAppName());
            GetDocument()->SetModifiedFlag(FALSE);                 // 3 Reset document's modified flag
        }
    }
}
```

The code is elementary WinForms data binding, where you use the `ReadXml` method of the `DataSet` class ❶ to read the XML data, and then bind that `DataSet` to the `DataGridView` by setting the latter's `DataSource` property ❷. Once you're done, you also reset the modified flag (in case it was previously set to `TRUE`) ❸.

Next, add the `OnFileSave` method, which uses the `WriteXml` method of the `DataSet` class to save any changes back to the XML file, and then resets the modified flag of the document:

```
void CDataGridView::OnFileSave()
{
    using namespace System;
    using namespace System::Data;
    try
    {
        DataSet^ ds = safe_cast<DataSet^>(
            GetControl()->DataSource);
        ds->WriteXml(gcnew String(m_XmlFile));
        GetDocument()->SetModifiedFlag(FALSE);
    }
    catch(Exception^)
    {
    }
}
```

Note how you catch a generic `Exception^`, which you use to make sure that if the user attempts a Save call when no XML is loaded, nothing happens.

Next, write the `OnFileSaveAs` method, which delegates the actual file-saving to the `OnFileSave` method:

```
void CDataGridView::OnFileSaveAs()
{
    CFileDialog fd(FALSE);
    fd.m_pOFN->lpstrFilter = _T("XML Files (*.xml)\0*.xml\0");
    fd.m_pOFN->lpstrDefExt = _T("xml");
    if(GetControl()->DataSource && fd.DoModal() == IDOK)
    {
        m_XmlFile = fd.GetPathName();                   <-- Set new
        AfxGetMainWnd()->SetWindowText(m_XmlFile            file path
            + _T(" - ") + AfxGetAppName());
        OnFileSave();    <-- Save file using
    }                        OnFileSave
}
```

You still need to write a handler for the New action where you first check to see if any Save is pending, and then clear the data source and thus the data grid view. Do that now, as shown here:

```
void CDataGridView::OnFileNew()
{
```

```
        if(DoModifiedCheck())
        {
            GetControl()->DataSource = nullptr;      Clear data
            GetControl()->DataMember = nullptr;      binding
            m_XmlFile = _T("");
            AfxGetMainWnd()->SetWindowText(m_XmlFile
                + _T("Untitled - ") + AfxGetAppName());
            GetDocument()->SetModifiedFlag(FALSE);
        }
    }
```

Next, add the corresponding command handlers that associate the menu/toolbar commands with the methods you just wrote:

```
BEGIN_MESSAGE_MAP(CDataGridView, CWinFormsView)
    ON_COMMAND(ID_FILE_OPEN, &CDataGridView::OnFileOpen)
    ON_COMMAND(ID_FILE_SAVE, &CDataGridView::OnFileSave)
    ON_COMMAND(ID_FILE_NEW, &CDataGridView::OnFileNew)
    ON_COMMAND(ID_FILE_SAVE_AS, &CDataGridView::OnFileSaveAs)
END_MESSAGE_MAP()
```

You now have a basically functional application that you can compile and run. There are still a few issues, though, which you'll address in the next couple of steps.

Step 11 Handle the `WM_CLOSE` message.

Despite all the checks you do to ensure that the modified flag of the document is set and reset appropriately, if you close the application when the modified flag is set, the default MFC save-prompt message box will pop up. If the user selects Yes at that prompt, the default MFC file-saving mechanism will be called—which is disastrous to the XML file, because it will be overwritten. The workaround to this problem is to handle `WM_CLOSE` in the frame window and to set the modified flag to `FALSE` before invoking the base class implementation of `OnClose`:

```
void CMainFrame::OnClose()
{
    CDataGridView* pView = dynamic_cast<CDataGridView*>(
        GetActiveView());
    if(pView)
    {
        if(pView->DoModifiedCheck())
        {
            pView->GetDocument()->SetModifiedFlag(FALSE);
        }
    }
    CFrameWnd::OnClose();
}
```

Step 12 Handle accelerator keys in `PreTranslateMessage`.

You've pretty much fixed the issues involved, but one nasty surprise is left. If you run the application now and open an XML file, you'll notice that the keyboard shortcuts for the cut, copy, paste, and undo functions don't work inside the `DataGridView` control. The default accelerator key-handling mechanism routes these keyboard messages to the main frame window, and they never reach the `DataGridView` control. To work around this problem, override the `PreTranslateMessage` message of the `CDataGridView` class:

```
BOOL CDataGridView::PreTranslateMessage(MSG* pMsg)
{
    switch(pMsg->message)
    {
    case WM_KEYDOWN:
    case WM_KEYUP:
        switch(pMsg->wParam)
        {
        case _T('C'):
        case _T('X'):
        case _T('V'):
        case _T('Z'):
            if(GetKeyState (VK_CONTROL) & 0x8000)
            {
                ::TranslateMessage(pMsg);
                return TRUE;
            }
        }
    }
    return CWinFormsView::PreTranslateMessage(pMsg);
}
```

You check for the Ctrl-X, Ctrl-C, Ctrl-V, and Ctrl-Z keyboard messages, call the `TranslateMessage` API directly, and then return `TRUE`, instead of calling the base-class implementation of `PreTranslateMessage`.

Now, you can rebuild and run the application. You'll find that it works just as expected.

That's the end of the example of hosting a WinForms control as an MFC view. You can use the same techniques and steps used in this example to host any WinForms control as an MFC view. Be aware that most WinForms controls weren't written with the purpose of hosting them in MFC applications, so sometimes you have to write workarounds to get things working as expected—such as the clipboard command shortcuts problem that you had to work around in this section, for the example.

Let's begin the step-by-step walkthrough to implementing an SDI application that uses a `DataGridView` as the view window.

6.4 Giving your MFC apps an Office 2003 style UI

In this section, we'll look at an example that takes an existing MFC SDI application and gives it an Office 2003 look and feel by using the WinForms 2.0 `MenuStrip` and `ToolStrip` controls. To continue the analogy, you're now replacing a Corolla's dashboard with that of a Pontiac.

You'll be using the `CWinFormsControl` class to host the WinForms controls in the MFC app. You'll also see how to remove the MFC menu and toolbar, and how you can hook the .NET menu and toolbar to the functionality originally associated with the MFC menu/toolbar. You may wonder why you don't replace the existing menu and toolbar with the WinForms versions. That's not possible because the WinForms controls are custom controls and not mere wrappers around a native toolbar or a menu. That's what makes things more complicated than they would be otherwise. The workarounds to those complications, however, aren't too difficult to implement.

For the example, you'll generate a simple MFC SDI application with a `CEditView`-derived class as the view class—which means you have a basic text file editor application (like Notepad). Figure 6.5 illustrates what the final application will look like. Please keep in mind that the code listings in the text may not be

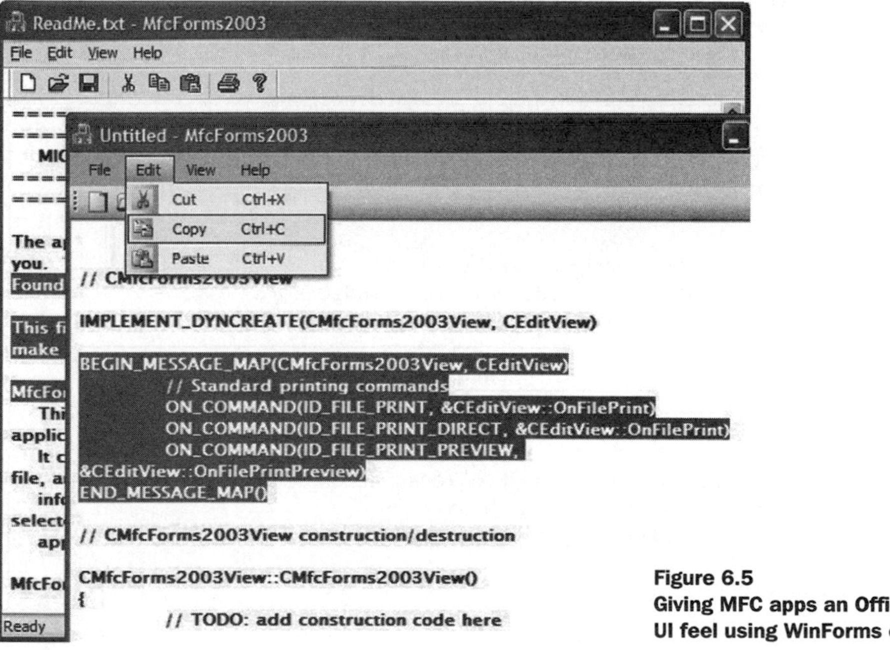

Figure 6.5 Giving MFC apps an Office 2003 UI feel using WinForms controls

complete (to save space and to avoid repetition), so you should refer to the accompanying source code for the actual source code.

You'll complete the following steps to get the application up and running with an Office 2003 look and feel:

Step 1 Create the MFC project.

Create an MFC SDI application, set the view base class to `CEditView`, and enable `/clr` compilation mode. Let's assume that this is the existing MFC application (which is why you don't unselect the toolbar option in the wizard—an existing app is pretty much assured to have a toolbar).

Step 2 Remove unwanted wizard-generated code.

Remove the MFC toolbar-creation code: You don't want that in the app, because you'll be using the WinForms `ToolStrip` control for the toolbar. The lines of code to remove (or comment out) are in `CMainFrame::OnCreate`; here's what the function looks like, after you remove the code associated with creating the toolbar:

```
int CMainFrame::OnCreate(LPCREATESTRUCT lpCreateStruct)
{
    if (CFrameWnd::OnCreate(lpCreateStruct) == -1)
        return -1;

    //if (!m_wndToolBar.CreateEx(this, TBSTYLE_FLAT,
    //  WS_CHILD | WS_VISIBLE | CBRS_TOP
    //  | CBRS_GRIPPER | CBRS_TOOLTIPS | CBRS_FLYBY
    //  | CBRS_SIZE_DYNAMIC) ||
    //  !m_wndToolBar.LoadToolBar(IDR_MAINFRAME))
    //{
    //  TRACE0("Failed to create toolbar\n");
    //  return -1;      // fail to create
    //}

    if (!m_wndStatusBar.Create(this) ||
        !m_wndStatusBar.SetIndicators(indicators,
          sizeof(indicators)/sizeof(UINT)))
    {
        TRACE0("Failed to create status bar\n");
        return -1;   // fail to create
    }

    //m_wndToolBar.EnableDocking(CBRS_ALIGN_ANY);
    //EnableDocking(CBRS_ALIGN_ANY);
    //DockControlBar(&m_wndToolBar);

    return 0;
}
```

As you can see, you comment-out the lines of code that create the toolbar and those that enable docking.

Step 3 Remove the MFC menu.

Next, remove the MFC menu. One way of doing this is in `PreCreateWindow`, where you can remove the menu style from the frame window; but you won't use that method. Instead, you'll use another approach that is more flexible: It can be used even while the application is up and running. Modify `OnCreate`, and add two lines that destroy the existing menu and set the menu handle to `NULL`, as shown here:

```
int CMainFrame::OnCreate(LPCREATESTRUCT lpCreateStruct)
{
    if (CFrameWnd::OnCreate(lpCreateStruct) == -1)
        return -1;

    CMenu* pMenu = GetMenu();
    if(pMenu)
    {
        pMenu->DestroyMenu();       <-- Destroy existing menu, if any
        SetMenu(NULL);              <-- Set frame's menu handle to NULL
    }

    . . .
```

At this point, you've removed the menu and the toolbar. If you run the application now, you'll see a plain frame window that houses an edit control—not impressive, eh? But you'll change that soon.

Step 4 Add the required header files and member variables.

Add `#include <afxwinforms.h>` to the stdafx.h file, so you can use the `CWinFormsControl` class. Then, declare the following two members in the header file for the frame window class (MainFrm.h):

```
CWinFormsControl<System::Windows::Forms::MenuStrip> m_MenuStrip;
CWinFormsControl<System::Windows::Forms::ToolStrip> m_ToolStrip;
```

The `MenuStrip` and `ToolStrip` controls are new controls that have been added to WinForms in .NET 2.0; they provide an Office 2003 look and feel.

Step 5 Initialize the WinForms controls.

To create and initialize the `MenuStrip` and `ToolStrip` controls, add the following code to the `OnCreate` method of the `CMainFrame` class:

```
    . . .

    m_MenuStrip.CreateManagedControl(WS_VISIBLE|WS_CHILD,
        CRect(0,0,0,25),this, 1001);
```

```
    m_ToolStrip.CreateManagedControl(WS_VISIBLE|WS_CHILD,
        CRect(0,25,0,50),this, 1002);

    CreateAndInitializeMenuStrip();
    CreateAndInitializeToolStrip();

    return 0;
}
```

You use the `CreateManagedControl` method of the `CWinFormsControl` class to create both the `MenuStrip` and the `ToolStrip` controls as children of the frame window, by specifying `this` as the parent. You put the `MenuStrip` initialization code into the `CreateAndInitializeMenuStrip` method. Similarly, you put the `ToolStrip` initialization code into `CreateAndInitializeToolStrip`. Listing 6.1 shows the `CreateAndInitializeMenuStrip` method.

Listing 6.1 Function to initialize the `MenuStrip` control

```
void CMainFrame::CreateAndInitializeMenuStrip()
{
    using namespace System::Windows::Forms;

    ToolStripMenuItem^ topitem;

    topitem = gcnew ToolStripMenuItem();          // Create File menu and subitems
    topitem->Text = "File";
    m_MenuStrip->Items->Add(topitem);

    AddToolStripMenuItem(topitem, "New", "Ctrl+N", IDI_FILENEW,
        MAKE_DELEGATE(System::EventHandler,File_New_Click));
    AddToolStripMenuItem(topitem, "Open", "Ctrl+O", IDI_FILEOPEN,
        MAKE_DELEGATE(System::EventHandler,File_Open_Click));
    AddToolStripMenuItem(topitem, "Save", "Ctrl+S", IDI_FILESAVE,
        MAKE_DELEGATE(System::EventHandler,File_Save_Click));
    AddToolStripMenuItem(topitem, "Save As...", "", 0,
        MAKE_DELEGATE(System::EventHandler,File_SaveAs_Click));
    AddToolStripMenuItem(topitem, "Exit", "Alt+F4", 0,
        MAKE_DELEGATE(System::EventHandler,File_Exit_Click));

    topitem = gcnew ToolStripMenuItem();          // Create Edit menu and subitems
    topitem->Text = "Edit";
    m_MenuStrip->Items->Add(topitem);

    AddToolStripMenuItem(topitem, "Cut", "Ctrl+X", IDI_EDITCUT,
        MAKE_DELEGATE(System::EventHandler,Edit_Cut_Click));
    AddToolStripMenuItem(topitem, "Copy", "Ctrl+C", IDI_EDITCOPY,
        MAKE_DELEGATE(System::EventHandler,Edit_Copy_Click));
    AddToolStripMenuItem(topitem, "Paste", "Ctrl+V", IDI_EDITPASTE,
        MAKE_DELEGATE(System::EventHandler,Edit_Paste_Click));
```

```
    topitem = gcnew ToolStripMenuItem();      <-- Create View menu
    topitem->Text = "View";                       and subitems
    m_MenuStrip->Items->Add(topitem);

    AddToolStripMenuItem(topitem, "Toolbar", "", 0,
        MAKE_DELEGATE(System::EventHandler,View_Toolbar_Click));
    AddToolStripMenuItem(topitem, "Statusbar", "", 0,
        MAKE_DELEGATE(System::EventHandler,View_Statusbar_Click));

    topitem = gcnew ToolStripMenuItem();      <-- Create Help menu
    topitem->Text = "Help";                       and subitems
    m_MenuStrip->Items->Add(topitem);

    AddToolStripMenuItem(topitem, "About", "", IDI_HELPABOUT,
        MAKE_DELEGATE(System::EventHandler,Help_About_Click));
}
```

You use the `Add` method of the `Items` property of the `MenuStrip` class to create the top-level menus. For the subitems of each top-level menu, you use a helper function called `AddToolStripMenuItem` to add individual menu items to a top-level menu. You pass the text for the subitem; the shortcut key text, if any; the icon to show, if any; and a delegate method to this helper function. You use the `MAKE_DELEGATE` macro to convert the MFC method to a .NET delegate, just as you did earlier when you put a WinForms control on an MFC dialog. Listing 6.2 shows the `AddToolStripMenuItem` method.

Listing 6.2 Function to add individual menu items

```
void CMainFrame::AddToolStripMenuItem(
        System::Windows::Forms::ToolStripMenuItem^ topitem,
        System::String^ text, System::String^ shortcutkey, UINT icon,
        System::EventHandler^ eh)
{
    using namespace System::Windows::Forms;

    ToolStripMenuItem^ item = gcnew ToolStripMenuItem();
    item->Text = text;
    if(shortcutkey->Length > 0)
        item->ShortcutKeyDisplayString = shortcutkey;
    if(icon)
        item->Image = System::Drawing::Bitmap::FromHicon(
            (System::IntPtr)
            LoadImage(AfxGetInstanceHandle(),MAKEINTRESOURCE(icon),
            IMAGE_ICON,0,0,LR_DEFAULTCOLOR));      <-- 1 Load icon and convert to Image object
    item->Click += eh;
    topitem->DropDownItems->Add(item);      <-- 2 Add subitem to top-level menu
}
```

You load the icon using `LoadImage` and convert the `HICON` to a `Bitmap` using the `FromHicon` method. `LoadImage` is preferred over `CWinApp::LoadIcon` to support higher-color icons ❶. Once the required members are set up, you call the `Add` method on the `DropDownItems` property of the passed-in top-level menu item ❷.

Initializing the `ToolStrip` is similar. Listing 6.3 shows what the `CreateAndInitializeToolStrip` method looks like.

Listing 6.3 Function to create the `ToolStrip` control

```
void CMainFrame::CreateAndInitializeToolStrip()
{
    using namespace System::Windows::Forms;

    AddToolStripButton("New",IDI_FILENEW,MAKE_DELEGATE(
        System::EventHandler,File_New_Click));
    AddToolStripButton("Open",IDI_FILEOPEN,MAKE_DELEGATE(
        System::EventHandler,File_Open_Click));
    AddToolStripButton("Save",IDI_FILESAVE,MAKE_DELEGATE(
        System::EventHandler,File_Save_Click));
    m_ToolStrip->Items->Add(gcnew ToolStripSeparator());
    AddToolStripButton("Cut",IDI_EDITCUT,MAKE_DELEGATE(
        System::EventHandler,Edit_Cut_Click));
    AddToolStripButton("Copy",IDI_EDITCOPY,MAKE_DELEGATE(
        System::EventHandler,Edit_Copy_Click));
    AddToolStripButton("Paste",IDI_EDITPASTE,MAKE_DELEGATE(
        System::EventHandler,Edit_Paste_Click));
    m_ToolStrip->Items->Add(gcnew ToolStripSeparator());
    AddToolStripButton("About",IDI_HELPABOUT,MAKE_DELEGATE(
        System::EventHandler,Help_About_Click));
}
```

You use a helper method called `AddToolStripButton` to add each individual button to the `ToolStrip`. This function takes the tool-tip text, the icon to show, and the event handler to call as parameters. Again, you use the `MAKE_DELEGATE` macro to convert the MFC method to a .NET delegate. Listing 6.4 shows the code for the `AddToolStripButton` method.

Listing 6.4 Function to add individual `ToolStrip` buttons

```
void CMainFrame::AddToolStripButton(
    System::String^ tooltip, UINT icon, System::EventHandler^ eh)
{
    using namespace System::Windows::Forms;
    ToolStripButton^ tbutton = gcnew ToolStripButton();
    tbutton->Size = System::Drawing::Size(25,25);
```

```
    tbutton->ToolTipText = tooltip;
    tbutton->Image =
            System::Drawing::Bitmap::FromHicon((System::IntPtr)
        LoadImage(AfxGetInstanceHandle(),MAKEINTRESOURCE(icon),
        IMAGE_ICON,0,0,LR_DEFAULTCOLOR));
    tbutton->ImageScaling = ToolStripItemImageScaling::None;
    tbutton->Click += eh;
    m_ToolStrip->Items->Add(tbutton);
}
```

Notice the difference from MFC toolbars, where you typically load the toolbar images from a bitmap; here, you load individual icons, which is the preferred WinForms method. The code is straightforward, and you set up the required members of the `ToolStripButton` object and then add it to the `ToolStrip` using the `Add` method of the `Items` property. Now that you've written code to initialize and set up the `MenuStrip` and `ToolStrip` controls, you need to write the event handlers as well as the delegate map.

Step 6 Add a delegate map.
Listing 6.5 shows the delegate map that you need to put into a public section of the `CMainFrame` class declaration.

Listing 6.5 Delegate map for the `CMainFrame` class

```
BEGIN_DELEGATE_MAP( CMainFrame )
    EVENT_DELEGATE_ENTRY( File_New_Click,
        System::Object^, System::EventArgs^)
    EVENT_DELEGATE_ENTRY( File_Open_Click,
        System::Object^, System::EventArgs^)
    EVENT_DELEGATE_ENTRY( File_Save_Click,
        System::Object^, System::EventArgs^)
    EVENT_DELEGATE_ENTRY( File_SaveAs_Click,
        System::Object^, System::EventArgs^)
    EVENT_DELEGATE_ENTRY( File_Exit_Click,
        System::Object^, System::EventArgs^)
    EVENT_DELEGATE_ENTRY( Edit_Cut_Click,
        System::Object^, System::EventArgs^)
    EVENT_DELEGATE_ENTRY( Edit_Copy_Click,
        System::Object^, System::EventArgs^)
    EVENT_DELEGATE_ENTRY( Edit_Paste_Click,
        System::Object^, System::EventArgs^)
    EVENT_DELEGATE_ENTRY( View_Toolbar_Click,
        System::Object^, System::EventArgs^)
    EVENT_DELEGATE_ENTRY( View_Statusbar_Click,
        System::Object^, System::EventArgs^)
```

```
    EVENT_DELEGATE_ENTRY( Help_About_Click,
        System::Object^, System::EventArgs^)
END_DELEGATE_MAP()
```

Again, the code is exactly the same as that shown earlier in this chapter when we discussed how to put a WinForms control on an MFC dialog. Now that you've written the delegate map, let's write the MFC handlers that are used in the delegate map.

Step 7 Add command-routing event handlers.
In each event handler, you'll use `PostMessage` to post a `WM_COMMAND` message to the frame window with the corresponding command-id of the menu/toolbar item. The code is nearly identical except for the command-id, which changes for each method; see listing 6.6.

Listing 6.6 Event handlers for the menu and toolbar controls

```
void CMainFrame::File_New_Click(
    System::Object^ sender,System::EventArgs^ e)
{
    PostMessage(WM_COMMAND,ID_FILE_NEW);
}
void CMainFrame::File_Open_Click(
    System::Object^ sender,System::EventArgs^ e)
{
    PostMessage(WM_COMMAND,ID_FILE_OPEN);
}
void CMainFrame::File_Save_Click(
    System::Object^ sender,System::EventArgs^ e)
{
    PostMessage(WM_COMMAND,ID_FILE_SAVE);
}
void CMainFrame::File_SaveAs_Click(
    System::Object^ sender,System::EventArgs^ e)
{
    PostMessage(WM_COMMAND,ID_FILE_SAVE_AS);
}
void CMainFrame::File_Exit_Click(
    System::Object^ sender,System::EventArgs^ e)
{
    PostMessage(WM_COMMAND,ID_APP_EXIT);
}
void CMainFrame::Edit_Cut_Click(
    System::Object^ sender,System::EventArgs^ e)
{
    PostMessage(WM_COMMAND,ID_EDIT_CUT);
}
void CMainFrame::Edit_Copy_Click(
```

```
    System::Object^ sender,System::EventArgs^ e)
{
    PostMessage(WM_COMMAND,ID_EDIT_COPY);
}
void CMainFrame::Edit_Paste_Click(
    System::Object^ sender,System::EventArgs^ e)
{
    PostMessage(WM_COMMAND,ID_EDIT_PASTE);
}

void CMainFrame::Help_About_Click(
    System::Object^ sender,System::EventArgs^ e)
{
    PostMessage(WM_COMMAND,ID_APP_ABOUT);
}
void CMainFrame::View_Toolbar_Click(
    System::Object^ sender,System::EventArgs^ e)
{
    m_ToolStrip->Visible = !m_ToolStrip->Visible;
    ResizeView();
}
void CMainFrame::View_Statusbar_Click(
    System::Object^ sender,System::EventArgs^ e)
{
    SendMessage(WM_COMMAND,ID_VIEW_STATUS_BAR);
    ResizeView();
}
```

As you can see, the last two methods differ from the other methods; they both call `ResizeView` (which you'll see in the next step). For the `View_Toolbar_Click` handler, you hide/unhide the `ToolStrip` control by toggling its `Visible` property. You have to resize the view window when that's done, and thus, you make a call to the `ResizeView` method. For the `View_Statusbar_Click` handler, you use a `SendMessage` instead of a `PostMessage` so that you can call `ResizeView` once the status bar has been shown or hidden. If you used `PostMessage`, the status bar might change its visibility state after `ResizeView` was called. This wouldn't serve the purpose because you need to resize the view window depending on whether the status bar is shown or hidden.

Step 8 Add a `ResizeView` method.

Write the `ResizeView` method that resizes the view so that it doesn't cover the `MenuStrip` or `ToolStrip` controls. In `ResizeView`, you also set the widths of the `MenuStrip` and `ToolStrip` controls to that of the view so they stretch to fill the view width. Listing 6.7 shows the code for the `ResizeView` method.

Listing 6.7 Function to resize the view to account for the WinForms controls

```
void CMainFrame::ResizeView()
{
    CRect rect;
    RepositionBars(AFX_IDW_CONTROLBAR_FIRST,
        AFX_IDW_CONTROLBAR_LAST,0,CWnd::reposQuery,&rect);

    m_MenuStrip->Size = System::Drawing::Size(
        rect.Width(),m_MenuStrip->Size.Height);
    rect.top += m_MenuStrip->Size.Height;
    if(m_ToolStrip->Visible)
    {
        m_ToolStrip->Size = System::Drawing::Size(
            rect.Width(),m_ToolStrip->Size.Height);
        rect.top += m_ToolStrip->Size.Height;
    }

    CView* pView = GetActiveView();
    if(pView)
    {
        pView->MoveWindow(rect);
    }
}
```

❶ Calculate required rectangle

❷ Stretch width of MenuStrip

❸ Stretch width of ToolStrip if visible

❹ Resize view to accommodate WinForms controls

You need to figure out the required rectangle that accounts for any other control bars (such as the status bar), and you use the MFC method `RepositionBars` with the `reposQuery` flag ❶. You then stretch the widths of the `MenuStrip` ❷ as well as the `ToolStrip` ❸ to match that of the view window. Finally, you resize the view so that it leaves enough space for the `MenuStrip` and `ToolStrip` controls ❹.

Step 9 Add a handler for `WM_SIZE`.

You also need to write a handler for `WM_SIZE` so that when the frame window is resized, the WinForms controls are resized accordingly:

```
void CMainFrame::OnSize(UINT nType, int cx, int cy)
{
    CFrameWnd::OnSize(nType, cx, cy);

    // If the menu strip is created
    if(m_MenuStrip.GetSafeHwnd())
    {
        ResizeView();
    }
}
```

You do a check to see if the `MenuStrip` has been created. If it has, you make a call to `ResizeView`, so that if the frame window is resized, the WinForms controls are appropriately resized, too.

Step 10 Add additional delegate map entries.
One thing you need to keep in mind is that you've replaced the regular MFC menu and toolbar with .NET WinForms controls. Because WinForms and MFC use different mechanisms in general, there may not be direct WinForms equivalents for every MFC mechanism you're used to. For example, an MFC app's menu items automatically support status bar prompts, and you can easily customize this further by using macros such as `ON_UPDATE_COMMAND_UI`. In the example, to do the same (or something similar), you need to use .NET functionality. As a simple example, let's add code so that the status bar reflects the text of each menu item in focus (you may alternatively want to use a lookup table and show a longer string in your application). First, add the following two delegate entries to the delegate map:

```
BEGIN_DELEGATE_MAP( CMainFrame )
. . .
    EVENT_DELEGATE_ENTRY( OnItemMouseEnter,
        System::Object^, System::EventArgs^)
    EVENT_DELEGATE_ENTRY( OnItemMouseLeave,
        System::Object^, System::EventArgs^)
END_DELEGATE_MAP()
```

Hook up the menu items to these delegate functions in the `AddToolStripMenuItem` method:

```
void CMainFrame::AddToolStripMenuItem(. . .)
{
    . . .
    item->MouseLeave += MAKE_DELEGATE(
        System::EventHandler,OnItemMouseLeave);
    item->MouseEnter += MAKE_DELEGATE(
        System::EventHandler,OnItemMouseEnter);
    topitem->DropDownItems->Add(item);
}
```

Listing 6.8 shows how you define the two methods. In `OnItemMouseEnter`, the status bar text is set to the menu item's `Text` property. In `OnItemMouseLeave`, you set it back to the default.

Listing 6.8 Mouse handlers for setting the status bar text

```
void CMainFrame::OnItemMouseEnter(
    System::Object^ sender,System::EventArgs^ e)
{
    using namespace System::Windows::Forms;
    ToolStripMenuItem^ item =
        dynamic_cast<ToolStripMenuItem^>(sender);
    m_wndStatusBar.SetPaneText(0,(CString)item->Text);
}

void CMainFrame::OnItemMouseLeave(
    System::Object^ sender,System::EventArgs^ e)
{
    using namespace System::Windows::Forms;
    ToolStripMenuItem^ item =
        dynamic_cast<ToolStripMenuItem^>(sender);
    if(IsWindow(m_wndStatusBar.m_hWnd))
        m_wndStatusBar.SetPaneText(0,_T("Ready"));
}
```

There's still one thing missing: Alt-keyboard shortcuts for the main menu! The problem is that the Alt-key shortcuts are sent via `WM_SYSKEYDOWN` messages to the menu associated with the main window of the application. But in the app, you've removed this main menu and replaced it with the menu strip WinForms control, which isn't really a menu but a simulated version of it. The workaround is to handle the `WM_SYSKEYDOWN` message in `PreTranslateMessage` and to manually drop down the specific menu associated with the shortcut key. Listing 6.9 shows one way of doing it, where you assume that the Alt-key shortcut for a top-level menu is always the first letter of the text for the menu. For your specific scenario, you may want to parse the menu text and locate the & character to decide which menu to drop down, but that's just an implementation detail. The technique remains the same.

Listing 6.9 The `PreTranslateMessage` override

```
BOOL CMainFrame::PreTranslateMessage(MSG* pMsg)
{
    using namespace System;
    using namespace System::Windows::Forms;
    if(pMsg->message == WM_SYSKEYDOWN)
    {
        for each(Object^ o in m_MenuStrip->Items)
        {
            ToolStripMenuItem^ item =
```

```
                safe_cast<ToolStripMenuItem^>(o);
            if(Char::ToUpper(item->Text[0]) == (Char)pMsg->wParam)
            {
                item->ShowDropDown();
                if(item->HasDropDownItems)
                    item->DropDownItems[0]->Select();
                break;
            }
        }
    }
    return CFrameWnd::PreTranslateMessage(pMsg);
}
```

That's it! Compile and run the code, and you'll see the same application that you had, with the same menu, toolbar, and functionality, except that the menu and toolbar now feature an Office 2003 style look and feel. You've left the functionality and basic behavior of the app untouched and changed the UI by interoping with the new WinForms controls. In the example, you use a simple `CEditView`-based application as the sample app, but the same techniques can be used with any functional MFC application. You just have to add suitable event handlers, depending on your original application's menu items and toolbar buttons, but the core techniques remain the same.

In the next section, you'll see yet another way to interop between WinForms and MFC by writing a small MFC program that will host a WinForms control as an MFC dialog.

Let's begin the step-by-step walkthrough to implementing an Office 2003–style sample application.

6.5 Using a Windows Forms control as an MFC dialog

You've already seen how to host a WinForms control in an MFC dialog as a child control. Sometimes, it may be more convenient to have the WinForms control itself be the MFC dialog. In this section, you'll write an example that does exactly that. You'll do so using the `CWinFormsDialog` class, which is a `CDialog`-derived class that provides functionality to host a WinForms control as the dialog. Of course, you may wonder why you need the `CWinFormsDialog` class when you can use the `CWinFormsControl` class to directly put WinForms controls on an MFC dialog. Technically, that is correct, and whatever you can do with `CWinFormsDialog` can be done using the `CWinFormsControl` class; but `CWinFormsDialog` is more convenient in some situations.

Because CWinFormsDialog is derived from CDialog, the calling code doesn't necessarily need to know that it uses a WinForms control; thus, fewer changes are involved. For example, say a software package includes a bunch of applications, all of which use a CDialog-derived class to show an About box; each app derives from a shared About box class. If you want to replace the base About box class with a WinForms control, you can change its base class from CDialog to CWinFormsDialog, and the individual apps that further derive from it needn't recode anything to continue using the class. In addition, CWinFormsDialog also handles resizing and appropriately resizes the embedded WinForms control to fit within the containing dialog. To continue the car analogy, this is like taking a Pontiac's light bulbs and putting them inside a Corolla headlight holder, thereby camouflaging the fact that the bulbs are those of a Pontiac. The mechanic fitting the headlight on the Corolla need not know that the bulbs are from a Pontiac.

For the example, you'll write a simple WinForms control that shows some basic program and copyright information typical of most About boxes, and then you'll use it as a dialog. Let's begin by writing the custom About box WinForms control that you'll use in the example. Figure 6.4, which shows the WinForms control in the VS 2005 designer, can be used as a reference.

Here are the steps to create the custom About box control:

Step 1 Create a new C++ WinForms Control Library project.

Step 2 Set the background color of the main control to Blue.

Step 3 Set both the MinimumSize and Size properties to (400,300).

Step 4 Add three Label controls, a read-only multi-line TextBox, and a Button control as in figure 6.6. Name them labelAppName, labelVersion, textInfo, labelCopyright, and buttonOK, respectively. Set the foreground color of the Label controls to White.

Step 5 Add the properties from listing 6.10 to the user control, which exposes the Text properties of the Label and TextBox controls to the calling client.

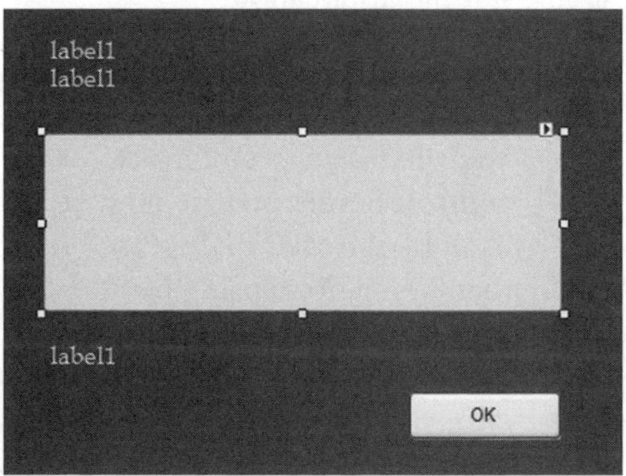

Figure 6.6 Creating the About box WinForms control

Listing 6.10 The various property definitions

```
property String^ AppName
{
    String^ get()
    {
        return labelAppName->Text;
    }
    void set(String^ value)
    {
        labelAppName->Text = value;
    }
}
property String^ AppVersion
{
    String^ get()
    {
        return labelVersion->Text;
    }
    void set(String^ value)
    {
        labelVersion->Text = value;
    }
}
property String^ AppCopyright
{
    String^ get()
    {
        return labelCopyright->Text;
    }
    void set(String^ value)
    {
        labelCopyright->Text = value;
    }
}
property String^ Info
{
    String^ get()
    {
        return textInfo->Text;
    }
    void set(String^ value)
    {
        textInfo->Text = value;
    }
}
```

Step 6 Add the following event to the user control. The event allows callers to hook onto the button click without having to directly access the `Button` control. This also lets the button-click event be handled by the containing dialog class, which allows you to map the event handlers to MFC methods:

```
event System::EventHandler^ OnAboutOK;
```

Step 7 Add an event handler for the `Button` control's `Click` event, and invoke the `OnAboutOK` event, as shown here:

```
System::Void buttonOK_Click(System::Object^  sender,
    System::EventArgs^  e)
{
    OnAboutOK(sender, e);
}
```

Compile and build the DLL, and the custom About box user control is ready. Now you'll write the sample MFC application that will use this WinForms control as a dialog. Once you're done, the app will look like Figure 6.7 (when the About box is invoked).

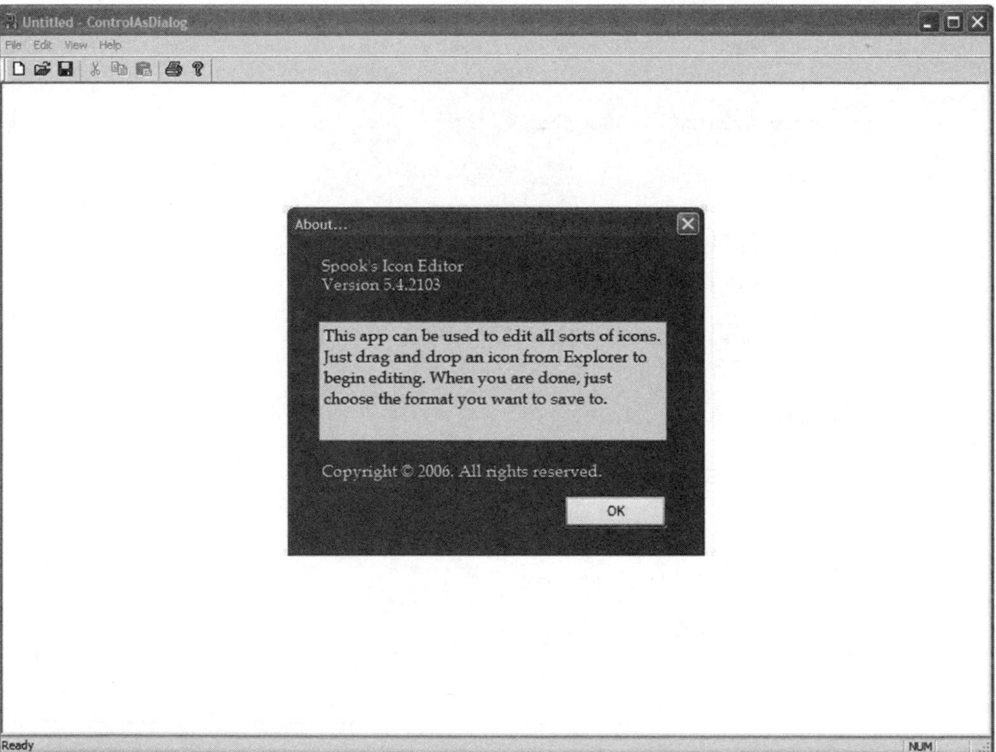

Figure 6.7 Hosting a WinForms control as an MFC dialog

You'll follow these steps to get the application started:

Step 1 Create the MFC project.
Create a standard MFC SDI application using the default settings, and turn on `/clr` compilation.

Step 2 Add the required header files.
Add `#include <afxwinforms.h>` to stdafx.h for the `CWinFormsDialog` class.

Step 3 Create a `CDialog`-derived class.
Using the wizard, add a new class called `CAboutBox` to your project, and set the base class as `CDialog`. Delete the dialog resources that are automatically generated by the wizard.

Step 4 Change the base class to `CWinFormsDialog`.
Modify the `CAboutBox` CPP and header files, and replace all instances of `CDialog` with `CWinFormsDialog<AboutBox::AboutBoxControl>`.

Step 5 Add a delegate map.
Add a delegate map to the public section of the `CAboutBox` class, as follows:

```
BEGIN_DELEGATE_MAP(CAboutBox)
    EVENT_DELEGATE_ENTRY( OnOkClick, System::Object^,
        System::EventArgs^ );
END_DELEGATE_MAP()
```

Step 6 Add the OK click handler.
Add an `OnOkClick` method to the `CAboutBox` class:

```
void CAboutBox::OnOkClick(System::Object^ sender,
    System::EventArgs^ e)
{
    CDialog::OnOK();
}
```

You call `CDialog::OnOK`, which closes the dialog when the button is clicked. You still need to hook up the event handler, which you'll do in `OnInitDialog`.

Step 7 Add initialization code.
Override `OnInitDialog`, and add code as shown here:

```
BOOL CAboutBox::OnInitDialog()
{
    CWinFormsDialog<AboutBox::AboutBoxControl>::OnInitDialog();
    CenterWindow();
    GetControl()->OnAboutOK +=
```

```
        MAKE_DELEGATE(System::EventHandler, OnOkClick);
    return TRUE;
}
```

The `CWinFormsDialog`'s `OnInitDialog` method sizes the dialog to match the size of the WinForms control and also sets the text of the dialog box to the `Text` property of the WinForms control. Thus, you don't need to do any initial resizing on your own.

Step 8 Add code to show the custom dialog.
Replace the default About box generated by the wizard to the WinForms control About box wrapped by the `CAboutBox` class. Modify the `ID_APP_ABOUT` command handler as shown here:

```
void CControlAsDialogApp::OnAppAbout()
{
    //CAboutDlg aboutDlg;
    CAboutBox aboutDlg;
    aboutDlg->Text = "About...";
    aboutDlg->AppName = "Spook's Icon Editor";
    aboutDlg->AppVersion = "Version 5.4.2103";
    aboutDlg->AppCopyright = "Copyright © 2006. "
        "All rights reserved.";
    aboutDlg->Info = "This app can be used to "
        "edit all sorts of icons. "
        "Just drag and drop an icon "
        "from Explorer to begin editing. "
        "When you are done, just choose the "
        "format you want to save to.";
    aboutDlg.DoModal();
}
```

Notice how you comment-out the declaration of the original About box class and replace it with the `CAboutBox` class. You also set the various properties exposed by the `CAboutBox` class and the `Text` property that will be used to set the window title of the dialog box. If you're wondering how you can directly access the properties of the WinForms control even before the MFC dialog has been created using `DoModal`, the underlying WinForms control gets created by the `CWinFormsDialog` constructor, and thus you can begin using them as soon as the dialog object is instantiated.

Compile and run the application. As I mentioned earlier, although you could probably achieve the same effect using the `CWinFormsControl` class, doing so would involve more changes both in the dialog class and in the calling client. The `CWinFormsDialog` class is mostly about convenience. I recommend that you use this class exclusively when you want to directly use a WinForms control as an MFC dialog, instead of directly using `CWinFormsControl` and writing a lot of plumbing code that `CWinFormsDialog` does for you.

Thus far in this chapter, we have been looking at techniques for using WinForms controls in MFC views and dialogs. It may be handy in certain situations to do the reverse—put an MFC control in a WinForms application. The good news is that this is possible, as I'll demonstrate in the next section.

Let's begin the step-by-step walkthrough to implement the sample application.

6.6 Using an MFC control in a Windows Forms form

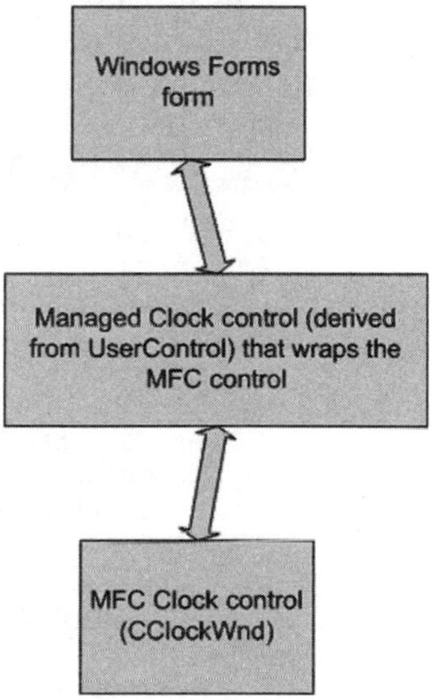

Occasionally, you may not have a WinForms equivalent for a custom MFC control you're using in your application (which you're now migrating to WinForms). Although you can rewrite the entire control using WinForms, that may not be the most efficient solution and may also take too much time. Obviously, the best solution is to reuse the MFC control in your WinForms application. To use the car analogy, this is like taking the Corolla's tires and using them on a Pontiac G6. This is an unlikely scenario, but if the Corolla's tires are brand-new and the Pontiac's tires aren't giving you the same traction, it may be something you'd consider doing.

Windows Forms form

Managed Clock control (derived from UserControl) that wraps the MFC control

MFC Clock control (CClockWnd)

Figure 6.8 MFC control in a WinForms form

In this section, you'll write a simple MFC clock control, write a managed wrapper for it, and use it in a WinForms application. Figure 6.8 shows how you can use an MFC control from a WinForms form.

Unlike in the previous scenarios, VC++ doesn't provide any interop helper classes such as `CWinFormsDialog` or `CWinFormsControl`; but writing your own custom wrapper isn't too much trouble. The only snag is that the Forms designer doesn't always work smoothly with custom WinForms controls that internally use MFC. This is more an issue with the Visual Studio 2005 Forms Designer than with MFC per se. On occasion, you may find that the Forms designer doesn't work at all and that you have to hand-code everything on your own. You can reduce the risk of this happening by making sure your custom code doesn't touch the wizard-generated code and by avoiding any custom UI rendering when the control is in the designer. If the designer still gets messed up, closing the solution and reopening it may fix the problem. You'll begin the example by putting together a simple MFC control that will render a digital clock on the screen.

6.6.1 The custom MFC control

`CClockWnd` is a `CWnd`-derived class you'll write that uses custom drawing to show a digital clock on-screen that is updated every second. It's a simple control. The primary aim is to see how you can write a managed wrapper for it and how the wrapper can be used in a WinForms application. You're going to put `CClockWnd` in a regular MFC DLL so the caller needn't be an MFC application.

Start by generating a new MFC regular DLL project called `ClockControl`. Add the code for the `CClockWnd` class; the declaration class (which should be put in a header file called ClockWnd.h) is shown in listing 6.11.

Listing 6.11 The `CClockWnd` header file

```
class CClockWnd : public CWnd
{
    DECLARE_DYNAMIC(CClockWnd)
public:
    CClockWnd();
    virtual ~CClockWnd();
    HFONT m_hFont;
    COLORREF m_BackColor;
    COLORREF m_ForeColor;
    UINT_PTR m_nTimer;
protected:
    DECLARE_MESSAGE_MAP()
public:
    afx_msg void OnPaint();
    afx_msg void OnTimer(UINT_PTR nIDEvent);
    afx_msg void OnClose();
private:
    CString m_strTime;
    void CalcTimeString();
protected:
    virtual void PreSubclassWindow();
};
```

Font and colors to render clock

MFC message handlers

Textual representation of time

Convert time to text

CWnd override for starting timer

`CClockWnd` is a `CWnd`-derived class and is fully custom-drawn. (`CWnd` doesn't do any drawing on its own.) Let's go through the methods that can be put into ClockWnd.cpp, the implementation file for the class. We'll start with the `CalcTimeString` method:

```
void CClockWnd::CalcTimeString()
{
    CTime t = CTime::GetCurrentTime();
    m_strTime = t.Format(_T("%H:%M:%S"));
}
```

It's just two lines long and retrieves the current time using the `CTime` class, converts it into a formatted string that represents the time, and stores it in the `m_strTime` member variable, which is used by the `OnPaint` handler. `CalcTimeString` is also called from the constructor, so that when the control is first shown on the window, the time is also displayed on it. Here's the constructor:

```
CClockWnd::CClockWnd() : m_hFont(NULL),
    m_ForeColor(RGB(255,255,255)),
    m_BackColor(RGB(0,0,0))
{
    CalcTimeString();
}
```

Note how you give default foreground and background colors to the control, just in case the caller doesn't set them. The `m_hFont` member is set to `NULL`, and this should compulsorily be set by the caller. These values are used by the `OnPaint` handler, which is shown in listing 6.12.

Listing 6.12 `OnPaint` handler for the `CClockWnd` control

```
void CClockWnd::OnPaint()
{
    CPaintDC dc(this);
    if(m_hFont)                                   <-- Check for valid font
    {
        COLORREF crOldTextColor = dc.GetTextColor();
        CRect rect;
        GetClientRect(&rect);
        dc.FillSolidRect(&rect, m_BackColor);     <-- Fill background
        dc.SetTextColor(m_ForeColor);
        CFont font;
        font.Attach(m_hFont);
        CFont* def_font = dc.SelectObject(&font);
        rect.MoveToX(5);
        dc.DrawText(m_strTime, m_strTime.GetLength(),
            &rect,DT_SINGLELINE);                 <-- Draw time string
        dc.SelectObject(def_font);
        font.Detach();
        dc.SetTextColor(crOldTextColor);
    }
}
```

This is straightforward drawing code. All you do is use the background color to fill the control, and draw the time string using the foreground color and the font specified using the `m_hFont` member.

You also have a timer-proc, where you recalculate the time and invalidate the control, forcing a repaint:

```
void CClockWnd::OnTimer(UINT_PTR nIDEvent)
{
    if(nIDEvent == 1000)
    {
        CalcTimeString();
        Invalidate();
    }
    CWnd::OnTimer(nIDEvent);
}
```

Obviously, for the timer shown previously to come into play, you need to set up the timer, and you accomplish that in the `PreSubclassWindow` override. You can't do so in the constructor because the `HWND` isn't valid yet, because the Win32 window hasn't been created at this point. Here's what the `PreSubclassWindow` override looks like:

```
void CClockWnd::PreSubclassWindow()
{
    m_nTimer = SetTimer(1000,1000,NULL);    // Run timer-proc every 1000 millisecs
    CWnd::PreSubclassWindow();
}
```

You set a timer that ticks every second, because you need to update the time string whenever the time changes. However, you may want to set the timer to 500 milliseconds, because a timer isn't guaranteed to fire when you expect it to, and the code can skip a second in rendering.

To elegantly remove the timer, you override `OnClose` as follows:

```
void CClockWnd::OnClose()
{
    KillTimer(m_nTimer);
    CWnd::OnClose();
}
```

You use `KillTimer` to kill the timer event. Because the window is being closed, this isn't strictly needed, but you want to keep the code well-written.

That's a full-fledged MFC custom control derived from `CWnd`. Next, you are going to write code to host this `CWnd`-derived control in a WinForms application.

6.6.2 Hosting the MFC control from WinForms

The following steps are required to wrap the CWnd-derived control and to host it in a WinForms form:

Step 1 Derive a class from UserControl.

You're going to put the wrapper class in the same DLL as the MFC class in the example. The first thing to do is to enable /clr compilation, so you can use CLI types in the project. Next, add a new WinForms user control to the project by choosing the Project menu's Add New Item option, and name the control Clock. Once you've done that, you have a managed class called Clock that's derived from UserControl. The basic idea is to create the MFC control as a child of the WinForms control and to resize it to fit the WinForms control, analogous to what CWinFormsDialog does (although there the situation is the reverse).

Step 2 Override the OnHandleCreated method of the WinForms control, and instantiate and create the MFC control as a child of the UserControl. Set the size of the MFC control to equal that of the WinForms control.

Add a CClockWnd* member to the class, and also add an override for the OnHandleCreated method, as shown here:

```
virtual void OnHandleCreated(EventArgs^ e) override
{
    UserControl::OnHandleCreated(e);
    if(DesignMode == false)                         <-- (1) Check for designer
    {
        AFX_MANAGE_STATE(AfxGetStaticModuleState());
        pClockWnd = new CClockWnd();
        CWnd wndThis;
        wndThis.Attach((HWND)Handle.ToPointer());
        pClockWnd->Create(NULL, _T("ClockWnd"),WS_CHILD|WS_VISIBLE,
            CRect(0,0,Size.Width, Size.Height),&wndThis,1000);   <-- (2) Create CClockWnd control
        pClockWnd->m_hFont = (HFONT)Font->ToHfont().ToPointer();
        pClockWnd->m_BackColor = RGB(
            BackColor.R,BackColor.G,BackColor.B);
        pClockWnd->m_ForeColor= RGB(
            ForeColor.R,ForeColor.G,ForeColor.B);
        wndThis.Detach();
    }
}
```

The OnHandleCreated method is called once a Handle has been associated with the user control, and that's the ripest moment for you to create the MFC control. As I mentioned earlier, the VS 2005 designer isn't stable with MFC controls. Thus, you check for the designer using the DesignMode property (1) before creating the MFC control. If you're in design mode, you don't create the MFC control; instead, you show a dummy mock-up of what the control will look like at runtime by adding a delegate handler for the `Paint` event. The `CClockWnd` MFC control is created as a child of the `Clock` WinForms control by specifying the WinForms control as parent window in the call to `Create` ❷. The control's size is kept the same as that of the parent window so that it will fully fit within the parent window (hiding the parent window in the process, which is what you want). You also transfer the WinForms control's font and color properties to the corresponding `CClockWnd` members.

Step 3 Delete the MFC control member in the finalizer (and make sure the finalizer is called from the destructor).

Because the `CClockWnd` member is a native object, you need to delete it in the destructor (and finalizer), as shown here:

```
~Clock()
{
    . . .
    this->!Clock();
}
!Clock()
{
    if(DesignMode == false)
    {
        AFX_MANAGE_STATE(AfxGetStaticModuleState());
        delete pClockWnd;
    }
}
```

You check the design mode before attempting to delete the native object, because the native object is created only when `DesignMode` is `false`, which implies that the control is running outside the VS 2005 designer.

Basically, this is all you need to use the control. To ease the design process, add a handler for the `Paint` event, and show a mock rendering of the time string using the user-specified font and colors. This way, during design time, the user can preview what the control will look like without having to run the app each time:

```
System::Void Clock_Paint(System::Object^  sender,
    System::Windows::Forms::PaintEventArgs^  e)
{
    if(DesignMode == true)
    {
        e->Graphics->DrawString("00:00:00", Font,
            gcnew SolidBrush(ForeColor),5,0);
    }
}
```

You use the default string "00:00:00" to render the mock time string in the designer. Note how this time you check if `DesignMode` is `true`, which implies that the control is in the VS 2005 designer.

The control is now ready to be used from a WinForms application. Let's go ahead and do that now.

The following sections describe these steps in detail.

6.6.3 Using the wrapped control from a WinForms app

Create a C++/CLI WinForms application using the wizard, and add the custom control you wrote earlier to the toolbox using the Choose Items dialog from the toolbox context menu. Now, drag and drop as many of those controls as you want into the form using the WinForms designer. You can customize the font, foreground color, and background color for each control individually. Figure 6.9 shows a sample form in the designer: It has three `Clock` controls, each with a different appearance. Figure 6.10 shows that form when the application is running.

When you put an MFC control on a WinForms form, remember that you're adding a dependency on the MFC DLLs to the WinForms application. Thus, for your application to run on a target machine, that machine needs to have the required MFC DLLs. But it's a handy technique that can help you reuse existing MFC controls in newly-developed WinForms applications. You can wrap just about

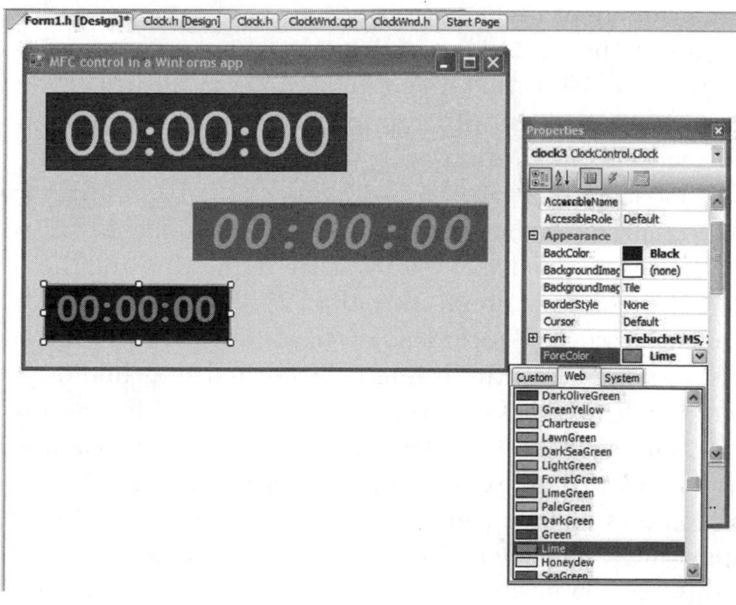

Figure 6.9 The MFC-based clock control in the VS 2005 Forms designer

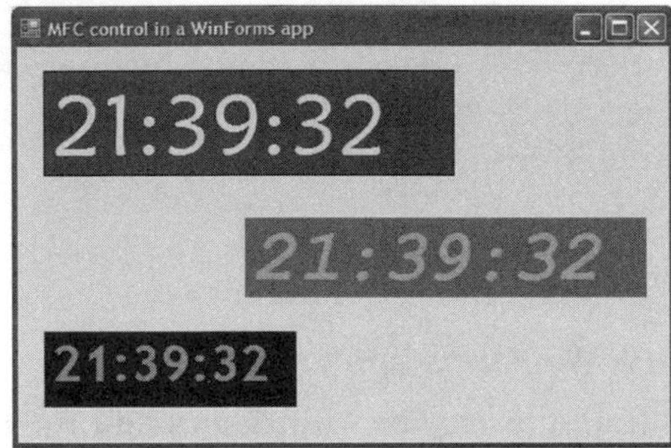

Figure 6.10
The MFC-based clock control on a live WinForms application

any MFC control using this technique; the basic process remains the same as that in the example. It's amazing what a little interop can do for you.

6.7 Summary

You saw several techniques for interoping MFC and Windows Forms in this chapter. For a real-life application that mixes WinForms and MFC, it's plausible to think that you'll need to use one or more of these techniques profusely. If you're replacing the UI layer and keeping the rest of the code intact, the `CWinFormsView` and `CWinFormsControl` MFC helper classes should be all you need. MFC applications are mostly made up of views and dialogs as far as UI goes, and using the classes covered in sections 6.2 and 6.3 of this chapter, you shouldn't have much trouble porting the UI to WinForms. You also saw an example where you took an existing MFC app, used WinForms interop to change its menu and toolbar, and ended up with the same application, with the same functionality, but with an Office 2003 style menu and toolbar. This technique has a lot of utility when you have legacy MFC applications that need to have their UI updated but you don't want to rewrite the entire code base; you just change the UI using the new WinForms classes and leave the rest of the code intact.

Other techniques we covered included how to use a WinForms control directly as an MFC dialog, where the control is internally created as a child of the dialog and resized to fit the dialog so as to cover it completely. You also saw the reverse of this technique, where you host an MFC control on a WinForms application by wrapping it within a WinForms user control and resizing it to fit the user control, so that the user control is hidden completely. This can also be a handy technique when you're upgrading your code to the .NET Framework and replacing the MFC UI with WinForms, but you have a few customized MFC controls that don't have direct replacements in WinForms. To rewrite them in WinForms from scratch would be a tremendously tedious task; in such scenarios, directly hosting the MFC control on a WinForms form using the technique we talked about in section 6.6 is a far more straightforward approach.

In the next chapter, we'll look at how you can interop native code with another managed framework: Windows Presentation Foundation (codenamed Avalon). Although Avalon is a future technology, Betas are already available, and people have begun coding for it. When Avalon is eventually released, you don't want to be left behind, do you? I'd say most definitely not—and with that mindset, we'll promptly move on to Avalon interop.

7 Using C++/CLI to target Windows Presentation Foundation applications

At the time of writing, the Windows Presentation Foundation (WPF) is still in Beta and will not be available until later this year. It's not easy to discuss future technology in a book, especially when it's months before it is scheduled to be released, and even more so when it's a massive framework like WPF. However, once WPF (formerly codenamed *Avalon*) is publicly available, the fact that C++/CLI can be used to interop native applications with Avalon applications should be a persuasive reason for Visual C++ developers to move to C++/CLI. Avalon is a completely different UI framework from anything previously available for Windows (with its declarative programming model, Direct3D-based rendering, HWND-less controls, and animation support, to name just a few of the new features); and the jump from MFC to WinForms would seem diminutive when compared to the jump from WinForms to Avalon. It's impossible to cover Avalon in a single chapter, and possibly a most difficult task to cover it in a single book. Thus, this chapter will only brush through some basic Avalon functionality and will also discuss how you can interop between Avalon and native code.

NOTE For more comprehensive coverage of WPF (Avalon), refer to another source of information. I recommend the book *Applications = Code + Markup: A Guide to the Microsoft Windows Presentation Foundation* by Charles Petzold.

For writing new Avalon applications, C++ may not always be the best option compared to other CLI languages such as C# or VB.NET, because there's lack of visual designer support for C++ (at least as of today). But as you'll find out in this chapter, if you want to stick to using C++, you can do that and still write fully-functional Avalon applications using three different mechanisms.

The advantage of using C++/CLI to target Avalon, however, is that it lets you interop Avalon code with existing native code—just as with WinForms, which you saw in chapter 6. In this chapter, we'll cover two mechanisms to use Avalon from within native MFC applications: one where you keep the caller application purely native, and the other where you use a mixed-mode caller application. We'll also look at the reverse scenario, that of using a native control from an Avalon application, although its uses may not be as practical as that of using Avalon from native apps.

NOTE The terms *Avalon* and *WPF* are used interchangeably in this chapter and mean the same thing. You'll notice the same (equivalent usage of the terms) in online publications and blogs, because the word *Avalon* became extremely popular before Microsoft gave the technology an official title. Most developers continue to use both words interchangeably.

Although Avalon is still in a Beta phase, it has established itself as a powerful way of writing user interfaces on Windows, and the developer world is getting ready to accept the UI framework of the future. Because this chapter was written based on the Betas and the CTP releases available at the time of writing, one important thing to keep in mind is that some of the namespaces used in the chapter's code snippets (especially those in the XAML) will change when the final version of Avalon is released. The core code snippets and the techniques discussed are mostly guaranteed to remain the same. I'll also upload updated versions of the sample code on the Manning website, so you can always get a version that will work with the latest release.

7.1 What is WPF?

WPF is a managed Graphical User Interface (GUI) subsystem for Windows that is implemented using the .NET Framework and DirectX technologies (see figure 7.1). Microsoft has unified the user interface, the application data, and multimedia and graphics capabilities into a single subsystem—the *Windows Presentation Foundation*.

WPF is one of the components that is natively included with Windows Vista—the latest operating system from Microsoft that was released recently. Windows

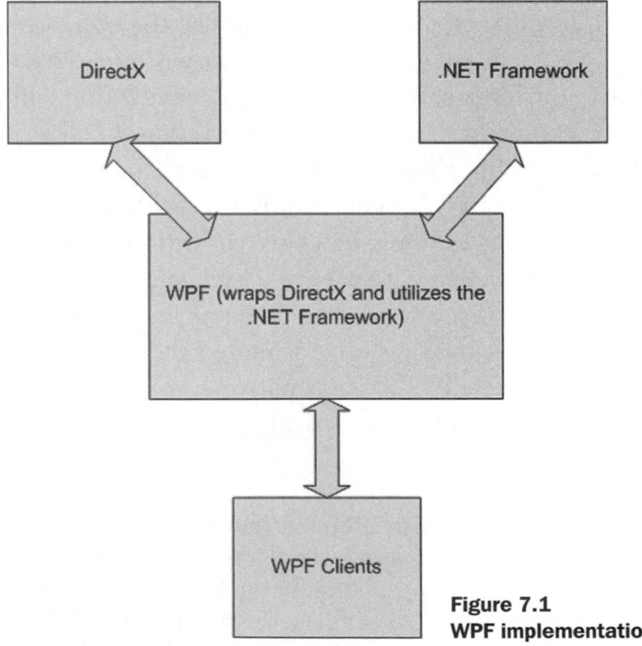

Figure 7.1 WPF implementation

Vista comes with a comprehensive managed API for application developers called .NET Framework 3.0 (formerly called WinFX), of which WPF is one of the components. The other components include

- .NET Framework version 2.0 (a subcomponent of .NET Framework 3.0; no one knows why Microsoft came up with such a confusing naming scheme)
- Windows Communication Foundation (which we'll talk about in the next chapter)
- Windows Workflow Foundation (still in an early Beta stage, and a topic that is outside the scope of this book)

Avalon, although natively supported in Windows Vista, will also be available for Windows XP and Windows 2003. That limits the scope of an Avalon-based application to Windows XP, Windows 2003, Windows Vista, and of course any post-Vista operating system. This means if you need to support legacy operating systems like Windows 98 and Windows 2000, you can't use Avalon. But if that isn't a restriction, the fact that Avalon is available for XP and Windows 2003 is wonderful, because you aren't forced to upgrade every client machine to Vista to take advantage of the powerful Avalon functionality.

The Avalon programming model is different from previous Windows programming models. If you've done any amount of Win32 UI development, either directly using plain API or indirectly using frameworks such as MFC or WTL, you may find the new approach to be totally unlike anything you've done previously. Even Windows Forms was essentially a wrapper around the Win32 API, and the underlying implementation was Win32 API-based; thus, having used Windows Forms won't prepare you any better for the Avalon culture shock, which inevitably everyone has to go through. WPF makes obsolete both Win32 API-based UI coding as well as Windows Forms. This isn't to say that your native applications or your Forms applications won't run on Windows Vista. They will be able to run on Vista, but they will be limited to the UI capabilities of their respective frameworks.

With WPF, you'll have full access to the new functionality, including but not limited to 2D and 3D vector graphics, built-in transformation and animation features, support for multimedia, rich text in the UI elements, and declarative programming using Extensible Application Markup Language (XAML). Ironically, Visual C++ doesn't directly support XAML (as of today), and thus in this chapter, you won't use a lot of XAML in the examples. That may seem incredible to those of you who have gone through other books dedicated to WPF, because those books use XAML everywhere. Of course, you'll see how you can indirectly take advantage of XAML and declarative programming, but before that, to refresh your memory, we'll take a quick look at using XAML to create Avalon applications.

7.1.1 Overview of XAML

XAML is the XML-based markup language supported by WPF. It can be used to create rich user interfaces for both desktop and web applications. (Note that XAML is popularly pronounced "Zammel," so you should say that instead of pronouncing each individual letter.) The XAML-based approach is to define the user interface declaratively using XAML and to put the program logic into the source code, thereby achieving a true separation of code (the business logic) that is in the source code from the UI definition in the XAML. XAML also allows specialist graphics designers, who may be nondevelopers, to design the UI for an application, because they don't need to write a single line of code. This lets a company have a team of graphics designers who design the GUI in XAML, which is then given to the developers, who then add the business logic in code.

Visual Studio Orcas (the next version of Visual Studio) will support a XAML designer called Cider (although the name may change), which provides a WYSIWYG editor for designing XAML interfaces. Microsoft is also working on a powerful graphics designer product called Expression that supports designing of power-user interfaces (with support for 2D and 3D graphics and animation) and then exporting the XAML for them. Alternatively, you can open any text editor such as Notepad or vi and directly hand-code your XAML. The .NET 3.0 SDK also comes with a tool called XAMLPad.exe, which lets you hand-code XAML while also showing you a preview of how the output will look. If you want to get a good understanding of how XAML works and how it's rendered, start playing with XAML using XAMLPad before moving on to more sophisticated editors like Cider where you can design your XAML UIs using the mouse and some drag/drop operations.

XAML and WPF are futuristic technologies that are still in a Beta phase; but the Betas are now publicly available, which means anyone interested can download and play with them. If you don't have your machine already configured properly for running WPF applications, you'll need to download and install the .NET 3.0 SDK before you can write WPF (and WCF) applications. At the time of writing this chapter, the latest version available is the Feb 2006 Community Technology Preview (CTP). I'm sure that by the time the book is published, you'll be using a far newer version of the Beta. Follow the instructions specified in the release notes that come with the specific version you download. Pay special attention to the order in which you install the various components, because it needs to happen in a specific order to do the installation correctly (this is specified in the release notes). Here are the various components you need to install on your system:

- *.NET 3.0 Runtime Components.* This contains the .NET 3.0 redistributables that are required for running .NET 3.0 applications (including WPF- and WCF-based applications). The analogous entity for .NET is the .NET redistributable that's required to run a .NET application.
- *Windows Vista SDK.* This includes the header files, libraries, SDK tools, and documentation for developing and distributing Vista applications. It also includes the .NET 3.0 SDK, which contains the libraries, tools, and documentation for designing and developing applications that leverage XAML, WPF, WCF, and so on. The analogous entity for .NET would be the .NET Framework SDK that's used to develop .NET applications.
- *Visual Studio Orcas .NET 3.0 Development Tools.* This is an optional component that adds support for .NET 3.0 development to Visual Studio 2005. Some of the components added to Visual Studio include a set of app-wizard project templates to generate WPF and WCF projects, Cider (a visual designer for XAML), intellisense when hand-coding XAML, and integration of the .NET 3.0 documentation with the VS 2005 documentation browser.

Although we won't focus on XAML in this chapter, I'd like to show you an example of using XAML to create a simple Avalon window. For the example, you'll use XAMLPad.exe, which comes with the .NET 3.0 SDK; you can start it from the Tools subfolder of the Windows SDK Start Menu folder. It's a simple application with a horizontally split view: The top view gives a preview of the rendered XAML, and the bottom view is your XAML editor. Type the following XAML code into the editor window:

```
<Page
  xmlns="http://schemas.microsoft.com/winfx/2006/xaml/presentation"
   xmlns:x="http://schemas.microsoft.com/winfx/2006/xaml"
   Width="200" Height="100">
 <Canvas  Background="Green">
   <TextBlock FontSize="20"
       Foreground="White">Hello World</TextBlock >
   <TextBlock FontSize="20" Canvas.Top="40"
       Foreground="Yellow">from XAML</TextBlock >
 </Canvas>
</Page>
```

Figure 7.2 shows the output that will be rendered on the preview window of the XAMLPad tool. The Auto Parse option is on by default, so you can see the changes even as you type in your XAML into the editor window.

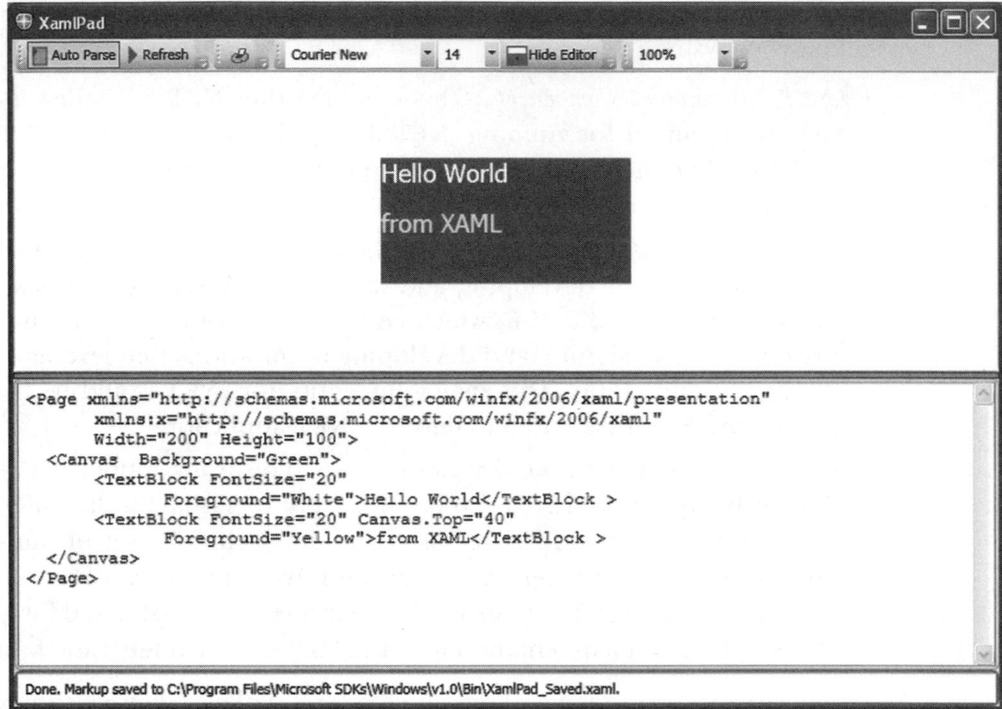

Figure 7.2 Hello World in XAML

You have a `Page` element as the root element of the XAML code. This `Page` element maps to the `Page` class in the `System::Windows::Controls` namespace. You specify `Width` and `Height` attributes to the `Page` element; these map to the `Width` and `Height` properties of the `Page` class. A `Page` element is typically used as a root element for browser-based XAML applications, although there's nothing stopping you from using them for desktop applications as well. Within the `Page` block, you have a `Canvas` element that maps to the `Canvas` class in the `System::Windows::Controls` namespace and serves as an area (or a canvas) where you can place other WPF controls. Notice how you set the `Background` attribute of the `Canvas` element to Green, which is equivalent to setting the `Background` property of the `Canvas` object to `Brushes::Green`. Inside the `Canvas` block, you have two `TextBlock` elements; you also set their `FontSize` and `Foreground` attributes (which map to the corresponding properties in the `TextBlock` WPF class).

By now, you must understand the basic pattern—every XAML tag you've used corresponds to a WPF class, and every attribute you set on a tag correspondingly maps to a property of the WPF object that's being used. As a real-life analogy, think of XAML as being similar to the blueprint for an apartment. Just as the blueprint defines what the apartment will look like, the XAML defines what the user interface will look like. Instead of writing imperative code, as was done in the pre-WPF days, you declaratively use XAML to define the UI.

This doesn't rule out imperatively defining the UI using procedural code. This is important to C++ developers because Visual C++ (as of today) doesn't directly support XAML! There are ways to use XAML directly and indirectly using Visual C++, and you'll see how to do that in this chapter. But you can't use Cider to design XAML user interfaces with a Visual C++ project; you have to do that using a C# or VB.NET project. We'll briefly discuss the ramifications of this lack of direct XAML support for C++ in the next section, because I think it's important that you understand exactly how this affects WPF development using C++.

7.1.2 Anatomy of a simple WPF application

When you create a C# WPF project, you end up with XAML files that define the UI with corresponding *code-behind* source files. This isn't supported in a VC++ project (at the time of writing).

To give you an idea of how this code-behind model works in C#, assume that you have a file called Window1.xaml that defines the main window for an application. In addition, you have a Window1.xaml.cs file, which is a sort of code-behind file for the XAML. This is analogous to the ASP.NET code-behind model, where the ASPX files define the user interface and the code-behind files (like aspx.cs) define the program logic.

The XAML files are analogous to the ASPX files, whereas the XAML-code-behind achieves the same purpose as the ASP.NET code-behind files.

Here's what the Window1.xaml file looks like:

```
<Window x:Class="CsHelloAvalon.Window1"                        <-1
    xmlns="http://schemas.microsoft.com/winfx/2006/xaml/presentation"
    xmlns:x="http://schemas.microsoft.com/winfx/2006/xaml"
    Title="CsHelloAvalon" Height="300" Width="300"
    >
  <Grid>
    <Button VerticalAlignment="Top" HorizontalAlignment="Right"     <-2
            Grid.Column="0" Grid.ColumnSpan="1"
            Grid.Row="0" Grid.RowSpan="1"
            Margin="0,26,30,0"
            Width="75" Height="23" Name="button1"
            Click="OnButtonClk">Close</Button>
  </Grid>
</Window>
```

An `x:Class` attribute ❶ links the `Window` element to a *partial class* defined in the code-behind file. In this code, it's defined as `CsHelloAvalon.Window1`, where `CsHelloAvalon` specifies the namespace and `Window1` specifies the name of the class. Partial classes are a C# feature where the definition of a class (or even a struct or an interface) is split into multiple source files. Also note how the `Button` element ❷ has defined an attribute called `Click` with the value `OnButtonClk`, which basically means that the `Click` event handler for the `Button` is a method called `OnButtonClk` defined in the code-behind file.

Corresponding to the Window1.XAML file, the Window1.xaml.cs file completes the definition of the `Window1` class and looks like the following:

```
namespace CsHelloAvalon
{
    public partial class Window1 : Window
    {
        public Window1()
        {
            InitializeComponent();      <-❶
        }
        public void OnButtonClk(Object sender, RoutedEventArgs e)    <-❷
        {
            Close();
        }
    }
}
```

The code-behind file completes the definition of the class, and you can see the definition of the `OnButtonClk` method ❷ that's the `Click` event handler for the `Button` element. Pay attention to the call to a function named `InitializeComponent` in the constructor ❶, although you haven't defined such a function.

The compilation process

The compilation process involves converting the XAML to a binary format, generating a partial class based on the XAML, and compiling the partial classes into a single class in the IL. Figure 7.3 shows what happens during compilation of the XAML.

The figure shows the four marked-out steps in the process, as described here. The XAML parser compiles the XAML into a binary format called Binary Application Markup Language (BAML), and a file named Window1.baml that contains the equivalent BAML for the XAML is generated.

The XAML parser also generates a partial class called `Window1.g.cs` (which will contain a partial definition for `CsHelloAvalon.Window1`), which will contain a field for every element in the XAML with a `Name` attribute. In this case, there will be a

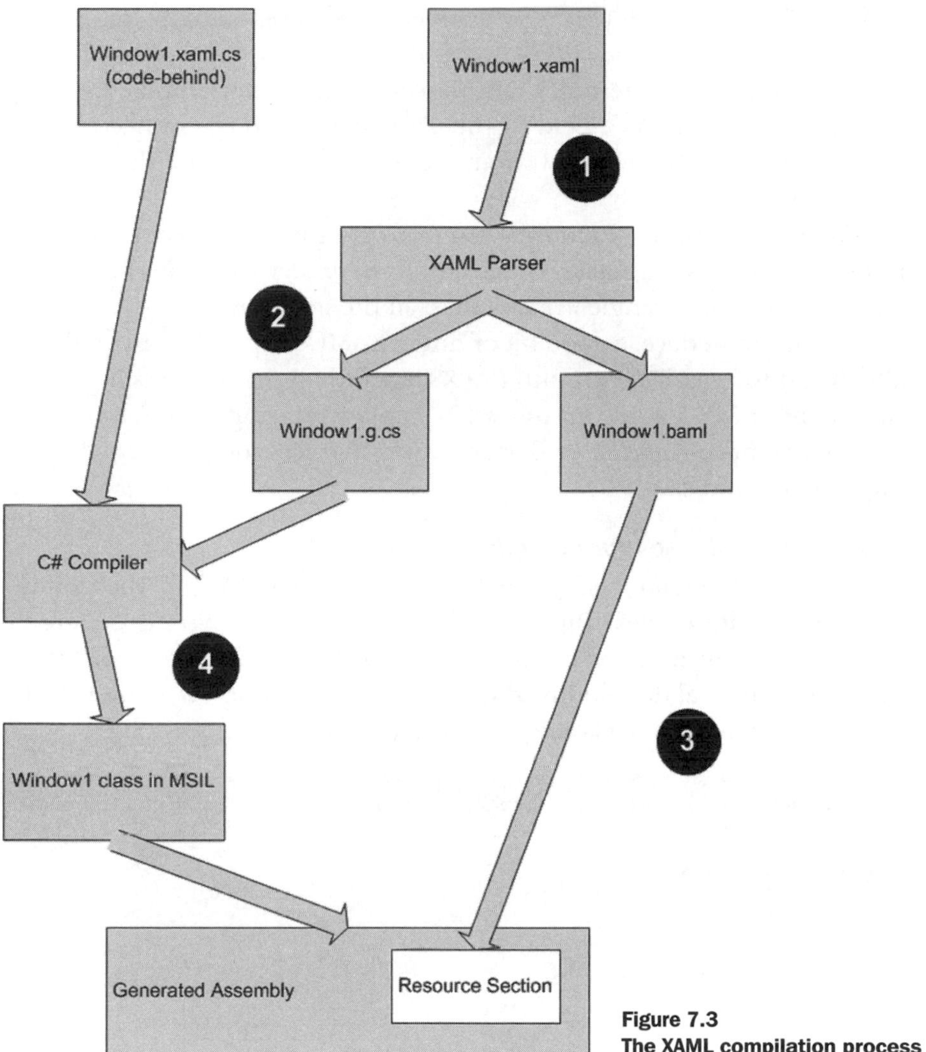

Figure 7.3
The XAML compilation process

`Button` field named `button1` (the name of the field is the same as the specified `Name` property in the XAML). The partial class also implements the `IComponent-Connector` interface, which defines two methods: `InitializeComponent` (which you saw called by the constructor in `Window1.xaml.cs`) and `Connect`. The `Initialize-Component` method uses `Application.LoadComponent` to load the BAML file (Window1.baml), whereas the `Connect` method hooks the event handlers with the various member objects. In this case, `button1.Click` is hooked onto the `OnButtonClk` method. Internally, `Application.LoadComponent` uses the internal static method `LoadBaml` of the `XamlReader` class to create the `Window` object from the BAML, and `LoadBaml` uses some internal BAML parser classes and methods. Eventually, `Connect` gets called for each field in the class that has to be connected with an element in the BAML, and any event handlers specified in the BAML are also associated appropriately.

The BAML (Window1.baml) is inserted into the generated assembly as a .NET resource. The two partial class definitions in `Window1.g.cs` and `Window1.xaml.cs` are compiled into a single `Window1` class in the generated MSIL.

As you can deduce, a good bit of direct XAML support is provided; this is what allows you to put all the UI into the XAML and all the business logic into the C# code-behind file. I went through what happens during compilation to show you the important role played by partial classes that lets you associate the XAML with the code-behind class.

Using partial classes for compilation

As I've already mentioned, partial classes allow you to split the definition of a class into multiple files. During compilation, a single type is generated in the MSIL. For instance, you can have two source files, Window1.cs and Window2.cs, which have partial definitions of the same class. Listing 7.1 demonstrates a class `Window` that has been declared partially in two separate source files.

Listing 7.1 Example of a partial class definition

```
//Window1.cs
partial class Window
{
    public void Hello()
    {
    }
}

//Window2.cs
partial class Window
{
    public void World()
    {
    }
}

//Program.cs
class Program
{
    static void Main(string[] args)
```

```
        {
            Window w = new Window();
            w.Hello();               <-- Call Hello defined in Windowl.cs
            w.World();        <-- Call World defined in Window2.cs
        }
    }
```

Although `Window` is defined partially in two separate source files, in Program.cs it's treated as a single type (because that's how it will be in the generated MSIL). This same principle is used during XAML compilation. The XAML file is compiled into BAML, and a partial class is generated that represents the type of the root element in the XAML. The code-behind source file also contains a partial definition for the same type and thus can access the elements defined in the XAML directly. In the generated MSIL, it's all generated as a single type that uses the BAML resource that's embedded in the assembly. The key mechanism is the use of partial classes to unify the type definitions in the XAML and the code-behind source file.

The problem with using XAML from C++

Because C++ doesn't support partial class definitions, it isn't possible to directly support XAML in VC++ projects using this mechanism. That isn't, however, the core reason why VC++ doesn't directly support XAML. In addition to using the `x:Class` attribute, you can also use the `x:Subclass` attribute so that the XAML gets compiled into the class specified by the `x:Class` attribute, and the code-behind will define the class specified by `x:Subclass`, which will be derived from the `x:Class` type. Thus, the lack of partial classes isn't that big of a block. The main issue is that, right now, no 100-percent CodeDOM support is available to convert the XAML to C++, and that is the single biggest reason why VC++ doesn't support XAML intrinsically. I don't know this for sure, but it's possible that on a later date, the Visual C++ team may work on their CodeDOM support and provide a fully functional XAML-to-C++ converter. Once that's available, XAML support can be integrated into VC++ projects. As of today, however, that isn't an option.

NOTE *CodeDOM* is a term used to represent a bunch of types available in the `System.CodeDom` namespace that lets you abstract code into an object model. Source code is represented using the CodeDOM tree and can be converted into source code for a specific language using the CodeDOM code generator for that specific language.

Still, the fact that you can't directly use XAML in a Visual C++ project doesn't mean that WPF applications can't be written with Visual C++.

Three ways to write WPF apps using VC++

You can use three different approaches to write WPF applications using Visual C++. Each has its pros and cons, and we'll cover each of these approaches in the next section:

- *Use procedural code.* For one thing, you can directly use procedural code to write Avalon-based applications and avoid using XAML. Of course, if you do that, you automatically give up the advantages of declarative programming that XAML brings in, but for certain scenarios, procedural code often serves the purpose well.
- *Dynamically load XAML.* Alternatively, you can dynamically load XAML during runtime to create your Avalon windows, although the disadvantage is that you'd be distributing a bunch of XAML files with your application.
- *Derive from a class in a C# DLL.* A third technique uses a C# project to create your XAML-based Avalon controls and have a class (or classes) in your C++ project that derives from the classes in the C#-based Avalon DLL. With that mechanism, the UI is created using XAML in the C# project, and the business logic is kept in the C++ project.

When you're developing WPF applications with C++, you can use one or more of these approaches to achieve whatever functionality you want. In the next section, you'll see how to write a simple WPF app with C++/CLI using each of the three techniques mentioned here.

7.2 Using C++/CLI to write a WPF application

If Visual C++ doesn't have support for XAML, and there are no project templates for building an Avalon application (as of the June 2006 CTP), how much extra effort does it take to write Avalon applications using C++? In this section, you'll find out. You'll put the three different techniques I described at the end of section 7.1.2 into action. All three mechanisms have their advantages and disadvantages; you can decide which is most suitable for your specific scenario. First, though, let's briefly go over how to create a new C++/CLI project for Avalon.

7.2.1 Creating a new C++/CLI Avalon project

Avalon is a managed framework, and as such any Visual C++ project that needs to access and use Avalon needs to have the /clr compilation mode turned on. Creating a new C++/CLI project with support for Avalon is fortunately not a difficult task. Table 7.1 lists the few simple steps you need to follow each time you create an application (or library, as the case might be) that uses Avalon.

Table 7.1 Steps to create a C++/CLI Avalon project

Step	Action	How To
1	Generate a new project	Using the application wizard, specify the CLR Empty Project template.
2	Set the `SubSystem` to `/SUBSYSTEM:WINDOWS`	Apply this change in the Project properties, Linker settings, System sub-setting.
3	Set the Entry Point to `main`	From Project properties, choose Linker settings and then the Advanced subsetting.

4	Add references to the following assemblies:
	`System`
	`PresentationCore`
	`PresentationFramework`
	`WindowsBase`
		Note: Except for `System`, the other three are required for Avalon.

At this point, your empty project is ready for writing Avalon code. Of course, you don't have any code yet to compile, but you'll fix that soon.

7.2.2 Using procedural code

You'll now write your first Avalon application using C++/CLI, and you'll do so entirely using procedural code. Think of it as analogous to an instruction book for putting together a table that contains only textual instructions (analogous to the procedural code) and no pictures (analogous to the XAML).

Create a new CLR project using the steps outlined in the previous section, and add an App.cpp file to it (you can call it whatever you want). Listing 7.2 shows the code for the simplest Avalon application that shows a window onscreen.

Listing 7.2 A simple Avalon app in procedural code

```
using namespace System;
using namespace System::Windows;
[STAThread]
```

❶ Set threading model to STA

```
int main(array<String^>^ args)
{
    return (gcnew Application())->Run(gcnew Window());
}
```

❷ **Create and show main window**

If you compile and run the application, you'll see a window onscreen that can be moved, resized, minimized, maximized, and closed. Avalon requires you to set the COM threading model to single threaded apartment (STA). You do so using the `STAThread` attribute on the main function ❶. You then create a new instance of the `Application` object (using `gcnew`) and invoke the `Run` method on that instance, passing in a new instance of a `Window` object (again using `gcnew`) ❷. The `Application` class represents an Avalon application and provides the core functionality for running the application. It has a `Run` method that is called to initiate the application's main thread. The `Run` method has an overload that accepts a `Window` object, which you use in the code. This overload launches the application and uses the specified `Window` as the main application window. The `Window` class represents the core functionality of a window and by default provides you with basic windowing functionality such as moving, resizing, and so on, which you verified when you ran the application and saw a fully functional window onscreen.

NOTE Those of you who have an MFC background may see a faint similarity between this model and MFC, where the `CWinApp` class is analogous to the `Application` class, and the `CFrameWnd` class is analogous to the `Window` class. `CWinApp` has a `Run` method that provides the default message loop, and `Application::Run` does something similar. Of course, you shouldn't infer too much from these minor similarities because they're totally different UI programming models, but it's possible that a similar design model was used by the architects of Avalon.

This little program doesn't have a lot of functionality; it just uses the default `Window` object to create and show a window onscreen. Let's write a more refined application with its own `Application`-derived object as well as a window with some controls. Figure 7.4 shows a screenshot of what the enhanced application will look like.

The main steps involved would be to derive two classes—one from the `Window` class, and the other from the `Application` class. You'll start with the `Window`-derived class.

Figure 7.4 Enhanced WPF app in C++ (procedural code)

Writing the Window-derived class

The first thing you'll do is add a new class called `FirstWindow` to your project, which will be derived from the `Window` class. You'll also add some member variables for the various controls and set some of the window properties in the constructor. Listing 7.3 shows the code once you've done that.

Listing 7.3 A more functional Avalon app in procedural code

```
using namespace System;
using namespace System::Windows;
using namespace System::Windows::Controls;

ref class FirstWindow : Window
{
    Canvas^ maincanvas;
    ListBox^ listbox;           // ❶ Member variables for child controls
    TextBox^ textbox;
    Button^ addbutton;
public:
    FirstWindow(void)
    {
        Title = "First Avalon App";
        Width = 400;                // ❷ Initialize window properties
        Height = 400;
        ResizeMode = System::Windows::ResizeMode::NoResize;
```

```
        InitControls();        <-- ❸ Method to initialize child controls
    }
    . . .
};
```

It's much like Windows Forms programming, except that the controls you declare ❶ are from the `System::Windows::Controls` namespace (which contains various WPF controls). You set properties like `Title`, `Width`, `Height`, and so on on the window object in the constructor ❷. There's also a call to a method called `InitControls` ❸, where you initialize the child controls (I put it into a separate method to improve the code's readability). Listing 7.4 shows the `InitControls` method. Basically, you instantiate each of the child controls, instantiate a container control, add the child controls to the container controls, and finally set the container control as the main `Content` of the parent window.

Listing 7.4 Function to initialize the Avalon controls

```
void InitControls(void)
{
    listbox = gcnew ListBox();
    listbox->Width = 180;
    listbox->Height = 350;                        ❶ Set up ListBox control
    Canvas::SetTop(listbox, 10);
    Canvas::SetLeft(listbox, 10);

    textbox = gcnew TextBox();
    textbox->Width = 180;
    textbox->Height = 25;                         ❷ Set up TextBox control
    Canvas::SetTop(textbox, 10);
    Canvas::SetLeft(textbox, 200);

    addbutton = gcnew Button();
    addbutton->Width = 80;
    addbutton->Height = 25;                       ❸ Set up Button control
    addbutton->Content = "Add";
    Canvas::SetTop(addbutton, 45);
    Canvas::SetLeft(addbutton, 200);
    addbutton->Click += gcnew RoutedEventHandler(this,
        &FirstWindow::OnAddButtonClick);     <-- ❹ Set button's Click event handler

    maincanvas = gcnew Canvas();
    maincanvas->Children->Add(listbox);           ❺ Add child controls to Canvas
    maincanvas->Children->Add(textbox);
    maincanvas->Children->Add(addbutton);
    Content = maincanvas;     <-- ❻ Set Canvas as window's Content
}
```

Again, you probably notice the similarity with Windows Forms programming. You instantiate the child controls ❶, ❷, and ❸, and set various properties like `Width` and `Height`, and you also use the `Canvas::SetTop` and `Canvas::SetLeft` methods to position them on their container. For the button control, you also add an event handler for the `Click` event ❹. Then, you instantiate the `Canvas` control (which is a container control for other child controls) and add the child controls as its children ❺. Finally, you set the `Content` property of the window to this `Canvas` control ❻.

Now, you need to add the `Click` event handler for the button control, where you add the text entered into the `TextBox` to the `ListBox`:

```
void OnAddButtonClick(Object^ sender, RoutedEventArgs^ e)
{
    listbox->Items->Add(textbox->Text);
    textbox->Text = "";
    textbox->Focus();
}
```

Notice that you set the text of the `TextBox` to an empty string once you've added it to the `ListBox`. You also call the `Focus()` method so that the user can continue adding more entries into the `ListBox`. The `Window`-derived class is ready. Let's now write the `Application`-derived class.

Writing the Application-derived class

You derive a class called `FirstApp` from `Application` and add an override for the `OnStartup` method where you create and show the main window:

```
#include "FirstWindow.h"

ref class FirstApp : Application
{
public:
    FirstApp(void){}
protected:
    virtual void OnStartup(StartupEventArgs^ e) override
    {
        Application::OnStartup(e);
        FirstWindow^ mainwnd = gcnew FirstWindow();
        mainwnd->Show();
    }
};
```

The `OnStartup` method is called, not surprisingly, when the application has just started. You override that function so that you can instantiate and show the window. The base function is responsible for invoking any event handlers associated with the `Startup` event, and thus you need to call the base method in the override. Now, all that's left is to modify the main function to use the custom `Application` object instead of the default, as shown here:

```
#include "FirstApp.h"

[STAThread]
int main(array<String^>^ args)
{
    return (gcnew FirstApp())->Run();
}
```

Notice that you don't specify a window object to the `Run` method, because the window object is created in the `OnStartup` override of your `Application`-derived class. Compile and run the application, and try entering some text into the `TextBox` and clicking the Add button. You should see the text being entered into the `ListBox`.

When you use procedural code with Avalon, it's much like using Windows Forms, where you derive classes from the default controls, set some properties, add some event handlers, and are done. Procedural code is all right to develop WPF applications for simple user interfaces, but sometimes it makes better sense to take advantage of XAML and declarative programming. As I've mentioned a few times already, XAML isn't directly supported in VC++, so you'll have to look at alternate options to make use of XAML. One such option is to dynamically load the XAML at runtime.

7.2.3 Dynamically loading XAML

In this section, you'll rewrite the application you wrote in the previous section, using dynamically loaded XAML. This way, you get to leverage the power of XAML and declarative programming (which you couldn't in the procedural code technique you used in the previous section). Continuing the instruction-book analogy, this will be like one that has textual instructions that refer to pictures (which describe the various steps needed) and are loosely distributed along with the book but not directly printed in the book. You'll define the UI using XAML instead of procedural code. When you're done, you'll have an identical application to the one you previously created.

Create a new C++/CLI Avalon project using the steps mentioned in the introduction to section 7.2, and call it FirstAvalonDynamic (or whatever you want to call it). The first thing you'll do is write the XAML (MainWindow.xaml) that represents the UI; see listing 7.5.

Listing 7.5 XAML for the main window

```
<Window
    xmlns="http://schemas.microsoft.com/winfx/2006/xaml/presentation"
    xmlns:x="http://schemas.microsoft.com/winfx/2006/xaml"
    Title="First Avalon App (dynamically load XAML)"
    Height="400" Width="400"
    ResizeMode="NoResize"
    >
  <Canvas>
    <ListBox Canvas.Left="10" Canvas.Top="10"
      Width="180" Height="350"
      Name="listbox" />
    <TextBox Canvas.Left="200" Canvas.Top="10"
      Width="180" Height="25"
      Name="textbox" />
    <Button Canvas.Left="200" Canvas.Top="45"
      Width="80" Height="25"
      Name="addbutton">Add</Button>
  </Canvas>
</Window>
```

The XAML shown does exactly what you did with the procedural code earlier. For the control elements, you use the same names using the `Name` attribute as you use for the member variables in the procedural code. Next, you need to hook an event handler to the `Button` so that the text entered into the `TextBox` is inserted into the `ListBox`. For that, you'll write a helper class, as shown in listing 7.6.

Listing 7.6 `WindowHelper` class that implements the event handler

```
using namespace System;
using namespace System::Windows;
using namespace System::Windows::Controls;
using namespace System::Windows::Markup;
using namespace System::IO;

ref class WindowHelper
{
    ListBox^ listbox;
    TextBox^ textbox;
    Button^ addbutton;
public:
    WindowHelper(Window^ window)
    {
        addbutton = (Button^)window->FindName("addbutton");
        textbox = (TextBox^)window->FindName("textbox");
        listbox = (ListBox^)window->FindName("listbox");
```

Map elements to control variables ❶

```
        addbutton->Click += gcnew RoutedEventHandler(      <-- ❷ Add Click event handler
            this,&WindowHelper::OnAddButtonClick);
    }
    void OnAddButtonClick(Object^ sender, RoutedEventArgs^ e)
    {
        listbox->Items->Add(textbox->Text);              Event handler ❸
        textbox->Text = "";                                 definition
        textbox->Focus();
    }
};
```

The `WindowHelper` constructor accepts a `Window` argument and uses the `FindName` method ❶ to get the control with the specified identifier (which maps to the `Name` attributes you used in the XAML). You also hook an event handler to the `addbutton` control ❷. Finally, you have the event handler ❸, which is identical to the one you used in the procedural code project. Listing 7.7 shows the code for the `Application`-derived class, where you override `OnStartup` as before, except that you create a window dynamically by loading the XAML file from the disk.

Listing 7.7 The `Application`-derived class

```
ref class FirstAppDynamic : Application
{
public:
    FirstAppDynamic(void)
    {
    }
protected:
    virtual void OnStartup(StartupEventArgs^ e) override
    {
        Application::OnStartup(e);
        Stream^ st = File::OpenRead(                   ❶ Get Stream to XAML
            "MainWindow.xaml");
        Window^ mainwnd = (Window^)XamlReader::Load(st);    <-- ❷ Create Window from XAML
        st->Close();
        WindowHelper^ mainwndhelper = gcnew WindowHelper(mainwnd);   <-- Instantiate helper class ❸
        mainwnd->Show();   <-- ❹ Show window
    }
};
```

You open a file stream to the XAML using `File::OpenRead` ❶ and use the overload of `XamlReader::Load` ❷ that takes a `Stream^` as parameter to create a `Window` object. This `Load` method works the magic, by reading and parsing the XAML and building a `Window` object out of it. You instantiate the `WindowHelper` object and pass this `Window` object as the argument, so that the event handler for the `addbutton` control is properly set up ❸. You then show the window ❹ with a call to `Show()`. The `main` method is much the same as before, where you instantiate the `Application` object and call `Run` on it:

```
[STAThread]
int main(array<String^>^ args)
{
    return (gcnew FirstAppDynamic())->Run();
}
```

The advantage of using this technique over using procedural code is that you get to design your UI in XAML, thereby achieving a level of UI/code separation. You can also use Cider or some other XAML designer to quickly design flexible user interfaces, which would involve a good bit of hand-coding in procedural code.

The disadvantage is that you have to distribute the XAML file with your application, and if you have multiple windows, you then need that many XAML files. There's always the risk of a loosely-distributed XAML file getting corrupted (accidentally or otherwise) or even being deleted. You can embed all the XAML files as resources in the C++/CLI assembly and load them at runtime, but even that involves a lot of extra work. To avoid distributing XAML files loosely with your application or embedding them as resources, you may want to use the technique we'll discuss in the next section: putting the XAML into a C# project and accessing it via a derived class in a C++ project.

7.2.4 Deriving from a class in a C# DLL

You'll write a third variation of the same application in this section. You'll use a C# control library project for the XAML, and a C++ project that will utilize that XAML control by deriving a control from it. Using the instruction-book analogy again, this is essentially a picture-based, step-by-step guide with the textual instructions printed alongside each picture providing some meta-information for the step indicated by that picture. First, use the New Project Wizard to generate a new C# .NET 3.0 Custom Control Library project, and delete the default XAML file generated by the wizard. The default XAML is derived from `UserControl` and isn't what you want. Add a new XAML file to the C# project that represents a `Window`, and either use Cider or hand-code the XAML from listing 7.8 into that file.

Listing 7.8 The `Window` class definition using XAML

```
<Window x:Class="CSXamlLibrary.BaseWindow"
    xmlns="http://schemas.microsoft.com/winfx/2006/xaml/presentation"
    xmlns:x="http://schemas.microsoft.com/winfx/2006/xaml"
    Title="First Avalon App (dynamically load XAML)"
    Height="400" Width="400"
    ResizeMode="NoResize"
    >
  <Canvas>
    <ListBox Canvas.Left="10" Canvas.Top="10"
      Width="180" Height="350"
      Name="listbox" x:FieldModifier="protected" />
    <TextBox Canvas.Left="200" Canvas.Top="10"
      Width="180" Height="25"
      Name="textbox" x:FieldModifier="protected" />
    <Button Canvas.Left="200" Canvas.Top="45"
      Width="80" Height="25"
      Name="addbutton" x:FieldModifier="protected">Add</Button>
  </Canvas>
</Window>
```

Specify class name

Specify protected modifier

The XAML is identical to that used in the previous project (where you dynamically loaded it) except for the `x:Class` attribute for the `Window` element, which specifies the name of the class that will be generated, and the `x:FieldModifier` attributes that are applied to the child control elements so they're generated as `protected` members in the class (rather than as `private` which is the default). Build the C# project, and generate the control library. Once that's done, create a new C++/CLI Avalon project (using the same steps as before), and then add a reference to this C# project. Now, you can write a new `Window` class that's derived from the class in the C# DLL, as shown in listing 7.9.

Listing 7.9 Deriving the main window from the XAML-defined `Window` class

```
using namespace System;
using namespace System::Windows;
using namespace System::Windows::Controls;

ref class AppMainWindow : CSXamlLibrary::BaseWindow
{
public:
    AppMainWindow(void)
    {
        addbutton->Click += gcnew RoutedEventHandler(
            this,&AppMainWindow::OnAddButtonClick);
    }
```

Derive from C# class

```
        void OnAddButtonClick(Object^ sender, RoutedEventArgs^ e)
        {
            listbox->Items->Add(textbox->Text);
            textbox->Text = "";
            textbox->Focus();
        }
    };
```

The code is similar to what you've seen thus far, except that it's a lot cleaner. Unlike the first example, you don't have a lot of clogged procedural code to create the UI. Unlike the second example, you don't need a helper class to map the XAML elements to the control variables and event handlers. It's definitely an improvement over the previous two examples, but you have to bring in the C# project just for the XAML. The rest of the code needed for the application is more or less similar to what you saw earlier:

```
ref class FirstAppDerived : Application
{
protected:
    virtual void OnStartup(StartupEventArgs^ e) override
    {
        Application::OnStartup(e);
        AppMainWindow^ mainwnd = gcnew AppMainWindow();
        mainwnd->Show();
    }
};

[STAThread]
int main(array<String^>^ args)
{
    return (gcnew FirstAppDerived())->Run();
}
```

In some ways, the third technique is a sort of hybrid of the previous two techniques. A lot of the code is identical to that in the first technique—as with the declaration of a custom class derived from `Window` and an `Application`-derived class with the `OnStartup` method creating the custom window. But, like the second technique, the UI definition is in the XAML, except that in this case, it's compiled into the C# DLL. You also reduce lines of code with each successive technique. You had the most lines of code with procedural code (as is to be expected) and improved on that considerably when you moved the UI definition to the XAML in the dynamically-loaded XAML example. In the last example, you saved even further on lines of code, such as the helper class from the second example that had to wire the XAML elements to the member variables. Of course, the total lines of code (LOC) isn't always the single deciding factor that determines what technique you choose. Table 7.2 shows a comparison of the three techniques; for each factor, the cells with the bold text reflect the technique (or techniques) that offer maximum performance (or convenience).

Table 7.2 Comparison of the three techniques

	Procedural code	Dynamically load XAML	XAML in C# DLL
Cluttered code that generates the UI	Yes	No	No
Dependency on loose XAML files	No	Yes	No
Dependency on C#-based DLL	No	No	Yes
Lines of code	Maximum	In-between	Minimum
UI design convenience	Poor	Excellent	Excellent
UI/business logic separation	Poor	Good	Excellent
Level of Visual C++ project support	Total	Partial	(Not applicable)

It's hard to pinpoint a specific technique and claim that it's the best one, because depending on your requirements, each has advantages and disadvantages. Of course, in the future, if Visual C++ has direct support for XAML (as I believe it will), that will be your best option for the majority of scenarios.

7.3 A brief look at some WPF Graphics features

Most of the Avalon code you'll encounter will use XAML. There won't be a lot of procedural code out there (for the simple reason that few people use C++/CLI to write Avalon apps—and that's because of the lack of project template support in Visual C++). In this section, I'll cover a select minority of the WPF Graphics features using procedural code. It will give you a good feel for writing WPF applications using straight procedural code without XAML dependencies.

We'll discuss the basic usage of brushes and look at creating common shapes such as rectangles and ellipses using the shape classes. We'll also cover a powerful Avalon feature: transformations.

7.3.1 Using brushes and shapes

Every UI component in Avalon, be it text or graphics, is rendered using a *brush*. You can think of this brush as being similar to a real-life brush—the name was intentionally chosen to reflect the fact that the Avalon brush behaves pretty much like a real brush. There is a Brush class (which is abstract), which is the base class for other brush classes, such as SolidColorBrush, LinearGradientBrush, and so on; these are declared in the System::Windows::Media namespace. It's merely a matter of setting a property or two to change the brush that's used to render a UI element. For instance, consider a ListBox where you'd like to set the color of the text to indigo and the background color to light blue. The following two lines of code achieve that purpose:

```
shapelistbox->Foreground = Brushes::Indigo;
shapelistbox->Background = Brushes::LightBlue;
```

The Brushes type is a sealed class that has a number of static properties that define predefined colors. For instance, in this code snippet, Brushes::Indigo returns a SolidColorBrush that corresponds to the indigo color. It gives you an easy way to specify a color—without having to remember the Alpha, Red, Green, and Blue (ARGB) component codes for each color. The same line of code can also be written by directly constructing a SolidColorBrush with the specified ARGB values, as shown here:

```
shapelistbox->Foreground = gcnew SolidColorBrush(
    Color::FromArgb(0xFF, 0x4B, 0x00, 0x82)); //ARGB for Indigo
```

Avalon also provides two specialized brush classes for rendering gradient backgrounds—LinearGradientBrush (for linear gradients) and RadialGradientBrush (for radial gradients). For example, let's see how to use a linear gradient with a Canvas control (you can use any other control if you prefer):

```
LinearGradientBrush^ linearbrush = gcnew LinearGradientBrush();
linearbrush->StartPoint = Point(0,0);        ❶ Starting and
linearbrush->EndPoint = Point(1,1);            ending coordinates
linearbrush->GradientStops->Add(
    gcnew GradientStop(Colors::LightGreen,0));   ❷ Set gradient
linearbrush->GradientStops->Add(                  stops
    gcnew GradientStop(Colors::Green,1));
canvas->Background = linearbrush;
```

The StartPoint and EndPoint properties ❶ are used to specify the start and end coordinates for the gradient. By specifying (0,0) and (1,1), you implement a diagonal linear gradient. Had you specified (1,0) as the EndPoint, you would have gotten a horizontal gradient, and (0,1) would have given you a vertical gradient. Once you've specified the start and end coordinates, you need to specify the gradient stops, which are basically points where the gradient is to arrive at a specific color. In the example, you use only two such gradient stops ❷: at 0 you specify light green, and at 1 you specify green. This results in a diagonal linear gradient that transitions smoothly from light green to green. Note that you could add more gradient stops if you wanted to. For instance, you could set a gradient stop at 0.5 and specify dark green, which would result in a transition from light green to dark green and then to green.

Rendering shape objects

In addition to the standard UI controls like `ListBox`, Avalon also provides a bunch of classes for rendering shape objects. And yes, though you probably saw this coming, the same brushes that you use with controls are also used with shapes. There is an abstract base class called `Shape` from which several other more specialized shape classes are derived—`Ellipse`, `Rectangle`, `Polygon`, and so on. Although we can't discuss every `Shape` class supported in WPF, let's take a quick look at a few basic examples. We'll begin with the `Ellipse` class, which can be used to render ellipses and circles (which are basically ellipses that have a width that's equal to the height):

```
Shape^ shape;
. . .
Shape^ CreateEllipse(int w, int h)
{
    Ellipse^ ell = gcnew Ellipse();
    ell->Width = w;
    ell->Height = h;
    ell->Stroke = Brushes::Black;
    return ell;
}
. . .
shape = CreateEllipse(200,200); // circle
shape = CreateEllipse(300,200); // ellipse
. . .
canvas->Children->Add(shape);
```

The code is straightforward and needs no explanation. The `Stroke` property is set to a brush that is used to render the shape. Adding the shape to the canvas is done in exactly the same way as adding a regular control. Both controls and shapes are indirectly derived from `UIElement` and can thus be added to a canvas directly. Instead of a `Background` property, `Shape` objects have a `Fill` property that can be set to any `Brush`-derived object. Before you see how to use that, I'd like to show you some code that creates a rectangle or a square (similar to creating the ellipse/circle) using the `Rectangle` class, and also how to create a triangle using the `Polygon` class.

Here's the code for a `CreateRectangle` function:

```
Shape^ CreateRectangle(int w, int h)
{
    Rectangle^ rect = gcnew Rectangle();
    rect->Width = w;
    rect->Height = h;
    rect->Stroke = Brushes::Black;
    return rect;
}
```

That's nearly identical to the `CreateEllipse` function. Again, you set the `Stroke` brush to black. Whether you get a square shape depends on how you set the width and height arguments to the function, as shown here:

```
shape = CreateRectangle(200,200); // square
shape = CreateRectangle(300,200); // rectangle
```

Creating a triangle is slightly different but again involves some fairly straightforward code:

```
Shape^ CreatePolygon(PointCollection^ pocoll)
{
    Polygon^ pgon = gcnew Polygon();
    pgon->Stroke = Brushes::Black;
    pgon->Points = pocoll;
    return pgon;
}

PointCollection pocoll;
pocoll.Add(Point(0,200));
pocoll.Add(Point(100,0));
pocoll.Add(Point(200,200));
shape = CreatePolygon(%pocoll);
```

A polygon shape is created by specifying a group of points, which are connected by lines, thereby forming a closed shape. In this example, you use three points that form a triangle, and as you did with the `Ellipse` and `Rectangle` classes, you set the `Stroke` property to a black brush. The level of consistency maintained across WPF classes is immaculate. This results in an extremely comfortable learning curve. The same function you used previously can be used to create a tetragon (four-sided quadrilateral), as shown here:

```
PointCollection pocoll;
pocoll.Add(Point(0,100));
pocoll.Add(Point(100,0));
pocoll.Add(Point(200,100));
pocoll.Add(Point(100,200));
shape = CreatePolygon(%pocoll);
```

Instead of three points, you use four to create the tetragon.

Now, let's see how to use a radial gradient fill with these shape objects. It doesn't matter which specific shape object you're trying to fill; you just set the `Fill` property to your brush of choice. In the following code, the `RadialFill` method uses two colors to create a radial gradient that is used to fill the shape. Instead of hard-coding the colors, you take the colors from two combo boxes, which specify the start and stop colors (please refer to the source code accompanying the book for the complete code—I haven't included full listings, to save space):

```
void RadialFill()
{
    if(shape && startcolorcombo->SelectedItem
        && stopcolorcombo->SelectedItem)
    {
        RadialGradientBrush^ radbrush = gcnew RadialGradientBrush();
        radbrush->RadiusX = 0.5;        Sets radii of outer
        radbrush->RadiusY = 0.5;        gradient circle
        radbrush->GradientOrigin = Point(0.5, 0.5);      Set focal point of gradient
        radbrush->GradientStops->Add(gcnew GradientStop(      ❶ Set gradient stops
            ((ColorComboItem)
              startcolorcombo->SelectedItem).mColor,0));
        radbrush->GradientStops->Add(gcnew GradientStop(
            ((ColorComboItem)
              stopcolorcombo->SelectedItem).mColor,1));
        shape->Fill = radbrush;
    }
}
```

As illustrated, you set up a minimal radial gradient fill. Just like with the linear gradient brush, you can set gradient stops where you specify the color at that point ❶. You specify only two stops—one at the beginning of the gradient and one at the finish—but you could add any number of gradient stops. Once you create the `RadialGradientBrush` objects, you set the `Fill` property of the `Shape` object, and the shape is filled using that brush—in this case, the radial gradient brush.

You've seen only a fraction of the capabilities available with brushes and shapes, but this section has given you a fundamental idea of how the various classes are implemented.

7.3.2 Transformations

Transformations refer to geometric transformations as applied to WPF UI objects. Every `UIElement`-derived object in Avalon can have a transformation (or transformations) applied to it. Applying a transformation is often as trivial as creating a specific transformation object and setting the `RenderTransform` property of the `UIElement` object. Objects derived from `FrameworkElement` also support a

LayoutTransform property, which is used to apply a transformation on the element during layout. In this section, we'll only look at examples of performing RenderTransform-based operations. You'll use three types of UIElement objects: a ListBox, an Ellipse, and a TextBlock; and you'll apply each transformation (or set of transformations) to all three objects. (Please refer to the source code accompanying the book for the complete code. I haven't included full listings to save space.)

Figure 7.5 shows what the controls normally look like—that is, when no transformations are applied to them.

The first example you'll try will apply a rotate transformation on the objects using the RotateTransform class. Here's the code listing that shows how this is done:

```
Transform^ transform = nullptr;
. . .
transform = gcnew RotateTransform(-30);      <-- Create Transform object
. . .
listbox->RenderTransform = transform;
ellipse->RenderTransform = transform;        Set RenderTransform property
textblock->RenderTransform = transform;
```

You create a RotateTransform object using the constructor that takes as an argument the angle (in degrees) by which the objects are to be rotated. This angle is specified in clockwise degrees, so you need to specify a negative number for counterclockwise rotation. Other constructors allow you to specify the center

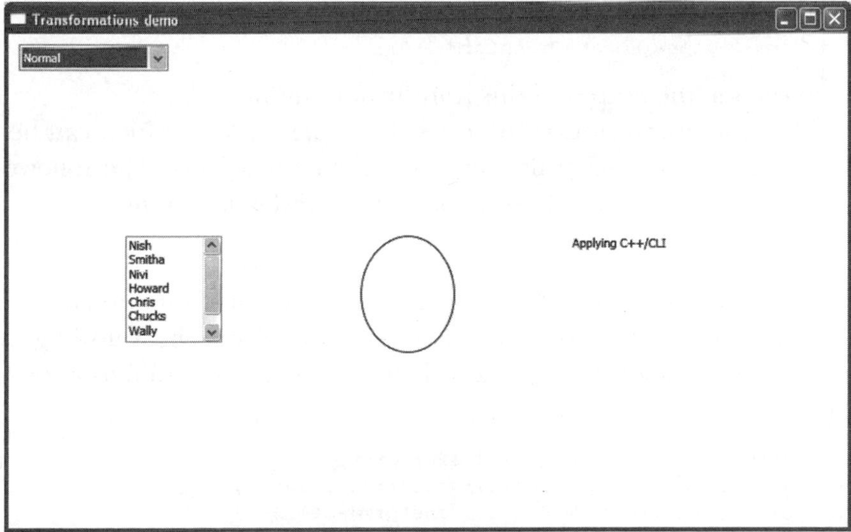

Figure 7.5 Normal rendering (without any transforms)

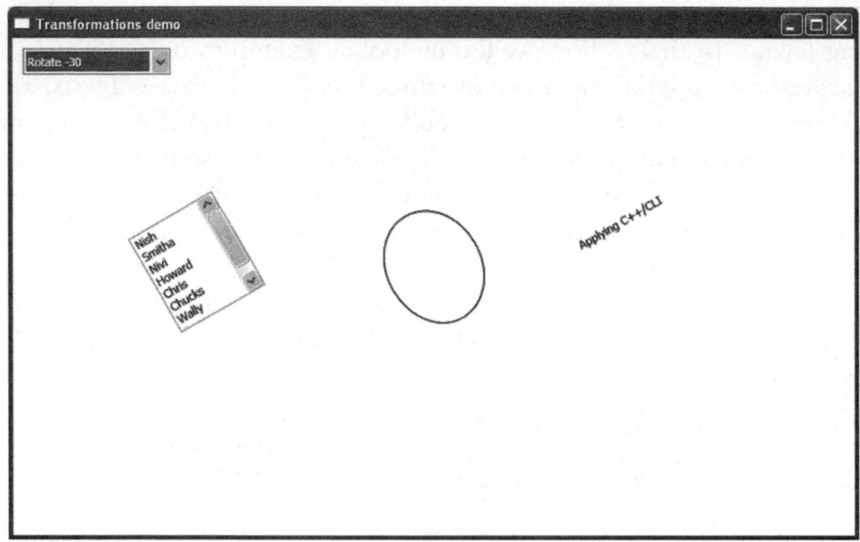

Figure 7.6 Rotated 30 degrees counterclockwise

coordinates on which the rotation is performed, but you don't use them here. Figure 7.6 shows the rotated objects, once this code is executed.

You can get some useful effects using the `RotateTransform` object. For example, by specifying a rotation angle of 180, you invert the object. The following code does just that:

```
transform = gcnew RotateTransform(180);
```

And you can see the output of this transform in figure 7.7.

Another useful transformation class is `ScaleTransform`, which can be used to perform two-dimensional scale transformations on objects. The following code scales an object by a factor of two in both the x and y directions:

```
transform = gcnew ScaleTransform(2,2);
```

Figure 7.8 shows the output of performing this scale transformation on the object.

You can apply multiple transformations on an object. The following code uses a `TransformGroup` object to apply a scale transformation as well as a rotate transformation on an object:

```
TransformGroup^ grp = gcnew TransformGroup();
grp->Children->Add(gcnew ScaleTransform(1.5,1.5));
grp->Children->Add(gcnew RotateTransform(-30));
transform = grp;
```

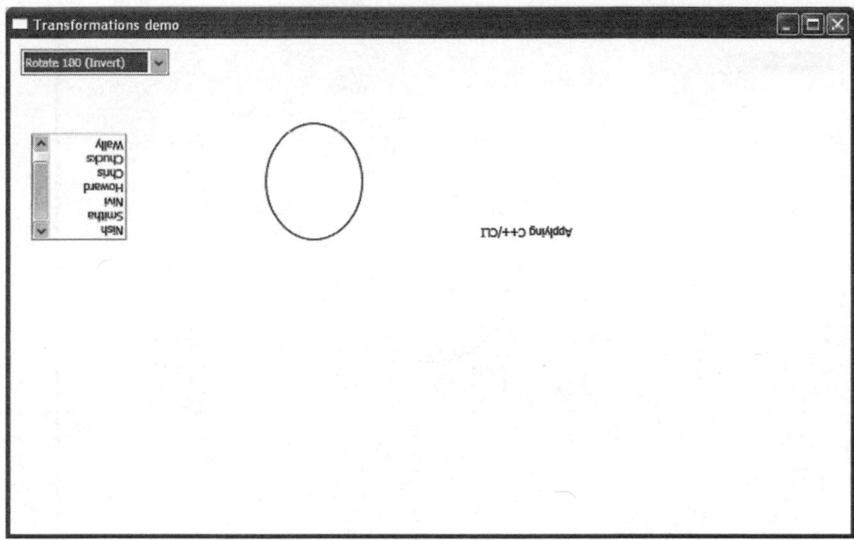

Figure 7.7 Inverted (rotated 180 degrees)

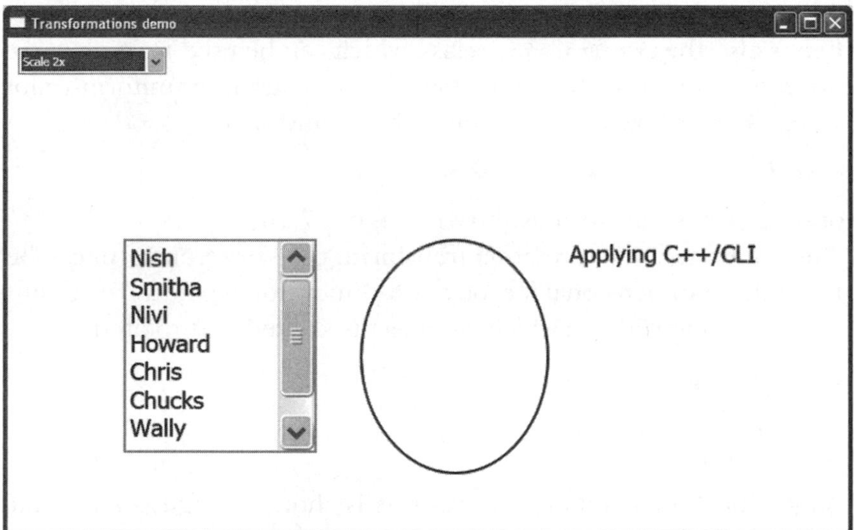

Figure 7.8 Scaled by 2x

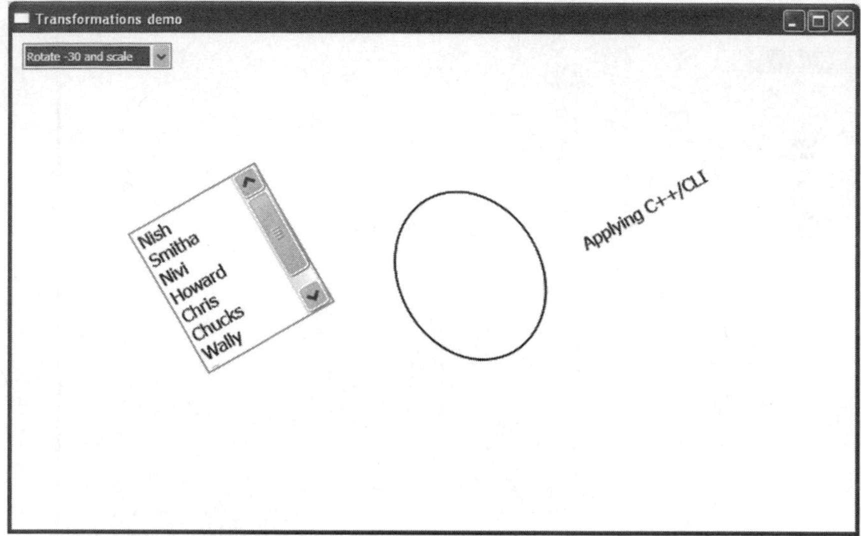

Figure 7.9 Rotated and scaled

The output of applying those transforms to your objects is shown in figure 7.9.

There's also the `SkewTransform` class, which can be used to apply a skew transformation on an object where the object is stretched non-uniformly along the x and y axes. Here's how you can apply a skew transform:

```
transform = gcnew SkewTransform(30,0);
```

The output of this transform is shown in figure 7.10.

When combined with a rotation transform, the skew transform can be used to simulate a three-dimensional feel on a two-dimensional object. For example, consider the following code, in which an object is skewed and rotated:

```
TransformGroup^ grp = gcnew TransformGroup();
grp->Children->Add(gcnew RotateTransform(-30));
grp->Children->Add(gcnew SkewTransform(-45,0));
transform = grp;
```

The output of these combined transforms is shown in figure 7.11. You can see how there's a 3D feel to the objects now.

The ability to create stunning user interfaces will be one of Avalon's biggest selling points. Obviously, we can't cover anything more than a negligible fraction of its capabilities in this chapter, so you should find an alternate source to get more information on what can be done using WPF.

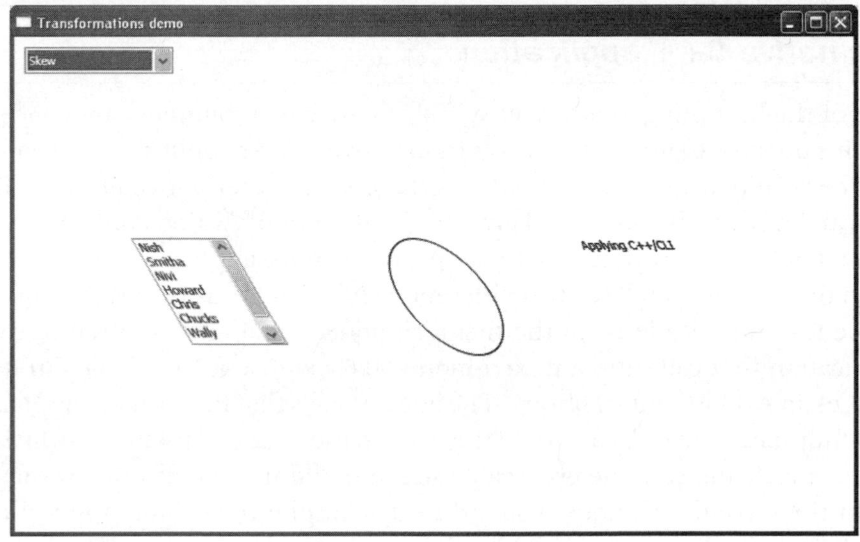

Figure 7.10 Skewed

Figure 7.11 Skewed and rotated

7.4 Hosting a WPF control in a native C++ application

One of the best things about WPF as far as native programmers are concerned is that it's possible to use WPF controls from native Win32 applications, regardless of whether you're using pure API, MFC, ATL, or some other native library. That way, you can leverage the powerful Direct3D capabilities of Avalon controls in existing native applications without having to port the entire application to Avalon.

In this section, you'll see two different techniques for using a WPF control from native C++ applications. In the first technique, you'll have a purely native MFC application that calls into a mixed-mode MFC extension DLL, which in turn references an Avalon control library. The advantage is that the primary application is kept fully native, thereby avoiding the need to use `/clr` compilation—which would unnecessarily increase the executable size and add managed code overhead.

In the second technique, you'll directly compile the calling application with the `/clr` compilation mode. This allows you to directly use an Avalon control library and avoids the need for the intermediary mixed-mode DLL.

7.4.1 Using a mixed-mode extension DLL

The key idea here is to keep the calling application purely native and to put all the interop code into an extension DLL. As a real-life analogy, think of a voice-operated television set that understands voice commands in English, and then imagine that a Japanese-speaking person wants to operate the TV. Instead of directly modifying the TV set so that it can respond to Japanese commands, you can use an add-on device that accepts commands in Japanese, and then invokes the corresponding functions on the TV. This way, the TV is untouched, the Japanese speaker needn't learn the English commands, and all the language-conversion work is done by the add-on device. The Japanese speaker is analogous to the native C++ app; the add-on device is analogous to the mixed-mode DLL; and the TV is analogous to the WPF control. Figure 7.12 shows how to use a mixed-mode DLL to host a WPF control in a native application.

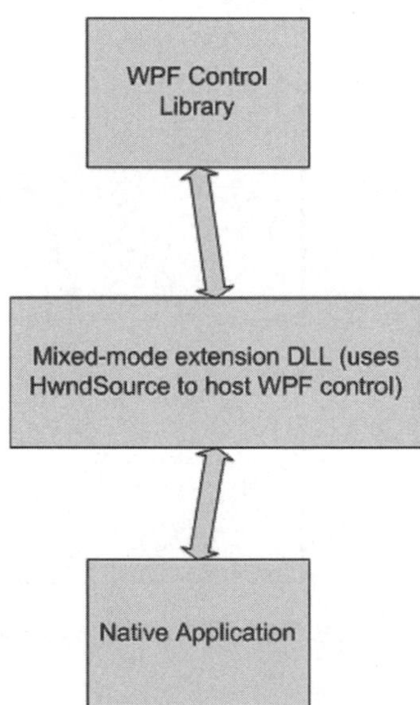

Figure 7.12 Hosting WPF using a mixed-mode extension DLL

For the example, you'll use an Avalon control called `MediaElement` to play a video file from within an MFC dialog-based application. Please note that I'm focusing on the interop process of hosting the WPF control in the MFC dialog rather than on trying to showcase a fancy WPF feature (because that isn't within the scope of this chapter). Essentially, the same techniques can be applied with any WPF control—with appropriate modifications depending on the nature of the control.

Creating the WPF control library

You'll use a C# project to create the WPF control library, except that you won't use any C# code. You'll use the project to generate the XAML and to take advantage of the XAML editor (Cider), which isn't available in a C++ project. Here are the two steps that are necessary to create a control library:

1. Generate a new C# .NET 3.0-based WPF control library project called CustomControlLibrary. Delete the C# source file that's automatically generated (you don't need any C# code for the example).
2. Delete the contents of the generated XAML file, and enter the XAML from listing 7.10 into it. (Note that for more sophisticated UIs, you can use Cider directly; this example is intentionally kept simple.)

Listing 7.10 XAML for the Avalon control

```
<Canvas x:Class="CustomControlLibrary.MyControl"
    xmlns="http://schemas.microsoft.com/winfx/2006/xaml/presentation"
    xmlns:x="http://schemas.microsoft.com/winfx/2006/xaml">

  <Canvas.Background>
  <LinearGradientBrush StartPoint="0,0" EndPoint="1,1">
    <LinearGradientBrush.GradientStops>
      <GradientStop Color="AliceBlue" Offset="0" />
      <GradientStop Color="LightBlue" Offset="0.5" />
      <GradientStop Color="Blue" Offset="1" />
    </LinearGradientBrush.GradientStops>
  </LinearGradientBrush>
  </Canvas.Background>

  <MediaElement Name="mVid" x:FieldModifier="public"
    LoadedBehavior="Manual"
    Width="{Binding RelativeSource={RelativeSource Self},
        Path=Parent.ActualWidth}"
    Height="{Binding RelativeSource={RelativeSource Self},
        Path=Parent.ActualHeight}">
```

```
      <MediaElement.LayoutTransform>
        <TransformGroup>
           <ScaleTransform ScaleX="0.7" ScaleY="0.7" />
          <SkewTransform AngleX="15" AngleY="15" />
           <RotateTransform Angle="-15" />
        </TransformGroup>
      </MediaElement.LayoutTransform>

    </MediaElement>
  </Canvas>
```

You use a linear gradient as the background using a `LinearGradientBrush` (discussed earlier in the chapter); you also use a bunch of transformations on the `MediaElement` object. The `MediaElement` control is used to play both audio and video and requires Windows Media Player 10 to be installed on the machine. You specify `LoadedBehavior` as `Manual` because you'll be performing operations on the `MediaElement` object through procedural code. Please refer to the WPF documentation for more details on customizing the `MediaElement` object. For the example, this XAML will suffice. Build the C# project to generate a DLL that will contain your custom control—the `MyControl` control in the `CustomControlLibrary` namespace.

The next step is to create the mixed-mode extension DLL that will wrap this WPF control for use from native applications.

Creating the MFC extension DLL

The extension DLL will bridge the native MFC caller application with the managed WPF control library you created previously. Follow these steps to generate the mixed-mode MFC extension project that you'll use for the example (please refer to the source code accompanying the book for complete code listings):

1. Generate an MFC Extension DLL project using the wizard, and call it AvalonHostLib.
2. Turn on `/clr` compilation, and add references to the core WPF assemblies.
3. Remove the `#include <afxdllx.h>` line from the source file that defines `DllMain` (AvalonHostLib.cpp).
4. Add a new CPP file to the project called NativeHeaders.cpp, change its properties to not use precompiled headers, and remove `/clr` compilation for this specific file. Put the following two `#include` lines in this CPP file : `#include <afxwin.h>` and `#include <afxdllx.h>`. (Note that these steps are mandatory and are done to avoid the loader-lock issues that come into play when `DllMain` is compiled as managed code. For our

purposes, it's not necessary that you understand the loader-lock issue; if you aren't aware of it, just make sure you follow these steps correctly, and you'll be fine.)

5 Add a project reference to the CustomControlLibrary project you created in the previous section.

6 Compile and build the project to make sure everything's all right. You'll now write a `CWnd`-derived class, which will be exported for use from the native caller. This means the header file must be compilable from a purely native context, because you'll be including this header in the native project. Listing 7.11 shows what the header file looks like.

Listing 7.11 Header file for the exported `CWnd`-derived class

```
class AFX_EXT_CLASS CMyWnd : public CWnd
{
    DECLARE_DYNAMIC(CMyWnd)

public:
    CMyWnd();
    virtual ~CMyWnd();

    void Stop(); [#1]
    void Play(); [#1]
    void SetSource(LPCTSTR strSource);
    virtual void OnMediaEnded();
protected:
    DECLARE_MESSAGE_MAP()

public:
    afx_msg int OnCreate(LPCREATESTRUCT lpCreateStruct);

protected:
#ifdef _MANAGED
    gcroot<CustomControlLibrary::MyControl^> m_ObjHandle;
#else
    intptr_t m_ObjHandle;
#endif
};
```

❶ Proxy functions for native caller

❷ Conditional member declaration for WPF control

The two important aspects of the class are the proxy functions ❶—`Stop`, `Play`, `SetSource`, and `OnMediaEnded`, which are used from the native code to communicate with the WPF control—and the conditional declaration of the `MyControl` member variable ❷, where you use a `gcroot` for the managed compilation and an `intptr_t` for the native compilation. You'll use a managed class called `HwndSource` (from the `System::Windows::Interop` namespace) to create the Avalon control as a child control of the `CWnd` class. As mentioned earlier, WPF controls aren't `HWND`-based Windows controls. The `HwndSource` creates an `HWND`-based window that will contain the WPF control. You can put this `HWND`-based window into any other native window. Listing 7.12 shows the `OnCreate` method, which creates the `HwndSource` that will be used to host the WPF control.

Listing 7.12 The `OnCreate` method, which sets up the `HwndSource`

```
int CMyWnd::OnCreate(LPCREATESTRUCT lpCreateStruct)
{
    if (CWnd::OnCreate(lpCreateStruct) == -1)
        return -1;

    CRect rect;
    GetClientRect(&rect);

    HwndSourceParameters sourceParams("CustomHost");
    sourceParams.PositionX = 0;
    sourceParams.PositionY = 0;
    sourceParams.Height = rect.Height();
    sourceParams.Width = rect.Width();
    sourceParams.ParentWindow = (IntPtr)m_hWnd;
    sourceParams.WindowStyle = WS_VISIBLE | WS_CHILD;

    HwndSource^ source = gcnew HwndSource(sourceParams);        <-1
    CustomControlLibrary::MyControl^ control =
        gcnew CustomControlLibrary::MyControl();     <-2
    control->InitializeComponent();
    control->mVid->RenderTransform =
        gcnew TranslateTransform(0, rect.Height() * .15);
    m_ObjHandle = control;
    EventHandlerHelper^ eventhelper = gcnew EventHandlerHelper(this);
    control->mVid->MediaEnded +=
          gcnew RoutedEventHandler(eventhelper,
        &EventHandlerHelper::OnMediaEnded);     <-3
    source->RootVisual = control;      <-4

    return 0;
}
```

The `HwndSource` ❶ and `MyControl` ❷ objects are created and connected together using the `RootVisual` property ❹. Once this is done, the WPF control is hosted within the `HWND`-based window that's associated with the `HwndSource` object. Although you don't use it in this example, you can use the `HwndSource::Handle` property to get the associated `HWND` for the `HwndSource` window. Notice how you associate the `MediaEnded` event with a handler defined in an `EventHandlerHelper` class ❸. As the name indicates, it's a helper class that is used to route the managed event to the native code. Here's the definition for the `EventHandlerHelper` class:

```
ref class EventHandlerHelper
{
    CMyWnd* _pWnd;
public:
    EventHandlerHelper(CMyWnd* pWnd):_pWnd(pWnd)
    {
    }
    void OnMediaEnded(Object^ sender, RoutedEventArgs^ e)
    {
        _pWnd->OnMediaEnded();          ❶ Route event to native code
    }
};
```

The event is proxied to the native class by issuing a call to the `virtual` `OnMediaEnded` method of the `CWnd` derived class ❶. The default implementation of the native `OnMediaEnded` method is an empty function that does nothing. It's up to the calling code to derive a class from `CMyWnd` and to provide a more functional implementation for the `OnMediaEnded` method. The proxy functions are implemented in a fairly straightforward manner and call the appropriate methods in the `MediaElement` object exposed by the `MyControl` object, as shown here:

```
void CMyWnd::Stop()
{
    m_ObjHandle->mVid->Stop();
}
void CMyWnd::Play()
{
    m_ObjHandle->mVid->Play();
}
void CMyWnd::SetSource(LPCTSTR strSource)
{
    m_ObjHandle->mVid->Source = gcnew Uri(
        gcnew String(strSource));
}
```

That's all there is to the mixed-mode DLL project. Compile and build the project to generate the extension DLL. Next, you'll consume this from the native caller application.

The native MFC caller

The caller app will be a purely native MFC application that will use the exported `CWnd`-derived control from the extension DLL. It will communicate with the WPF

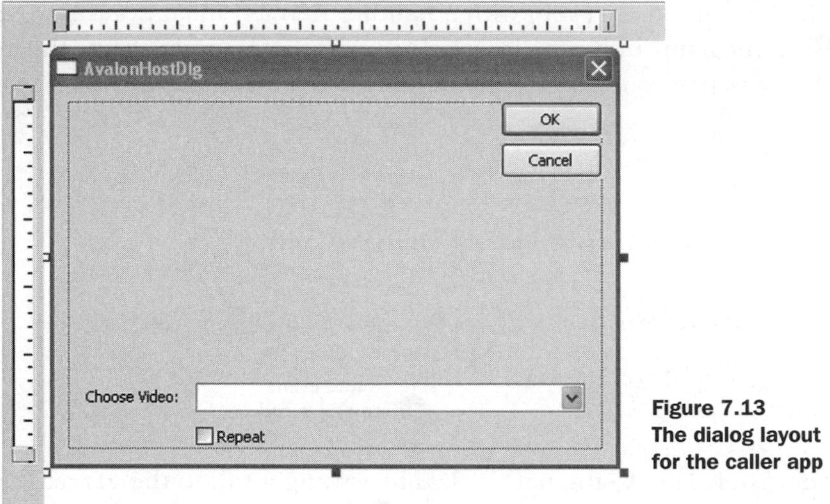

Figure 7.13
The dialog layout for the caller app

control through the proxy functions in the extension DLL. Figure 7.13 shows the dialog layout of the native MFC caller application.

Follow these steps to generate the project (you can also directly copy the full project from the source code accompanying the book):

1. Generate a new MFC dialog-based project called AvalonHostDlg, add a dependency to the extension DLL project created in the previous section, and add the following controls (use figure 7.13 as a reference).
   - A combo box with identifier `IDC_COMBOVIDEOS` and DDX variable `CComboBox m_ComboVideos`
   - A check box with identifier `IDC_CHECKLOOP`
2. Add static text next to the combo box that says `Choose Video:`.
3. Associate an event handler called `OnCbnSelchangeComboVideos` with the `ON_CBN_SELCHANGE` of the combo box.
4. Associate an event handler called `OnBnClickedCheckLoop` with the `ON_BN_CLICKED` of the check box.
5. Add a call to `AfxOleInit` in `CAvalonHostDlgApp::InitInstance`. This is done to ensure that you have an STA model (because Avalon requires STA).

The project is ready, and you can compile it once to make sure everything works. The basic idea is to populate the combo box with paths to video files and to play those videos in the `MediaElement` control contained in the `MyControl` custom control you wrote previously. If you remember, I mentioned how the `MediaEnded` event is routed to the native code handler (which is an empty stub function in the `CMyWnd` class). To handle this event, you need to derive a class from `CMyWnd` as follows:

```
class CMyDerivedWnd : public CMyWnd
{
public:
    CMyDerivedWnd():bRepeatVideo(false)
    {
    }
    bool bRepeatVideo;
    virtual void OnMediaEnded()
    {
        if(bRepeatVideo)      <-- (1) If repeat-mode is on,
        {                         play video again
            Play();
        }
    }
};
```

The `MediaEnded` event is fired when the video (or any media) has finished playing. You get this event in the derived class and check for repeat-mode (1). If repeat-mode is enabled, you call `Play` to play the video once again. This is simple, but it's an interesting mechanism because you're handling an event that was generated in the managed WPF control in the native `CWnd`-derived class. You create the `CMyDerivedWnd` control in the dialog's `OnInitDialog` method, as shown here:

```
BOOL CAvalonHostDlgDlg::OnInitDialog()
{
    . . .

    // TODO: Add extra initialization here
    m_ComboVideos.AddString(_T("c:\\windows\\clock.avi"));
    m_ComboVideos.AddString(_T("c:\\Videos\\greekpriest.wmv"));
    m_ComboVideos.SetCurSel(0);
    m_WpfWnd.Create(NULL, _T("Host"),WS_VISIBLE | WS_CHILD,
        CRect(0,0,200,200),this,1000);
    m_WpfWnd.SetSource(_T("c:\\windows\\clock.avi"));
    m_WpfWnd.Play();
    return TRUE;
}
```

In this code snippet, you populate the combo box with some video files, create the `CMyDerivedWnd` control with a call to `CWnd::Create`, set the source to a default video file, and call the `Play` method, so that the dialog shows up with the default video playing. The `OnBnClickedCheckLoop` is implemented as shown here and is used to set or unset the repeat-mode for the playing video:

```
void CAvalonHostDlgDlg::OnBnClickedCheckLoop()
{
    m_WpfWnd.bRepeatVideo = static_cast<CButton*>(
        GetDlgItem(IDC_CHECKLOOP))->GetCheck() == BST_CHECKED;
}
```

Similarly, the `OnCbnSelchangeComboVideos` method is used to play a different video by choosing it from the combo box:

```
void CAvalonHostDlgDlg::OnCbnSelchangeComboVideos()
{
    CString strVideoPath;
    m_ComboVideos.GetLBText(m_ComboVideos.GetCurSel(),
        strVideoPath);
    m_WpfWnd.Stop();
    m_WpfWnd.SetSource(strVideoPath);
    m_WpfWnd.Play();
}
```

Notice how you call `Stop` first to make sure you don't change the `Source` property of the `MediaElement` when a video is playing (this may result in an exception or other unexpected behavior). Compile and run the app, and you should see something similar to what's shown in figure 7.14.

One important thing to be aware of is that WPF internally uses Direct3D technologies, which require you to have a powerful 3D-accelerated video card. If your video card isn't good enough, you may see some extremely pathetic video quality, especially if you try to play a high-resolution media file.

Summarizing the example, you saw how to communicate between the native MFC app and the managed WPF control via the mixed-mode extension DLL. You saw how a managed WPF event can be handled from the native code, and how

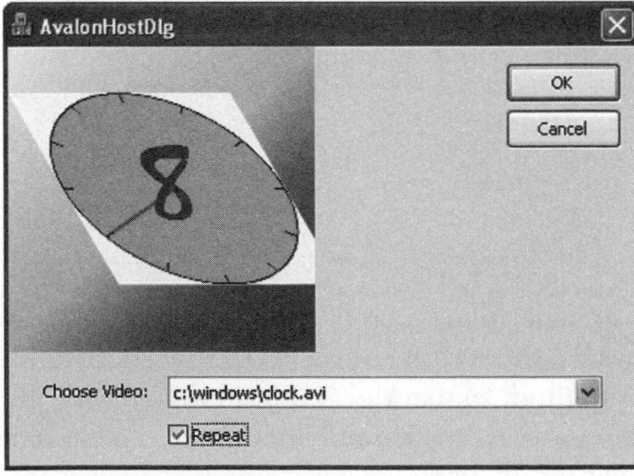

Figure 7.14
The dialog app that hosts the WPF control

the native code can indirectly invoke managed functions in the WPF control. You had to route all the communication through the extension DLL, because you needed to keep your caller native. But if that wasn't a restriction, you wouldn't need a proxy DLL in between, and you could directly use WPF controls from the calling application.

7.4.2 Using a mixed-mode application

Although the technique in the previous section, which use a mixed-mode extension DLL as a proxy between the native application and the managed Avalon control, works well, it introduces the complexity of having to use the extension DLL. If the calling app itself could be mixed-mode, then it could directly communicate with the Avalon control and thereby avoid the dependency on the proxy extension control. In this section, you'll write such a mixed-mode MFC application that will use an Avalon `Canvas`-derived control as its view. Using the voice-activated TV analogy, this is like directly modifying the TV so that it accepts Japanese commands in addition to English commands. The Japanese speaker can issue commands in their native language, and the TV will respond accordingly without the need for an add-on device. Figure 7.15 shows the base design of a mixed-mode MFC application that hosts a WPF control.

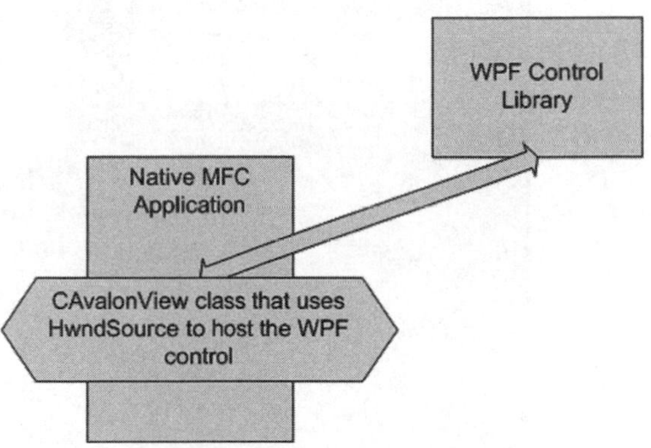

Figure 7.15 Hosting WPF using a mixed-mode app

Note that the primary aim of this example is to demonstrate how to host the Avalon control within the view, not to showcase a complex application of WPF. As such, the example is kept simplistic—but the techniques used to host the control can be used with any real-world WPF control (or controls). You'll write a class called `CAvalonView` that can be used to host any WPF control as the view. The example will show how to communicate between a native view and the view that hosts the WPF control. You'll also see how to use the `BEGIN_DELEGATE_MAP` and `MAKE_DELEGATE` macros to use an MFC class method as the event handler for a managed event raised by the WPF control.

Figure 7.16 shows a screenshot of the example application. As you can see, it's an MDI application with a split view.

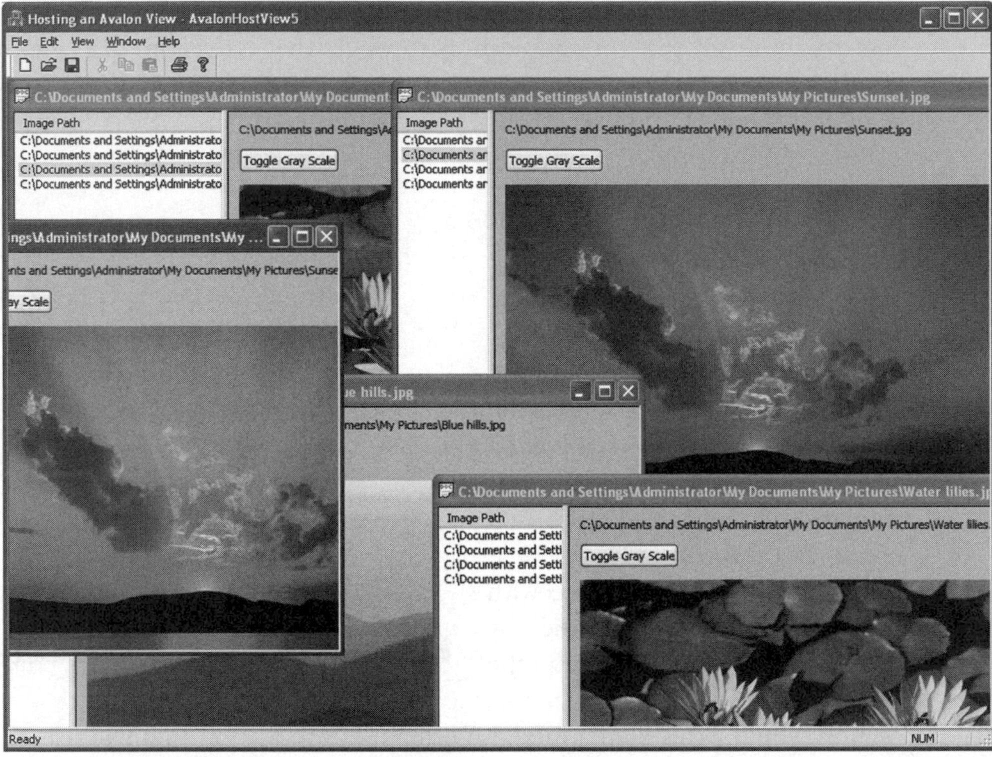

Figure 7.16 Mixed-mode app with an Avalon-based view

The view on the left (natively implemented) shows a list of images (the example program scans the My Pictures folder for JPG files); and the view on the right displays the image, along with a button that toggles the image between normal color mode and grayscale mode. The view on the right (`CAvalonHostViewView`) is implemented using an Avalon `Canvas`-derived control that contains an `Image` control that is used to display the JPG image. (For full code listings, please look at the AvalonHostView solution provided with the source code accompanying the book. The explanations will show only the most relevant code snippets.)

Let's begin by writing a `CView`-derived class (`CAvalonView`) that can be used to host any Avalon control. Listing 7.13 shows the declaration of the `CAvalonView` class.

Listing 7.13 The declaration of the `CAvalonView` class

```
class CAvalonView : public CView
{
    DECLARE_DYNCREATE(CAvalonView)

protected:
    CAvalonView(Type^ pType = nullptr);
    virtual ~CAvalonView();
    virtual void OnDraw(CDC*){};
    gcroot<FrameworkElement^> m_AvalonControl;     <-- ❶ WPF control member
    gcroot<Type^> m_ControlType;     <-- ❷ Type of WPF control

. . .

public:
    afx_msg void OnSize(UINT nType, int cx, int cy);
    virtual BOOL Create(LPCTSTR lpszClassName,
        LPCTSTR lpszWindowName,
        DWORD dwStyle, const RECT& rect, CWnd* pParentWnd,
        UINT nID, CCreateContext* pContext = NULL);
    afx_msg BOOL OnEraseBkgnd(CDC* pDC);
    virtual void OnInitialUpdate();
};
```

To avoid clutter, I've shown only the relevant portions of the class. There are two important member variables: `m_AvalonControl` ❶, which holds the WPF control that will be hosted by the view; and `m_ControlType` ❷, which instantiates the WPF control based on a `Type` argument. The `Type` of the control to be created is passed as an argument to the constructor, as shown here:

```
CAvalonView::CAvalonView(Type^ pType) : m_ControlType(pType)
{
}
```

The WPF control can be created in the `Create` override of the class using the `Activator::CreateInstance` method, which can be used to instantiate an object by passing its type as an argument:

```
BOOL CAvalonView::Create(LPCTSTR lpszClassName,
    LPCTSTR lpszWindowName, DWORD dwStyle, const RECT& rect,
    CWnd* pParentWnd, UINT nID, CCreateContext* pContext)
{
    BOOL bRet = CView::Create(lpszClassName, lpszWindowName,
        dwStyle, rect, pParentWnd, nID, pContext);
    ASSERT(m_ControlType);
    m_AvalonControl = safe_cast<FrameworkElement^>(
```

```
        Activator::CreateInstance(m_ControlType));
    return bRet && m_AvalonControl;
}
```

As you can see, the WPF control instance that is created is stored in the `m_AvalonControl` member variable. The control is then associated with an `HwndSource` control in the `OnInitialUpdate` method, where the `HwndSource` control is created as a child of the view; see listintg 7.14.

Listing 7.14 Hooking the Avalon control to the `HwndSource`

```
void CAvalonView::OnInitialUpdate()
{
    CView::OnInitialUpdate();

    HwndSourceParameters sourceParams("CustomViewHost");
    sourceParams.PositionX = 0;
    sourceParams.PositionY = 0;
    sourceParams.ParentWindow = (IntPtr)m_hWnd;
    sourceParams.WindowStyle = WS_VISIBLE | WS_CHILD;

    HwndSource^ source = gcnew HwndSource(sourceParams);
    source->SizeToContent = Windows::SizeToContent::WidthAndHeight;

    source->RootVisual = m_AvalonControl;

    CRect rect;
    GetClientRect(&rect);
    m_AvalonControl->Height = rect.Height();
    m_AvalonControl->Width = rect.Width();
}
```

The code is similar to what you saw in the previous example, where you put a WPF control on a dialog, except for the fact that you set the `SizeToContent` property of the `HwndSource` to `SizeToContent::WidthAndHeight`. Doing so ensures that the `HwndSource` window is automatically resized to fit the size of the contained WPF control. You then set the width and height of the WPF control to those of the view window. You also need to handle `WM_SIZE` and appropriately resize the WPF control to fit the view window whenever a resize is performed:

```
void CAvalonView::OnSize(UINT nType, int cx, int cy)
{
    CView::OnSize(nType, cx, cy);
    CRect rect;
    GetClientRect(&rect);
    if(m_AvalonControl)
```

```
        {
            m_AvalonControl->Height = rect.Height();
            m_AvalonControl->Width = rect.Width();
        }
    }
```

Every time the view is resized, so is the WPF control; you essentially cover the view client area with the WPF control at all times. This is the same paradigm used by the `CWinFormsView` class (discussed in the previous chapter).

You also handle `WM_ERASEBKGND` and return `TRUE`. If you don't do that, the `CView` class will keep repainting the view window background, even though the WPF control fully covers it, which results in a slight but annoying flicker:

```
BOOL CAvalonView::OnEraseBkgnd(CDC* pDC)
{
    return TRUE;
}
```

Now that you have the `CAvalonView` class, you're ready to host an Avalon control as a view. Before you do that, listing 7.15 shows the `Canvas`-derived control that you'll use as your view.

Listing 7.15 The `Canvas`-derived class that will act as the view

```
ref class MyCanvas : Canvas
{
public:
    TextBlock^ ImagePath;
    Image^ TheImage;
    Button^ GrayScaleButton;
    MyCanvas(void)
    {
        Background = Brushes::LightBlue;
        InitControls();
    }
    void InitControls()
    {
        . . .

        Children->Add(ImagePath);
        Children->Add(TheImage);
        Children->Add(GrayScaleButton);
    }
    void ShowImage(String^ path)        <-- Method shows image in color
    {
            ImagePath->Text = path;

            BitmapImage^ myBitmapImage = gcnew BitmapImage();
            myBitmapImage->BeginInit();
```

```
            myBitmapImage->UriSource = gcnew Uri(path);
            myBitmapImage->DecodePixelWidth = 500;
            myBitmapImage->EndInit();
            TheImage->Source = myBitmapImage;
            TheImage->Width = 500;
    }
    void ShowGrayScale()
    {
        FormatConvertedBitmap^ newBitmap =
            gcnew FormatConvertedBitmap();
        newBitmap->BeginInit();
        newBitmap->Source =
            safe_cast<BitmapImage^>(TheImage->Source);
        newBitmap->DestinationFormat = PixelFormats::Gray32Float;
        newBitmap->EndInit();
        TheImage->Source = newBitmap;
    }
};
```

Method shows image in grayscale

It's a simple control that contains an `Image` control as well as a `Button` control that toggles the image between color and grayscale modes. Note that you can use any WPF control here that's inherited from `FrameworkElement`, either directly or indirectly. The following steps explain how to derive a view from `CAvalonView` so you can host the WPF control within it:

1. Change the base class for the view from `CView` to `CAvalonView`. Your header file declaration of the class should look like this :

   ```
   class CAvalonHostViewView : public CAvalonView
   {
   ```

2. Replace `CView` with `CAvalonView` in the `IMPLEMENT_DYNCREATE` macro declaration of the cpp file:

   ```
   IMPLEMENT_DYNCREATE(CAvalonHostViewView, CAvalonView)
   ```

3. From the view constructor, pass the type of the WPF control to be created to the `CAvalonView` constructor:

   ```
   CAvalonHostViewView::CAvalonHostViewView()
       : CAvalonView(MyCanvas::typeid)
   {
       bGrayScale = false;
   }
   ```

4. Add a member variable to the view class that will hold a `gcroot`-ed reference to the WPF control:

   ```
   gcroot<MyCanvas^> m_Control;
   ```

5 Hook an event handler to the toggle button of the WPF control. You declare a delegate map (you can refer back to the Windows Forms chapter, where you used delegate maps to map managed event handlers to native MFC methods) in the public section of the view class declaration. The delegate map allows you to handle WPF control events using MFC methods as handlers, which is possible because the app is compiled using `/clr`:

```
BEGIN_DELEGATE_MAP( CAvalonHostViewView )
    EVENT_DELEGATE_ENTRY( OnToggleGrayScale,Object^,RoutedEventArgs^ )
END_DELEGATE_MAP()

void OnToggleGrayScale(Object^ sender, RoutedEventArgs^ e);
```

6 Override `OnInitialUpdate`, and store the underlying WPF control in the `m_Control` variable so that you can directly access the WPF control whenever you need to:

```
void CAvalonHostViewView::OnInitialUpdate()
{
    CAvalonView::OnInitialUpdate();

    m_Control = (MyCanvas^)(FrameworkElement^)m_AvalonControl;
    m_Control->GrayScaleButton->Click += MAKE_DELEGATE(
        RoutedEventHandler,OnToggleGrayScale);
    ShowImage();
}
```

Note how you call `CAvalonView::OnInitialUpdate`, because that's where the WPF control is associated with the `HwndSource` and created as a child of the view. Also note the use of the `MAKE_DELEGATE` macro, which is needed to hook the `OnToggleGrayScale` method as the event handler. Here's the code for the `OnToggleGrayScale` method:

```
void CAvalonHostViewView::OnToggleGrayScale(
    Object^ sender, RoutedEventArgs^ e)
{
    if(bGrayScale)
        ShowImage();
    else
    {
        m_Control->ShowGrayScale();          <-- 1 Invoke method on MyCanvas control
        bGrayScale = true;
    }
}
```

You can see how you directly invoke a method on the WPF control ❶. Communicating with the WPF control is straightforward because the view class has direct access to the WPF member variable. The rest of the example application uses standard MFC functionality, and I won't go through it.

In summary, this mechanism gives you more flexibility compared to the previous technique, where you went through a proxy mixed-mode DLL to communicate between the native code and the Avalon control. One big advantage here is that you don't need to write proxy native methods that route control to the corresponding WPF methods. Because your caller is managed (mixed-mode application), it can directly use the WPF control and invoke methods and properties on it. Another advantage is that by using the delegate map and the `MAKE_DELEGATE` macro, you can assign MFC methods as event handlers to the WPF control. Of course, you also need to use `/clr` compilation on your caller application. If you don't want to do that, then the other mechanism may be more suitable. Also note that the `CAvalonView` class can be reused with just about any WPF-based control. All you'd need to do would be to follow the steps mentioned in this section to derive your class from `CAvalonView` instead of from `CView`.

Both techniques have been for using WPF controls from native code. It's also possible, although perhaps not as beneficial, to host native controls in WPF applications.

7.5 Hosting a native control in a WPF application

Although the scenario may not be as common as using WPF from native code, the reverse scenario of using a native Win32 control from WPF may have its uses, however rare they may be. Think of it as the reverse scenario from the voice-activated television set analogy, where the TV set understands Japanese commands by default, and you're adding support for English to it.

Just as the `HwndSource` class is used to put a WPF control on a native window, the `HwndHost` class lets you put a native control on a WPF window (or container control). Let's write a simple example that will put a native `EDIT` control on a WPF application. You'll also put a WPF button in the window; clicking that button will broadcast the contents of the native `EDIT` control to all top-level windows using `WM_COPYDATA`. You'll also handle the `WM_COPYDATA` message to update the contents of the `EDIT` control. If you have multiple instances of the example app running, and you enter text into one instance and broadcast it, every instance will update its native `EDIT` control with the broadcasted text. The example is simple, but it demonstrates how you can put a native control in a WPF window; how you can

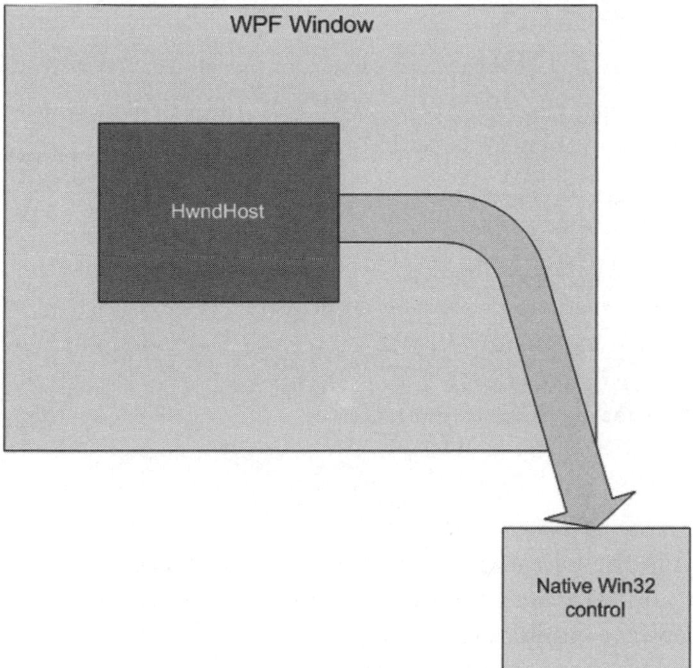

Figure 7.17 Native control in a WPF app using `HwndHost`

access it; and how a WPF window can handle native Windows messages that don't have an equivalent WPF event available. Figure 7.17 shows how a WPF window can host a native control using `HwndHost`.

The `HwndHost` class allows you (as the name indicates) to host an `HWND`-based native window as a child element of a WPF control (or window). It's derived from `FrameworkElement`, and when you add it as a child to a container control, the `BuildWindowCore virtual` method is called with a handle to the parent window; you need to create the native control as a child control of this parent window. For the example, you'll derive a class from `HwndHost` to create the `EDIT` control, as shown in listing 7.16.

Listing 7.16 The `HwndHost`-derived class

```
namespace MyWin32                    <-- ❶ Use namespace to avoid clash
{
    #include <windows.h>
    #include <tchar.h>
}

ref class EditHost : HwndHost
{
```

```
    MyWin32::HWND hwndEdit;
public:
    virtual HandleRef BuildWindowCore(HandleRef hwndParent) override
    {
        using namespace MyWin32;
        hwndEdit = CreateWindowEx(WS_EX_STATICEDGE,          <-- Create native
            _T("EDIT"),_T(""),                           (2)     control
            WS_VISIBLE|WS_CHILD|ES_MULTILINE|
            WS_VSCROLL|ES_AUTOVSCROLL,
            0,0,300,100,(HWND)hwndParent.Handle.ToPointer(),
            (HMENU)1000, NULL, NULL);
        return HandleRef(this, (IntPtr)hwndEdit);
    }
    virtual void DestroyWindowCore(HandleRef hwnd) override     <-- Destroy
    {                                                               native
        MyWin32::DestroyWindow(hwndEdit);                       (3) control
    }
};
```

Notice how you wrap the native `#include` calls in a namespace ❶ to avoid name clashes with .NET and WPF class names and methods. Without that, you'll often end up with numerous compiler errors due to name clashes, and it can be a real hassle to work around that. The `EDIT` control is created as a child of the `HWND` passed as parent via the `hwndParent` argument of the `BuildWindowCore` method ❷. Because the parent window is a WPF window, it won't destroy your native control when it's being closed, so you need to override `DestroyWindowCore` and call `DestroyWindow` on your own ❸. Putting this native control on a WPF window is now as simple as instantiating an `EditHost` object and adding it as a child element. You'll write a `MyWindow` class that's derived from `Window`, and add the `EditHost` object as a child element, as shown here:

```
MyWindow()
{
    canvas = gcnew Canvas();
    . . .

    edithost = gcnew EditHost();
    canvas->Children->Add(edithost);
    Canvas::SetLeft(edithost, 20);
    Canvas::SetTop(edithost, 20);
```

As far as the Avalon window is concerned, it's added a `FrameworkElement`-derived object as a child. The `HwndHost` class goes about creating the native control—in this case, the `EDIT` control. You'll also add a button that broadcasts the contents of the `EDIT` control to all top-level windows; see listing 7.17.

Listing 7.17 Adding a `Click` handler for the Send button

```
MyWindow()
{
    canvas = gcnew Canvas();
    . . .

    sndbtn = gcnew Button();
    sndbtn->Content = "Broadcast";
    sndbtn->Click += gcnew RoutedEventHandler(
        this, &MyWindow::OnSendBtn);
    canvas->Children->Add(sndbtn);
    Canvas::SetLeft(sndbtn, 340);
    Canvas::SetTop(sndbtn, 20);
    . . .
}

. . .

void OnSendBtn(Object^ sender, RoutedEventArgs^ e)
{
    using namespace MyWin32;
    HWND hEdit = (HWND)edithost->Handle.ToPointer();      ❶ Get underlying HWND
    TCHAR buff[1024];
    GetWindowText(hEdit, buff, 1023);
    COPYDATASTRUCT cds = {0};
    cds.lpData = buff;
    cds.cbData = sizeof(buff) + 1;
    SendMessage(HWND_BROADCAST,WM_COPYDATA,             ❷ Broadcast WM_COPYDATA message
        (WPARAM)hEdit, (LPARAM) (LPVOID)&cds);
}
```

In the click handler for the button, you obtain the `HWND` for the edit control using the `Handle` property of the `HwndHost` class ❶. Once you have the `HWND`, you can use API functions such as `GetWindowText` to retrieve the text contained in the `EDIT` control. After you retrieve the text, you broadcast it to all top-level windows using the `WM_COPYDATA` message ❷.

You now need to write code to receive this message and set the `EDIT` control's text to the data thus broadcasted. How do you get the message from the WPF window? No event is fired when a `WM_COPYDATA` message is received. You need to get an `HWND` for the WPF container window and also be able to handle messages that are sent to that HWND. You achieve that by adding an event handler to the `Loaded` event of the WPF top-level window and using the `WindowInteropHelper` to get an `HWND` for the WPF window. Once you do that, you also add an `HwndSourceHook` to the `HwndSource` associated with the `HWND` so that you can handle any native

Windows message received by the window, including `WM_COPYDATA` (which you're specifically looking for). The code in listing 7.18 shows how you do all this.

Listing 7.18 Setting up a message hook for the Avalon window

```
MyWindow()
{
    . . .

    Loaded +=  gcnew RoutedEventHandler(this,
        &MyWindow::OnLoaded);          <-- Add event handler for Loaded
}

void OnLoaded(Object^ sender, RoutedEventArgs^ e)
{
    HwndSource^ src = HwndSource::FromHwnd(
        (gcnew WindowInteropHelper(this))->Handle);    <-- Get HwndSource for window
    src->AddHook(gcnew HwndSourceHook(this,           <-- Add message processing hook
        &MyWindow::HwndProcHook));
}

IntPtr HwndProcHook(IntPtr hwnd, int msg,
    IntPtr wParam, IntPtr lParam, bool% handled)
{
    using namespace MyWin32;
    if(msg == WM_COPYDATA)          <-- (1) Handle WM_COPYDATA
    {
        PCOPYDATASTRUCT pCDS = (PCOPYDATASTRUCT)lParam.ToPointer();
        PTCHAR buff = (PTCHAR)pCDS->lpData;
        HWND hEdit = (HWND)edithost->Handle.ToPointer();
        SetWindowText(hEdit,buff);
    }
    handled = false;
    return IntPtr::Zero;
}
```

The crux of the code is in the `OnLoaded` method, where you get an `HwndSource` for the Avalon window and associate a message handler for it. This message handler (`HwndProcHook`) can handle any native message that's sent to the top-level window. As you can see, you handle `WM_COPYDATA` and use `SetWindowText` to set the received text to the `EDIT` control (1). You can run three to four instances of the app (see the book's accompanying source code for the full code listing), set the text in one of them, and broadcast the text using the button. The `EDIT` control in all instances of the application will show that text.

In summary, you use an `HwndHost`-derived class to create the native `EDIT` control and then add that to the WPF window's `Canvas` control. You access the native window by using the `Handle` property of the `HwndHost`-derived object. You also saw how to handle native messages from the WPF top-level window by using `WindowInteropHelper` to get an `HwndSource` for the WPF window, and by adding a hook that will receive native messages sent to the window.

7.6 Summary

In this chapter, you saw how WPF is a managed UI subsystem for Windows that internally uses DirectX technologies and is based on the .NET Framework. We also briefly covered some basic graphical operations using WPF, including rendering shapes, using brushes, and applying transformations on UI objects.

To recapitulate the prospects of using C++/CLI to write Avalon applications, if using XAML isn't a high priority, then you can use C++/CLI and procedural code to write wholly operative Avalon UIs. On the other hand, if you prefer to design your UIs in XAML, you can use C++/CLI to write your business logic, either by dynamically loading the XAML files or by using a precompiled XAML-based C# assembly.

The true potential of using C++/CLI and Avalon comes into play when you need to interop with native applications and libraries. Both forms of interop-hosting (hosting a WPF control in a native app or vice versa) are possible, and you can either put an Avalon control in a native window or put a native control in an Avalon window. One useful application of that would be to redesign your app's UIs using the powerful 2D and 3D graphics capabilities available in Avalon while reusing your existing C++ code base.

It's possible that direct support for XAML compilation may be added to Visual C++ in the future; if that happens, you could strictly use C++/CLI for writing all sorts of Avalon applications, including mixed-mode and purely managed apps. However, until that happens, native-interop with Avalon is the single most important reason to use C++/CLI with WPF.

WPF is, of course, only one of the two major components of the .NET 3.0 Framework, the other being the Windows Communication Foundation (WCF). In the next (and final) chapter of this book, you'll see how to take advantage of the WCF (formerly codenamed *Indigo*) from Visual C++ applications.

8

Accessing the Windows Communication Foundation with C++/CLI

The Windows Communication Foundation (formerly codenamed *Indigo*) is a framework for developing and running connected applications. It's distributed as part of the .NET Framework 3.0 (formerly known as WinFX) that also includes the Windows Presentation Foundation (WPF), which we covered in the last chapter. In some ways, WCF can be said to be an evolution of .NET remoting (which didn't take off for various reasons, performance being one of them). WCF attempts to provide a uniform programming model for building distributed applications over the range of APIs and communication mechanisms that exist in the Microsoft Stack. From the perspective of native Windows programmers, WCF is the apparent successor to the Distributed Component Object Model (DCOM). Most DCOM programmers will appreciate it when I say that configuring network security and firewalls for getting DCOM to work on any decently secure network was an unadulterated pain. Firewall settings had to be modified at the server as well as the clients, and DCOM security had to be configured to allow clients to connect to the server. WCF, on the other hand, makes it almost effortless to write, deploy, and distribute client/server applications.

WCF, as a part of .NET 3.0, will be an intrinsic part of the Windows Vista operating system. However, as I mentioned in the last chapter, .NET 3.0 will also be available for Windows XP and Windows 2003 operating systems. Thus, you aren't restricted to using Vista if you want to write WCF applications. WCF applications can be hosted within regular GUI applications (including Windows Forms apps), console applications, Windows services, and Internet Information Services (IIS) servers. For the foreseeable future, WCF will be the de facto communications framework for the Windows platform, so you can expect that most new networking applications will use the WCF framework. Consequently, if you're writing new applications with C++ or upgrading your existing applications, it will be extremely useful to be able to support WCF, especially if you want to interact with frameworks that internally use WCF.

WCF includes a vast set of classes that provide a unified programming model for developing service-oriented systems. It would be highly implausible to attempt to cover anything more than an insubstantial portion of it in a single chapter. I'll focus mainly on how to use WCF from C++/CLI. The first two sections cover some simple WCF client/service examples that are fully implemented in managed code using C++/CLI. The meat of this chapter will be an example of migrating a DCOM-based client/server application to WCF. We'll discuss two approaches to doing the migration. You'll also see how to host a C++/CLI-written WCF service within an IIS server. We'll start the chapter with a simple Hello World example of a WCF service and a WCF client.

8.1 Hello World with the Windows Communication Foundation

In this section, you'll write a simple console application that will contain code to host a WCF service as well as code to consume the service. Essentially, both client and server are in the same application, which would be a highly unlikely scenario in real-life applications. It's a little like calling your cell phone from your land phone; both caller and the receiver are the same person—you. For your first app, I wanted to keep the code as simple as possible so that you can quickly get a feel for the basic WCF concepts and how to implement them in your code. In the example, you'll bring up a service that exposes a simple interface with a single method, and write client code that will connect to this service and invoke that method.

To create a basic VC++ project that can use the WCF classes, let's create a CLR console application and add a reference to the `System.ServiceModel` assembly. The following namespace declarations are put on top for convenience:

```
using namespace System;
using namespace System::ServiceModel;
using namespace System::ServiceModel::Channels;
```

A WCF service exposes one or more endpoints that can be consumed by calling clients. Each endpoint consists of three entities—a contract, a binding, and an endpoint address:

- The contract specifies the operations that are exposed by the service to the calling clients.
- The binding abstracts the network protocols, transport mechanisms, security modes, buffering options, and so on that are used for communication.
- The address specifies a Universal Resource Identifier (URI) as well as some address properties.

Think of a WCF service as analogous to a kiosk where you can renew your car's registration, change your address, purchase a new license plate, and so on, by yourself. The contract here would be the set of functionalities offered by the kiosk, such as registration renewal and new license plates. The binding defines how you interact with it—most kiosks have a simple keypad for entering data, a slot for inserting a credit card, and a slot that throws out a registration sticker or a receipt. The address or URI would be where the kiosk is located—say, on the first floor of the mall between the Walmart and Sears stores.

In its simplest form, a WCF service is created by defining its contract, specifying the binding, and then associating it with an address that clients can connect to. Let's define the contract for the Hello service:

```
[ServiceContract]                  <-  Specify interface as
interface class IHello          (1)   service contract
{
    [OperationContract]            <-  Mark method as
    void Greet(String^ s);      (2)   service operation
};
```

You define a simple interface called `IHello` and used the `ServiceContract` attribute on it (1), which indicates that the service will expose the `IHello` interface through an endpoint. Service contracts are often defined using interfaces, and these interfaces are put into a contract definition DLL that can be used by both server-side and client-side code. Note that the interface is just one way to define a service contract. There are WCF tools that can translate between that and other representations, such as Web Services Description Language (WSDL). You also need to mark those methods in the interface that you need to expose using the `OperationContract` attribute (2). The `OperationContract` attribute specifies that the method implements an operation that is part of the service contract. A service contract needs at least one method that's marked with the `OperationContract` attribute, or else during instantiation of the service, an `InvalidOperationException` will be thrown. Also, if you attempt to invoke a method in a service contract interface that isn't marked with the `OperationContract` attribute, a `NotSupportedException` will be thrown.

You've defined the contract interface, so let's now write the service implementation, which is basically a class that implements the `IHello` interface:

```
ref class HelloService : IHello
{
public:
    virtual void Greet(String^ s)
    {
        Console::WriteLine("Hello " + s);
    }
};
```

The calling client isn't aware of the exact nature of this class and sees only the `IHello` interface, but this class provides implementations for each of the exposed service operations.

You've defined the contract interface as well as the implementation. Now you can write code to create the service and bring it up:

```
WSHttpBinding^ binding = gcnew WSHttpBinding();      ❶ Specify HTTP binding
Uri^ baseAddress = gcnew Uri("http://localhost:8088/Hello");

ServiceHost^ servicehost = gcnew ServiceHost(         Specify URI for
    HelloService::typeid, baseAddress);               client connections ❷
servicehost->AddServiceEndpoint(
    IHello::typeid, binding, baseAddress);             Create service
servicehost->Open();                                 ❸ endpoint
Console::WriteLine("The service is running...");
```

You've used the `WSHttpBinding` class ❶ to specify that you'll be using an HTTP-based binding. WCF comes with a bunch of other binding classes, all of which are either directly or indirectly derived from `System.ServiceModel.Channels.Binding`. If you wish, you can create custom binding mechanisms by deriving from this class. Because you specified an HTTP-based binding, you also specify an HTTP address as the URI for the service ❷. The service is instantiated using the

Bindings available in WCF

This example uses the `WSHttpBinding` class, which provides HTTP protocol support, secure sessions, and distributed transactions. The framework comes with other binding classes, which you can use by replacing the binding used, appropriately changing the URI to match the binding protocol, and setting some protocol- and security-related properties as required. Here's a partial list of binding classes available in the WCF:

- `BasicHttpBinding` provides basic HTTP protocol support and is compatible with ASP.NET Web Services (ASMX)-based web services. When you host a service using IIS, this is a good binding option to use.
- `NetNamedPipeBinding` uses named pipes and is most suited for interprocess communication.
- `NetTcpBinding` is a binding that provides generic TCP protocol support and is well suited for intranet-based cross-machine communication. This may not be well suited for Internet communication because firewall issues would come into play.
- `NetPeerTcpBinding` is a TCP-based binding protocol that is specifically intended to be used for peer-to-peer communications.
- `WSDualHttpBinding` is an extended version of the `WSHttpBinding` binding with support for duplex communications.
- `CustomBinding` allows you to define your own binding protocols, if you so desire.

ServiceHost class; the type of the service implementation as well as the service URI are specified. You still need to create an endpoint so clients can connect to the service. This is done using an overload of the AddServiceEndpoint method ❸, where you specify the type of the service contract interface, the binding to be used, and the base address where the service will be exposed. Finally, a call to Open changes the service from the created state to the open state, which basically means that it's up and running and is ready for client connections.

Next, you'll write the client code that will connect to this service and invoke a call to the Greet method:

```
String^ url = "http://localhost:8088/Hello";
EndpointAddress^ address = gcnew EndpointAddress(url);
ChannelFactory<IHello^>^ channelFactory =
      gcnew ChannelFactory<IHello^>(binding, address);
IHello^ channel = channelFactory->CreateChannel();
channel->Greet("Nish");
```

Each client connects to an endpoint using what is called a *channel*, where the channel abstracts the connection between the client and the service. Figure 8.1 shows a diagrammatic representation of how WCF clients connect to a WCF service via endpoints and channels.

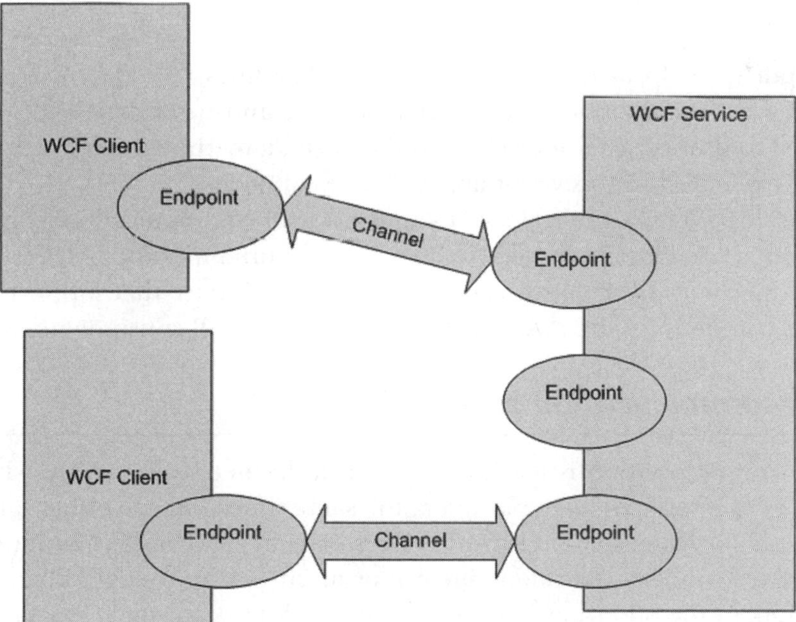

Figure 8.1 WCF endpoints and channels

You use the `ChannelFactory` class to create a channel that can be used to communicate with the Hello service. You use the same binding object that was used to create the service, and also specify the address to connect to (which is the same URI that was defined earlier when you created the service). A call to `CreateChannel` creates a channel to the `IHello` type using the endpoint specified in the `ChannelFactory` constructor. You can now invoke methods on the `IHello` object just as if it was a local object. Of course, you can only invoke those methods that are part of the service contract: namely, those marked with the `OperationContract` attribute.

Finally, you need to close the channel as well as the service host and dispose of the objects:

```
((IChannel^)channel)->Close();
delete channelFactory;
servicehost->Close();
delete servicehost;
```

Notice how you need to cast to `IChannel` before calling `Close`, because the variable is of the type `IHello`.

You can compile and run the application now. You should see the following output:

```
The service is running...
Hello Nish
```

The output is far from impressive; but in the few lines of code you wrote, you specified a service contract, created that service, and instantiated it. You then connected to the service from a client and invoked a method that was exposed by the service. That's impressive for about 25 lines of code.

In the Hello service example, you saw one way of communication from the client to the service. Often, you need to do two-way communication between the service and the client. In the next section, you'll write a service that supports duplex (two-way) communication and then write a client that will consume it.

8.2 Duplex communication in WCF

One-way communication is like using an old fashioned walkie-talkie where two people can talk to each other, but not at the same time. You can either talk to the other person or listen to what the other person is saying. Duplex communication is more like a modern-day telephone call or an instant messenger chat, because you can talk to the other person, and they can talk back to you at the same time. Figure 8.2 shows a diagrammatic representation of a WCF duplex service.

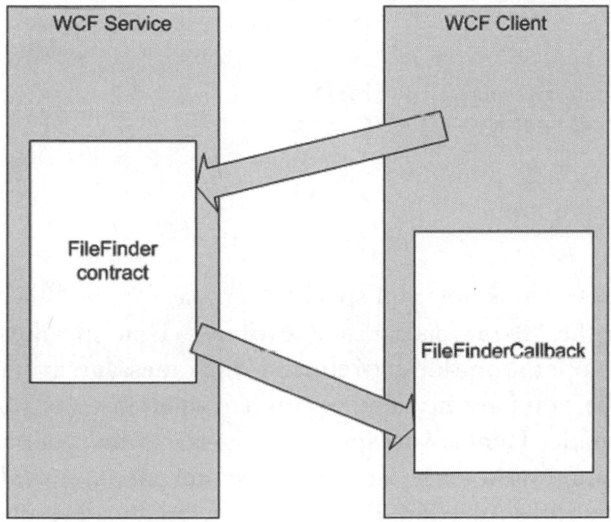

Figure 8.2
A duplex service

Unlike the previous sample, client and server are separate applications here; and because the contract will be shared by both of them, you'll put it in a separate DLL. The service is simple; it exposes a method that searches a specific folder recursively for a file pattern and returns files that match the pattern to the calling client via duplex communication. Essentially, it's a library that can be used to search for specific files within a directory structure.

The first step is to create a new C++/CLI library project (you can call it FileFinderContract) and add a reference to `System.ServiceModel`. Then, put the code from listing 8.1 into the FileFinderContract.h file where you define the interface that defines the service contact and the interface that defines the callback method.

Listing 8.1 Interfaces for the service contract

```
using namespace System;
using namespace System::ServiceModel;

namespace FileFinder
{
    public interface class IFileFinderCallback
    {
        [OperationContract(IsOneWay = true)]
        void OnFoundFile(String^ filefound);
    };

    [ServiceContract(
```

❶ Definition for client-invoked callback

```
        CallbackContract=IFileFinderCallback::typeid)]    <- Specify CallbackContract
    public interface class IFileFinder
    {
        [OperationContract(IsOneWay = true)]
        void FindFile(String^ rootfolder,
            String^ filter);
    };
}
```

One thing that will interest you is how you specify `IsOneWay = true` ❶ when you mark the methods with the `OperationContract` attribute. That specifies to the WCF framework that the operation doesn't return a reply message at the transport layer. In the example, you have no need to confirm whether a method invocation was successfully made. Hence, you specify `IsOneWay` to be `true`, as is the norm for most duplex communication services, because there are always alternate means to detect whether a call succeeded. For instance, a failed call results in the callback not being invoked, thereby indicating an error. For the service contract interface, the `ServiceContract` attribute's `CallbackContract` property is set to the type of the callback interface: `IFileFinderCallback`. This is so the server knows what interface it can expect to reside on the client and make calls into that interface accordingly. Both server and client projects will add a reference to this DLL, so that the contract and callback interfaces can be accessed without code duplication. Let's move on to writing the WCF service code.

8.2.1 Creating the service

For your service project, create a console application (call it FileFinderService), and add a reference to the `System.ServiceModel` namespace. Add a project reference to the FileFinderContract interface project. The first step is to define the service implementation class that will implement the `IFileFinder` contract interface; see listing 8.2.

Listing 8.2 Implementation of the service class

```
using namespace System;
using namespace System::IO;
using namespace System::ServiceModel;

namespace FileFinder
{
    ref class FileFinderService : IFileFinder
    {
        IFileFinderCallback^ pCallback;    <- Reference to callback
```

```
        bool bInit;
    public:
        FileFinderService():bInit(false) , pCallback(nullptr)
        {
        }
        virtual void FindFile(String^ rootfolder,
            String^ filter)
        {
            bool bRootCall = (bInit == false);
            bInit = true;
            if(pCallback == nullptr)
                pCallback = OperationContext::Current->
                    GetCallbackChannel<IFileFinderCallback^>();    ❶ Get channel to caller
            for each(String^ file in
                Directory::GetFiles(rootfolder, filter))
                pCallback->OnFoundFile(file);
            for each(String^ file in
                Directory::GetDirectories(rootfolder))
                FindFile(file, filter);                          Recursively search for pattern
            if(bRootCall)
                pCallback->OnFoundFile(nullptr);    Pass nullptr signaling last call
        }
    };
};
```

The call to `OperationContext::Current` ❶ returns an `OperationContext^` that represents an execution context for the current method. By calling the generic `GetCallbackChannel` method, you get a reference to an `IFileFinderCallback` object that's a channel to the callback object residing in the calling client. The `FindFile` implementation is standard .NET framework code, where you use the `GetFiles` and `GetDirectories` methods of the `Directory` class to recursively go through each folder looking for files that match the pattern. For every file that is a match, you invoke `OnFoundFile` on the callback channel object, which results in the method getting invoked at the client. Once all directories are searched, you call `OnFoundFile` and pass a `nullptr` to specify that the search has ended. This also signals to the client that it needn't keep the callback object alive if it doesn't want to.

Now that you've defined the service implementation, you can write code to start the service; see listing 8.3.

Listing 8.3 Code to create and start the service

```
int main(array<System::String ^> ^args)
{
    using namespace FileFinder;
    WSDualHttpBinding ^ binding = gcnew WSDualHttpBinding();    ❶ Specify duplex binding protocol
```

```
    Uri^ baseAddress = gcnew Uri(
        "http://localhost:8086/FileFinder");      <-- Endpoint address

    ServiceHost^ servicehost = gcnew ServiceHost(
        FileFinderService::typeid, baseAddress);    <-- Instantiate service
    servicehost->AddServiceEndpoint(IFileFinder::typeid,
        binding, baseAddress);    <-- Associate endpoint
    servicehost->Open();    <-- Start service
    Console::WriteLine("Service up! Press any key to stop...");
    Console::ReadKey(true);
    servicehost->Close();
    delete servicehost;
    Console::WriteLine("Service stopped!");
    return 0;
}
```

Most of the code is identical to what you saw in the Hello World example in the previous section. The only change is that you use `WSDualHttpBinding` ❶ as the binding protocol instead of `WSHttpBinding`. `WSDualHttpBinding` is a secure binding that is appropriate for duplex service contracts and is thus ideal for the example. All that's left to complete the example is to write the client application, which is what you'll do next.

8.2.2 Creating the client

For the client project, create a console application (call it FileFinderClient), and add a reference to the `System.ServiceModel` namespace and a project reference to the FileFinderContract interface project. Because you're going to access a duplex communication service, you need to define the class that implements the callback interface, so that the service can invoke a method in the client context; see listing 8.4.

Listing 8.4 Implementing the callback class

```
using namespace System;
using namespace System::Threading;
using namespace System::ServiceModel;
using namespace System::ServiceModel::Channels;

namespace FileFinder
{
    ref class FileFinderCallback : IFileFinderCallback
    {
        ManualResetEvent^ blockevent;    <-- ❶ Event used to block client code
    public:
        FileFinderCallback() : blockevent(
            gcnew ManualResetEvent(false))
```

```
        {
        }
        void WaitTillSafe()                    ❷ Method waits on event
        {
            blockevent->WaitOne();
        }
        virtual void OnFoundFile(String^ filefound)   ❸ Call method implementation
        {
            if(!filefound)
                blockevent->Set();             ❹ Set event when nullptr is encountered
            else
                Console::WriteLine(filefound);
        }
    };
}
```

Because the server will call back into the client code (shown in listing 8.5), you need to keep the callback object alive until you're sure the server has finished its work. You use a `ManualResetEvent` object ❶ and also a method called `WaitTill-Safe` ❷ that block on the event object until its state is set to `true`. The `OnFoundFile` method ❸ is the callback that is repeatedly invoked by the server, and which executes in a client context for every file that matches the search pattern. You know that the method will be called with a `nullptr` when the search is completed. Thus, you check for a `nullptr` ❹ and set the event state, so that the `WaitTillSafe` method can return.

Listing 8.5 Client code to connect to and utilize the WCF service

```
int main(array<System::String ^> ^args)
{
    using namespace FileFinder;                ❶ Same duplex binding protocol as server
    WSDualHttpBinding ^ binding =
        gcnew WSDualHttpBinding();
    binding->ClientBaseAddress =               ❷ Base address for duplex connection
        gcnew Uri("http://localhost:8087/FileFinderClient");
    String^ url = "http://localhost:8086/FileFinder";
    EndpointAddress^ address = gcnew EndpointAddress(url);
    FileFinderCallback^ callback =
        gcnew FileFinderCallback();            Instantiate callback object
    InstanceContext^ instcontext =
        gcnew InstanceContext(callback);       Create InstanceContext object

    DuplexChannelFactory<IFileFinder^>^ channelFactory =
        gcnew DuplexChannelFactory<IFileFinder^>(
            instcontext,binding, address);     Use DuplexChannelFactory
    IFileFinder^ pFileFinderChannel =
```

```
        channelFactory->CreateChannel();      <-- Create duplex channel
    pFileFinderChannel->FindFile(    <-+  Invoke method
        "C:\\windows",                  3  on server
        "*.txt");
                                   4  Wait as callbacks
    callback->WaitTillSafe();    <-+  are invoked
    ((IChannel^)pFileFinderChannel)->Close();
    delete channelFactory;
    return 0;
}
```

You need to use the same binding protocol as is used by the WCF service, and thus you use the `WSDualHttpBinding` class ❶. One extra chore is to set the `ClientBaseAddress` property of the binding object ❷. You need to do this so that the service can connect to your client to establish the duplex communication. Because you're running both client and service on the same machine, you choose a different port (by the way, the 8087 was the math coprocessor for the 8086 chip, for those old enough to remember). The rest of the code is indistinguishable from the Hello World client you wrote in the previous section, except for using `DuplexChannelFactory` instead of `ChannelFactory`. The `DuplexChannelFactory` constructor has an extra argument: an `InstanceContext` object that represents the callback object's client instance, which is accessed at the server when it retrieves a duplex channel back to the client. Once you invoke the service method ❸, you block the client code using a call to `WaitTillSafe` ❹ so that the app doesn't exit until the service finishes the file-search operation. To test the example, compile and run the server, and then run the client, which will display the search results and then exit.

8.3 Migrating a native DCOM application to WCF

As I mentioned at the beginning of this chapter, the future of communication technology on Windows operating systems is WCF. Whether you're maintaining an existing native application or writing a new one, it's important to be able to support WCF. One of the most popular technologies for writing distributed apps with C++ is DCOM, and DCOM applications are ideal candidates for migrating to WCF. For one thing, this will allow them to communicate with any app that uses WCF. For another, it will help avoid DCOM's disadvantages, such as security issues, firewall issues, and deployment problems, which don't exist in WCF.

In this section, you'll see two approaches for migrating a DCOM-based client/server application to WCF. The first approach is quicker to implement and involves writing a WCF proxy that routes the calls to the DCOM server. The second approach reuses the existing program logic; you'll write a fully managed WCF server. Why would you want to do this? WCF is a newer technology, firewall-friendly, easy to configure, and a managed framework, whereas DCOM is now pretty much an obsolete technology and won't be further improved. It's firewall-unfriendly, and configuring it for security can be an absolute abomination (as DCOM people will readily accede to). Figure 8.3 shows a diagrammatic representation of how you'll design the various parts of the application. It also shows how the WCF client communicates with the DCOM server via the WCF proxy and how it connects directly to the pure WCF service.

For the example, you'll use a DCOM server that generates prime numbers. Once the numbers are generated, the server invokes a callback on the client. The

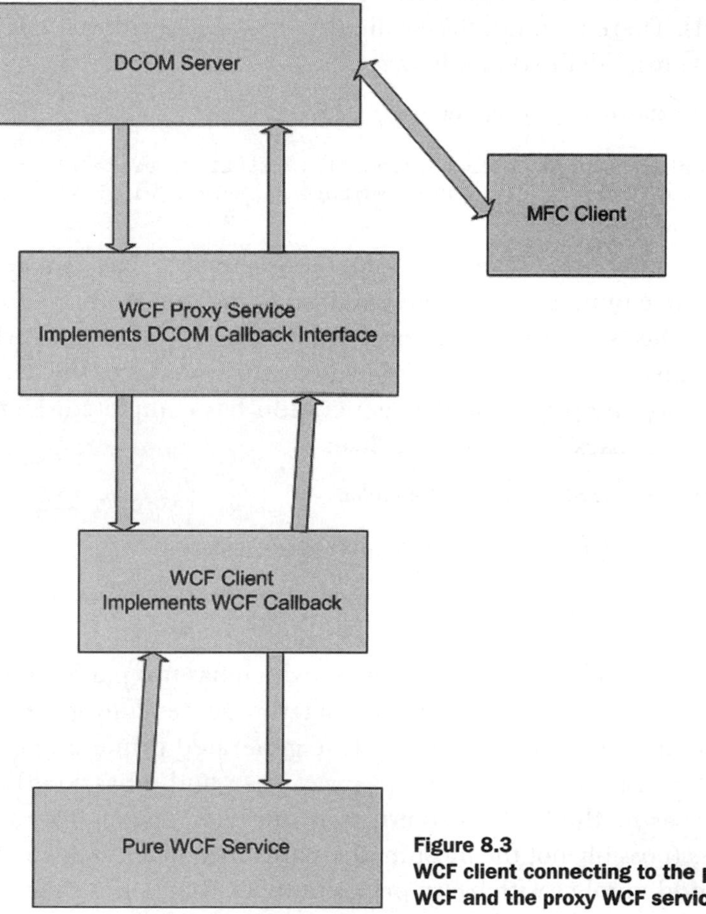

Figure 8.3
WCF client connecting to the pure WCF and the proxy WCF service

DCOM application will have two parts: the DCOM server and an MFC client that calls into it. Before you see how to migrate the application to WCF, let's quickly look at how the DCOM application is implemented, so that later, when you change code in appropriate locations, you can understand how most of the original code has been retained. We'll start with a look at how the DCOM server is implemented and what interfaces it exposes.

8.3.1 The example DCOM server

The DCOM server is an out-of-process, ATL-based executable, and is available in the source code accompanying the book (the DCOM server code is in the project named PrimeNumberServer). I won't describe how to create the DCOM server project, because it's not useful to our discussion, but I'll go through the interfaces and the methods. There is an interface called `IPrimeNumber` with a single method called `GeneratePrimes`, defined as follows:

```
interface IPrimeNumber : IUnknown
{
    [, helpstring("method GeneratePrimes")] HRESULT GeneratePrimes(
        [in] LONG nCount, [in] IPrimeNumberCallback* pCallback);
};
```

The `GeneratePrimes` method takes two `[in]` parameters: a `LONG` that represents the number of prime numbers to be generated, and a pointer to an `IPrimeNumberCallback` object. The `IPrimeNumberCallback` interface is the callback interface that will be implemented at the client side. Through this interface, the server calls back the client once the prime number generation has completed. Here's what the `IPrimeNumberCallback` interface looks like:

```
interface IPrimeNumberCallback : IUnknown
{
    [, helpstring("method OnNumbersGenerated")] HRESULT
        OnNumbersGenerated([in] LONG nCount,
        [in, size_is(nCount)] LONG* pNumbers);
};
```

There's only one method, `OnNumbersGenerated`, which has two parameters: a `LONG` that specifies the number of prime numbers that were successfully generated, and a `LONG*` that contains an array of numbers (the generated prime numbers). The coclass for the `IPrimeNumber` interface is `CPrimeNumber`, and it has a definition for the `GeneratePrimes` method that is shown in listing 8.6. The algorithm used to generate primes (possibly not the most mathematically efficient way to do this) is to divide each odd number with every prime number that is less than its square root to decide whether the number is a prime.

Listing 8.6 Method to generate prime numbers

```
STDMETHODIMP CPrimeNumber::GeneratePrimes(
    LONG nCount, IPrimeNumberCallback* pCallback)
{
    LONG* pNumbers = (LONG*)CoTaskMemAlloc(
        nCount * sizeof LONG);              <-- Allocate memory for array

    pNumbers[0] = 2;
    pNumbers[1] = 3;

    int i = 2;
    int nextPrimeCandidate = 5;
                                            Loop through and generate primes
    while(i < nCount)                    <--
    {
        int maxNumToDivideWith = (int)sqrt(
            (double)nextPrimeCandidate);

        bool isPrime = true;

        for(int j = 0;
            (j < i) && (maxNumToDivideWith >= pNumbers[j]); j++)
        {
            if ((nextPrimeCandidate % pNumbers[j]) == 0)
            {
                isPrime = false;
                break;
            }
        }

        if(isPrime)
            pNumbers[i++] = nextPrimeCandidate;

        nextPrimeCandidate += 2;
    }
                                                         ❶ Pass array to client
    pCallback->OnNumbersGenerated(nCount, pNumbers);  <--
    CoTaskMemFree(pNumbers);              <-- Clean up memory on server

    return S_OK;
}
```

It's standard C++ code. The interesting line of code is the call to `OnNumbersGenerated` ❶ using the `pCallback` pointer, which is a pointer to the `IPrimeNumberCallback` object that resides on the client.

That's all there is to the DCOM server. Now, let's look at the MFC client that will connect to this server.

8.3.2 The native MFC client

It's this application that you'll later port to, acting as a WCF client instead of a DCOM client. The DCOM client is an MFC dialog-based application that contains a virtual list view that displays the prime numbers generated. The full project is available in the book's accompanying source code; I won't explain how to create the project. Instead, we'll look at the bits of code that interest us, which include how the application connects to the DCOM server and how it implements the callback method. It's important that you see this, so that later, when you migrate to WCF, you can easily see what code needs to be changed. Figure 8.4 shows the MFC client application.

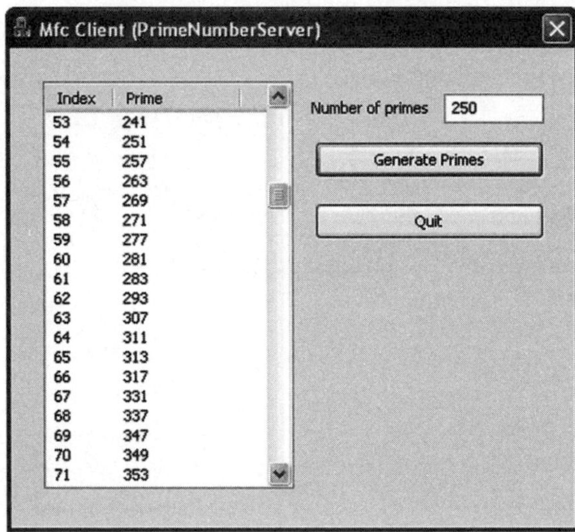

Figure 8.4 MFC client

You'll declare the callback method as a member function of the `CDialog`-derived class. The dialog header file contains the following declarations:

```
DECLARE_INTERFACE_MAP()

BEGIN_INTERFACE_PART(PrimeNumberCallback, IPrimeNumberCallback)
    STDMETHOD(OnNumbersGenerated)(LONG lCount, LONG* rglNumbers);
END_INTERFACE_PART(PrimeNumberCallback)
```

Corresponding to that is the following declaration in the dialog CPP file:

```
BEGIN_INTERFACE_MAP(CMfcClientDlg, CDialog)
    INTERFACE_PART(CMfcClientDlg, IID_IPrimeNumberCallback,
        PrimeNumberCallback)
END_INTERFACE_MAP()
```

The CDialog-derived class is the IPrimeNumberCallback implementation. Because IPrimeNumberCallback is derived from IUnknown, you need to provide implementations for QueryInterface, AddRef, and Release as shown in listing 8.7. Although not directly pertinent to WCF, these are pieces of code that you'll be removing (or commenting out) during the WCF migration.

Listing 8.7 IUnknown implementation

```
STDMETHODIMP CMfcClientDlg::XPrimeNumberCallback::QueryInterface(
    const IID &iid, LPVOID *ppvObj)
{
    METHOD_PROLOGUE(CMfcClientDlg, PrimeNumberCallback);
    return pThis->ExternalQueryInterface(&iid, ppvObj);
}

STDMETHODIMP_(ULONG) CMfcClientDlg::XPrimeNumberCallback::AddRef()
{
    METHOD_PROLOGUE(CMfcClientDlg, PrimeNumberCallback);
    return pThis->ExternalAddRef();
}

STDMETHODIMP_(ULONG) CMfcClientDlg::XPrimeNumberCallback::Release()
{
    METHOD_PROLOGUE(CMfcClientDlg, PrimeNumberCallback);
    return pThis->ExternalRelease();
}
```

As you may have observed, you don't have to provide full implementations. Instead, you call the corresponding default implementations provided by CCmdTarget, which is an indirect parent class of the CDialog class. Before you see how the OnNumbersGenerated callback method has been implemented, I'd like to talk about how you implement the user interface to display the prime numbers.

For the list view that displays the prime numbers, you implement a virtual list, because a list view is too slow and unresponsive when a large number of items are added to it. You use an std::vector<int> to store the prime numbers that are generated; in the LVN_GETDISPINFO notification handler, you access the required prime numbers from this vector. I won't show the LVN_GETDISPINFO handler here, but you can go through it in the source code provided.

Getting back to the OnNumbersGenerated callback method, all that needs to be done is to repopulate the vector<int> with the newly-generated prime numbers. Listing 8.8 shows how the OnNumbersGenerated method is implemented.

Listing 8.8 The callback in the MFC client

```
STDMETHODIMP CMfcClientDlg::XPrimeNumberCallback::OnNumbersGenerated(
    LONG lCount, LONG* rglNumbers)
{
    METHOD_PROLOGUE(CMfcClientDlg, PrimeNumberCallback);

    pThis->m_vecnums.clear();

    for(int i=0; i<lCount; i++)
    {
        pThis->m_vecnums.push_back(rglNumbers[i]);    <-- Store numbers into vector
    }
                                                        Set number of items (for virtual list)
    pThis->m_NumList.SetItemCount(lCount);          <--
    pThis->EnableGenerate();     <-- Enable Generate button

    return S_OK;
}
```

Once the numbers have been populated into the `vector`, the list is refreshed by the call to `SetItemCount`, and the `LVN_GETDISPINFO` handler comes into play. The last bit of code that's of interest in the MFC client is the code in the OK button's handler, which connects to the DCOM server; see listing 8.9.

Listing 8.9 Code that connects to the DCOM server

```
void CMfcClientDlg::OnBnClickedOk()
{
    CString str;
    m_NumPrimes.GetWindowText(str);             Get number of primes to generate
    int count = _ttoi(str);                 <--
    if(count < 1 || count > 1000000)        <-- Do range check
    {
        return;
    }

    CComPtr<IPrimeNumber> pPrime;
    HRESULT hr = pPrime.CoCreateInstance(CLSID_PrimeNumber);   <--
    if(FAILED(hr))
    {                                                   Create remote COM object (1)
        _com_error e(hr);
        AfxMessageBox(e.ErrorMessage());
    }
    else
    {
        DisableGenerate();
        pPrime->GeneratePrimes(count,        <-- Invoke DCOM method
```

```
            static_cast<IPrimeNumberCallback*>(
            GetInterface(&IID_IPrimeNumberCallback)));
    }
}
```

For the example, both client and server are running locally; hence, you use `CComPtr` and its `CoCreateInstance` method to create the COM object ❶. If you want to remotely run the MFC client, you need to do something like the code shown here:

```
COSERVERINFO csi = {0};
csi.pwszName = "<Put DCOM machine name here>";
MULTI_QI mqi = {0};
mqi.hr = S_OK;
mqi.pIID = &__uuidof(IPrimeNumber);
HRESULT hr = CoCreateInstanceEx(__uuidof(PrimeNumber),
    NULL,CLSCTX_ALL,&csi,1,&mqi);
CComPtr<IPrimeNumber> spPrime = mqi.pItf;
```

To keep the example simple to install and run, I've assumed that client and server are on the same machine. To test out the MFC client, build the DCOM server project (as well as the generated proxy project), and then build and run the MFC client. Obviously, if you want to run the MFC client remotely, you'll have to fiddle with security configurations, so that the client has permission to access the server, and also make appropriate firewall changes at both client and server to enable the DCOM communication to work. Those of you who have worked with DCOM in the past may appreciate it when I say that sometimes it can be an absolute pain to configure.

8.3.3 Writing a WCF proxy service

In this section, you'll write a WCF service that will act as a bridge between a WCF caller and the DCOM service. The basic purpose of the WCF proxy is to allow WCF clients to leverage the functionality of the DCOM service. The business logic is still in the DCOM server, and the WCF service merely proxies it across and exposes a managed WCF API to calling clients. The basic advantage of doing this is that the caller applications need not use DCOM to connect with the server; the proxy effectively hides the DCOM server from calling clients. What the proxy does here is analogous to those email-to-post services that were around a few years ago, when email was just coming out and not everyone had an email address. Say you were in the United States, and you wanted to send a letter to a friend in India who didn't have internet access. Posting a letter would be expensive, and there'd be a few days lag before the letter arrived. An email-to-post service let you send an email, which was received by the service (whose offices were in India); they locally sent a letter (a copy of the email) to the recipient (your friend). Not only was this less expensive, but it was also faster. In this case, the sender is analogous to the WCF caller, the recipient is analogous to the DCOM service, and the email-to-post service is analogous to the WCF proxy.

The first step is to write a contract DLL that will contain the contract interfaces that define the service and the callback. This isn't something new—you've done it before. Create a new C++/CLI library project, add a reference to `System.ServiceModel`, and then add the two interface definitions from listing 8.10.

Listing 8.10 Definition of the prime number service contract

```
using namespace System;
using namespace System::ServiceModel;

namespace PrimeNumberContract
{
    public interface class IPrimeNumberManCallback        <-- WCF callback interface
    {
        [OperationContract(IsOneWay = true)]
        void OnNumbersGenerated(int nCount,
            array<int>^ pNumbers);
    };

    [ServiceContract(
        CallbackContract=IPrimeNumberManCallback::typeid)]
    public interface class IPrimeNumberMan        <-- WCF service interface
    {
        [OperationContract(IsOneWay = true)]
        void GeneratePrimes(int nCount);
    };
}
```

The two interfaces are similar to the COM interfaces used by the DCOM server. The `OnNumbersGenerated` has an `array<int>^` as the second argument instead of a `LONG*` as in DCOM. The `GeneratePrimes` doesn't have an argument for the callback reference because WCF uses a different mechanism to specify the callback interface to the server.

Let's now look at the wrapper service. To maintain simplicity, you'll write it as a console application, although a more common way to deploy it is as a Windows service. In the next section, when you write a pure WCF service, you'll use a Windows service. In case you want to write the present example as a Windows service, you can look at the next section for example code.

The WCF wrapper service acts as the server for calling WCF clients. Because it also needs to connect to the DCOM server, it acts as a DCOM client too. You'll need to implement the following set of functionalities:

- Implement the DCOM callback interface. In the DCOM callback, it has to then proxy the call into the WCF calling client using the WCF callback interface.
- Implement the WCF service contract. In the WCF class's `GeneratePrimes` implementation, it needs to proxy the call into the DCOM server by instantiating the DCOM object and invoking the DCOM version of the method. It also needs to host a duplex service that exposes the wrapper service contract.

Figure 8.5 is a diagrammatic representation of how the WCF wrapper bridges the WCF caller with the DCOM server. Let's start by implementing the class that will implement the DCOM callback interface; see listing 8.11.

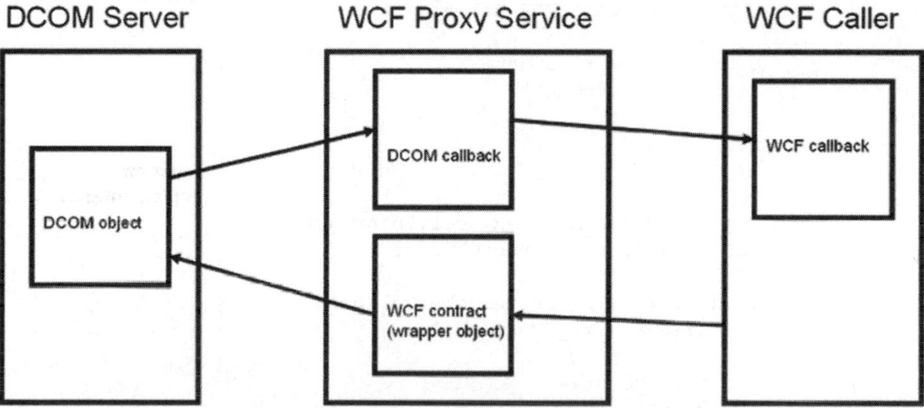

Figure 8.5 Block diagram that shows the design of the WCF wrapper

Listing 8.11 Implementation of the DCOM callback

```
class PrimeNumberCallback : public IPrimeNumberCallback
{
    DWORD m_refcount;
    gcroot<PrimeNumberContract::IPrimeNumberManCallback^>
        pCallback;                                    <-- (1) Member holding WCF callback reference
public:
    PrimeNumberCallback() : m_refcount(0)
    {
    }
                                                      Setter function for WCF callback
    void SetCallback(   <--
        gcroot<PrimeNumberContract::IPrimeNumberManCallback^> value)
```

```
    {
        pCallback = value;
    }
                                                  ❷ DCOM callback
    STDMETHODIMP OnNumbersGenerated(          <─┘   implementation
        LONG nCount, LONG *pNumbers)
    {
        array<int>^ nums = gcnew array<int>(nCount);
        Marshal::Copy((IntPtr)pNumbers, nums, 0, nCount);
        pCallback->OnNumbersGenerated(nCount, nums);       <─┐ Invoke WCF
        return S_OK;                                       ❸   callback
    }

    ULONG STDMETHODCALLTYPE AddRef()
    {
        m_refcount++;
        return m_refcount;
    }

    ULONG STDMETHODCALLTYPE Release()
    {
        ULONG rc = m_refcount--;
        if(0 == m_refcount)
            delete this;
        return rc;
    }                                                   IUnknown
                                                        implementation
    HRESULT STDMETHODCALLTYPE QueryInterface(
        REFIID iid, void **ppvObject)
    {
        if((iid == IID_IPrimeNumberCallback) ||
            (iid == IID_IUnknown))
        {
            m_refcount++;
            *ppvObject = (void *)this;
            return S_OK;
        }
        return E_NOINTERFACE;
    }
};
```

You use a `gcroot`'d variable to hold a reference to the WCF callback interface ❶. In the `OnNumbersGenerated` method ❷, the `LONG*`-based array of prime numbers is converted to an `array<int>` and then passed to the WCF caller by invoking the WCF callback method via the `pCallback` variable ❸. In short, the DCOM callback that's running in the context of the WCF server proxies the call to the WCF callback that's running in the context of the calling client. Listing 8.12 shows the implementation of the WCF contract.

Listing 8.12 Implementation of the WCF contract

```
using namespace System;
using namespace System::IO;
using namespace System::ServiceModel;
using namespace PrimeNumberContract;

ref class PrimeNumberMan : IPrimeNumberMan
{
    IPrimeNumberManCallback^ pCallback;
public:
    PrimeNumberMan()
    {
        pCallback = OperationContext::Current->
            GetCallbackChannel<IPrimeNumberManCallback^>();     <-- Get callback channel to WCF client
    }

    virtual void GeneratePrimes(int nCount)
    {
        CComPtr<IPrimeNumber> pPrime;
        HRESULT hr = pPrime.CoCreateInstance(
            CLSID_PrimeNumber);     <-- Instantiate DCOM object
        if(FAILED(hr))
        {
            _com_error e(hr);
            std::cout << e.ErrorMessage() << std::endl;
        }
        else
        {
            PrimeNumberCallback* pPrimeNumberCallback =
              new PrimeNumberCallback();     <-- Instantiate DCOM callback
            IPrimeNumberCallback* p;
            hr = pPrimeNumberCallback->QueryInterface(
                IID_IPrimeNumberCallback,(void**)&p);
            if(FAILED(hr))
            {
                _com_error e(hr);
                std::cout << e.ErrorMessage() << std::endl;
            }
            else
            {
                pPrimeNumberCallback->SetCallback(pCallback);     <-- Pass WCF callback to DCOM callback class
                pPrime->GeneratePrimes(nCount,p);     <-- (1) Invoke DCOM method
                pPrimeNumberCallback->Release();
            }
        }
    }
};
```

The class acts as a proxy to the DCOM class. The `GeneratePrimes` method instantiates the DCOM object and invokes the DCOM version of `GeneratePrimes` ❶. The callbacks are all set up properly so that the DCOM server's callback is correctly passed to the WCF client.

All that's left to do is to write code to bring up a duplex WCF service, as shown here:

```
WSDualHttpBinding ^ binding = gcnew WSDualHttpBinding ();
Uri^ baseAddress = gcnew Uri(
    "http://localhost:9000/PrimeNumber");

ServiceHost^ servicehost = gcnew ServiceHost(
    PrimeNumberMan::typeid, baseAddress);
servicehost->AddServiceEndpoint(IPrimeNumberMan::typeid,
    binding, baseAddress);
servicehost->Open();
Console::WriteLine("Service up! Press any key to stop...");

Console::ReadKey(true);
servicehost->Close();
delete servicehost;
Console::WriteLine("Service stopped!");
```

If you compile and run the application, you have a WCF service ready and listening on port 9000, waiting for clients to connect to it.

8.3.4 Modifying the MFC client to use WCF

In this section, you'll change your MFC DCOM client so that it connects to the WCF service instead of to the DCOM service. The basic idea is to demonstrate how a typical native DCOM-based client can be converted into a WCF client with as few code changes as possible, so that you retain the vast majority of the original code base. Make a copy of the MFC client, and rename the project to avoid confusion. Turn on `/clr` compilation, and add a reference to the `System.ServiceModel` assembly and a project reference to the PrimeNumberContract project.

The first thing to do is to write a class that implements the `IPrimeNumberMan-Callback` interface, so that the WCF service can callback into your client. Listing 8.13 shows the code for the implementation.

Listing 8.13 Implementation of the callback class

```
using namespace System;
using namespace System::Threading;
using namespace System::ServiceModel;
using namespace System::ServiceModel::Channels;
```

```
using namespace PrimeNumberContract;

ref class PrimeNumberManCallback : IPrimeNumberManCallback
{
    ManualResetEvent^ blockevent;                    <-- Event object used for blocking
    CMfcClientDlg* pMfcClientDlg;                    <-- Pointer to MFC dialog
public:
    PrimeNumberManCallback(CMfcClientDlg* pDlg) :    <-- Constructor sets MFC
            blockevent(gcnew ManualResetEvent(false)),    dialog pointer
            pMfcClientDlg(pDlg)
      {
      }
                                            Event-based
      void WaitTillSafe()                <-- blocking function
      {
          blockevent->WaitOne();
      }
                                                       (1) Implement
      virtual void OnNumbersGenerated(int nCount,      <-- callback method
        array<int>^ pNumbers)
      {
          pMfcClientDlg->m_vecnums.clear();
          for each(int i in pNumbers)
          {
              pMfcClientDlg->m_vecnums.push_back(i);
          }
          pMfcClientDlg->m_NumList.SetItemCount(nCount);
          pMfcClientDlg->EnableGenerate();
          blockevent->Set();
      }
};
```

Most of the code is similar to the earlier examples. In the `OnNumbersGenerated` method ❶, you mimic the behavior of the DCOM callback method used in the original MFC client. You can remove the COM-based maps from the dialog header file. You can comment out or delete from the dialog's header file the code shown here:

```
/*DECLARE_INTERFACE_MAP()*/

//BEGIN_INTERFACE_PART(PrimeNumberCallback, IPrimeNumberCallback)
//     STDMETHOD(OnNumbersGenerated)(LONG lCount, LONG* rglNumbers);
//END_INTERFACE_PART(PrimeNumberCallback)
```

Similarly, from the dialog's CPP file, remove the `BEGIN_INTERFACE_MAP` block, as well as the definitions of the `QueryInterface`, `AddRef`, `Release`, and `OnNumbersGenerated` methods.

The last step is to modify the `OnBnClickedOk` function so that it connects to the WCF service instead of the DCOM server. The modified `OnBnClickedOk` function is shown in listing 8.14.

Listing 8.14 Code to connect to the WCF service

```
void CMfcClientDlg::OnBnClickedOk()
{
    CString str;
    m_NumPrimes.GetWindowText(str);
    int count = _ttoi(str);
    if(count < 1 || count > 1000000)
    {
        return;
    }

    WSDualHttpBinding ^ binding = gcnew WSDualHttpBinding();
    binding->ClientBaseAddress = gcnew Uri(
        "http://localhost:9001/PrimeNumberClient");
    String^ url = "http://localhost:9000/PrimeNumber";
    EndpointAddress^ address = gcnew EndpointAddress(url);
    PrimeNumberManCallback^ callback =
        gcnew PrimeNumberManCallback(this);
    InstanceContext^ instcontext = gcnew InstanceContext(
        callback);
    DuplexChannelFactory<IPrimeNumberMan^>^ channelFactory =
        gcnew DuplexChannelFactory<IPrimeNumberMan^>(
            instcontext,binding, address);
    IPrimeNumberMan^ pFileFinderChannel =
        channelFactory->CreateChannel();
    DisableGenerate();
    pFileFinderChannel->GeneratePrimes(count);
    callback->WaitTillSafe();
    ((IChannel^)pFileFinderChannel)->Close();
    delete channelFactory;
}
```

The code is pretty much the same as that you wrote for the duplex communication example in section 8.2. That's all; your WCF client is ready. If you compile and run it, you'll see that it behaves identically to the old version, although now it connects to a WCF service instead of to a DCOM server. In summary, you changed only the code related to the DCOM connection and left the rest of the application intact. The DCOM callback was replaced by the WCF callback; and instead of remotely instantiating a DCOM object, you connect to the WCF service.

I know I've said this many times in this book, but I'm going to say it again: C++/CLI lets you reuse existing native code as no other CLI language can. If you were converting the client to a C# app, not only would you have to rewrite the WCF client code (as you did here), but you'd also have to implement the rest of the application in C#, including the UI and any other business logic. The example used a trivial scenario, so the savings in terms of recoding time may not be stupendous. However, for any real-life scenario, it shouldn't be hard to imagine the magnitude of resource and time savings you can achieve and how advantageous this is. Your WCF service is still dependent on the DCOM server, and thus while you've eliminated the client side of the DCOM application, the server side still exists.

In the next section, you'll write another version of the server that will purely use managed code and WCF. Your WCF MFC client can connect to it because the WCF contract will remain the same. The WCF MFC client will be oblivious as to which version of the service it's connecting to.

8.3.5 Writing a pure WCF service

In this section, you'll write a WCF service that will reuse the business logic from the original DCOM server. Once you're done, because this service fully includes the functionality of the original DCOM server, you'll no longer have a dependency on the DCOM server. As before, you'll reuse as much of the original DCOM server code as is possible, thereby minimizing code-rewrite. To continue the earlier email-to-post analogy, this is like setting up an Internet connection at your friend's place so that you can directly send email to them (and vice versa).

This time, you'll use a Windows service (instead of a console application as you did in the wrapper version). It's easy to create a Windows service with VC++ 2005. All you need to do is create a new project and choose Windows Service from the list of project templates offered by the wizard. Add a reference to the `System.ServiceModel` assembly as well as a project reference to the PrimeNumberContract project. The first step is to create the class that will implement the service contract, as shown in listing 8.15.

Listing 8.15 Implementation of the service contract

```
using namespace System;
using namespace System::IO;
using namespace System::ServiceModel;
using namespace PrimeNumberContract;

ref class PrimeNumberMan : IPrimeNumberMan
{
    IPrimeNumberManCallback^ pCallback;
public:
```

```
    PrimeNumberMan()
    {
        pCallback = OperationContext::Current->
            GetCallbackChannel<IPrimeNumberManCallback^>();
    }

    virtual void GeneratePrimes(int nCount)
    {
        array<int>^ pNumbers = gcnew array<int>(nCount);

        pNumbers[0] = 2;
        pNumbers[1] = 3;

        int i = 2;
        int nextPrimeCandidate = 5;

        while(i < nCount)
        {
            int maxNumToDivideWith = (int)sqrt(
                (double)nextPrimeCandidate);

            bool isPrime = true;

            for(int j = 0;
                (j < i) && (maxNumToDivideWith >= pNumbers[j]);
                j++)
            {
                if ((nextPrimeCandidate % pNumbers[j]) == 0)
                {
                    isPrime = false;
                    break;
                }
            }

            if(isPrime)
                pNumbers[i++] = nextPrimeCandidate;

            nextPrimeCandidate += 2;
        }

        pCallback->OnNumbersGenerated(nCount, pNumbers);
    }
};
```

The implementation of the `GeneratePrimes` method is pretty much identical to that used by the DCOM server. You've minimized code rewrite by reusing the existing business logic instead of rewriting it from scratch for .NET. In the simplistic example, this was exemplified by a copy/paste of the original code. In a real-life scenario, this would more likely involve reusing entire libraries and sets of classes exactly as they were in their native versions, which would mean little rewrite of core business logic. Now, all that's left is to add code to bring up the WCF service when the Windows service is started. Add the following member to the service class (derived from `ServiceBase`):

```
ServiceHost^ servicehost;
```

You make it a member because you'll be accessing it from two different methods in the service class. The WCF service start-up code is put into the `OnStart` implementation of the `ServiceBase`-derived class, as shown here:

```
virtual void OnStart(array<String^>^ args) override
{
    WSDualHttpBinding ^ binding = gcnew WSDualHttpBinding ();
    Uri^ baseAddress = gcnew Uri(
        "http://localhost:9000/PrimeNumber");

    servicehost = gcnew ServiceHost(
        PrimeNumberMan::typeid, baseAddress);
    servicehost->AddServiceEndpoint(
        IPrimeNumberMan::typeid, binding, baseAddress);

    servicehost->Open();
}
```

There's not much to explain, because the code is exactly the same as that used earlier to bring up a WCF service. Similarly, you dispose off the `servicehost` object in the `OnStop` override, as shown here:

```
virtual void OnStop() override
{
    servicehost->Close();
    delete servicehost;
}
```

Add an installer component to the service, and set the service to use the LocalSystem account. I won't go into how that's done because it's not within the scope of this book; but you can look at the sample project provided with the book, which includes full source code for all the samples we covered in this chapter. Start the service from the Services Control Panel applet, and run the WCF MFC client. You'll see that it functions the same as it did with the wrapper WCF service. At this point, you've eliminated DCOM from both the server application as well as the calling client, and thus the migration has been successfully completed.

8.3.6 Comparison of the two migration methods

In the first method, you didn't get rid of the DCOM server. You just wrote a WCF service that proxied all incoming calls to the DCOM server and all callbacks back to the calling client. The advantage with that mechanism is that it's easy to implement. All you need to do is define the service contracts and write a thin wrapper that invokes the corresponding DCOM methods. Any existing DCOM-based clients can continue to connect to the DCOM server, whereas newer WCF clients, including those written in languages other than C#, can connect to the WCF wrapper and be oblivious to the presence of the DCOM server. If the WCF wrapper and the DCOM server are on the same machine, then this also solves the security and connectivity issues involved with using DCOM on any secure network. The disadvantage of this method is that you retain the dependency on the DCOM code. Any modifications to the DCOM code will mean partially redundant changes in the WCF wrapper as well. There's also the extra overhead of going from the managed WCF environment into the unmanaged DCOM environment. My recommendation is to use this wrapper technique as step one of a two-step migration process. The wrapper isn't hard to write, and you can quickly provide a WCF interface for managed clients to connect to. That will give you extra time to completely port the code and avoid the dependency on the DCOM code.

With the second method, which I suggest be step two in the migration process, a little more code-rewriting is required. But you'll find that you can reuse just about all the business logic code. Most of the rewrite involves removing the COM-based objects and replacing them with .NET objects. Of course, once you've done a full port to WCF, native DCOM clients can't connect to it. One option is to maintain the DCOM server for older clients, except that newer changes to functionality will be implemented only in the purely-managed WCF version.

8.4 Hosting a WCF service in an IIS server

Another way to host a WCF service is to host it within an IIS server. The trick is to use an SVC file and to put this SVC file in a virtual IIS directory. The SVC file supports inline code for C# and VB.NET, but it doesn't support C++. That isn't a major hassle because you can use a precompiled binary file (a .NET DLL) that contains the service implementation. The advantage of hosting the service this way is that you avoid the need to have a separate application to act as the service host.

Let's write a simple Hello service implementation in a .NET DLL project. The code in listing 8.16 shows the contract interface and two different service implementations. (You have two because you'll define two different services in your SVC file.)

Listing 8.16 English and French service implementations

```
using namespace System;
using namespace System::ServiceModel;

namespace HelloWorld
{
    [ServiceContract]
    public interface class IHelloContract          <-- Contract interface
    {
        [OperationContract]
        String^ Hello(String^ name);

    };                                              English version implementation

    public ref class EnglishHelloService : IHelloContract    <--
    {
    public:
        virtual String^ Hello(String^ name)
        {
            return "Hello World, " + name;
        }
    };                                              French version implementation

    public ref class FrenchHelloService : IHelloContract     <--
    {
    public:
        virtual String^ Hello(String^ name)
        {
            return "Bonjour Le Monde, " + name;
        }
    };
}
```

The next step is to create a virtual IIS directory. Choose any folder on your hard disk, or create a folder specifically for hosting the SVC files. Three preliminary steps must be performed before the SVC files are created:

1. Use the IIS administration tool, and create a virtual web directory on the chosen folder.
2. Ensure that the virtual directory is configured to use ASP.NET 2.0 (by default, it may be set to use .NET 1.1) and that anonymous access is turned on (the default setting).

3 Change the folder's security settings, and give the ASP.NET account read and execute permissions on the folder. If you don't set the permissions correctly, it won't work as expected or may not work at all.

Create a bin folder within the virtual folder, and copy the DLL containing the service contract and implementations to this folder. Next, create the following two SVC files, and put them in the virtual directory:

File : HelloEnglish.svc

```
<%@ServiceHost Service="HelloWorld.EnglishHelloService"%>
```

File : HelloFrench.svc

```
<%@ServiceHost Service="HelloWorld.FrenchHelloService"%>
```

Each file contains only a single line that contains a header tag (which may look familiar to ASP.NET developers). The only attribute you set is `Service`, which you set to the fully-qualified name of the implementation class for the specific service. You aren't done yet; you still need to create a web.config file that will describe the services hosted within that virtual ISS directory. For the example, create the following web.config file, and put it in the same folder as the SVC files:

```
<?xml version="1.0" encoding="utf-8"?>

<configuration>
  <system.serviceModel>
    <services>
      <service name="HelloWorld.EnglishHelloService">      ❶ English version service
        <endpoint binding="basicHttpBinding"
            contract="HelloWorld.IHelloContract" />
      </service>
      <service name="HelloWorld.FrenchHelloService">       ❷ French version service
        <endpoint binding="basicHttpBinding"
            contract="HelloWorld.IHelloContract" />
      </service>
    </services>
  </system.serviceModel>
</configuration>
```

The web.config file describes the services hosted by IIS within that virtual directory, and you specify the English ❶ and French ❷ service versions. You also specify the endpoint by explicitly stating the binding that will be used as well as the contract interface. Notice how you specify `"basicHttpBinding"` as the binding that corresponds to the `BasicHttpBinding` WCF class and that clients will need to use.

If your client was written in C# or VB.NET, you could use svcutil.exe, which can generate a proxy class for the WCF service when a URL to the service is passed to it. Although svcutil.exe can be used to generate a C++/CLI proxy (by specifying CPP as the language), the proxy class generated throws hundreds of warnings and won't even compile by default. It may be theoretically possible to fix the generated class to get it to compile, but that approach would be highly inefficient and would waste time. A more level-headed option is to use imperative code and to directly connect to the service, as you did earlier in the chapter. The code in listing 8.17 shows a simple console client that will prompt the user to choose between French and English versions of the service and will then connect to the selected service and invoke the `Hello` method on it.

Listing 8.17 Client code to connect to the two services

```
using namespace System;
using namespace System::ServiceModel;
using namespace System::ServiceModel::Channels;

namespace HelloWorld
{
    [ServiceContract]
    public interface class IHelloContract          <-- (1) Define contract interface
    {
        [OperationContract]
        String^ Hello(String^ name);

    };
}

int main(array<System::String ^> ^args)
{
    using namespace HelloWorld;
    BasicHttpBinding^ binding = gcnew BasicHttpBinding();   <-- Specify same binding as service

    String^ url = "";

    Console::Write("Press E for English, and F for French : ");
    ConsoleKeyInfo cki = Console::ReadKey();
    Console::WriteLine();

    if(cki.Key == ConsoleKey::E)          <-- Choose service to connect to
        url = "http://localhost/Hello/HelloEnglish.svc";
    else if(cki.Key == ConsoleKey::F)
        url = "http://localhost/Hello/HelloFrench.svc";
    else
        return 0;

    EndpointAddress^ address = gcnew EndpointAddress(url);
    ChannelFactory<IHelloContract^>^ channelFactory =
        gcnew ChannelFactory<IHelloContract^>(binding, address);
```

```
        IHelloContract^ channel = channelFactory->CreateChannel();

        Console::WriteLine(channel->Hello("Nish"));     <-- Invoke method on chosen service

        ((IChannel^)channel)->Close();
        delete channel;
        return 0;
    }
```

Notice how you define the service contract interface in the client code ❶. Only the contract matters, not the type of the interface (which includes the containing assembly). As long as the interface you define in the client matches the service contract interface defined on the server, you're OK. The advantage of hosting services within IIS is that you not only avoid having to run and maintain a stand-alone server application, but also, with a stand-alone service, you'd have to open up additional ports in the firewall (if one is present). With IIS, because all traffic will go through the HTTP port, which is firewall-friendly, you won't run into firewall-related connection problems.

8.5 Summary

There's a lot more to WCF than we covered in this chapter. But the techniques you used can more or less be reused without any major changes due to the unified programming model used by WCF. It won't be a trivial task to convert a large-scale native DCOM-based application to use WCF—but eventually, once .NET 3.0 becomes the norm for Windows development and Windows Vista is the standard OS, you'll have to do a migration. With C++/CLI, you'll be able to make the migration path a lot less painful and time-consuming than it might otherwise have been. For quick deployment, you can use a proxy WCF server like in the first migration example, which routes calls into the native DCOM server. Gradually, you can complete a full port to WCF and do so with extensive code reuse. Little code-rewriting will be required in the business logic.

With this chapter, we have also come to the end of this book. Through the chapters, we covered C++/CLI syntax and semantics, examined mixed-mode programming techniques, saw examples of interoping between native code and Windows Forms, and finally, in the last two chapters, glanced at what the future holds in store for Visual C++ in terms of the ability to consume .NET 3.0 technologies such as WPF and WCF. Visual C++ may not be the most popular CLI language compiler today, but where interop and mixed-mode application scenarios are concerned, it's king; no other language can remotely compare to it. Let me conclude this book by saying that I think the future of C++ development on Windows platforms will be C++/CLI, and that it will serenely coexist with Standard C++ in a glorious amalgamation of the two forms.

Appendix: A concise introduction to the .NET Framework

This appendix is meant as a quick introduction to the .NET Framework and has been kept as brief as possible. It doesn't comprehensively talk about every aspect of .NET (that would have been impossible for such a short piece), but it does touch on all the major facets associated with the .NET Framework. If you've used .NET in the past, this should serve to freshen your memory; if you've never used .NET, you can think of this as an initial step to understanding the .NET Framework, but you should enhance your knowledge of the topic from other, more extensive sources. We'll look at what this .NET Framework is all about and what its major components are. We'll also briefly touch on how a managed executable is run on Windows, the role of Visual C++ in the framework, the various sublibraries that form the Base Class Library, the different types available under .NET, AppDomains, and reflection. We'll begin with a look at what the .NET Framework is from a Microsoft perspective.

What is the .NET Framework?

The .NET Framework provides an abstraction layer on top of the native operating system that allows applications compiled into a special intermediate language called *Microsoft Intermediate Language* (MSIL) to run under a managed environment—where both execution and memory are managed by various parts of the framework. Its two primary components are the *Common Language Runtime* (CLR) and an extensive *Base Class Library* (BCL). The CLR is responsible for the execution of .NET applications, inducing memory management through its built-in *Garbage Collector* (see the section on memory management for more information), whereas the BCL provides various hierarchical class libraries for creating rich user interfaces (UIs), both for the desktop and for the Web—accessing data, security, web services, and many more commonly-performed programming chores.

The first version of the framework that was publicly available was .NET 1.0, which was soon followed by .NET 1.1. The current (third) public release of the framework is .NET 2.0, which coincided with the release of Visual Studio 2005. Multiple .NET Framework versions can coexist on the same machine, and a .NET application can target a specific version of the framework. This allows an application coded for a specific .NET version to execute successfully on a target machine that contains more than one framework version. Most machines these days that run Windows 2000 or later operating systems from Microsoft have one or more versions of the .NET Framework installed, either directly via a Windows update, or indirectly via some .NET application that's installed on that machine, which installed the framework through its installer.

Because the .NET Framework abstracts away the underlying OS, an application that runs on the .NET Framework can theoretically run on any OS that has a .NET implementation that matches the application requirements. Practically, though, Microsoft is the only company today that releases full framework editions for the various .NET versions, although it does so for a variety of its OS versions including Windows 98, Windows 2000, Windows XP, and Windows 2003. This allows developers to write code in an OS-agnostic fashion, and the actual OS calls are done by the .NET framework. As a proof of concept that the .NET Framework can exist on non-Microsoft operating systems, Microsoft has made publicly available a shared source .NET implementation called *Shared Source CLI* that supports (in addition to Windows 2000 and XP) FreeBSD 4.7 and Mac OS X 10.2. This version is mostly (but not fully) compatible with the Microsoft .NET Framework version 1.1 release. In addition to the Shared Source CLI, a third-party open source project called *Mono* provides an implementation of the .NET Framework. Mono allows you to run your .NET applications on Linux and other UNIX variants.

The .NET Framework only understands MSIL—its machine language equivalent—and thus any compiler capable of producing MSIL can be used to write .NET applications. Microsoft provides four languages, each of which can be used to write MSIL applications:

- *C#*. A C++-like language that was introduced by Microsoft specifically for .NET.
- *Visual Basic .NET*. A variant of classic Visual Basic with .NET-specific syntax and semantics.
- *J#*. A Java-like language with a lot of compatibility with regular Java.
- *C++/CLI*. C++ with some additional keywords and semantics that support .NET.

All of these compilers can be downloaded for free as part of the .NET Framework Software Development Kit, and they're all included as part of Visual Studio 2005 (the latest release of Microsoft's integrated development environment). Figure A.1 shows an abstract block diagram that represents the various layers that form the .NET Framework implementation on Windows.

Although .NET was greeted with apprehension by the Windows developer community when it was first released, more and more developers are switching from traditional programming methodologies to using the .NET Framework. My personal observations are that most companies are choosing .NET for their new applications and are also upgrading some of their existing applications to use the

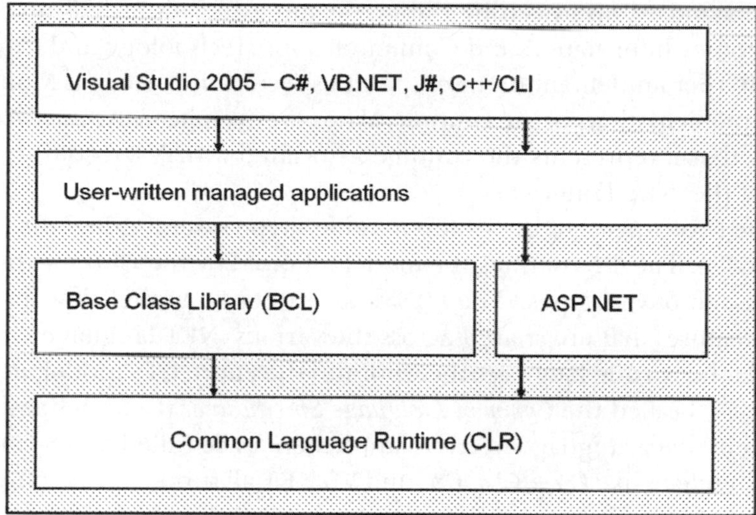

Figure A.1 Hierarchy of layers in the .NET Framework

.NET Framework. Microsoft has promoted .NET as its primary user development tool by including the .NET Framework in Windows Update and using it partially or fully in writing the company's own applications. Visual Studio 2005 and SQL Server 2005 both use the .NET Framework, and BizTalk Server 2006 (currently in Beta) is a fully-managed application (written using the .NET Framework). Microsoft has also made classic Visual Basic obsolete. It's no longer officially supported and has been replaced with Visual Basic .NET (which is backward-incompatible with classic VB). Windows Vista, the next OS from Microsoft, comes with some purely-managed frameworks such as Windows Presentation Foundation (WPF) and Windows Communication Foundation (WCF). It's a trivial conclusion to say that the future of Windows programming will be primarily .NET based.

One of the most fundamental aspects of the .NET Framework is the CLR, which is effectively the virtual machine on which the MSIL is executed. I'll talk about the CLR next.

The Common Language Runtime

The CLR is the core of the .NET Framework. It includes an execution engine that can directly execute MSIL using a Just in Time (JIT) compiler that converts the MSIL into the native code for the underlying OS/CPU. Note that the CLR specifically refers to Microsoft's implementation of the CLI specification, which is an international standard approved by the ECMA (an association dedicated to the standardization of Information and Communication Technology and Consumer Electronics). Other implementations of the CLI specification, such as Mono, have their own implementations of the runtime. Whenever you hear the term *CLR*, you should know that it represents the runtime associated with Microsoft's commercial release of the .NET Framework.

One of the core aspects of the CLR is a unified type system called the *Common Type System* (CTS). The CTS defines the model followed by the CLR for the declaration and usage of CLI types. The CTS is an extensive model that includes a super set of features that are shared across the various .NET language compilers that are available. No one language incorporates the entire CTS model; instead, a subset of the CTS called the *Common Language Specification* (CLS) defines a minimal type system that a language needs to implement to be called a CLS-compliant language. Languages like C++/CLI, C#, and VB.NET all support CLS compliance; in addition, each language has a set of features from the CTS that is outside the CLS, although when you're writing portable libraries, it's highly advisable to refrain from using the non-CLS features, because applications written in other languages aren't guaranteed to be able to consume those non-CLS features. The majority of the BCL types are CLS-compliant and can be consumed by any CLS-compliant language. Figure A.2 shows a diagrammatic representation in which the shaded portion in the center represents the CLS—which is common to all the three CLS-compliant languages shown in the figure.

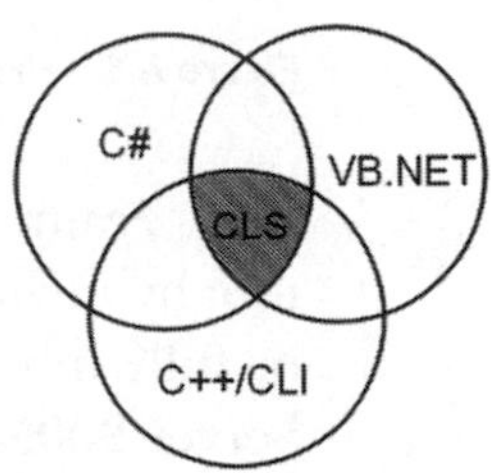

Figure A.2 The Common Language Specification

One of the primary functions of the CLR is to execute MSIL code through its execution engine, which is called the Virtual Execution System (VES). The VES enforces the CTS model and is responsible for loading and executing .NET assemblies. An *assembly* contains various types, resources, and metadata and provides the basic building block for a .NET application. A type is always associated with an assembly and doesn't have an existence of its own outside the assembly. The VES invokes the JIT compiler to compile the MSIL into native code as and when required. The fact that the VES executes MSIL natively gives .NET its language-agnostic disposition, because as long as a language compiler supports compilation into MSIL, the VES (or, in other words, the CLR) can execute that application. Regardless of whether you code using C#, VB.NET, J#, C++/CLI, any other third-party compiler (such as COBOL.NET or Forth.NET), or straight MSIL, eventually the CLR is executing pretty much the same MSIL instructions. The diagram in figure A.3 shows the various components that make up the CLR.

MSIL is the Microsoft-specific implementation of the Common Intermediate Language (CIL) instruction set. MSIL is a simple stack-based instruction set that has been designed with portability as one of its main objectives. It doesn't support the concept of CPU registers, making it convenient for CLI implementations to create separate runtimes for different CPUs and operating systems. The .NET Framework SDK includes the MSIL Assembler (ilasm.exe), which can be used to generate a Portable Executable (PE) file that runs on Windows from an MSIL source file. There is also the MSIL Disassembler (ildasm.exe), which can open a PE file and reveal the types and the MSIL in readable text format. It may interest you that although the .NET Framework doesn't come with full source code, a considerable percentage of the BCL can be directly examined as readable MSIL using the MSIL Disassembler. You don't even have to do that, because higher-level third-party decompilers (such as Anakrino and Reflector) decompile the MSIL into higher-level languages like C# and VB.NET, making them all the more readable.

When you hear the term *.NET executable* on Windows, it essentially means a PE file that contains MSIL but isn't entirely MSIL. Windows is a native OS (as opposed to a virtual OS, such as the CLR); as such, it can only execute native code—specifically, PE files. Even if you use a purely-managed compiler like C# or VB.NET, the executable produced by the compiler will be a native PE file with a native stub that loads and executes the MSIL body. We'll cover that process of loading and executing a .NET executable in the next section.

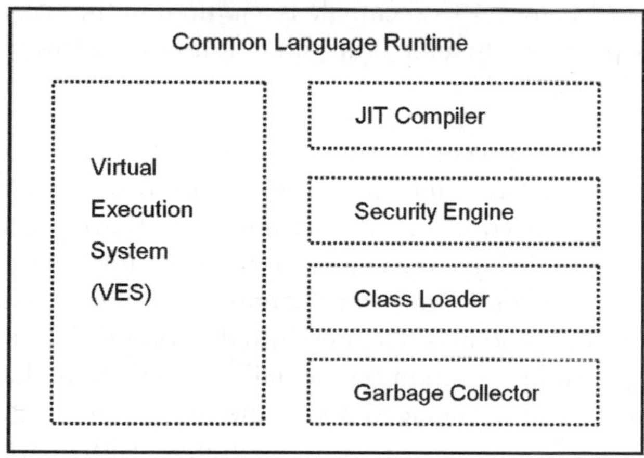

Figure A.3
Components of the CLR

Executing a .NET program

Before we look at how a .NET executable (also called a *managed executable*) is loaded and executed by the CLR, let's quickly look at the contents of such an executable file. A .NET executable (which is a PE file) contains the following blocks:

- *PE header.* This contains standard PE file information such as whether the file is a DLL or an EXE; and, if it's an EXE, whether it's a console application or a windows application. In general, the PE header of a managed executable is similar to the PE header in a regular native executable.
- *CLR header.* This contains information required by the CLR to execute the application, including the expected CLR version, the managed entry-point function, the location of metadata, and relocation addresses for the MSIL.
- *Metadata.* The metadata section includes information about the types in the module (the executable or DLL) and their members, external references to assemblies, version information, and other data that may be required by the CLR. Because metadata contains all the required information to run an application, it eliminates the need for external import libraries or header files.
- *MSIL.* This is the managed IL code generated by the compiler (whether it is C#, VB.NET, or C++/CLI). During program execution, this code is JIT-compiled into native code by the CLR on an as-required basis.

Every .NET executable references a DLL called mscoree.dll in its import library section; this is the *Microsoft Component Object Runtime Execution Engine* of the CLR. The first native instruction in any .NET executable is a jump into the `_CorExeMain` exported function of mscoree.dll. On an x86 machine, it looks like this :

```
JMP _CorExeMain
```

When you run a .NET executable, execution begins as normal in native mode, and a jump is made into the `_CorExeMain` function in mscoree.dll (which is automatically loaded because it's referenced in the import library section). `_CorExeMain` initializes the CLR, determines the managed entry point by reading that information from the CLR header, compiles the code for the entry-point method (which is in MSIL) using the JIT compiler, and makes a jump into the compiled native code. At this point, the managed code execution has actually started. Note that if this was a managed DLL (instead of a managed EXE), the jump would have been made to `_CorDllMain` (instead of to `_CorExeMain`). Of course, with `_CorDllMain`, there would be no attempt to compile and jump into an entry-point method (for there would be none), and so the CLR would be initialized, and control would return to the calling code.

Before the entry-point method is executed, all types referred by the method are listed, and a table is created that contains the type's members and their entry addresses (which are initially set to point to the JIT compiler stub). As a method is executed, the JIT compiler loads the MSIL for that method, JIT-compiles it into native code, and changes the table so that the entry address for the method points to the compiled native code. Any further calls to this function won't require JIT compilation and will instead jump straight into the native code for that function. This explains why some .NET applications are slow during startup, because a lot of JIT compilation is taking place; once they're up and running, they run as fast as a native application, because the JIT compilations are minimal. Note that the JIT compiler performs some runtime optimizations on the generated native code, because it has more knowledge of the exact runtime environment, unlike a regular compiler that doesn't have enough runtime data to perform some of the optimizations. As an example, if a switch block checks for the Windows version, the JIT compiler can remove the entire block and jump straight into the code for the specific Windows version on which the application is running. In some cases, the JIT-compiled code is faster than similar code written using a native compiler.

In addition to JIT compilation, the CLR also performs MSIL verification before invoking the JIT compiler. Verification checks to see whether the code is safe to execute; for instance, it may check to see if an unsafe memory access is made, or if an argument passed to a method is of the expected type. By doing this verification, the CLR ensures that your managed application won't corrupt memory that doesn't belong to it. Application domains take advantage of this aspect of code safety, as we'll discuss later; multiple managed applications can be run in a single process address space, and the underlying OS sees only a single process. Now that you know how a managed application is loaded and executed, let's see how Visual C++ fits into the picture.

Visual C++ and .NET

Visual C++ 2005 is the only .NET-capable language that can create native executables, managed executables, and mixed-mode executables (containing both managed and native code). Section 1.2.1 of chapter 1 covers the various compiler options that are set to create managed and mixed-mode applications using Visual C++. In safe-compilation mode, Visual C++ produces managed executables that are verifiable, just as a C# or VB.NET compiler would. In this mode, only pure managed constructs that adhere to the C++/CLI specification can be used in the source code. C# supports an unsafe compilation mode (not available in VB), where it can perform certain unsafe operations such as direct pointer access. The Visual C++ equivalent is the compiler's pure compilation mode, where a purely-MSIL executable is produced that may not necessarily be verifiable (just as with using C# in unsafe mode). In addition to these modes, Visual C++ supports a third option, where it produces an assembly that contains both native code blocks and managed code blocks; hence the term *mixed-mode assembly* (or executable, if it's an EXE). Figure A.4 shows the execution flow of a typical mixed-mode executable generated using Visual C++.

Because of the Visual C++ compiler's ability to have mixed-mode code, it serves as a powerful mechanism to bridge managed and unmanaged code. The mixed-mode assembly can use both managed and unmanaged libraries and can bridge any communication between them. Thus, a managed application that wishes to use a native (unmanaged) library can use a mixed-mode library that acts as a wrapper for the unmanaged library. Similarly, a native application can use a managed library via a mixed-mode proxy library (that acts as the wrapper). Section 1.1 of chapter 1 describes in more detail the capabilities and advantages of having a compiler that can support mixed-mode compilation.

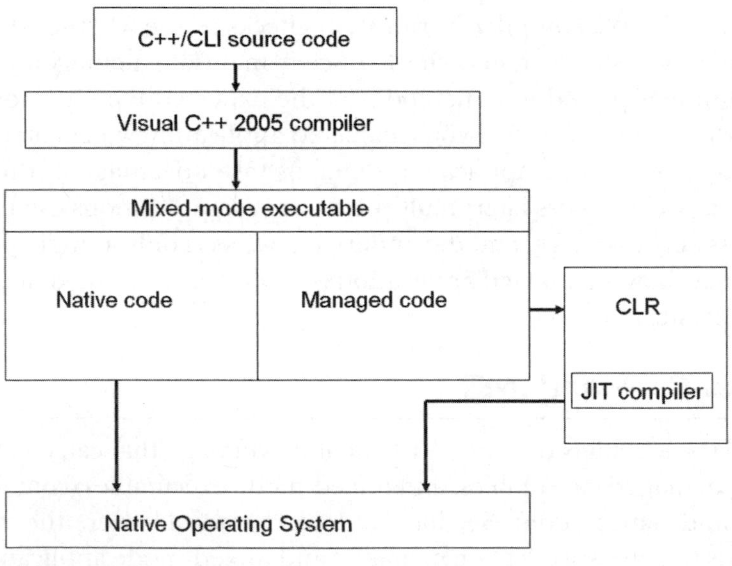

Figure A.4 Mixed-mode program execution flow

I've observed a certain amount of confusion as to the purpose of Visual C++ in the Visual Studio ladder of languages. Some people are ignorant about what Visual C++ can do; often, in forums and newsgroups, you can observe people posting questions about whether they can continue to build native applications using Visual C++. The answer is that they absolutely can continue to do so. Visual C++ 2005 supports an excellent Standard C++ compiler that's ahead of several other compilers in terms of ISO-standard compliance. Others believe that Visual C++ is only good for mixed-mode applications. Although it's true that the ability to create mixed-mode applications (or libraries) is one of its greatest features, most people don't realize that it's possible to create a purely-managed assembly using Visual C++. Someone coming from a C++ background can target managed applications using a language syntax they're familiar with. The semantics and syntax changes added to Visual C++ as part of the C++/CLI implementation do deviate from regular C++, but that deviation is a minor syntactic difference when compared to learning a whole new language such as C# or VB.NET.

Whenever people talk about the classes in the .NET Framework, they're talking about the .NET BCL, which is perhaps one of .NET's biggest selling points. We'll briefly discuss the BCL and its various component libraries in the next section.

The Base Class Library

The BCL is a set of managed assemblies distributed with the .NET Framework that contains thousands of types that can be directly used by managed applications. The BCL is vast, and no comparable programming library is available for Windows. Think of it as a library that encompasses and far exceeds the combined functionality provided by MFC, ATL, WTL, STL, and the Win32 API. Most of the Win32 API has been wrapped by various BCL classes, and there are also tons of utility classes that don't have equivalents in the Win32 API. When I say *wrapped*, I don't mean a thin wrapper such as the MFC classes—the .NET classes are high level and abstract in nature, and they hide the underlying API from the developer.

Here is a partial set of libraries (or subframeworks) provided as part of the BCL. The importance and utility value of a specific library varies depending on your developmental requirements, so the list is in alphabetical order:

- *ADO.NET.* ADO.NET is to .NET what ADO was to COM. It provides a consistent API that lets your applications use a number of data sources such as SQL Server, Oracle, Sybase, MySQL, Postgres, Microsoft Access, XML flat files, and so on. ADO.NET provides components such as Connection objects, Command objects, DataAdapter objects, DataReader objects, DataSet objects, and more. As long as a data store has a .NET Framework data provider, ADO.NET can be used with it.

- *Collection classes*. The BCL has extensive container classes (including generic container classes), including support for popular containers like arrays, hash tables, stacks, queues, lists, and so on. It's also straightforward to create your own custom collection classes; doing so merely involves implementing a few interfaces that all collections need to have.
- *Console API*. The BCL includes the `Console` class that lets you do standard input/output operations with a console window. These are particularly useful when you want to quickly test out a library's functionality or when you're writing command-line tools for your application.
- *Cryptography*. An extensive set of classes lets you add cryptographic support to your applications. There are classes for performing encryption and decryption of your data using popular cryptographic algorithms such as DSA, RSA, RC2, Rijndael, and so on. In addition, there are classes that perform various types of hashing, generating random numbers and Base64 transforms.
- *File I/O*. The `System.IO` namespace contains classes for performing common file I/O operations such as creating and managing files and directories. In addition, a bunch of stream-based readers and writers can be used for file manipulation.
- *Graphics classes*. The BCL includes the `System.Drawing` namespace, which provides access to GDI+ functionality through a large set of wrapper classes. There are classes to create and manipulate images, brushes, fonts, icons, colors, and shapes.
- *Math support*. The `System.Math` class provides functionality for most of the common mathematical operations, including trigonometry and logarithms.
- *Network I/O*. With .NET, you no longer need to directly access Winsock to write network applications. The `System.Net.Sockets` namespace provides classes for manipulating TCP and UDP socket connections. There's also stream-based support for reading and writing from a network stream, which is similar to using file streams.
- *Regular expressions*. Regular expressions are fully supported in .NET through the `System.Text.RegularExpressions` namespace.
- *Threads*. The BCL has classes that fully support multithreaded programming; and it includes classes to create and manage threads, as well as

synchronization classes such as the Mutex, Monitor, re-settable event classes, and so on. There is also support for thread pooling and timers.

- *Web Forms / ASP.NET.* ASP.NET is .NET's version of classic ASP. It provides a framework for creating power web applications. Note that ASP.NET also encompasses web services (which run on the ASP.NET engine). Web Forms is an ASP.NET feature that lets you design flexible user interfaces for web applications. Visual Studio 2005 includes a convenient Web Forms designer that you can use to quickly design Web Forms applications.
- *Web services.* The BCL includes support for XML-based web services that are consumed over HTTP. All the standard web-service protocols, such as XML, HTTP, XSD, WSDL, and SOAP, are supported intrinsically. It's also trivial to write a .NET application that consumes a web service, and often, all that's required is to add a reference to the web service, and then the components of the web service can be used as if they were local classes.
- *Windows Forms*: Windows Forms is a GUI framework that's part of the BCL. It lets you develop rich, powerful user interfaces. Windows Forms lets you take advantage of standard Windows desktop application features such as toolbars, menus, mouse handling, dialogs, common controls, and so on, all using a consistent programming model. Visual Studio 2005 includes a full-fledged Windows Forms designer that lets you quickly design a form by dragging and dropping controls from the toolbox. The first section in chapter 6 gives you a brief introduction to using Windows Forms with C++/CLI.
- *XML classes.* The BCL includes many XML classes that provide standards-compliant features for processing and manipulating XML documents. These classes can be found in the `System.Xml` namespace.

Again, the preceding list is merely a subset of the full functionality of the BCL, but the items mentioned give you an idea of the BCL's imposing capabilities. Any CLS-compliant language can consume and use any of these BCL classes. This has the side effect that .NET programs written in two different languages that perform the same functionality look much the same (ignoring syntactic differences), because they eventually use the same set of BCL classes and methods. In the next section, I'll briefly discuss the various types that are supported by the CLI.

CLI types

All types in .NET automatically derive from `System.Object`. This includes primitive types such as `int` and `wchar_t` (both of which have corresponding types in the BCL: `System.Int32` and `System.Char`). The CLR (actually, the CLI—the CLR is an implementation of the CLI) supports two categories of types: reference types and value types. Reference types are always allocated on the CLR heap and are subject to garbage collection by the CLR's GC. Value types are lighter objects that are normally allocated on the thread's stack. Sections 1.4 and 1.6 of chapter 1 cover how you can declare such types in C++/CLI and how they differ in various implementation details. A value type is always implicitly derived from the `System.ValueType` class (which itself is derived from `System.Object`). Primitive types such as `Int32` (`int` in C++/CLI) and `Char` (`wchar_t` in C++/CLI) are value types. If there were no value types, such primitive types would have to use reference-type semantics, which would involve the overhead of CLR heap allocation, garbage collection, and so forth; and performance-wise, this would be a bad thing. Note that value-type objects may end up on the CLR heap when they're used as member objects of a reference type.

The C# language treats all value types as `structs` and all reference types as classes. C++/CLI doesn't follow that semantic and instead uses the contextual keywords `ref` and `value` to specify whether a class is a reference type or a value type. Thus, in C++/CLI, a `struct` can either be a value type or a reference type, and the same goes for a class. A C# `struct` is equivalent to a C++/CLI `value class` or `value struct`, whereas a C# `class` is equivalent to a C++/CLI `ref class` or `ref struct`. Programmers who have used C# should keep note of this, because it may otherwise be a cause for confusion.

A special value type called an *enumeration value type* derives every enumeration type implicitly from `System.Enum` (which itself is derived from `System.ValueType`). Enumeration types are treated specially by the CLR as well as by the CLS-compliant languages. Enumerations are typically used as named constants, and by default they use `Int32` as the underlying type, although other primitive types are also allowed (barring `Char`).

Programmers coming from a native C++ background may be a little confused initially by the two different types (reference types and value types). In native C++, an object can be declared on the stack or the CRT heap depending on how you declare it; in .NET, reference types automatically go into the CLI heap, and value types automatically go into the thread stack. Note that value types can be converted to a reference type (the process is called *boxing*), and the reference type thus obtained is referred to as the *boxed value type*. This boxed value type can be unboxed to retrieve the underlying value type. Boxing and unboxing are covered in detail in section 1.6 of chapter 1. In the next section, we'll talk about memory management in .NET.

Memory management

The .NET Framework has a Garbage Collector that takes care of freeing memory when it's no longer required. The GC uses a trigenerational algorithm; section 3.1 of chapter 3 covers this GC algorithm in some detail. In native C++, if you create a heap object using the `new` operator, you're responsible for deleting that object when it's no longer being used, using the `delete` operator. But when you're coding in .NET, your reference objects are created on the CLI heap; the GC keeps track of each object thus allocated, and when the object goes out of scope and has no variable references to it, it gets cleaned up during the next GC cycle. The framework manages memory deallocation for you, saving you the trouble of doing so and thereby removing any chance of memory-management errors such as memory leaks or accidentally using a pointer after its object has been deallocated. Because GC cleanup is nondeterministic—it's impossible to predict when the next GC cycle will occur—the GC doesn't support destructors, which means that reference types can't have them. Instead, they have something similar called *finalizers*, which are executed by the GC during object cleanup. Deterministic cleanup is simulated using a pattern called the *Dispose pattern*, and VC++ 2005 supports this intrinsically through pseudo-stack semantics; all this and more is covered in chapter 3 when we discuss stack semantics and deterministic destruction.

Most people were apprehensive about the GC-based memory management when .NET was first released, because they feared this would bring in overheads that would result in a serious decline in performance. But performance analysis showed that the GC doesn't slow down an application as much as a lot of people feared; in some scenarios, it shows an improvement in performance. The GC algorithm has been further improved and optimized in .NET 2.0, and for most purposes, you won't find any noticeable performance hits (although there are always a few .NET critics who may try to make you believe otherwise). Of course, attempting to use .NET to write a real-time application would be an immensely injudicious thing to attempt, and in such scenarios the GC overhead may be a crucial bottleneck. One danger with an automatic memory-managed environment is that programmers tend to be careless about how they allocate and use objects, because they know that the GC will clean up after them. The effect of this carelessness is inefficient code that uses a lot more memory than is ideally required. Keep in mind that, regardless of whether the memory is freed by you or the GC, it's the developer's responsibility to make judicious use of your memory resources.

Next, let's talk about a concept that was introduced in .NET: application domains (also called AppDomains).

Application domains

The Windows OS has separate address spaces for each process, and processes aren't permitted to access memory from other processes. One big advantage is that a misbehaving process can't take the rest of the system down with it when it crashes. Processes are expensive entities, because each process has a set of kernel objects associated with it, along with its own heaps and thread stacks, process memory, and other process-distinctive objects. Now, under .NET, because every managed process executes under the strict control of the CLR, it's possible to have multiple lightweight processes associated with a single Windows process—and these lightweight processes are called *AppDomains* (short for application domains).

Whereas a process is an abstract entity created and managed by the OS, an AppDomain is an abstract entity created and managed by the CLR. Every AppDomain is associated with a process, and there can be more than one AppDomain in an OS process. AppDomains are similar to OS processes, but they have some advantages:

- Creating an AppDomain is less expensive than creating an OS process.
- Although inter-AppDomain communication (assuming both AppDomains to be in the same OS process) has much the same difficulties as interprocess communication, once again, it's cheaper than the latter, because the AppDomains are within the same process address space.
- An AppDomain can be unloaded without having to terminate the containing process.
- Different AppDomains in a process can be given different security permissions, which improves the flexibility of the whole application.

Every managed application has a primary AppDomain, and most managed applications typically have only a single AppDomain (the primary). In a process with more than one AppDomain, every type that's loaded exists once per AppDomain; this includes the static members. If you have an app with two AppDomains, remember that any static members *are not shared* between the AppDomains. Again, there are exceptions to this rule; some assemblies, such as mscorlib.dll, are loaded in a domain-neutral manner and shared by all AppDomains in the process, and this includes static members. The `System.AppDomain` class can be used to create and manage AppDomains in your applications, although as I mentioned, it wouldn't be a common scenario. One real-world application that uses App-Domains is ASP.NET: Each web application is run as a separate AppDomain within the containing ASP.NET worker process.

Let's now move on to one of the most remarkable features in the .NET Frame-work: reflection.

Reflection

Every .NET assembly contains metadata that includes information about the types contained in the assembly, the methods in those types, fields in those types, and so on. Because this metadata is present, any type is basically self-describing: Its methods and field structure are detailed in the metadata. The BCL provides the `System.Reflection` namespace, which provides lots of classes that let you *reflect* over this metadata—essentially by querying information stored in the metadata. Given an unknown managed assembly, using reflection, it's possible to list the types present in that assembly, along with the members for each type—including private, protected, and public members. It's also possible to dynamically load an assembly and instantiate a type from that assembly merely by knowing its fully-qualified name. This makes reflection particularly useful in plug-in development. An application can specify a CLI interface that a type needs to implement to be used as the plug-in, and you can provide multi-ple plug-ins by providing assemblies that contain types that implement the required plug-in interface.

This ability of a .NET type to describe itself eradicates the need for header files and import libraries. All you need is access to the containing assembly, and you can then access any type in that assembly and also instantiate and use types as required. The `System.Object` class has a `GetType` method that returns a `Type` object that represents the type of that object instance. Because every CLI object automatically has `System.Object` as a direct or indirect parent, `GetType` can be used on any .NET object. The `Type` class is your primary access to the metadata associated with a CLI type. `GetType` works for any CLI object due to reflection—basically, the fact that every instance can describe its type intrinsically because of the metadata. Note that reflection can be used for some advanced purposes, such as emitting fresh metadata and MSIL, which means you can build types, methods, and even assemblies dynamically in-memory during program execution. The classes that are used for such purposes are in the `System.Reflection.Emit` namespace and are normally used by .NET compilers, interpreters, or scripting engines; they aren't usually used by regular programs.

index

Symbols

A

B

C

D

E

F

G

S

T

U

V

ABOUT THE AUTHORS

Called "the brightest young author team on the culinary scene today" on National Public Radio, Andrew Dornenburg and Karen Page are co-authors of a groundbreaking trilogy of books chronicling America's vibrant restaurant culture: *Becoming a Chef: With Recipes and Reflections from America's Leading Chefs*; *Culinary Artistry*; and *Dining Out: Secrets from America's Leading Critics, Chefs and Restaurateurs.*

Dornenburg has cooked professionally in some of the best restaurants on the East Coast, including Biba and the East Coast Grill in Boston, and three-star restaurants Arcadia, Judson Grill, and March in New York. He attended the School for American Chefs at Beringer Vineyards in 1992, where he studied cooking with Madeleine Kamman. He currently heads his own catering company in New York City, which has been featured in two editions of *America's Elite 2000*.

Page has consulted with leading companies on issues related to marketing, strategy, and business development. She is a graduate of the Harvard Business School, whose alumnae network she heads, and of Northwestern University, whose president appointed her to the Council of 100, an organization of Northwestern's one hundred leading alumnae. She previously served a term on the board of directors of Women Chefs and Restaurateurs.

The authors can be reached at:

Andrew Dornenburg and Karen Page
527 Third Avenue, Box 130
New York, NY 10016
www.becomingachef.com
Dornenburg@aol.com or KarenAPage@aol.com.